ESSENTIALS OF INTERNATIONAL HUMAN RESOURCE MANAGEMENT

To our students

*The more that you read, the more things
you will know. The more that you learn,
the more places you'll go.*

Dr. Seuss

ESSENTIALS OF INTERNATIONAL HUMAN RESOURCE MANAGEMENT

MANAGING PEOPLE GLOBALLY

SECOND EDITION

MILA LAZAROVA

Canada Research Chair of Global Workforce Management, Associate Professor of International Business and Director of the Centre for Global Workforce Strategy, Beedie School of Business, Simon Fraser University, Canada

DAVID C. THOMAS

Professor of International Business, Gustavson School of Business, University of Victoria and Professor Emeritus, Simon Fraser University, Canada

ELAINE FARNDALE

Professor of Human Resource Management and Director of the Center for International Human Resource Studies, School of Labor and Employment Relations, The Pennsylvania State University, USA

Edward Elgar
PUBLISHING

Cheltenham, UK • Northampton, MA, USA

Published by
Edward Elgar Publishing Limited
The Lypiatts
15 Lansdown Road
Cheltenham
Glos GL50 2JA
UK

Edward Elgar Publishing, Inc.
William Pratt House
9 Dewey Court
Northampton
Massachusetts 01060
USA

A catalogue record for this book
is available from the British Library

Library of Congress Control Number:
2021943525

Printed on elemental chlorine free (ECF)
recycled paper containing 30% Post-Consumer Waste

ISBN 978 1 78897 677 0 (cased)
ISBN 978 1 78897 679 4 (paperback)
ISBN 978 1 78897 678 7 (eBook)

Printed and bound in the USA

CONTENTS

FIGURES

TABLES

BOXES

PREFACE

This textbook is the product of a collaboration of subject experts, who happen to be friends with a shared passion of international human resource management (IHRM) and cross-cultural management. Having found existing IHRM textbooks lacking in one aspect or another, we felt that the vast and interesting practice of IHRM could use a fresh treatment and published the first edition of *International Human Resource Management: Managing People Globally*.

Nearly a decade later, taking this book as a base, we invited a third author to draw from a wider range of expertise and then updated and expanded on this earlier volume. A lengthy process, which included the challenges of the COVID-19 pandemic, as well as researching new topics and updating our knowledge on more traditional topic areas in IHRM, finally resulted in this latest edition. We hope that some of our passion and dedication to the IHRM field reaches you through the pages that follow.

If you share our intense interest in IHRM, we hope that you will enjoy this second edition and the greater details it offers about the broad global spectrum that creates the backdrop for international HRM, including cultural, institutional and organizational contexts. The book does not focus exclusively on managing global mobility, nor is it limited to managing HRM in multinational enterprises. Rather, it integrates comparative approaches to HRM with an understanding of the strategic management of people in all types of organizations embedded in a global context.

Specifically, in this second edition you will find the following new elements:

- Increased coverage of institutional contexts
- A new chapter on the HR function's role globally
- A deeper focus on global talent management
- Extended coverage on research on career management across national contexts
- Greater detail on global employment relations
- Deeper insights into the challenges of global corporate social responsibility
- Updated case studies and learning opportunities through discussion questions.

Accompanying resources can be accessed on: https://www.e-elgar.com/textbooks/lazarova

We send our thanks to our families, friends and colleagues who have helped us in publishing this second edition of our book, as well as to you for choosing to read this. We also thank our home institutions for their ongoing support of our work. We now welcome you into a world of discovery as you start your journey into the second edition of *Essentials of International Human Resource Management: Managing People Globally*…

Mila Lazarova, David Thomas, Elaine Farndale
December 2020

PUBLISHER'S NOTE

Every effort has been made to trace all the copyright holders but if any have been inadvertently overlooked the publishers will be pleased to make the necessary arrangement at the first opportunity.

1
Globalization and human resource management

CHAPTER LEARNING OBJECTIVES

After reading this chapter you should be able to:

1. Describe what is meant by the term globalization.
2. Define global HRM.
3. Discuss the factors in the external environment that influence global HRM.
4. Outline the important differences between global and domestic HRM.
5. Outline the historical development of global HRM.
6. Describe the role of the Global HR professional.

The new normal

Jeremy Greenblatt, Chief People Officer at Hypermarket dismounted from his exercise bicycle on the deck of his Seattle home overlooking Lake Washington. "I need to squeeze in a quick shower before my Zoom meeting with the regional HR managers," he thought. The bike was his main form of exercise as a result of the "work from home" order or "lockdown" as some called it that had resulted from the COVID-19 pandemic. The global spread of this deadly new virus had shut down many industries, but Hypermarket, a big box retailer with operations in a dozen countries was thriving. People still needed the food and other necessities that were the staple products offered by Hypermarket and most governments considered them an essential service. Travel restrictions, along with people's reluctance to be in close contact with others had increased the percentage of home delivery, but the retail outlets were still busy.

Hypermarket's retail stores had all changed their operations to provide for "social distancing" of shoppers (physical separation of people by at least 2 meters/6 feet) as mandated by the health authorities in the various countries in which the company operated. The wide variety of government mandates to try and stem the spread of the virus combined with social norms had made it difficult to come up with best practices that the company could adopt worldwide. The same was true for providing for the health and welfare of Hypermarket employees, which was the subject of today's online meeting. Jeremy was hoping that he and his regional managers could create some policy guidelines that could be implemented company wide.

His team at headquarters in Seattle had already dealt with the immediate needs of office staff who were working from home such as office chairs, desks, noise-cancelling headphones and computer cameras, as well as assisting with childcare and elder care issues. The needs of the in-store workers had so far been left up to local managers and there was no company-wide policy. It made Jeremy uncomfortable to leave decisions like this up to individual store managers, without any central guidance. He had heard that car maker Ferrari had hired a team of virologists and health experts to help them craft a plan for a safe working environment and that Disney was planning to use thermal scanners to check guests' temperatures to protect employees. Many companies had already set up hotlines to deal with the increased stress of working in this new environment. There were a great many things to consider.

Refreshed from his workout and shower, Jeremy signed into the Zoom meeting a few minutes early so he could welcome each of his subordinates as they arrived. Under normal circumstances he would have been welcoming them to dinner at Altura or another of his favorite Seattle restaurants. But, of course, all the restaurants were closed and air travel between countries was almost impossible. As he was waiting for everyone to sign in, Jeremy reviewed his agenda. He wanted to hear from each regional manager about the kind of issues they were facing. He knew that Ken Park, regional HR manager for Asia/Pacific had been facing a wide range of issues because of the vastly different political and socio-cultural climates of Japan, Korea, Taiwan, and Australia. Sarah Hughes, the HR manager for Europe had, until this situation arose, been primarily concerned with the exit of Great Britain from the European Union. And, Billy Nichols had been exasperated by the slow pace of the new trade agreement between the United States, Mexico, and Canada (USMCA). These changes in the international business environment and their effects on HRM policy and practice were still there but were now outweighed by the urgency of how to respond to a global pandemic.

Now in his fourth month of operating from his home office, Jeremy wondered, as did everyone else, how long it would be before things got back to normal. He mused that while it was the finance team that saved the company during the financial crisis of 2008, it might be his own team that was most critical now. Employee welfare had always been part of HR's job, but it seemed to him that he and his team were now truly in the health care business. The faces popping up on his screen interrupted his thoughts. "Welcome to the new normal," he said to open the meeting.

INTRODUCTION

Human resource management (HRM) activities may not often involve the dramatic global events of our opening case. However, HRM in an international context (involving multiple nations) or global context (involving all nations across the world) must respond to a dynamic and complex set of factors. HRM consists of the activities, policies and practices of *attracting, engaging, developing, rewarding* and *retaining* the employees that an organization needs to accomplish its goals. It involves all the management decisions that affect the relationship between employees and the organization.[1] *Global* HRM means conducting these activities across countries, cultures and contexts. And, not only must global HRM bridge across environments, it must also operate in a worldwide context characterized by the rapid and discontinuous change that is called *globalization*.[2]

GLOBALIZATION

Definitions of the term globalization vary widely. Some see globalization in economic terms as the absence of borders and barriers to trade and economic activity or more broadly as the overlapping of the interests of business and society.[3] Others focus on the rapid advances in information and communications technology, suggesting that the world is flat or has crystalized as a single place.[4] Here, we focus on the central idea that globalization is the process whereby worldwide interconnections in every sphere of activity are growing.[5] That is, globalization is not an end result or caused by a single force, but the dynamic interconnectedness that results from shifts that are taking place across a range of contexts including technological, political, economic, and cultural spheres.

These interconnections operate within and across levels. For example, Thomas Friedman talks about how ten events and forces including political (fall of the Berlin Wall and later the opening of China, Russia, and Eastern Europe), technological (the advent of Netscape and later other online search and collaborative tools such as Google), cultural (the popularization of the internet), and economic (the use of thousands of Indian software engineers to work on the Y2K problem from all over the world, and waves of outsourcing, offshoring and global supply chaining) that converged to flatten the world.[6] These forces have created a world that allows for multiple forms of collaboration without regard to geography, time zones, or in many cases even language.

Globalized environments interact with and influence each other. As an event occurs in any one of the external environments (e.g., the introduction of Netscape in the technological sphere), it influences other spheres (e.g., the popularization of the internet in the cultural sphere). These interrelated shifts in external environments affect organizations whose leaders respond by integrating *people*, *processes*, and *structures* to shape organizational outcomes.

In addition, other elements such as intergovernmental and non-government organizations (IGOs and NGOs), buyers, sellers, competitors, unions, and other mediating organizations influence elements of the external environment on the firm. For example, while the fall of the Berlin Wall touched off a worldwide rush to capitalism, NGOs in representing the interest of society, advocate (either through opposition to or through dialogue with organizations) for workers' rights in the absence of unions or legal protection.[7] And, as in our opening case, the COVID-19 pandemic has caused organizations to become more directly involved in the health and welfare of their employees.[8] These four spheres are not independent. Together they create a complex interconnected external environment in which the organization operates and across which the global organization must function. Despite their interconnectedness, it is useful to consider each individually with respect to global HRM.

Global technology

The aspect of globalization with perhaps the most potential to shape the organizational environment is the dramatic advances being made in information and communication technology.[9] Technological breakthroughs seem to be occurring on an almost daily basis with the latest communication or computing device even more powerful, smaller, less expensive, and more user-friendly than its predecessor. The pace of technological change is breathtaking. For example, the computer in your mobile phone today is a million times cheaper, a thousand times more powerful and about a hundred times smaller than the one computer owned by the Massachusetts Institute of Technology (MIT) in 1965.[10] The effects of technology largely result from two interlinked activities.

First, advances in information technology reduce the cost of communication, leading to more global goods and capital markets. This globalization in turn increases competition and contributes to the spread of technology and to its further development. The decreasing price and increasing sophistication of computing systems has placed technological capability in the hands of a wide range of organizations that was available only to large multinational firms only a few years ago.

Second, access to information, resources, products and markets are all affected by this improved technology. This means that small firms can now compete globally. This is of considerable significance given that across countries of all levels of development, the majority of firms are small and medium sized (SMEs). Now, even they have to think globally about HRM. It also means that all organizations are less limited by physical location; for example, making it possible for teams of individuals to be rapidly assembled and just as rapidly disassembled throughout the world; even creating virtual organizations in which employees do not meet face-to-face but are linked by computer technology.[11] Organizational boundaries are less rigid and the value chain functions of production, sales and marketing, and distribution might all be located in different countries.

Recently, we have seen the rise of "digital MNEs" (such as PayPal, Google, eBay, and Amazon, to name but a few) that perform activities based on or strictly linked to the internet. They offer such things as search engines, digital solutions like payments services, internet retail or provide digital content such as online games or digital media. In these firms the majority of their sales, but a minority of their assets are abroad. For example, in 2015, 58% of eBay's sales, but only 7% of their assets were international.[12]

Technological advances allow for various HR administrative functions to become easily automated or outsourced.[13] As recently as 30 years ago, there was a widespread belief that technology is largely irrelevant in HR as computers do not have people skills and could not handle HR work. And while the "transition from paper to pixels" has taken a couple of decades, today there are very few HR tasks that do not require technology. Organizations in many countries depend on it to manage recruitment, hiring, employee evaluation, compensation, and outsourcing.[14]

An example of the impact of technology on HR is the influence of social media such as LinkedIn, Facebook, and Twitter on staffing. Although the appropriateness and legality of using an individual's social media profile in recruitment and selection is still being debated,[15] there is mounting evidence that examining job candidates' social media presence is increasingly becoming commonplace.[16] The days of posting job openings only in newspapers and/or professional publications are a thing of the past. Now, the majority of organizations (especially large organizations that operate across borders) spend much more time and resources engaging in online recruitment. As illustrated by these examples, rapid technological change is challenging traditional thinking about organizing and the HR function. And of course, the work roles of employees in all organizations will change to reflect an increasingly information-driven environment.

Global economics

It is possible to argue that globalization is nothing new – just business as usual. For example, international trade as a percentage of gross world product was only slightly higher at the end of the 20th century than it was before 1914.[17] However, the number of new economic entrants to the international business arena is difficult to ignore. And, global economic interconnections are increasingly evident in shifting patterns of trade, foreign direct investment, capital and labor. In particular, globalization has resulted in worldwide capital markets that were previously closely aligned with nations, allowing both large and small firms around the world to participate in the global economy. A "flat world" is one in which the economic playing field has been leveled for all participants, small and large, from developed countries and emerging economies, and one in which value chains in both manufacturing and service industries are becoming (or can become) truly global.[18]

The global business landscape is changing and the center of economic activity is shifting. While US multinational firms dominated the international business landscape just after World War II, in 2011 Tokyo, Beijing and Paris were home to most of *Fortune* magazine's Global 500. In 2018, over 20% of the Fortune 500 companies were headquartered in China, with China ranking second only to the US. The US had four and China had three companies in the Global Top 10. The McKinsey Global Institute forecasted that it was likely that more than 45% of the Fortune Global 500 could be based in emerging regions (up from 5% in 1990 and 17% in 2010) by 2025.[19] In addition, the service sector of the global economy is increasing rapidly with as much as 69% of world economy in 2015 (up from 63% in 1997). The respective share in advanced economies was 74% in 2015 (up from 69% in 1997) and its share of global trade is rising faster than that of manufactured products.[20] At the time of writing, the economic impact of the COVID-19 pandemic is only beginning to be felt. The length and depth of the recession that this event creates is unknown. The story of whether the pace of globalization will return or if protectionism stalls global growth is still being written.

In summary, the players on the global economic stage are now more likely to include firms headquartered in Asia or Europe as opposed to the United States, previously the home country of many of the world's biggest and most internationalized companies. They are also more likely to be small to medium sized businesses and to be involved in the service sector. Although globalization has encountered a number of obstacles since the 2008 economic crisis (to which we return ahead in the chapter), most people would agree that it is not a trend or a passing

Table 1.1   Migrants as a percentage of total population[21]

WORLD	**3.5**
World Bank income groups	
High-income countries	14.0
Middle-income countries	1.4
Upper-middle-income countries	2.1
Lower-middle-income countries	0.9
Low-income countries	1.7
Geographic regions	
Africa	2.0
Asia	1.8
Europe	11.0
Latin America and the Caribbean	1.8
Northern America	16.0
Oceania	21.2
Select countries	
United Arab Emirates	87.9
Monaco	68.0
Luxembourg	47.4
Singapore	37.1
Australia	30.0
New Zealand	22.3
Canada	21.3
Ireland	17.1
Germany	15.7
United States of America	15.4
Estonia	14.4
France	12.8
Puerto Rico	9.1
Russian Federation	8.0
South Africa	7.2
Hungary	5.3
Argentina	4.9
Mexico	0.8

Source: International migrant stock as % of the total population, UN Migration Stock Workbook 2019 https://www.un.org/en/development/desa/population/migration/data/estimates2/estimates19.asp.

phenomenon, but rather an "overarching international system" that shapes not only economic activity but also domestic politics and foreign relations of nearly every country on the planet.[21]

Related to changes to the increased interconnectedness of economies and permeability of political boundaries, the number of permanent migrants (i.e., people relocating to other regions or countries, particularly in search of work) is changing the composition of the work-force in many countries. The magnitude of migration is large and increasing. Between 1990 and 2005 the world gained 36 million international migrants,[22] and between 2005 and 2015 – 71 million migrants.[23] In 2015, the number of international migrants in the world was over 243 million,[24] and in 2019, 272 million, which was 3.4% of the world population (compared to 2.8% in 2000).[25] If migrants were the population of a country, this country would be the fifth most populous country in the world.[26] The global number of international migrants has grown faster than the world's population.[27] Table 1.1 shows migration data by income groups and geographic regions, as well as some select country examples. In 2019, two thirds of the world's migrants live in a relatively small number of countries, with most migrants residing in the US (51 million, or 19% of the world's total migrants), followed by Germany, Saudi Arabia, the Russian Federation, and the United Kingdom. While there is more diversity in terms of where migrants come from, in 2019 one third of migrants originated in ten countries with India being the leading country of origin, followed by Mexico, China, the Russian Federation and the Syrian Arab Republic.[28]

The ease of movement of workers of all skill levels across borders combined with low birth rates in the developed world have and will likely continue to change the characteristics of the workforce in many countries, with increased levels of cultural diversity and more women in the workforce becoming key features. Therefore, global HRM policies and procedures must reflect the differing needs of this new workforce demographic. On a larger scale, nation states that receive migrants become more multi-ethnic and multicultural and face an increased challenge of integrating migrants and maintaining their own national and cultural identity (see also Box 1.1).[29]

BOX 1.1   AN IMMIGRATION STORY[30]

When Balnoor Gill arrived in Canada he already held a law degree from a university in the UK and had practiced law in Delhi as a senior associate in a corporate law firm. In fact, his law degree provided much-needed points in Canada's points-based immigration system. Balnoor knew however, that his British degree and Indian experience would not be enough to secure the kind of position he wanted in his new country. So, he enrolled in a Master of International Law degree program at an Ontario university. His wife, Jaspinder, went to work full-time to provide financial support and after a year of hard work, armed with his new degree, and with finances running low, he hit the job market. One law firm after an-other told him that while they appreciated his prior experience, they couldn't find a way to fit him into their organization. Finally, one firm took him on as a summer intern. However, at the end of the summer they offered positions to several other interns, but not to him. Undiscouraged, he broadened his search and finally found a good position working in the international division of a large Canadian bank. While not the job he had hoped for, he was now able to provide for his family and they were finally able to settle into their new home.

While Canada has long prioritized bringing in skilled migrants, and about 20% of the population was born outside of the country, Balmoor's situation is not unique to Canada. Skilled immigrants struggle in the labor markets in many countries and they tend to have lower salaries than native born individuals. The recognition of foreign credentials and experience is one issue, but also the cost of training upgrades, licensing fees and so on, can drain finances. All this is on top of adjusting to a new way of life. While government policies can have a positive impact, in the end it may be the willingness of employers to give an opportunity to people who come to a new country to make a new life that will allow countries to capitalize on these new resources.

Global political and legal environments

Many of the economic interconnections described previously are forged or brokered by intergovernmental financial institutions (such as the World Bank or the European Investment Bank), which underscores the link between economics, politics and organizations.[31] Political systems are the structures and processes by which a nation integrates the parts of society into a functioning unit. At the core of every political system is the need to balance between individual and national interests. The global shift from command (central control) to market (free market) economy structures suggests that many countries believe that free markets can help to achieve that balance. However, the world continues to be organized around nation-states that operate with different political structures and their different laws, rules and regulations that apply to organizational practices.

There is a wide range of political systems around the world. However, they can be roughly classified along a continuum that represents the degree to which citizens participate in decision-making. The two extremes are the pure democracy advocated in ancient Greece at one end and totalitarianism at the other. Totalitarianism typically takes one of two forms, theocratic or secular. In theocratic totalitarianism religious leaders are also the political leaders, as in Islamic countries in the Middle East such as Iran and Saudi Arabia. Secular totalitarianism includes socialism and communism, where ideological as opposed to religious concepts form the basis of the political system and leaders rely on bureaucratic power, military power or both. Key elements of political systems affecting organizations are political rights and civil liberties. The extent to which these freedoms exist in a country is often used to anticipate the degree of government interventions with business. For example, in their 2019 survey report, Freedom House ranked 194 countries on a scale of 1–7.[32] Around 20% of the world received a rating of 1 as the most free in terms of political rights and civil liberties including Australia, New Zealand, Canada, Japan, and most of Europe, while 5% were classified as the least free with a rating of 7 on the index, including Syria, North Korea, and Saudi Arabia.

The last two decades have produced enormous political change and have transformed the world's political landscape. After four decades of Cold War, the fall of the Berlin Wall in 1989 marked the beginning of a democratization process in many former secular totalitarian countries, notably those in Central and Eastern Europe. Many of these countries have seen great improvements in political rights and civil liberties. These political changes were closely intertwined with economic liberalization and privatization, leading to the increased participation of these countries in the global marketplace. But economic liberalization is not always matched by political change within countries.[33] For example, China is currently implementing some characteristics of a market economy while still maintaining a political hard line. While pressures to democratize are visible, the government has shown readiness to use various unpopular measures to suppress dissent and maintain order.

Other countries too have started on the path to democracy only to find themselves regressing back to totalitarianism. Initially, the Middle Eastern countries were excluded from this democratization process. But the arrival of the Arab Spring pro-democracy movement throughout much of the Middle East that erupted in late 2010 signaled that these countries too might be ready for a change. Throughout 2011, there was a wave of protests sparked by popular discontent with unlimited political power concentrated in the hands of small minorities, corruption, lack of political freedom and civil liberties and extremely high unemployment, especially among youth, which represents the majority of the population in the region.[34] By early 2012, three governments had been overthrown, others had announced their intent to step down or had made significant concessions, and protests in some countries continue. This illustrated the interconnectedness of the spheres of globalization: technology was widely credited with having played a significant role in these events, as protesters used social media to plan their actions and mobilize support. However, nearly a decade after the Aran Spring began, hopes for democracy have all but disappeared. Egypt remains an authoritarian state, Syria and Yemen are embroiled in civil wars. Even Turkey has abandoned its earlier shift toward openness and democracy and now resembles an autocracy.[35]

In 2019, Freedom House reported that 2018 had seen the 13th straight year of decline in global freedom. This change spanned a broad range of countries including longstanding democracies as the United Kingdom and the United States.[36] After years of increasing globalization and opening of borders, both political and economic, the last few years have seen an increased return to nationalism as evidenced through events like Brexit, the United Kingdom's vote to leave the European Union (EU), and Donald Trump's election to the US presidency and his and his supporters' commitment to "Make America Great Again!"

Such shifts in the political landscape underscore the need to estimate the likelihood that a government will undergo political changes, and how these changes may affect the organization. It is also important to consider the extent to which governments are involved in the activities of organizations and the overall legal environment associated with doing business in a particular country. With respect to global HRM, companies in some countries have relative freedom when it comes to handling HR issues, whereas in other countries many HR activities are strictly regulated (e.g., employment discrimination, minimal wage, maximum work hours, unionization rights, pension benefits). Such regulations are typically established at the national level (i.e., within a country) but they may stem from harmonized legislation that spans several countries, as is the case of members of the EU. There is also rising pressure to comply with voluntary guidelines introduced by intergovernmental organizations such as the UN, OECD, or the ILO, especially in the area of corporate social responsibility which is often tightly linked to HR issues.

In this context, political and legal pressure for organizations to fit into the local environment can sometimes conflict with a more global orientation toward economic activities. For example, organizations may wish to strategically deploy personnel wherever in the world they are most needed, but laws regarding immigration or the national composition of a workforce with a country can limit this ability. Further, as illustrated by the various national reactions to (and resulting restrictions in response to) the COVID-19 pandemic, in times of crisis even countries with stable (and thus typically predictable) political regimes may swiftly impose regulations that affect businesses in unexpected and profound ways.

Globalization of culture

Culture stems from the fundamental way in which a society learns to interact with its environment. The economic, legal and political systems that have developed over time are the visible elements of a more fundamental set of shared meanings in the society. As described in more detail in Chapter 2, culture also affects the goals of the institutions of society, the way the institutions operate, and the reasons that their members have for their policies and behavior. The cultural context deserves special attention because unlike the economic legal and political aspects of a country which are observable, culture is largely invisible. That is, the influence of culture is difficult to detect and is often overlooked.

Some people suggest that the rapid technological and economic development associated with globalization will have a homogenizing effect on culture.[37] For example, products ranging from cola beverages to denim jeans are consumed throughout the world, English is increasingly the global language for business, global travel is inexpensive and fast, and popular culture from films and television is transmitted worldwide. However, others argue that cultural diversity will persist or even expand, as people with different cultural orientations respond differently to this development.[38] For example, while values associated with economic development are converging, this is not true for other elements of culture;[39] and these aspects of culture can be seen to affect behavior in societies.[40] The seemingly identical McDonald's restaurants that exist almost everywhere actually have different meanings and fulfill different social functions in different parts of the world.[41] Although the physical facilities are similar, eating in a McDonald's is a very different social experience in Japan, or China, or the United States, or France.

Both convergence and divergence (see Chapter 3 for a more detailed discussion) of culture are probably oversimplifications. The reality is that although different environments produce different social systems, different environments can also produce similar social systems, and similar environments can produce vastly different cultures.[42] Thus, a reliance on the idea that the influence of the cultural context on global HRM will diminish as a result of globalization is probably not well founded. Global HRM must consider the systematic differences in values, attitudes, beliefs and assumptions about appropriate behavior that exist across societies and among members of today's increasingly culturally diverse workforce.

Global talent management

Given the multifaceted impact of globalization on technology, economics, political and legal structures, and culture, described here in detail, it is not surprising that globalization has spawned a new term related to international HRM: global talent management (GTM). Let's first unpack the meaning of these words. Talent is sometimes used as a synonym for human resources, that is, everyone in an organization brings some element of valued skill, knowledge, or abilities to the workplace.[43] Others use the term talent to refer specifically to those "A players" or "stars" who make up the top performers or high potentials who add the greatest value to the organization.[44] Talent management in either scenario is about attracting these people to the organization, and consequently rewarding, developing, and retaining them.[45] Applying the "global" lens, we can now see that in order to attract, reward, develop, and retain talent, organizations need to consider the effects of technologies, economics, politics, legal systems, and cultures globally to do this effectively. In other words, the study and practice of global talent management involves understanding how to manage talent in different countries across the globe, as well as understanding why differences in practices exist between countries.[46]

ORGANIZATIONAL INTEGRATION

Organizations function within the environment established by the interconnected elements of technology, economics, culture, and political and legal systems. Organizations respond to this environmental context through different configurations of *people, processes* and *structures*.[47]

All organizations create *structure* to coordinate and control the actions of their members. However, the forms that organizations take both domestically and globally vary considerably. The influence of these different organizational forms on global HRM and the relationship of HRM to the overall organization structure is the subject of Chapter 4. However, it is important to note here that because structures are related to both processes and people, change in one results in change in the others. For example, when Ford changed from a geographic to a product line structure, it saved billions of dollars, but sales processes and the roles of some managers were affected, and new managers were needed in its European operations. To remedy the problems Ford relocated some employees, but also restored some of the authority that regional managers had lost.[48]

Organizational *processes* are flows of activity that link together to accomplish the goals of the organization. Organizational processes are of course linked to both structures and people. For example, process innovations such as just-in-time manufacturing or concurrent engineering can transform the way organizations are structured and the way in which people do their jobs.[49] Of particular importance to HRM is the strategic management of the organization, which is a continuous process involving specifying the organization's mission, vision and objectives, and developing policies and plans to achieve these objectives. Sometimes an organization's business strategy can be its HRM strategy. That is, developing human capital can be a competitive advantage and it is therefore a strategically important consideration for global HRM.[50]

Organizations are created by and consist of *people*. As organizations globalize differences in how people think about their jobs, the time they are willing to devote to work, the skills and abilities they have, and the compensation they expect become apparent.[51] Designing and implementing structures and processes require engaging a diverse workforce.

In summary, organizations must engage with a dynamic and complex set of factors in the global environment. They do this through different configurations of people, processes and structures. The remainder of this book focuses on how an organization can attract, engage, develop, and retain the employees that it needs to thrive in today's global environment. To set the stage for this discussion, it is useful to examine the historical development of HRM.

EVOLUTION OF GLOBAL HRM

The roots of modern HRM in an international context can be traced to the Industrial Revolution of the late 18th century.[52] The forces of industrialization drove employment policies and practices until the rapid internationalization of organizations that followed World War II. The idea of internationalization was a dominant factor until the 1990s when the distinction between domestic and international business began to blur with many firms becoming exposed to international competition. While the seeds of globalization had been sown much earlier, it was from the early 1990s on that forces of globalization began to have a significant influence on HRM policies and practices. Therefore, the three broad phases of development of global HRM can be categorized as the eras of *industrialization, internationalization* and *globalization.*

Era of industrialization

The spread of industrialization in Europe and the United States prompted a global search for the raw materials to fuel this development. Trading firms, shipping companies, banks and utilities were all involved in international expansion. By the mid-19th century cross-border manufacturing began to emerge. The level of development of transportation and communications made it difficult to exercise control over geographically distant operations. Family members were often sent abroad to ensure that distant subsidiaries acted in the best interest of the parent firm. For example, when Siemens from Germany set up a factory in St Petersburg, Russia, in 1855, a brother of the founder was put in charge and in 1863 another brother established a manufacturing subsidiary in Britain.[53]

During this era, the way in which firms were organized was influenced by new manufacturing techniques such as interchangeable parts and the resultant division of labor. To alleviate punctuality, attendance, and supervisory problems created by the mechanical pacing of work, some individuals, such as Scottish textile mill operator Robert Owen in 1810, began attending to the welfare of employees. Under his direction workers were provided with housing, dining facilities, recreation centers and so on, and the minimum wage for children and schooling was introduced. By the late 1880s these ideas had spread to the United States in the form of a philosophy called *industrial betterment.*[54] The industrial betterment movement resulted in the creation of the first managers whose main responsibilities revolved around the workers, rather than the work process, called *welfare secretaries* who were initially engaged in education, health and safety, and social issues.[55]

By the early 1900s, multinational activity had become an important element of the world economy with numerous large multinational manufacturing firms supported by a global infrastructure of service firms. This period saw the emergence of the *scientific management* movement in the United States with its emphasis on making the most efficient use of a poorly educated immigrant labor pool. The focus of what were now increasingly called *personnel directors*, shifted to conducting time and motion studies, preparing job specifications, and financial incentive programs as well as a continuing focus on employee morale. Thus, modern HRM has a dual legacy in both the industrial betterment and scientific management initiatives.

Two World Wars and the great depression saw a retrenchment of international business activity, but saw *personnel management* emerge as a function quite separate from line management with an emphasis on systematic recruitment, testing, and assessment of employees, some of which had spilled over from the psychological testing used by the military.[56] The personnel department was further strengthened during this time because of its role in managing the relationship with labor unions.

Era of internationalization

While international commerce had long existed in Europe and Asia, it was the rapid post-World War II international expansion of US firms that gave rise to institutions that truly transcended national borders – the modern multinational corporation. The drivers of this internationalization were the fact that the US had emerged as the unprecedented leader of the world economy following the war, coupled with advances in transportation and technology such as the introduction of commercial jet travel, transatlantic telephone links and the use of computer technology. The rush to internationalize created an increase in the international job market that could not be filled by the sons of internationally experienced military or diplomatic fathers. The focus of the expanding *personnel* departments was on expatriation.[57] Initially this activity focused on persuading managers to accept overseas assignments, usually through financial incentives. In the 1970s the costs of expatriation, reports of expatriate failure, and increased employee resistance to moving overseas refocused activities to support for expatriates to assure success. The use of the term *human resource management* (HRM) became popular[58] at this time and, coupled with the study of expatriation, gave rise to the academic study of international HRM.[59]

The rapid growth of multinational organizations created issues regarding the coordination and control of far-flung operations. The problem of how to best organize to meet this challenge resulted in two approaches to organizational structure, both of which contributed to the internationalization of HRM. One approach was implementing matrix organizational structures involving both product and geographic reporting lines, while the other was to have more headquarters staff in coordinating roles. In the first case, the difficulties associated with matrix structures, in particular dual authority relationships and horizontal communication linkages, created people management challenges that involved HRM as opposed to strategy and structure. In the second case, the increase in headquarters staff required for coordination led to top-heavy bureaucracies that eroded competitiveness. Downsizing staff bureaucracies began with the US-based firms but was followed by European, and then following the financial crisis of the 1990s, by Asian firms. Therefore, HRM turned its attention to outplacement and redesigning jobs to manage this change. Coupled with expatriation, the need to coordinate and control the activities of the multinational organization recognized during this era continues to be a major element of global HRM.

During the 1980s the idea that the management of human resources could be a strategic advantage began to take hold, which in turn questioned the notion that there was a single best approach to HRM. Growing research on cultural differences in management practice,[60] along with the ability of Japanese firms to make such an amazing recovery after World War II, with people as their only natural resource, awakened Western managers to the fact that very different approaches to the management of people could be successful. The recognition that organizations who were expanding overseas did not necessarily have superior management practices coupled with pressure from local governments to hire and develop local employees shifted HRM focus to also include recruiting and developing local executives to run foreign subsidiaries. As organizations began to adopt the approach that talent mattered more than nationality, the challenge for global HRM became how to identify, develop, and transfer and repatriate talent that was spread out across the world.

Era of globalization

The accelerating global competition of the 1990s caused organizations of all sizes and types to consider the global context in which they were operating. Previously HRM had a heavily functional focus primarily on managing international assignments. However, the erosion of traditional sources of competitive advantage by the forces of globalization emphasized the need for organizations to create sustainable competitive advantage through HRM. This has brought HRM to center stage regarding management practice and stimulated many innovations that have improved operational effectiveness.

More important perhaps is the recognition that in order to be competitive in today's global environment HRM must be aligned with organizational strategy. An important development in thinking about the alignment of HRM and strategy is what is called the *resource-based view* of the organization.[61] The idea that the organization can be viewed as a bundle of resources gave rise to notion that HRM-related capabilities (such as staffing practices, performance appraisals, training and development, compensation, or union–management relationships) could be sources of competitive advantage.[62] For example, Hewlett-Packard's organizational strategy requires continuous innovation of products and services. HP's competitive advantage stems in part from the entrepreneurial behavior that is stimulated by their reward system.[63]

Globalization has also caused multinational organizations to recognize that a critical aspect of maintaining their competitive advantage is the ability to learn across its geographic boundaries.[64] Valuable knowledge can originate anywhere in the network of subsidiaries and concerted efforts are needed to ensure that knowledge and innovative practices are transferred not only from headquarters to subsidiaries but within and across all organizational units, regardless of their geographic location. The importance of transferring and recombining knowledge effectively reinforces the role of HRM as central to organizational effectiveness. While explicit knowledge can be easily passed on to others through texts or manuals, complex tacit knowledge (knowledge you don't know you have), which is based on experience and is difficult to put into words, can be a source of competitive advantage.[65] This knowledge is embodied in individuals and for organizations to leverage it, these individuals must be retained and assigned to roles in which the knowledge can be used.

The positive influence of globalization is not universally acknowledged. Opponents to globalization point out such things as the environmental damage caused by increased use of fossil fuels, the negative effects of global price competition, and the job insecurity caused by outsourcing.[66] Also, at the time of writing, the COVID-19 pandemic has thrown world economies into disarray. If previous levels of economic interdependence as a result of globalization will remain or if protectionism will have an increased influence is, at the time of writing, an open question. In any case, however, HRM will have an important strategic role to play.

Today HRM continues to be concerned with the challenges of foreign assignments and the coordination and control of geographically distributed organizations. However, there is a growing recognition that organizational effectiveness involves tracking and developing a global talent pool and that talent not nationality is key. Furthermore, while HRM was initially seen as a means to implementing organizational strategy, it is increasingly viewed as a source of competitive advantage, in particular as the transfer and recombination of knowledge increases in its strategic importance (see also Box 1.2).

BOX 1.2 CX SOLUTIONS COMPETITIVE ADVANTAGE = HRM

CX Solutions offers business processes outsourcing (BPO) to corporate clients, from their 27 offices in 10 countries. From these facilities, they provide services over the telephone or computer interfaces to customers in 30 different languages. What started out as "call centers" had now expanded along with the boom in e-commerce to provide non-voice back office services, which now made up 25% of its business. Key to CX Solutions success is creating and maintaining a positive customer experience. And that's not easy when the customer has contacted you because something is not working properly, or they have a complaint.

CX Solutions learned that the most important factor to a good customer experience was intelligent and well-trained staff. Certainly, locating their offices offshore was partly because of lower labor costs. But, just as important was the ability to attract and retain the front-line employees they needed. These employees, they felt, could be a source of competitive advantage that competitors would find it difficult to copy. That's why they had avoided the fierce competition for staff in the BPO hotspots such as India, the Philippines, and Ireland in favor of Eastern Europe locations, such as Romania and Bulgaria, and Latin American ones in Guatemala and El Salvador. By locating in major cities with universities they had been able to hire just the kind of college educated staff they needed. Combined with a rigorous training program and ongoing mentoring they were able to create a workforce that gave them one of the highest customer experience ratings in the industry. And to keep these employees happy their bright and modern workplaces included a wide range of amenities including fitness centers, games rooms and on-site health care. Their low turnover resulted in a more capable workforce but also lowered labor costs through reduced recruitment and training expense.

GLOBAL VERSUS DOMESTIC HRM

The internationalization of business requires HRM in all types of organizations to consider the broader context of its activities and the interests of different stakeholders.[67] However, global organizations need to manage the additional challenge of successfully navigating diverse institutional, social, cultural, political, and economic environments. It is the need to leverage all these differences that makes the HRM activities in global organizations much more complex than the HRM activities of purely domestic organizations.[68] This complexity affects the people, processes and structures required to deliver the functions of HRM. Global HRM must (a) consider more and different contextual influences, (b) operate under higher levels of risk, (c) engage in a broader set of activities, (d) fulfill many strategic roles, and (e) balance the forces toward differentiation versus internal consistency of HR operations.[69]

More and different contextual influences

Domestic HRM is concerned with a single national context including its legal, economic, political, and cultural elements. In global HRM policies and procedures must be constructed and implemented with the variety of national contexts in mind. For example, in Islamic countries religion dictates numerous work practices including time and space for daily prayers, a work week that includes a Saturday–Wednesday (e.g., Saudi Arabia) or a Sunday–Thursday (e.g., Egypt, Jordan, UAE) schedule, compared to the Western Monday–Friday schedule.

Higher risk exposure

Global HRM often involves higher levels of risk than domestic HRM. For example, the additional expense associated with sending expatriates on overseas assignments (see Chapter 8) creates a financial risk associated with the potential of these employees to return without completing the assignment or to underperform. Ultimately, the simple fact that international organizations operate in multiple geographies exposes them to greater risk from both natural and manmade sources.

Broader set of HR activities

Operating in multiple national environments makes several activities necessary that are not required in a purely domestic context. Global HR departments are engaged in complex processes such as global redistribution and relocation of work, the integration of organizational units following international mergers, acquisitions or joint ventures (see Chapter 7), and providing input in the designing of HR practices in greenfield investments overseas. Global HR is also involved in creating conditions for successful transfer of HRM practices across countries, disseminating corporate culture, facilitating knowledge transfer across borders (see Chapter 6), and creating and maintaining formal and informal HR networks that span the globe.[70]

Balancing differentiation and internal consistency[71]

In contrast to HRM in domestic organizations, which operate in fairly homogenous national contexts, global HRM needs to continuously balance being both responsive to local environments *and* internally consistent (discussed in more detail in Chapter 4). On the one hand, MNEs need to ensure that the HRM policies and practices they introduce will fit with local employment regulations, broader institutional conditions and local cultural values. For example, introducing a compensation practice that foregoes union consultation in a country with strong union presence may not only alienate workers but may also be in violation of local laws. On the other hand, global HRM also needs to create coherence and internal consistency between HRM strategy and the HRM policies and practices in the different locations of the organization. Local adaption of HRM practices in each national subsidiary may diminish the competitive advantage of the organization as it is no longer using its global experience to distinguish itself.

MAPPING GLOBAL HRM

Models of HRM vary depending on the extent to which they emphasize the fit between HRM and business strategy with a goal of improving organizational effectiveness[72] or a more pluralistic perspective that considers multiple stakeholders and situational factors as antecedents to HRM policy choices.[73] Here we map the domain of HRM onto the multiple contexts that influence HRM in a global environment. This framework is presented in Figure 1.1.

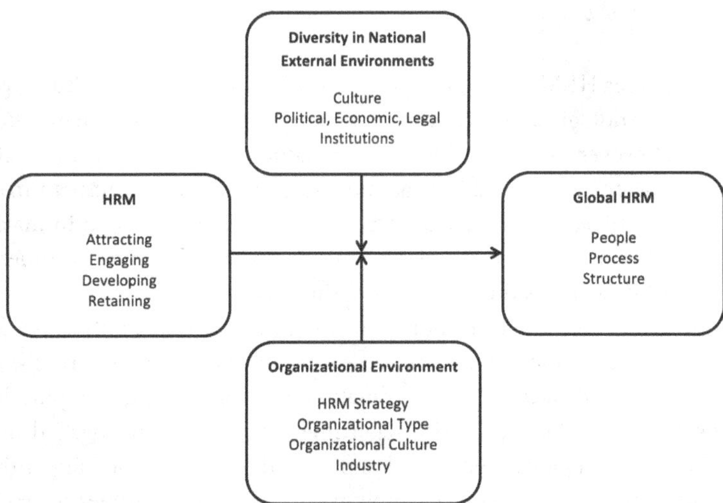

Figure 1.1   Map of global HRM

Factors in an organization's external environment include culture and the institutions that reflect different legal, political, and economic systems. In this book Chapters 2 and 3 focus on the external (cultural and institutional) factors, while Chapter 4 deals with the internal (organizational) context for global HRM. These factors interact with the core functions of HRM to result in different configurations of people, processes, and structures involved in decision-making about the human resources of the organization.

The result is not only the definition of particular HRM policies or practices, but also the relative importance of a particular activity, the feasibility and mechanisms for implementing a particular policy or procedure, and how that policy or procedure might be organized.[74] For example, by drawing on the various elements outlined in Figure 1.1, we could define the domain of a particular HRM activity as attracting computer technicians in a joint venture in the petroleum industry to work on drilling rigs off the coast of Norway. The feasibility of engaging particular people (HRM professionals and/or line managers), a particular process (university on-campus recruiting or professional associations), or particular structures (local Norwegian HR, headquarters HR, or both) might vary depending on other factors such as the HRM strategy of the firm or its organizational culture.

In other words, this framework does not prescribe the configuration of global HRM activities nor does it suggest a strictly contingent relationship. For example, the configurations of HRM activities might be as influential in shaping organizational strategy as the reverse and as we discussed at the outset, the interconnectedness of the environmental and organizational factors means that a change in one affects the others. However, this static diagram is useful in mapping the various elements that must be considered by HRM in a global context.

CHAPTER SUMMARY

This chapter examines HRM in the global context, which includes the cultural, political, legal, economic, and technological aspects of the various national environments in which firms might operate. However, it also includes the dynamic interconnectedness called *globalization*. Organizations engage with this dynamic and complex set of factors through different configurations of people, processes, and structures, which are included in making decisions concerning the human resources of organizations in today's global environment. This is the focus of global HRM, which is the core focus of this book.

Global HRM has its origins in responses to the forces of industrialization, later of internationalization, globalization, and, most recently, anti-globalization trends. HRM is still concerned with the challenges of the coordination and control of geographically distributed organizations. However, the Global HR department is increasingly engaged in the development and utilization of a global talent pool and viewed as a source of competitive advantage. While all organizations need to consider how the global context influences HRM, organizations that operate in multiple countries face several additional challenges that are not present in a purely domestic context. This increased complexity has implications for the activities, policies and procedures of HRM as well as for the role of HR professionals.

QUESTIONS FOR DISCUSSION

1. Discuss the key elements of the external environment that shape global HRM.
2. Describe how global HRM differs from purely domestic HRM.
3. Describe how the eras of industrialization, internationalization, and globalization have influenced HRM.
4. Describe an example of how an organization might engage with its environment by configuring its people, processes and structures.

NOTES

1. See Beer, Spector, Lawrence, Mills, & Walton (1984) for a discussion of this definition of HRM.
2. For more on globalization and business see Parker (2005).
3. See Ohmae (1995); Renesch (1992).
4. See Friedman (2005); Robertson (1995).
5. Parker (2005).
6. Friedman (2005).
7. See for example, Chen (2009).
8. McKinsey Global Institute (2020).
9. See Naisbett (1994).
10. Mcleod, Fisch, & Bestler (2009).
11. See Erez & Earley (1993).
12. https://unctad.org/en/PublicationChapters/wir2017ch4_Annex_en.pdf; https://unctad.org/en/Publication Chapters/wir2017_KeyMessage_en.pdf; https://unctad.org/system/files/official-document/diaeia2018d3a5 _en.pdf
13. See Marler (2009).
14. Caudron, Gale, Greengard, & Hall (2002).
15. Dery, Tansley, & Hafermalz (2014).
16. Spencer (2018) and Stam (2018).
17. Farnham (1994).
18. Friedman (2005).
19. Dobbs, Remes, Smit, Manyika, Woetzel, & Agyenim-Boateng (2013).
20. Buckley & Najumdar (2018).
21. Friedman (1999).
22. Population Division of the United Nations Secretariat (2006).
23. https://refugeesmigrants.un.org/infographics
24. https://refugeesmigrants.un.org/infographics
25. https://www.un.org/en/development/desa/population/migration/publications/migrationreport/docs/ MigrationStock2019_TenKeyFindings.pdf
26. Calculations by authors, based on data reported by the US Census Bureau: https://www.census.gov/ popclock/print.php?component=counter

27. https://www.un.org/en/development/desa/population/migration/publications/migrationreport/docs/MigrationStock2019_TenKeyFindings.pdf

28. https://www.un.org/en/development/desa/population/migration/publications/migrationreport/docs/MigrationStock2019_TenKeyFindings.pdf

29. Menipaz & Menipaz (2011).

30. This case is fictional, but based on the story of Ramanuj Basu as reported on the BBC.

31. See Parker (2005) for a discussion.

32. https://freedomhouse.org/report/freedom-world/2020/leaderless-struggle-democracy

33. See Napier & Thomas (2004).

34. http://www.guardian.co.uk/world/interactive/2011/mar/22/middle-east-protest-interactive-timeline

35. https://www.thetimes.co.uk/article/whatever-happened-to-the-arab-spring-0lqkc6mgq

36. https://freedomhouse.org/report/freedom-world/2019/democracy-retreat

37. For example, see Dunphy (1987).

38. For example, see Lincoln, Olson, & Hanada (1978).

39. Inglehart & Baker (2000).

40. See Smith & Bond (1999).

41. Watson (1997).

42. See Cohen (2001).

43. Iles, Xin, & Preece (2010).

44. Cappelli & Keller (2017).

45. Tarique & Schuler (2010).

46. King & Vaiman (2019).

47. See Parker (2005).

48. Lublin (2000).

49. See Carter & Baker (1991).

50. See Evans, Pucik, & Barsoux (2002).

51. See Thomas, Au, & Ravlin (2003).

52. Our discussion of the historical development of HRM draws on Evans, Pucik, & Barsoux (2002).

53. Evans, Pucik & Barsoux (2002).

54. George (1968).

55. Crichton (1968).

56. Jacoby (1985).

57. See Thomas (1994) for a discussion.

58. The term possibly originated from the Japanese word jinzai (human material) which gained use in post-war Japan or from early economics research on "human capital."

59. For a discussion see Thomas (2008).

60. See Hofstede (1980).

61. See Barney (1991) for a discussion from a management strategy perspective.

62. Schuler & MacMillan (1984).

63. Scanlon (2009).

64. See Kogut & Zander (1992).

65. See Nonaka & Takeuchi (1995) for a discussion.

66. https://www.marketing91.com/what-is-globalization/

67. See Beer, Spector, Lawrence, Mills, & Walton (1984) for discussion of the stakeholder interests served by HRM.
68. Dowling, Festing, Engle, & Gröschl (2009), and Sparrow, Brewster, & Harris (2004).
69. This classification is based on Dowling (1988), Evans, Pucik, & Björkman (2011), and Farndale, Scullion, & Sparrow (2010).
70. Sparrow, Brewster, & Harris (2004).
71. Discussion based on Evans, Pucik, & Björkman (2011).
72. Fombrun, Tichy, & Devanna (1984).
73. Beer, Spector, Lawrence, Mills, & Walton (1984).
74. Murray, Jain, & Adams (1976).

2
Cultural context of IHRM

CHAPTER LEARNING OBJECTIVES

After reading this chapter you should be able to:

1. Define national culture and describe the dimensions along which national cultures differ.
2. Recognize how national cultures impact organizational practices and employees' behaviors.
3. Evaluate the limitations of cultural frameworks for use by IHR managers.
4. Compare and contrast the arguments for and against cultural convergence/divergence.
5. Outline the differences between societal culture and organizational culture.

Springtime in Paris

As she savored the last bite of her croissant Martha Pereaux, HR Director for C3 Technologies thought about how she would approach her latest "cross-cultural collision" as she had come to think of them. In the year since she had moved to Paris from Houston, there had been many, but none quite as bizarre as this one.

Martha had taken the big promotion to head up the HR Division of the joint venture between Houston-based SuperChem and the French company. C3 developed technology for the oil industry, primarily new types of concrete that formed the barrier wall for offshore oil and gas wells. The joint venture was meant to take on the likes of the giant Schlumberger on its own turf and competed with them for valuable technical staff.

Everyone said she was the perfect choice, having grown up in a bi-lingual family in Canada, with a chemical engineering degree and an MBA with an emphasis in international management. But, nothing had really prepared her for the day-to-day challenges she faced in Paris. Every time she thought she had the French figured out something new would arise that mystified her. They could be so "French" she thought.

She had called the meeting this morning with the lead chemist Dr. Bertrand to discuss his rejection of Frank Reynolds, a recently graduated PhD in Chemistry from MIT, an expert in synthetic polymer chemistry which C3 desperately needed, and whom Martha had recruited. Despite what to Martha seemed impeccable credentials, Bertrand had refused even to interview him. "The graphology report shows him to be unreliable," said Bertrand. Graphology, "hand writing analysis," thought Martha, what will it be next?

"It's still early," she thought as she paid for her breakfast. "I might as well walk the few blocks over to the office in the 7th ar-

INTRODUCTION

While the use of handwriting analysis as a selection technique, as mentioned in the opening vignette, may be peculiar to a few countries such as France, HRM policies and practices do vary substantially between the different cultures in which multinational firms operate. Thus, global HRM is not only about understanding the HRM practices of international organizations but also about the ways in which the cultural context that different countries provide influences human resource management. In this chapter we discuss how societal culture influences HRM.

CULTURAL CONTEXT

Culture is a widely recognized word, but its exact meaning can be elusive. A useful way of thinking about culture is that it is the mental programs that are shared by groups of people and that condition their responses to their environment.[1] Therefore, in terms of establishing the context for HRM, culture consists of values, attitudes, beliefs and assumptions about appropriate behavior that are shared in a society. To understand how this cultural context influences HRM, it is important to know some basic characteristics of culture, the way in which cultures vary in a systematic way, and how culture has its influence both on individuals who make up organizations and the context in which organizations operate.

Characteristics of culture

Several general characteristics of culture are important to keep in mind to understand the effect that the cultural context has on HRM. These are that culture is *shared*, it is *learned*, and it is *systematic and organized*. Also, cultures can be *tight or loose*. By definition, culture is something that is shared by a specific group of people and is not readily available to individuals outside this group. If we think of culture as mental programming, culture exists at the middle of three levels as shown in Figure 2.1.

At the base level, all human beings share certain biological characteristics. At the highest level are the personality characteristics that are unique to each of us. Culture occurs at an intermediate level and consists of the elements of mental programming that we share with others in our specific group. Also, as indicated in Figure 2.1, culture is transmitted through the process of learning and interacting with the environment. Over time, societies develop patterned ways of dealing with all the different parts of their environment and this knowledge is passed on from generation to generation. Guidance about appropriate behavior in a particular culture is often contained in the stories that parents tell their children.[2] For example, people in the United Sates know that the (probably fictional) story of George Washington chopping

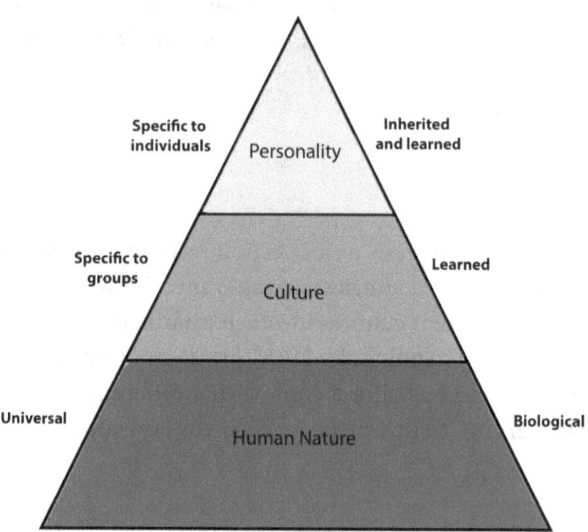

Source: From Thomas (2008), p. 28 (adapted from Hofstede 1980).

Figure 2.1   Three levels of mental programming

down a cherry tree, and confessing that he had done so, demonstrates the American values of honesty and truthfulness. In China, people show the value of education by honoring teachers on September 28, the anniversary of the birth of Confucius. It is unusual for a person to be a member of a society without having been taught its core values.

A third important characteristic of culture is that culture is not a random assortment of customs and beliefs, but is an organized system of values, attitudes, and meanings that are related to each other. The visible artifacts of culture (language, customs, dress, and so on) are related to a deeper set of meanings that are not accessible to outsiders but are taken for granted by members of a cultural group. Often members of a society know that they should behave in a particular way but cannot say why this is so. Because this mental programming is imposed by our own culture, the cultures of others often seem strange and illogical. Much of culture is hidden and the superficial and visible elements of culture have been likened to the tip of an iceberg, with more fundamental aspects well below the surface.[3] Icebergs have as much as 90% of their mass below the surface of the water, leaving only a small percentage visible. Like the iceberg, it is the deep underlying assumptions of culture that are the ultimate source of values and action. It is at this level that the logic and coherence of a culture can be understood. Thus, a deeper understanding can often reveal the logic in beliefs and behaviors that seem strange and illogical on the surface.

Cultures differ not only in their details, but also in the extent to which they are shared among members of society. Some cultures have widespread agreement about correct behavior, while others have greater diversity and tolerance of difference.[4] So-called *tight* cultures, such as Japan, have broad agreement on cultural norms and are often based on homogeneous populations or the dominance of particular religious beliefs. Countries with diverse populations, such as Canada, have relatively *loose* cultures with more variability of thought and action accepted and even encouraged. Thus, it is important to remember that there can be very different degrees of agreement among members of society on culturally based values, attitudes, beliefs and assumptions about appropriate behavior.[5] That is, not everyone in a society will know everything about its culture, nor will people from the same culture behave identically to each other. As shown in Figure 2.1, culture is only one of several factors influencing how people behave.

Societal culture is best expressed in the complex interactions of values, attitudes and behavioral assumptions among its members. A definition of culture that captures this idea and that informs the discussion of culture's influence on IHRM in this chapter is that *culture is a set of knowledge structures, consisting of systems of values, norms, attitudes, beliefs and behavioral assumptions that are shared by members of a social group (society) that are embedded in institutions and learned from previous generations.*

Sources of cultural differences

There are so many factors that contribute to cultural variation that we cannot cover them all in this chapter. However international managers will often find themselves in situations where cultural norms that may have been developed many centuries earlier influence their employees or business associates today. From a practical perspective, if managers can understand something about the source of cultural differences they may be able to anticipate the ways in which people from different cultures are likely to react to technological, social, and economic conditions that today's organizations face. Many cultural characteristics originally developed to aid the survival and safety of society's members. For example, the Western practice of shaking hands with the right hand as a form of greeting originated as an indication that the dominant hand held no weapon. Other culturally based forms of greeting developed as a way of showing respect and deference for social ranks, as in the case of bowing in Japan. In addition to such norms about interpersonal interactions some societal norms relate directly to the geography in which the culture developed. For example, the more casual attitude toward time observed in tropical climates stands in contrast to the view of time as a scarce resource that must not be wasted, but must be saved or used wisely found in more temperate climates. The more relaxed view of time may have originally reflected the fact that in tropical climates crops can be planted and harvested year-round as opposed to at certain times.

People encode the things they observe and the feelings they have in terms of language. Therefore language defines their view of the world and plays a significant role in spreading and maintaining culture.[6] For example, the Inuit language of the indigenous people of the northern part of North America contains numerous words describing snow because they have the need to distinguish the different types. However, the existence of many more terms for snow does not necessarily indicate the ability to distinguish types of snow.[7] That is, just because non-Inuit people do not have a term for a particular type of snow does not mean they cannot recognize it. Language varies by culture, but does not limit thought. For example, when we do not have a word for something and need one, we invent or borrow one. *Pochemuchka*, the unique Russian term for someone who asks too many questions, would seem to be a candidate for widespread use if it was easier for non-Russians to pronounce. Even the way we think about time may be influenced by language.[8] For example, English speakers mainly think of time horizontally as *behind* followed by *ahead*, whereas Mandarin speakers think of time vertically as up *(shang)* followed by down *(xia)*. Language, therefore, is an artifact of culture that helps to perpetuate its values, attitudes, beliefs, and behavioral routines. Because we use language to interact with others, it has a powerful role in shaping behavior and in perpetuating beliefs and habitual, cultural, patterns of interaction.[9]

A number of other factors contribute to the origins of culture and the persistence of cultural differences. These include the following:

- *Religion and ideologies* reflect the beliefs and behaviors shared by social groups that cannot be verified by empirical tests. They have a cultural influence through the content of their belief systems, the structure of their beliefs and rituals, and the identities that they promote.
- *Climate, topography and the indigenous economy* affect the origin of traditions and behavior of modern societies as our discussion of the relationship between climate and time suggested.
- *Geography* affects the exchange of culture among societies. Geographic features such as mountains and oceans, limit the opportunities for cross-cultural interaction.
- *Economic systems and technology* affect the exchanges between cultures and therefore the opportunity for the transfer of culture.
- *Political boundaries* define areas where there is more, or less, interaction among cultural groups.

A practical example of the usefulness of recognizing the factors that contribute to the source of cultural differences is provided by the unique culture of the Japanese. For many Westerners Japan seems the strangest of cultures. However, when we consider such factors as its relative geographic isolation, its limited natural resources, its population density, and its homogenous population, many of the strange rites and rituals of this culture become understandable. For example, the need for order in the very densely populated island developed a system of *tateshakai* (vertical society) which translates to the ritualistic exchange of business cards to establish status and deference to one's *senpai* (superior) in modern Japanese organizations. The reason for the persistence of seniority as a key variable in HRM decisions in Japanese organizations is thus more obvious. Deep-rooted cultural concepts, which have their foundation in ancient beliefs and have become fundamental beliefs about right and wrong in a society, are programmed at a very deep unconscious level in its members. Their meaning might not be apparent to the outsider and can even be obscure to members of the cultural group. Once a cultural pattern is established it is very resistant to change even when surrounding circumstances change.

Issues with the concept of culture

There are a number of issues regarding the concept of culture that are important to IHRM. The ability to draw on culture to understand, explain, and predict behavior in organizations is dependent on considering the following:

- The concept of national culture
- Cultural convergence or divergence
- The concept of organizational culture
- The effects of acculturation and biculturalism.

An important practical consideration for managers is the extent to which a nation has its own distinctive culture. For example, Canada contains both Anglophone and Francophone Canadians, each with their distinct culture, and the First Nations people of North America span the border between Canada and the United States. Any North American city will have many distinct cultures represented within its boundaries. Despite the existence of sub-cultures in a country, a solid argument can be made in favor of the concept of a national culture. Because nations are political entities, each has a distinctive form of government, its own legal framework and educational and employment systems, which reflect the cultural consensus of society.[10] In addition, the concept of nation has a symbolic value that reinforces the idea that people from that country have a shared and distinctive culture.

The fact that national culture is related to other societal factors, such as political, legal, educational, and employment relations systems leads some people to suggest that the rapid technological and economic development around the world has the effect of making cultures more similar.[11] This is called the *convergence* theory of national cultures – the view that all cultures are converging to be more similar to each other. Others focus on processes that maintain cultural stability, and argue that as societies with different cultural traditions respond to rapid technological development, cultural diversity will persist or even expand.[12] The stability of cultures is fostered by the large number of complex links between the various elements within the nation and the long history of its distinctive culture.[13] Because of their unique origins and complexity, cultures evolve in different and unpredictable ways, making the idea of convergence toward some common end point highly unlikely. Thus, while economic development brings pervasive cultural changes, the historical basis for a society has an enduring effect (called "path dependence") on the character of this development.[14] Also, cultural systems may be able to combine traditional and modern elements in unique ways. For example, Hong Kong Chinese seem to have been able to retain the traditional Chinese respect for authority while rejecting its fatalism and adopting modern competitiveness.[15]

Researchers and managers have long been aware that the social characteristics of organizations in some ways resemble the cultural characteristics of societies.[16] The term to describe this informal structure is *organizational culture*, which we discuss in detail ahead in Chapter 4. The idea of an organization having its own culture raises the questions of how national culture and organizational culture are related and how are they similar or different?

Organizational culture is a somewhat different idea to national culture and is composed of different elements.[17] While national culture consists of deeply held values which result in a shared understanding, organizational culture largely consists of shared behaviors or norms for how things are done in the organization. In addition, entry to, and transmission of, organizational culture occurs in different ways from national culture. We are born into our national culture but socialized into an organizational culture as an adult. Moreover, individuals are only partially involved with an organizational culture but are totally immersed in their national culture. Overall, probably the best way to consider the influence of organizational culture is to think of organizational *norms* operating in, and in concert with, societal *culture*. For example, national culture can influence the type of organizational culture that exists within a firm. The bureaucratic precision and centralized decision-making of Daimler Benz and the fast-paced trial and error approach to encourage creativity at Chrysler reflected the societal cultures of Germany and the US. However, the inability to reconcile these differences is often mentioned as a primary cause of the failure of the merger of these two firms (see Chapter 7).

While the cultural beliefs of individuals are relatively stable over their lifetimes, changes do occur. Acculturation concerns the psychological and behavioral changes that occur in people because of contact with different cultures. The term is most frequently used to describe the changes in individuals who relocate from one culture to another. The gradual process of psychological acculturation that occurs during immigration results in changes in individual behavior, identity, values, and attitudes. Also, some individuals with experience of living in multiple cultures acculturate to such an extent that they are able to function very effectively in more than one culture. These so-called bicultural individuals have, through time living in another culture or through intensive daily interaction with culturally different others, developed so much cultural flexibility that they can adjust their behavior to the immediate cultural context. Biculturals do not just adapt their superficial behavior but they can also hold different views of themselves, reflecting two different cultures.[18] The issues of acculturation and biculturalism add complexity to our understanding of culture and its influence. However, they do not diminish the need for IHRM to consider the influence of the cultural context.

In summary, societal cultures are resistant to change and this resistance is typically too strong for organizational cultures to overcome. However, cultures are not static and can change through the process of acculturation as people move from one society to another.

COMPARING CULTURES

For the concept of culture to be useful in studying IHRM, we need a method of systematically comparing cultures. Much of our understanding of cultural variation has been achieved by reducing the analysis to the study of values. Values are relatively stable and differences arise from the solutions that different societies have devised over time for dealing with fundamental problems. Because there are a limited number of ways in which a society can manage these problems it is possible to develop a system that categorizes and compares societies on this basis.[19] That is, by examining the choices that societies have made we have been able to infer their values, that is their preferences for the way things ought to be or the way one should behave.

Despite being devised at widely different times and with different methods, some very similar sets of cultural dimensions have been identified. Because none of these dimensional approaches is entirely satisfactory as a basis for cultural comparison, we briefly review the major frameworks that have been devised for categorizing and comparing cultures. This review leads to a more in-depth look at the concept of individualism and collectivism and its relationship to other elements of the socio-cultural system.

Kluckhohn and Strodtbeck's cultural framework

Early studies in comparative anthropology produced a framework that has influenced the way the management literature has conceptualized cultural variation.[20] This categorization identified six dimensions along which a society can be categorized. These variations in value orientations concern the following issues:

- *Relationship to nature* – People have a need or duty to control or master nature (domination), to submit to nature (subjugation), or to work together with nature to maintain harmony and balance (harmony).
- *Beliefs about human nature* – People are inherently good, evil, or a mixture of good and evil.
- *Relationships among people* – The greatest concern and responsibility is for one's self and immediate family (individualist), for one's own group that is defined in different ways (collateral), or for one's groups that are arranged in a rigid hierarchy (hierarchical).
- *Nature of human activity* – People should concentrate on living for the moment (being), striving for goals (achieving), or reflecting (thinking).
- *Conception of space* – The physical space we use is private, or public, or a mixture of public and private.
- *Orientation to time* – People should make decisions with respect to traditions or events in the past, events in the present, or events in the future.

Hofstede's cultural framework

A framework that has received a great deal of attention is Hofstede's now-classic study of work values.[21] Based on attitude surveys of 117,000 employees of a large US multinational corporation (later identified as IBM), Hofstede extracted four dimensions with which he could classify the 40 different countries represented. These dimensions were named *individualism–collectivism, power distance, uncertainty avoidance*, and *masculinity–femininity*.

Individualism–collectivism is the extent to which one's self-identity is defined according to individual characteristics or by the characteristics of the groups to which the individual belongs on a permanent basis, and the extent to which individual or group interests dominate. Power distance refers to the extent that power differences are accepted and sanctioned in a society. Uncertainty avoidance is the extent to which societies focus on ways to reduce uncertainty and create stability. Masculinity–femininity refers to the extent to which *tradi-*

tional male orientations of ambition and achievement are emphasized over *traditional* female orientations of nurturance and interpersonal harmony.

By giving each of the 40 countries (later 50) a score, ranging from 0 to 100 on each of the dimensions, Hofstede derived a classification of national cultures. To investigate the possibility of a Western bias in this classification, a subsequent study in 23 countries[22] revealed a new cultural value orientation important in Chinese culture, Confucian work dynamism (later called long-term/short-term orientation),[23] interpreted as dealing with society's search for virtue. Societies with long-term orientation tend to show preference for order, thrift, and persistence. Recently, a sixth value orientation called indulgence versus restraint was identified. Indulgence stands for pursuit of gratification of basic needs and desires, and hedonistic behaviors, while restraint describing societies with strict social norms where gratification of needs is suppressed.[24]

It is particularly important to point out that Hofstede's value scores were the average score for all participants in each country. Therefore, it is not appropriate to be confused by ecological fallacy and infer that because two nations differ on a particular value dimension that any two individuals from those countries will differ in the same way. That is, within each nation, there might be variation on a particular dimension, such that a particular individual will not be at all representative of the mean score. For example, Figure 2.2 shows the hypothetical distribution of individual scores on individualism–collectivism between a collectivist country (Malaysia) and an individualist country (New Zealand).

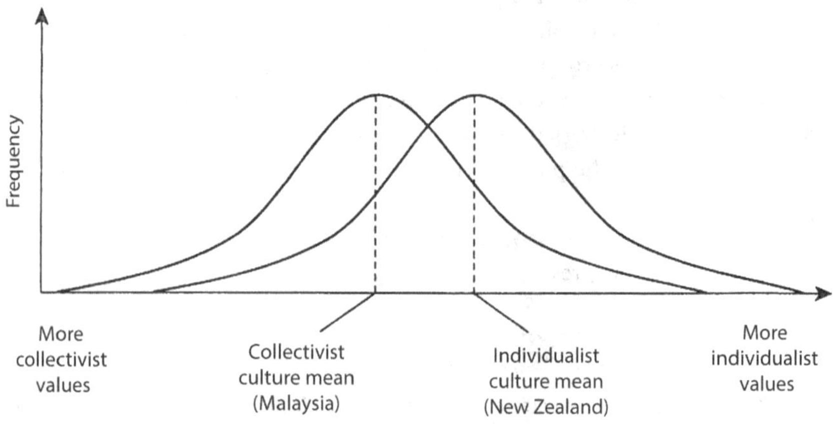

Source: From Thomas (2008), Figure 3.2.

Figure 2.2   Hypothetical distribution of individualism–collectivism scores

As shown in Figure 2.2, it is entirely possible to find an individual in New Zealand who scores lower on individualism than someone in Malaysia.

Schwartz Value Survey

In what can be seen as a refinement of Hofstede's earlier work, several additional large-scale surveys of values have been conducted.[25] Each of these studies adds something new to our understanding of cultural differences. The first of these is the Schwartz Value Survey.[26] Based on a review of previous theory and research, Shalom Schwartz and his colleagues conducted a series of studies on the content and structure of human values based on three universal human requirements. The first is the nature of the relationship between the individual and the group, the second is the preservation of the society itself, and the final problem relates to the relationship of people to the natural world. From these requirements that all societies share, Schwartz and his team derived values that reflected various ways of satisfying these needs.

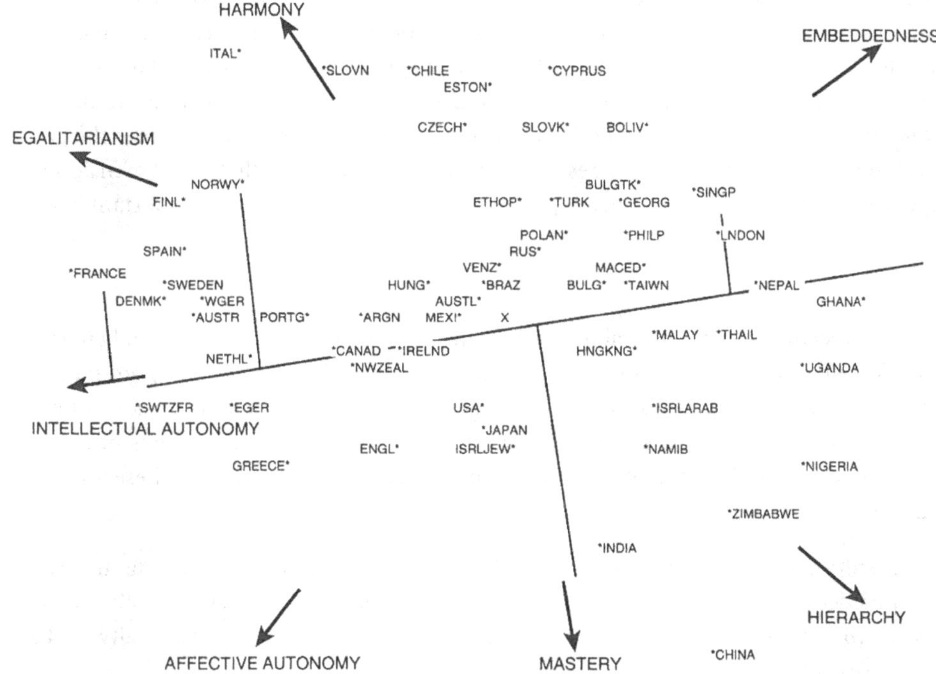

Source: From Thomas (2008), p. 58 (original source: Sagiv & Schwartz 2000).

Figure 2.3   Co-plot of value dimensions across 57 national cultures

To define cultural dimensions at the level of national culture, Schwartz and colleagues performed an analysis that yielded seven value types that were labeled as the following:

1. *Egalitarianism*, recognition of people as moral equals;
2. *Harmony*, fitting in harmoniously with the environment;
3. *Embeddedness*, people as embedded in the collective;
4. *Hierarchy*, unequal distribution of power is legitimate;
5. *Mastery*, exploitation of the natural or social environment;
6. *Affective autonomy*, pursuit of positive experiences; and
7. *Intellectual autonomy*, independent pursuit of own ideas.

A procedure that generates a two-dimensional graphic representation of the relationship of countries to each other on all seven dimensions simultaneously produces the diagram shown in Figure 2.3.[27]

As shown in Figure 2.3, the location of countries along the seven value vectors indicates their relationship to each other. The direction of the vector indicates the increasing importance of the value type in relationship to the center of the diagram marked by the X. For example, the line drawn on Figure 2.3 indicates the importance that each country attributes to *intellectual autonomy*. To locate a country on this dimension, a perpendicular is drawn from the position of the country to the vector. The lines drawn on the figure indicate that this dimension is very important in France, less so in Norway, India, and Singapore, and very unimportant in Ghana.

The GLOBE study

The most recent study of cultural differences in value orientations was undertaken as a part of the Global Leadership and Organizational Behavior Effectiveness (GLOBE) program.[28] One of the outcomes of the GLOBE research was the construction of nine dimensions of cultural variation. The first four of these dimensions are described as direct extensions of Hofstede's work, with the exception that two dimensions of collectivism are presented. These four dimensions are:

- *Institutional Collectivism:* The degree to which organizational and societal institutional practices encourage and reward collective distribution of resources and collective action.
- *In-Group Collectivism:* The degree to which individuals express pride, loyalty, and cohesiveness in their organizations or families.
- *Power Distance:* The degree to which members of a collective expect power to be distributed equally.
- *Uncertainty Avoidance:* The extent to which a society, organization, or groups relies on social norms, rules, and procedures to alleviate unpredictability of future events.

The next two dimensions can be seen as re-conceptualization of Hofstede's masculinity–femininity dimension. They are:

- *Gender Egalitarianism:* The degree to which a collective minimizes gender inequality.
- *Assertiveness:* The degree to which individuals are assertive, confrontational, and aggressive in their relationships with others.

The next two dimensions have their origins in the work of Kluckhohn and Strodtbeck on the *nature of people* and *time orientation* presented previously, and are:

- *Humane Orientation:* The degree to which a collective encourages and rewards individuals for being fair, altruistic, generous, caring, and kind to others.
- *Future Orientation:* The extent to which individuals engage in future-oriented behaviors such as delayed gratification, planning and investing in the future.

The final dimension is derived from work on achievement motivation,[29] but is also related to Hofstede's masculinity concept.[30] This dimension is:

- *Performance Orientation:* The degree to which a collective encourages and rewards group members for performance improvement and excellence.

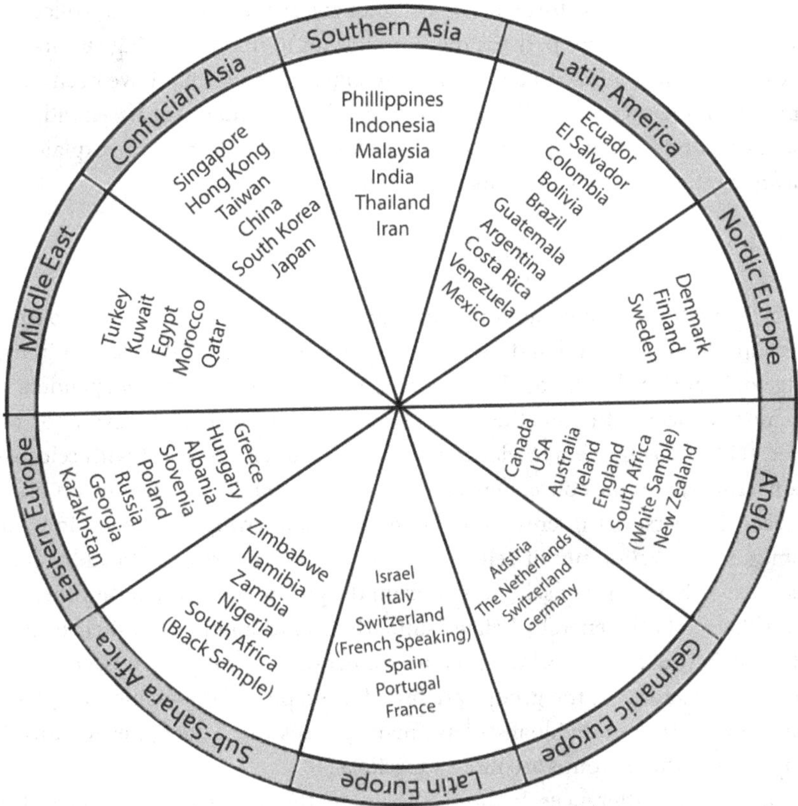

Source: From Thomas and Inkson (2009), p. 38 (reprinted from House, Hanges, Javidan, Dorfman, & Gupta 2004).

Figure 2.4   Country clusters according to GLOBE

The country scores for GLOBE data are available from the GLOBE website (https://globeproject.com/results#country). However, an additional way of understanding similarities and differences across cultures is to examine which countries cluster together in their positions on measures of cultural values. Based on the GLOBE data these clusters are shown in Figure 2.4.

As shown in Figure 2.4 the clusters of countries reflect such factors as common language, common religion, common climate, common economic systems, and shared political boundaries, some aspects of which are discussed in Chapter 3, as culture and the institutions of society share a common history.

As the previous discussion indicates, the results of the major studies of national variation in value orientations have some remarkable similarities, despite being conducted at widely different times, with different samples, and using different methods. This consistency of findings shows the utility of this approach to describing cultural variation. In addition, however, because they appear in some form in all the frameworks, individualism–collectivism and power distance (verticality) are perhaps more important to understanding cultural variation. That is, these dimensions relate to two of the fundamental issues that have been identified as being common among societies.[31] The first has to do with boundaries between individuals and groups and the second with the preservation of order in society. Both can be explained through horizontal and vertical individualism and collectivism.

Horizontal and vertical individualism and collectivism

Because they relate to fundamental differences among societies, individualism and collectivism are perhaps the most useful and powerful dimensions of cultural variation in explaining a wide range of behavior.[32] Individualism refers to viewing one's self as independent of others and to be more concerned about the consequences of a particular behavior for one's self. Alternatively, collectivism refers to viewing one's self as interdependent with selected others, to being concerned about the consequences of behavior for one's reference group, and to being willing to sacrifice personal interests for the good of this group. However, individualism–collectivism is not a dichotomy of self-interest and group interest. Both individualists and collectivists derive their sense of self, in part, from the groups with which they identify – their in-groups. Although both generally behave similarly toward members of their in-group, they differ in the way in which they decide who is a member of this group. That is, collectivists have very few of these groups, but the groups are broad in scope encompassing many interrelated relationships. By contrast, individualists have many groups with which they identify, but their relationships within these groups are more superficial.

In addition to the differences in motives and in the specification of reference group members, it is possible to differentiate between different kinds of individualism and collectivism. Significant among these is the concept of vertical and horizontal dimensions that relate to the way in which people view their status relationship with others.[33] In combination with individualism and collectivism, these dimensions correspond to the four types of self, independent or interdependent[34] and same or different.

Table 2.1 Culture, self-orientation, and politics

	Vertical		Horizontal	
	Collectivism	*Individualism*	*Collectivism*	*Individualism*
Kind of self	Interdependent	Independent	Interdependent	Independent
	Different from others	Different from others	Same as others	Same as others
Fake orientation	Communal sharing	Communal sharing	Communal sharing	Communal sharing
	Authority ranking	Authority ranking	Equality matching	Equality matching
Rokeach values	Low equality	Low equality	High equality	High equality
	Low freedom	High freedom	Low freedom	High freedom
Political system	Communalism (e.g., Indian village)	Market democracy (e.g., US, France)	Communal living (e.g., Israeli kibbutz)	Democratic socialism (e.g., Sweden, British Labour party)

Source: From Thomas (2008), p. 66 (reprinted from Triandis 1995).

Table 2.1 indicates how the different combinations of vertical and horizontal individualism and collectivism correspond to how people define themselves, their value orientations, their dominant political systems, and their typical patterns of social behavior.

As shown in Table 2.1, this distinction between vertical and horizontal individualism and collectivism results in four different cultural profiles. However, vertical collectivism and horizontal individualism might be the dominant cultural profiles around the world.[35]

Vertical collectivists see themselves as an aspect of an in-group, but members of the in-group are different in terms of status. These cultures are characterized by patterns of social relationships that emphasize communal sharing according to need and authority ranking, or the distribution of resources according to rank. They typically have social systems that do not reflect the values of individual freedom or equity. Inequality is the accepted norm, and serving and sacrificing for the in-group feature prominently.

In *horizontal individualism*, the self is autonomous and people are generally equal. These cultures are characterized by patterns of social behavior that emphasize equity in resource sharing according to contribution and distribution of resources equally among members. They have social systems that emphasize both the values of equality and individual freedom.

What these two dominant syndromes suggest is that verticality serves to reinforce collectivism, and horizontalness reinforces individualism.

The previous discussion has examined the main attempts that have been made to identify dimensions along which cultures could be systematically described and compared. Of the dimensions identified, the constellation of concepts encompassed by individualism and collectivism appear to be especially important in describing and comparing social behavior.

Cultural tightness and looseness

Another important issue when it comes to comparing cultures is the idea of cultural *tightness* and *looseness*.[36] Tightness refers to the extent to which members of a culture agree about what correct behavior is, and believe that they must behave according to cultural norms, and that they will receive sanctions for even small deviations from cultural norms. Loose cultures often have multiple and sometimes conflicting norms about appropriate behavior, and tolerance is shown to those who deviate from the norm. For example, Japan is a relatively tight culture, whereas Canada is a relatively loose culture.[37] Tight cultures tend to be homogeneous, and often occur in societies with high population density. Canada has high cultural heterogeneity compared to Japan's mono culture. Although a culture may be tight or loose overall, both tightness and looseness can occur in a society in different contexts. For instance, China provides an example of a culture that is tight in its political orientation (the country is ruled by a single party) but loose in terms of religion (many religions are recognized and practiced).

USE OF CULTURAL DIMENSIONS

Being able to systematically define cultural variations provides a foundation for explaining and predicting HRM on a comparative basis. However, the ability to profile national cultures along a limited number of dimensions also opens up the possibility for a dramatic oversimplification of the effect of culture. This oversimplification results in stating that people from this particular type of culture behave this way, whereas those from that other type of culture behave like that. Often, this is done by referring to an existing typology of attributes of national culture (very typically Hofstede's numeric ratings stemming back to the 1970s). In effect, by suggesting that culture works in this way, we have substituted *sophisticated stereotypes* of a culture for the complex reality that exists.[38] Therefore, instead of explaining cultural effects, it can have the opposite effect of constraining the way in which people regard members of another culture.

For example, we run the risk of thinking of all Japanese people as high on *masculinity*, and uncertainty *avoidance*, and moderate on *individualism* and *power distance*. The fallacy of this approach is apparent to anyone who has encountered behavior in members of another culture inconsistent with the picture painted by the profile. However, these problems do not render the systematic description of cultural variation useless. On the contrary, they can be valuable in selecting national cultures to compare when trying to assess the degree of similarity or difference on responses to HRM questions. In addition, they are useful tools, provided their limitations are understood. It is also important to understand how culture exerts its influence, which is this topic that we discuss next.

Influence of cultural context on HRM

To avoid the oversimplification of the influence of cultural context, that suggests that all people in a country behave in a particular way, we discuss the employee-level mechanisms through which variation in national culture influences IHRM. That is, it is important to understand that individuals are embedded in specific national-level cultures and are affected by and express their cultural orientation through both *cognitive* (what is perceived and interpreted) and *motivational* (what is desired) individual-level mechanisms.[39] Each individual will be different in the degree to which aspects of their culture are influential, but in general there is more similarity within cultural groups than between cultures.[40]

First, from a *cognitive* perspective, culturally different individuals learn different sets of values (as discussed previously), which develop into cognitive frameworks (mental programs) that are used to help organize and process information about situations and events such as HRM practices. Different priorities for what activities deserve attention, and the meaning we attach to these activities, are formed by gradually internalizing prevailing cultural patterns.[41] That is, individuals only attend and respond to those things that they have learned in their culture are important.

From a *motivational* perspective, the appropriateness of HRM practices is fundamentally tied to how people view themselves and their relationship to others. Everyone evaluates activities according to the extent to which they contribute to their personal self-worth and well-being.[42] Motives to maintain a positive self-image are probably universal. However, what constitutes a positive self-view depends on the extent to which individuals see themselves as connected to or separate from others as learned in their culture. That is, the extent to which an HRM policy or practice has benefit to the individual or to others with whom they feel connected can be seen as more or less appropriate in different cultures.

In sum, the mechanisms of cultural influence at the individual level fall into these cognitive and motivational domains. Together, these mechanisms produce a reasonably complete picture of the mechanics of cultural influence. They are the mechanisms through which cultural factors influence individuals to see a particular HRM policy or practice as important and also evaluate the extent to which it is beneficial. For example, the reasons why employee ownership plans are more likely to be found in some countries (e.g., the US) than others (e.g., Brazil) is influenced at least in part by individual preferences based on the cultural values of low power distance, high individualism and low uncertainty avoidance.[43]

Cultural differences have been found to exist in a wide variety of HRM practices including recruitment and selection (Chapter 8), reward allocation policies and compensation programs (Chapter 10). For example, organizations in countries in which culture is characterized by high uncertainty avoidance are more likely to offer seniority-based compensation than organizations from low uncertainty avoidance cultures. However, the fact that societies might, in general, exhibit a culturally based preference for a particular set of HRM policies or practices should not be interpreted as requiring that firms adopt these practices in order to be effective.

While the idea that culture influences HRM across countries has long been embraced, culture can become "the catchall for complexity"[44] if any differences between countries are quickly attributed to culture. Cultural differences are only one of many country differences and variations in HRM practices can be caused by a multitude of factors. Also, the assumption that culture drives HRM practices implies that organizations have only very limited managerial discretion in adopting different practices.[45] While HRM practices may be culture-bound on average, diversity within countries does exist and some evidence suggests adopting counter-cultural practices may pay off for the organization.[46] For example, individual pay for performance systems would seem to be incompatible with collectivist cultures, but in fact has been implemented with some success in China.[47] In fact, it is doing things that are unique (i.e., not average) that can result in a competitive advantage and make an organization more successful. Adopting atypical HRM practices may also attract employees that are more open to change, easily adaptable, and less constrained by prevalent norms, which can result in additional benefits for the organization.[48]

In the absence of clear evidence that shows that adapting HRM practices to local cultural values results in better organizational performance, organizations are best advised to use cultural values as only very general guidance as to what practices may or may not be culturally appropriate. Specific decisions on HRM practices should be driven not by the desire to achieve cultural fit but rather to build strong organizational identity and achieve superior performance.[49] This reminds us that culture is only one aspect of the context in which global HRM must operate and that other factors such as the institutions of society, discussed ahead in Chapter 3, and the organizational context (Chapter 4) are important.

CHAPTER SUMMARY

This chapter examines the cultural contexts that shape HRM in different countries. Societal cultures are relatively stable, but are not static and can be influenced by such factors as acculturation. Culture exerts its influence and constraints informally, through internalized socially acceptable norms for behavior. Numerous attempts have been made to categorize national cultures on a set of value dimensions. While these dimensional approaches are an oversimplification, they provide a systematic basis for explaining and predicting HRM on a comparative basis. They are useful provided their limitations are understood. The cultural context influences not only HRM practices but also the expectations that employees have about their relationship with organizations.

QUESTIONS FOR DISCUSSION

1. What are the three key characteristics of national culture?
2. Describe some of the reasons why culture originally became different and why these differences continue to exist.
3. Discuss how the major studies of cultural values are similar or different.
4. Describe the differences between organizational culture and societal culture.
5. How should national cultural dimensions be used by IHR managers?
6. Describe the ways in which societal culture influences the behavior of individuals.

NOTES

1. Hofstede (1980).
2. Howard (1991).
3. Schein (1985).
4. The idea of tight and loose cultures comes from Pelto (1968) as cited in Triandis (1995). See also Chan, Gelfand, Triandis, & Tzeng (1996).

5.   Au (1999); Gelfand, Raver, Nishii et al. (2011).

6.   See Hall (1966); Whorf (1956).

7.   Pinker (1994).

8.   Boroditsky (2001).

9.   Berger & Luckman (1966).

10. See Hofstede (1983).

11. Dunphy (1987).

12. Huntington (1996).

13. Goldstein (1999).

14. Inglehart & Baker (2000).

15. Bond & King (1986).

16. Smircich & Calas (1986).

17. See Hofstede, Neuijen, Ohayv, & Sanders (1990).

18. Benet-Martínez, Leu, Lee, & Morris (2002).

19. Kluckhohn & Strodtbeck (1961).

20. Kluckhohn & Strodtbeck (1961); Maznevski, DiStefano, & Nason (1993).

21. Hofstede (1980); Hofstede (2001).

22. Chinese Culture Connection (1987).

23. Hofstede (1991).

24. Hofstede & Minkov (2010).

25. Smith & Bond (1999).

26. Sagiv & Schwartz (1995); Schwartz (1992); Schwartz (1994); Schwartz & Bilsky (1990).

27. Sagiv & Schwartz (2000).

28. House, Hanges, Javidan, Dorfman, & Gupta (2004).

29. McClelland (1962).

30. Peterson (2004).

31. See work by Schwartz and colleagues.

32. Triandis (1995).

33. This concept is conceptually similar to Hofstede's (1980) power-distance dimension and relates to the SVS (Schwartz, 1992) value orientations of hierarchy and harmony.

34. Markus & Kitayama (1991).

35. Triandis (1995).

36. Gelfand, Raver, Nishii, et al. (2011).

37. Chan, Gelfand, Triandis, & Tzeng (1996).

38. Osland & Bird (2000).

39. See Thomas (2008) for an expanded discussion of these mechanisms.

40. Schwartz & Sagie (2000).

41. Markus & Kitayama (1991).

42. Erez & Earley (1993).

43. Schuler & Rogowsky (1998).

44. See Evans, Pucik, & Barsoux (2002).

45. Milkovich & Bloom (1998).

46. Caprar (2011).

47. Du & Choi (2010).
48. Gerhart (2008); Gerhart & Fang (2005).
49. Milkovich & Bloom (1998).

3
Institutional context of IHRM

CHAPTER LEARNING OBJECTIVES

After reading this chapter you should be able to:

1. Explain why HRM practices differ between countries.
2. Describe how the institutions of society can shape HRM policies and procedures.
3. Recognize the effects of institutional context on employee expectations.
4. Compare and contrast the arguments for and against HRM convergence/divergence globally.

Jane in the HR jungle

Jane Freeman, the newly appointed Vice President of Human Resources for Humanico, poured herself a fairly large glass of red wine, kicked off her shoes and settled down to watch the sunset from her midtown Manhattan high rise. As she reflected on her meeting with her three Regional HR Managers, she wasn't sure how she could satisfy the needs for HR practices to reflect Humanico's corporate strategy and also conform to the local requirements of their subsidiaries in the US, Germany and Japan. Humanico was a significant player in the design and production of medical testing equipment. For years they had done very well by continuously improving their products, which were well known in the industry for their reliability and service life. But, new entrants in the industry along with technological changes meant they could no longer survive on just improving their products. They knew they needed to innovate. Jane had been hired because top management felt that Human Resources had a big part to play in creating a global culture that supported this strategy.

When she had bounced some of her ideas off Phil Blakely the HR Manager of Humanico's subsidiary in Raleigh, North Carolina they had quickly come to an agreement with regard to best HR practices to foster innovation. But, today, when she and Phil had met with the other two Regional Managers, Riku Sasaki and Elias Schneider, they received a lot of negative feedback. She had outlined a process of aligning HR practices with the overall business strategy through efficient reward and appraisal systems. Both Riku and Elias raised objections to ideas such as individual performance appraisals and merit based individual rewards. For example, Elias had reminded Jane that in Germany because of codetermination, "we can't just do as we wish, but have to respect the perspective of the works council." And Riku stressed the need in Japan to consider collective achievements in order to foster the inclusion and involvement of everyone in the company.

Jane was beginning to understand why,

despite globally consistent approaches to product design and manufacturing, Human Resource Management had largely been left to be managed by the local subsidiary. The national contexts of both Japan and Germany were so different from the US, particularly in right to work states like North Carolina. She knew she needed a new approach for tomorrow's follow-up meeting. But, right now she was hungry, and with nothing in the fridge it was time to call Uber Eats.

INTRODUCTION

While designing standardized HRM practices may not always face the challenges as mentioned in the opening vignette of codetermination as in Germany and a more collective mentality as in Japan, in every country where Humanico is operating, policies and practices do vary substantially between the different countries in which MNEs operate. Thus, IHRM is not only about understanding the HRM practices of international organizations but also about the ways in which the context of different countries influence human resource management. Building from Chapter 2 in which we focused on cultural differences between countries, in this chapter we discuss the institutional factors of societies that shape HRM.

INSTITUTIONAL DIMENSION OF COMPARATIVE HRM

In attempting to answer the questions raised by comparative HRM, our knowledge of national cultures can explain some of the reasons why HRM practices differ between countries. The other important factor to take into account is institutional differences, which some argue are the artifacts of cultural values (even those who insist on examining institutional differences in their own right agree that culture and institutions are interrelated at least in some way).[1] Institutions are the structures and activities that provide stability to a society and consist of the elements such as family, education, economic, religious, and political systems. These institutions shape organizations in that they are built into the fabric of society and constrain the actions of organizations and their members. Failure to conform to these societal demands can be costly, increase risk, and potentially reduce the organization's license to operate.

Similar to the case of cultural frameworks, those who study institutions have demonstrated how countries differ fundamentally in terms of the systems established around employment. To accomplish their goals, organizations need to interact with societal institutions, each of which has its own goals, but which overlap with other institutions in creating the employment infrastructure within a society. There are two main streams in institutional theory: one from an economic perspective and the other from a sociological perspective. The first is known as "economic institutional theory" and it highlights how an institutional infrastructure is created by the "rules of the game" which reduce uncertainty through formal regulations and informal norms.[2]

The second approach, coming from sociology, is known as "neo-institutional theory."[3] Neo-institutional theory too considers what the formal and informal "rules of the game" are, and it also explains how the process of institutionalization works, that is, how rules and norms become embedded in the everyday operating environment of firms. First, there are *coercive* mechanisms (such as laws and regulations) within any society that mandate what an organization is permitted to do regarding employment issues. Second, there are *mimetic* mechanisms, which means that organizations often copy the employment practices of other successful organizations around them. For example, in the 1980s, GE were known for their forced ranking performance management system which was seen as highly successful. Many businesses copied this system as they saw this as a way of achieving the high performance levels of GE. Finally, there are *normative* mechanisms, such as professional bodies, consultancies and universities, that set guidelines and standards within an industry on employment issues. In the USA, for example, the Society for Human Resource Management produces many guidelines on best HRM practices that its members apply in their organization.

Organizations operate within four interrelated institutional systems: they function within (1) economic systems to gain access to essential financial resources to be able to function effectively; interact with (2) governmental and legal systems and (3) employment relations systems to regulate wages and working conditions; and rely on (4) labor market and education systems to gain access to required talent. We describe each institutional system in turn here.

Economic systems

How organizations generate essential financial resources has a fundamental impact on how employment systems develop. If the primary focus of an organization is to deliver wealth to shareholders through a powerful stock market (such as in the USA), the emphasis will be on minimizing employment costs to maximize profits. This means, for example, ensuring wage costs are kept as low as possible and therefore minimum wage legislation could be minimal to non-existent. In contrast, where the emphasis of a society is less on the dominant power of financial markets and instead on building more of a welfare-based society (such as in Sweden or Germany), governments work together with organizations and financial markets to ensure a long-term focus on employment rights rather than short-term financial gains.

Furthermore, national economic wealth impacts employee expectations of the rewards and benefits in exchange for labor. In more wealthy economies such as Canada, the focus of employees might be on having a luxury company car as part of their benefits package. In less wealthy economies such as Vietnam, employees may be more focused on earning a living wage. The relationship between national economic wealth and employment practices is studied widely in the field of comparative labor economics.[4]

Governmental and legal systems

Employment legislation varies between countries in the extent to which the law is predominantly biased toward looking after the interests of the employer or the employee. The HRM practices adopted in organizations are thus at least in part determined by mandatory employment regulations aimed at *employee protection* and/or *minimum employment conditions*. *Employee protection* refers to how easy it is for organizations to hire and fire employees based on the type of contract (if any) that is issued. Compare, for example, the concept of "employment-at-will" in many states across the USA (where an employee can be dismissed for any reason at any moment, provided the reason is not illegal) with the elaborate procedures for dismissing an employee in Italy (involving substantial compensation and permission from the courts).[5, 6] Costs for dismissing an employee in Italy (as well as other Western European countries) for business rather than performance reasons can end up being considerably higher than the individual's annual salary. *Minimum employment conditions* refer to criteria such as any applicable minimum wage, payment for overtime, or the maximum number of working hours in a specified period. Countries that are part of the European Union, for example, all have legislation providing these and other baseline protections for employees.[7]

In some countries (for example, throughout Western Europe), legislation requires employment to be established through *formal contracts*, whereas in other countries (for example, in India), employment happens more commonly through informal agreements between individuals, sometimes also known as the "informal labor market" or "grey economy." The more formalized the employment relationship, the more diverse and sophisticated the HRM practices available to support that relationship. It is also important to note that the existence of a law designed to protect employees does not necessarily mean that the law is fully and correctly applied. For example, research evidence from Cyprus[8] and Ghana[9] indicates very little legislative back-up for employee protection despite the presence of applicable laws. Another issue that can occur is that legislation becomes cumbersome and outdated as business practices progress. India is a case in point here where a myriad of outdated legislation is seen as neither protecting employees nor supporting business growth.[10]

Governments can influence the employment relationship between the employer and the employee through many channels including, but not limited to, the following. First, in countries with strong welfare systems (such as in Northern Europe), the government provides substantial benefits to those out of work and seeking employment as well as offering back-to-work programs to help people find work (such as those with disabilities or returning from a long absence from the workplace). As a result, employers in such countries need to be less concerned about reaching people outside of the current employment system as the government programs are helping to identify potential talent. Moreover, when substantial benefits (such as health care, retirement pensions, disability pay) are available to employees through government programs, this means that companies do not have to provide such benefits themselves.

Another way in which a government can exert influence over employment practices is by being a majority employer. For example, the traditionally strong role of state-owned enterprises (SOEs) in China means that the majority of employees in that country are covered by typical SOE HRM practices. The extent of intervention can range from almost complete control of employment systems (such as in China) to a much more hands-off approach where organizations have much greater freedom to implement the HRM practices they choose (such as in the USA). We discuss this further when we explore the different "institutional ideologies" ahead.

Employment relations systems

In some countries (such as France), agreements bargained with trade unions substantially influence HRM practice adoption, yet in other countries (such as the USA), such agreements are rare and of little consequence. When trying to understand where trade unions may be more influential, country comparisons are often made based on the extent of trade union membership, with the implication that high union membership density equates to strong union power, and conversely low membership density means weak unions. Although this can be true (for example, membership density rates in 2018 of around 10% in the USA[11] is indeed indicative of low union influence in general across US organizations), it is not the whole story. In some countries, such as the Netherlands (see also Chapter 12 for further details), union membership density is relatively low (around 17% in 2016[12]) yet unions are highly influential.

Why is this? Another important piece of information that is needed to understand the level of influence of trade unions beyond membership density is collective bargaining coverage. In the Netherlands, around 80% of employees in 2016 were covered by agreements bargained with trade unions (i.e., both union members and non-union members are covered by collectively bargained agreements),[13] so this creates a very different image than when we only knew that membership density was 17%. Areas of employment regulations typically covered by collective bargaining agreements include wages, working hours, pensions, and working conditions.

Labor market and education systems

The extent to which employees expect to switch between employers as they develop their career is an indicator of whether a labor market is predominantly either internal or external.[14] Internal labor markets rely on promotion from within or horizontal moves of employees to different positions as needs arise. This means that employers need to offer opportunities for further career development and promotion for existing employees, rather than turning to the external labor market to fill vacant positions. An external labor market, in contrast, exists when organizations rarely seek to appoint from within and instead seek people outside the organization who have the competencies required. Internal labor markets have the advantage that the candidate is well known already inside the organization and is thus a less risky hire than recruiting externally. External labor markets have the advantage of bringing new ideas and competencies into an organization, avoiding the potential stagnation that can occur when hires are usual made from among existing employees.

Research has shown that both internal and external recruitment can have not only beneficial but also detrimental effects for organizations and employees,[15] demonstrating that one approach is not necessarily more effective than another. The sense of organizational loyalty that an internal labor market creates can be a great advantage when attracting employees who are seeking job security. Japanese organizations have, for example, been known for offering long-term commitments to their employees.[16] In contrast, in organizations operating with more of an external labor market (such as in the USA), the emphasis is on developing short-term HRM practices with the knowledge that human capital will be sought externally but equally can frequently be lost to competitors.

The human capital available to employers in any labor market is an accumulation of competencies that people develop initially through national education systems. Where the education system does not provide "job-ready" skills, organizations provide a greater amount of in-house training to rectify the skills gap. More vocational educational systems tend to demonstrate stronger linkages with industry, hence curricula for students are more closely aligned with the needs of businesses and fewer training opportunities need to be provided to employees. The German "dual training" system that combines schooling and apprenticeships is an example of organizations and schools working closely together to produce valuable human capital that can meet employers' needs.[17] However, many countries (including the USA and UK) have more academic rather than vocational educational systems, whereby the latter has traditionally been seen as less prestigious. This puts a greater burden on organizations to provide more training to employees on-the-job.

GROUPING COUNTRIES BY THEIR INSTITUTIONAL APPROACH TO HRM

Looking across this broad range of institutional factors that affect the employment relationship, patterns emerge across countries. There are some nations that are more like others and can be grouped together in their approach to HRM, while being substantially different from another group of countries. These groupings (or clusters) can be explained based on different varieties of capitalism,[18] each of which adopts a distinct approach to HRM: (a) liberal market economies; (b) coordinated market economies; and (c) socialist market economies. We discuss each in turn here, explaining the dominant ideologies[19] and corporate governance systems,[20] including how the institutional systems described earlier (economic systems; governmental and legal systems; labor and employment relations systems; labor market and education systems) create the employment infrastructure, as well as describing typical countries representing each system.

Liberal market economies

Economic systems: Liberal market economies (LMEs) are based on the principles of free markets, adopting a *neo-liberalist* ideology. This means that LMEs are "outsider systems" with *shareholder* corporate governance systems. In other words, the primary purpose of corporations is to deliver value to external shareholders. Organizations therefore need the freedom to be able to react quickly to changes in the market to deliver short-term profit maximization.

Governmental and legal systems: Free markets translate into a liberal employment framework (i.e., with limited legislation or collective bargaining agreements mandating HRM practices), minimum government intervention in the employment relationship, and anti-government ownership. The result is high levels of managerial freedom, which maximize the opportunities for corporate financial competitiveness. Ultimately, the company is King.

Employment relations systems: Given the *neo-liberalist* ideology, in organizations in LMEs there is weak employee voice and organizations frequently adopt an anti-union stance, that is, management makes HRM-related decisions with minimum input from employees or their representatives. It is argued that if employees were given the opportunity to participate widely in organizational decision-making, the consultation processes would slow down considerably the speed at which these decisions could be made, and hence the short-term financial goals of corporations would be in jeopardy (see also Chapter 12).

Labor market and education systems: LME labor markets tend to be externally focused and fluid, that is, employees are willing to switch between organizations for new opportunities and promotion. This is supported by an academic-focused formal education system through high schools and colleges, in which people develop general skills that they are able to apply across a range of different organizations and jobs. Links between educational establishments and industry are generally weak, further reducing the focus on developing skills for a particular industry or organization.

Typical country: The United States of America (USA) is the archetypical LME, with an emphasis on ensuring that organizations have maximum leeway to deliver short-term financial returns and shareholder value. We noted earlier that the USA is known for the system of "employment-at-will" in many states: this is an example of a practice that maximizes flexibility in the employment relationship. By having the freedom to make decisions about how to hire, fire, and otherwise manage employees with minimal legal constraints, organizations can be maximally responsive to trends in the market, allowing changes to be implemented swiftly to deliver high firm profits. This is the context in which "human resource management" was first developed, that is, employees are human resources to be used to maximize firm financial performance.

The traditionally anti-union stance of firms (based on a history of violence and intimidation in the USA) means that employees have little opportunity for formal, independent representation. Instead, employers who choose to look after their employees adopt a system of welfare capitalism, whereby enlightened employer initiatives are introduced to forestall unionization (such as high involvement or high commitment work systems). Due to the success of the US economy operating under this model, there has been a significant impact of US MNEs spreading this model of HRM worldwide. This LME's highly individualistic and masculine culture and many HRM "best practices" based on these core values, motivates employees through opportunities to earn more than their peers through systems such as individual performance-related-pay.

Coordinated market economies

Economic systems: Coordinated market economies (CMEs) are based not on free markets but on access to capital through reputation rather than share value. The *neo-corporatist* ideology is at the heart of such economies. Neo-corporatism is characterized by *stakeholder* corporate governance systems (also termed "insider systems"), which, in contrast to shareholder systems, take a broader group of people or entities who have a stake, that is, stakeholders, in the organization into consideration when deciding on employment practices. This includes not only the role of shareholders in successful corporations, but also the role of other stakeholders such as employees, the government, customers, suppliers, and all entities that in some way interact with or are affected by the organization. CMEs encourage a system based on equity (rather than the "survival of the fittest" free market principles) whereby employment systems are directed at achieving consensus where possible among the various stakeholders involved.

Governmental and legal systems: Compared to LMEs, CMEs have a much higher level of state involvement through social insurance programs, greater regulation of the economy, a more dominant role of the state as an employer, and higher levels of spending on labor market programs. The government plays an active role as mediator between employers and employees. This results in highly regulated, extensive employment systems and a long-term view on investing in employees. Employment regulation includes both employee protection through greater regulation of recruitment and dismissal, and baseline employment conditions including minimum wage, leave, working hours, and contract forms. Overall, this creates a context in which formalized HRM practices are well-established and employee rights and benefits clearly delineated, with the belief that this is in the best interests of all stakeholders.

Employment relations systems: Worker participation is encouraged in CMEs through employee representation because of the multi-stakeholder corporate governance system. This is often described as a tripartite model of social partnership whereby the government, employers and employees work together to create mutually beneficial employment systems. This creates strong employee voice, whereby employee representatives are party to the strategic decision-making of the organization. Consequently, firms can be financially successful at the same time as employee rights being protected. For example, *neo-corporatist* ideology supports long-term investment in human resources (such as multi-year development plans) as the organization's stakeholders are not demanding instant returns and are prepared to wait for their investment to pay off.

Labor market and education systems: In CMEs, labor markets are more internally focused and less fluid, meaning that people tend to stay with employers for a longer period of time than in LMEs. This is at least in part due to the strong vocational education systems in place alongside more generalist academic education opportunities. Vocational education and the use of apprenticeships mean that employees become more tied to an organization or job in which they are working. Consequently, there is a strong link between industries or organizations and education providers, resulting in collaborative training programs to develop specific skills that are required in the workplace.

Typical country: Germany is the prototypical CME with a strong stakeholder corporate governance system. Rather than firms in Germany demanding the freedom to make quick decisions to be able to provide short-term profits, they are instead part of a coordinated employment framework that ensures the interests of not only the firm and its shareholders but also those of the other stakeholders, including employees, are represented. There is consequently a legal industrial relations framework that includes employee rights to formal representation and consultation (see also Chapter 12). Moreover, as part of the European Union, employee rights legislation is underpinned by a baseline of supranational regulations that are further developed and incorporated into German law.

As noted, Germany is known for its highly effective vocational education system (also known as the "dual training" system). This system combines academic education with training through apprenticeships to maximize an employee's impact in a specific industry or workplace.[21] Firms work closely with local colleges to develop appropriate training and education programs that are regulated by law (the Vocational Training Act of 1969) to ensure quality. Trade unions also have an input into establishing the required skills that are then taught, ensuring buy-in from government, employee and employer representatives.

Socialist market economies

Economic systems: Socialist market economies[22] are built on *state corporatist* ideological principles. State corporatism implies that the state, that is, the government, is in control of corporations. The basic principles of this ideology stem from the fundamental views of Marxism that inequalities can lead to power struggles, and hence the role of the government is to avoid such struggles by providing centralized control.

Governmental and legal systems: Given the state corporatist principles, socialist market economies are characterized by a high level of SOEs. The government is thus the dominant employer. Employment legislation exists to ensure that government control can be implemented through legal mechanisms, however, this legislation has traditionally tended to focus less on employee protections such as might be found in CMEs, and instead more on employee compliance. Developments in Chinese employment law (with the introduction of the 2008 Labor Contract Law, for example) have, however, increased the focus on employee rights and protections, although these legal requirements are not always being enforced.[23]

Employment relations systems: State-controlled trade unions are the only legal form of employee representation in socialist market economies. Given that the majority of employees also work in state-owned organizations, or organizations influenced greatly by the state, this means there is very little employee voice. There are underground (i.e., illegal) unions that form through the activities of activists wishing to increase employee voice, but their activities are largely halted by the government.[24]

Labor market and education systems: socialist market economies focus on providing guaranteed job security to employees within the dominant state-owned enterprises. This means that people have a job for life with steady income and benefits. Less attention is therefore paid to building links between education and businesses because all necessary training will take place inside the organization once the employee has joined. The education system in general is therefore focused primarily on core academic rather than vocational skills.

Typical country: Typical of a socialist market economy is China,[25] although economic reforms in recent years are slowly changing employment systems in this country. China has traditionally operated a high number of SOEs so that the government maximizes control of employees. In order to maintain its status as a low-cost employment country, a low wage policy has been implemented, which minimizes employment costs and maximizes the ability to export products to more developed economies. State-controlled unions are mandated at enterprise level and employee strikes are illegal. Due to the system of worker suppression, the trade union movement has remained underdeveloped for many years although the incidence of labor disputes is now rising.[26]

The Chinese labor market has traditionally relied on an internal system of life-long employment (referred to as the "iron rice bowl"), although the shift toward a socialist market economy means that management autonomy is increasing (see also Box 3.1). The education system is also predominantly academic focused, however, the introduction of the 2019 Government Work Plan[27] implies that there is increasing attention being paid to develop more vocational education opportunities.

Summary

Summarizing across these country groupings, we can see how institutional systems affect employment relationships. We linked the shareholder corporate governance system with the neo-liberalist ideology in the liberal market economy (e.g., the USA), the stakeholder corporate governance system with the neo-corporatist ideology in the coordinated market economy (e.g., Germany), and the state corporatist ideology in the socialist market economy (e.g., China). Table 3.1 summarizes the important aspects of each market economy type based on the elements of the institutional systems and ideologies.

CONVERGENCE, DIVERGENCE, OR EQUILIBRIUM?

Because of the effects of globalization (discussed in Chapter 1) and the tendency of MNEs to be consistent wherever they operate (discussed ahead in Chapter 4), it is often argued that HRM policies and procedures are isomorphic, that is, they are in the process of becoming more similar around the world. The key argument in support of this idea is that as the world moves toward a single economic system[28] and technology produces an increasingly information-driven business environment, business executives receive the same type of training, and so on, organizations and their HRM systems become more similar. This suggests the possibility of a universal set of best HRM practices that all organizations should adopt in order to be successful.[29] This is ultimately what we might term *final convergence*, that is, the same practice is in use in all organizations globally. However, as discussed in the previous chapter and here, HRM systems are embedded in the cultural and institutional context of their home country. That is, HRM may not be as influenced by the forces of globalization because its ability to change is limited by regulatory structures, interest groups, public opinion and cultural norms, which are all relatively slow to change.[30] In fact, national differences in HRM practice in Europe persist in the face of globalization.[31] The reality is, however, that it is probably somewhat more complex than simply converging or diverging practices.

Two examples of the complexity of convergence are provided by the concepts of *directional similarity* and *club convergence* (see Figure 3.1). *Directional similarity* implies that over time organizations from different countries move their HRM practices in the same direction, but because of different starting points they remain relatively parallel (i.e., one country still has greater use of a particular HRM practice than another country). In other words, directional similarity is indicated by the presence of similar trends across countries, but without final convergence. For example, between 1992 and 2004 organizations in both Norway and Greece decreased their investment in employee training and development. However, despite following the same trend (both reducing training and development), they had different levels of

Table 3.1 Comparison of economies based on ideologies and institutional systems

Ideology	Liberal Market Economy	Coordinated Market Economy	Socialist Market Economy
	Neo-liberalism	Neo-corporatism	State corporatism
Corporate governance system	Shareholder	Stakeholder	State controlled
Economic system	Free markets, external finance depends on market valuation	Access to capital based on reputation as opposed to share value	Centralized control of organizations and the economy
Governmental and legal system	Managers have a great deal of authority over organizational activities, including most aspects of the employment relationship	Regulated employment framework in place to balance needs of governments, employers, and employees	High level of state-owned enterprises with legislation that reinforces central control
Employment relations system	Trade unions are relatively weak, employment protection and employee voice are low	Strong employee voice through representation and high levels of employment protection	State-run trade unions, very limited employee voice
Labor market and education system	Labor markets are fluid, workers develop general knowledge and skills through academic education that can be transported to other jobs	Labor markets internally focused, workers develop industry/organization-specific skills through greater emphasis on vocational education	Life-long job security means very limited external labor market, education systems focused primarily on academic skills
Typical countries	United States of America, United Kingdom	Germany, Japan, South Korea, Sweden, Norway, Finland, Denmark, Belgium, The Netherlands	China, Vietnam

adoption of training and development practices at the end of this twelve-year period because of different initial levels.[32] Another example is the adoption of Western-style HRM practices across Asian countries where the economies have been developing, such as in China, Taiwan, Singapore, Malaysia, Thailand, Vietnam, and India.[33] Traditional Asian practices are being replaced by the practices of Western MNEs as they become established in these markets, but relative to the Western countries, they remain behind in the rate of adoption due to being in a developmental phase.

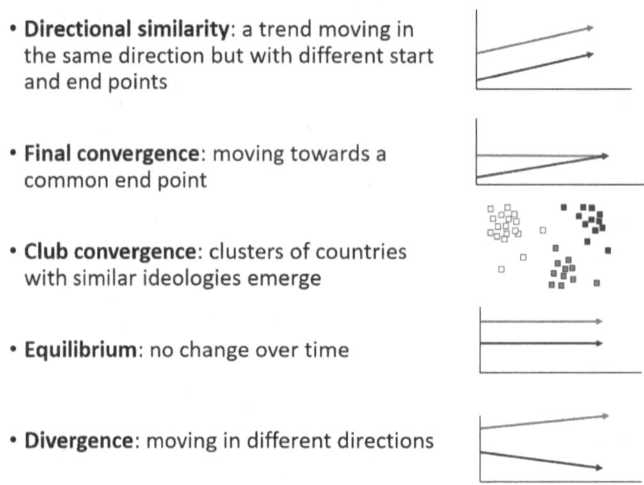

Figure 3.1   Definitions of convergence

Club convergence[34] is the idea that countries with similar degrees of labor legislation tend to cluster together in that they look more like other countries belonging to the same cluster over time.[35] This means that HRM practices are more similar *within* than *across* clusters of countries. This follows the market economy reasoning discussed earlier in this chapter in that we would expect the liberal market economies such as the UK and the USA to have more similar HRM practices in place than when compared to countries in the coordinated market economies, such as Germany or Japan, or in the socialist market economy of China. This phenomenon is described in the business systems literature,[36] explaining how institutional systems combine to create the infrastructure in which organizations conduct their business.

Groupings can also be defined by geographical regions in which cultural values play a role in defining how business is conducted. For example, as noted in Chapter 2, researchers[37] have identified cultural clusters among Germanic (Germany, Austria, Switzerland), Nordic (Sweden, Norway, Iceland), Latin European (Spain, Portugal, Italy, Belgium, France), Near East (Turkey, Greece), Arab (Kuwait, Morocco, UAE), and Confucian (China, Taiwan, Singapore) countries, among others. While any classification of countries into clusters has its inherent problems, countries do exhibit certain similarities to other countries and framing the study of HRM in terms of clusters can be a useful way of examining HRM across the globe.

Global changes in HRM are a result of the complex, dynamic interaction of forces of convergence and the embeddedness of national business systems.[38] For example, some practices may be converging, others may exhibit directional similarity, while others may actually be diverging. There is evidence, for example, that more institutionally constrained practices such as compensation and wage-bargaining level practices are less likely to converge when compared with less institutionally constrained practices such as contingent employment, training, and direct information provision practices.[39] This is because practices such as compensation and wage-bargaining are often the result of either legislation or collectively bargained agreements and as such, a firm cannot introduce alternative practices without being perceived as not following the norms. In other words, in neo-institutional theory terms, the coercive mechanisms in an organization's operating environment are affecting practice adoption. As a result, there is minimal isomorphism (practices becoming more similar) across national boundaries, unless the regulatory context is similar. For contingent employment, training, and direct information provision practices, however, there is more leeway for firms to adopt the practices that they consider appropriate for their business, as fewer, if any, coercive mechanisms are at play. Convergence can still occur if, for example, firms copy other firms that appear to be performing well. Hence, mimetic mechanisms may still have a role to play, but this is based more on organizational choice than on mandated actions, and therefore we see more variance in practices adopted and less convergence.

Coming back to the concept of *final convergence* (where all organizations globally converge on the adoption of the same HRM practice), studies have increasingly encouraged us to think about this in a more nuanced way due to the passage of time needed to establish patterns of change. The convergence/divergence continuum ranges from constant no difference (practices have always been alike), through robust convergence/divergence (a consistent trend of convergence or divergence over time) and non-robust convergence/divergence (some years practices are converging or diverging but not as part of a consistent trend), to constant difference (practices have always been different and still are).[40] In other words, what is important is the timing of when we look for trends of convergence or divergence.[41] Taking the example of forced ranking in performance management at GE mentioned earlier as an example, if we look at firms in the 1980s, there was a clear trend of robust convergence in that many firms were starting to adopt this practice. Over time, however, new ideas about how performance management should be conducted have emerged (such as abandoning annual or semi-annual performance reviews) and a greater variety of performance management systems have been implemented, leading to a trend of robust divergence of practices in this area of HRM.

Overall, as discussed in Chapter 6 ahead, organizations may develop approaches in which they maintain some local management values and practices but can adapt with regard to using *best practices* developed in other countries.[42] Similarly, different environments produce different institutional systems, but different environments can also produce similar systems, and similar environments can produce vastly different institutions.[43] This creates multiple different equilibrium conditions in the institutional environments to which organizations must attend.[44] Institutions result from social interaction and form the structure of society based on patterns of thinking that persist over time.[45] Any change must consider the historical as well as current conditions that create the present institutional environment. The remnants of state socialism in transitional economies provide a case in point, which is discussed in Box 3.1.

BOX 3.1   LEGACY OF STATE SOCIALISM

The essence of economic transition is the replacement of one set of institutions that govern economic activity with another. In former socialist countries (such as Croatia, Slovenia, Serbia, Bulgaria, and Poland, to name but a few), the institutions that support a Western style market-based economy have had to be adopted very rapidly, but they must also be acceptable within their society.[46] Therefore it is not surprising that the institutions in transition economies retain some vestiges of their socialist past. Therefore, understanding the institutional context of former socialist countries requires some understanding of the previous environment.

The key to understanding state socialism is recognizing the importance of three factors: undivided political power, state ownership of key elements of the economy, and bureaucratic coordination. These three factors motivated all the actors in the social system. In pre-transition socialist economies, the single party system set rules for organizations as a form of legal power. Thus, there was no need for laws regarding business since formal constraints on organizations were part of the central planning regime. The various institutions of society were designed to have a monopoly in their own field: one labor union movement, one association of engineers, one academy of sciences, and so on. Power and prestige were determined by one's level in the hierarchy, with appropriate privileges (e.g., housing, medical care, access to goods and services, holidays) proportionate to rank. Individuals in power maintained their position through paternalism. Also, a kind of labor aristocracy in which reliable and skilled workers were recruited into the party existed.[47] With the transition to a market orientation, a shift in the balance of power came about with the previous hierarchical distinctions becoming blurred.

A fundamental tenet of socialism is that labor is not a commodity, but a resource to be employed. A central belief of the labor collective is that a worker had a right to a job and its associated benefits.[48] For example, in China, factories approximated institutions, providing for all of the worker's needs: they fed, housed, hospitalized, and generally protected the working class as part of the wider social contract. The bureaucratic control of employment began with education where choices open to individuals were severely limited or individuals were channeled to a particular type of work and extended through all aspects of organizational life including central determinations of wage rates. Pre-transition managerial behavior was also influenced by this bureaucratic control. As the state gradually relinquished its role in controlling organizations, institutions were required to fill the void. However, developing an institutional framework takes time and the capacity of society to accept institutions and enforce their norms is questionable.[49]

Former socialist countries have faced several difficulties including a slower than expected pace of change, growing differences between rural and urban areas, large income disparities, and in some cases declines in health care and life expectancies as well as social unrest.[50] In some countries, the reality of economic transition can cause a resurgence of communist parties and move toward more conservative policies. Thus, the institutional context in these societies is far from being stable.

CHAPTER SUMMARY

National-level institutional systems (in addition to the national culture systems described in Chapter 2) create the operating context of organizations and hence impact on HRM practice adoption in different countries. The influence of institutions is often formal and supported by enforceable sanctions. Each type of institution discussed here (e.g., economic, governmental, legal, employment relations, labor markets, education) does not operate in isolation but combines with the others to form a contextual business system in which organizations are embedded.

Over time, given the globalization trends described in Chapter 1, it is also interesting to explore the extent to which HRM practices might be becoming more alike. Convergence is therefore one area of research that is hotly debated, with those who believe that HRM practices are changing as organizations are constantly in search of best practice, while others believe that HRM practices are too embedded in local institutions and cultures to change so quickly, and hence divergence of HRM remains strong. One part of this debate is fueled by the activities of MNEs that operate across national contexts, projecting their own institutional (or cultural) context overseas, but we should also expect the local institutional (and cultural) context to influence HRM practice. Chapter 4 considers this and other aspects of organizational context so that we can understand better the forces at play.

QUESTIONS FOR DISCUSSION

1. What are the major institutions that can impact on employment relationships?
2. How might employee expectations about their relationship with their employer differ across the three market economy types described here?
3. What is implied by convergence and divergence of HRM practices? Does the evidence provide support for either idea?

NOTES

1. In distinguishing between these two factors we do not take a position as to whether culture is an institution of society or if institutions of society reflect the more fundamental societal characteristic of culture. Again, this academic debate is largely irrelevant to practice.
2. Gooderham, Mayrhofer, & Brewster (2019).
3. Lewis, Cardy, & Huang (2019).
4. Michie (2009).
5. https://www2.deloitte.com/content/dam/Deloitte/global/Documents/Legal/dttl-legal-international-dismissal-survey-2018.pdf provides an interesting comparison of dismissal costs by country.
6. Baker & McKenzie International (2006).
7. https://ec.europa.eu/social/main.jsp?langId=en&catId=82
8. Stavrou-Costea (2004).
9. Debrah (2000).

10. Budhwar, Varma, & Patel (2016).
11. https://www.bls.gov/news.release/union2.nr0.htm
12. https://stats.oecd.org/Index.aspx?DataSetCode=TUD
13. https://stats.oecd.org/Index.aspx?DataSetCode=TUD#
14. Schwan & Soeters (1994).
15. Bidwell & Mollick (2015).
16. Tachibanaki (1987).
17. Eichhorst, Rodríguez-Planas, Schmidl, & Zimmermann (2015).
18. Hall & Soskice (2001).
19. Hollinshead (2010).
20. Martin, Farndale, Paauwe, & Stiles (2016).
21. https://www.bmbf.de/en/the-german-vocational-training-system-2129.html
22. Schmitter (1979).
23. Gallagher, Giles, Park, & Wang (2013).
24. Pringle (2011).
25. Warner (1993).
26. Hualing & Choy (2001).
27. https://monitor.icef.com/2019/07/chinas-push-to-expand-vocational-education/
28. Eisenhardt (1973).
29. See Mayrhofer, Brewster, Morley, & Ledolter (2011) for a discussion.
30. Brewster (2006).
31. Gooderham & Nordhaug (2011).
32. Mayrhofer, Brewster, Morley, & Ledolter (2011).
33. Budhwar, Varma & Patel (2016).
34. Fischer & Stirböck (2006 cited in Mayrhofer, Brewster, Morley, & Ledolter (2011).
35. Mayrhofer, Brewster, Morley, & Ledolter (2011); Brewster (2004); Brewster (2007); Sparrow, Schuler, & Jackson (1994).
36. Hall & Soskice (2001).
37. Ronen & Shenkar (2013).
38. McGaugley & De Cieri (1999); Tregaskis & Brewster (2006).
39. Farndale, Brewster, Ligthart, & Poutsma (2017).
40. Farndale, Brewster, Ligthart, & Poutsma (2017)
41. Kaufman (2016).
42. See Rowley, Poon, Zhu, & Warner (2011) for a discussion.
43. Cohen (2001).
44. Dewettinck & Remue (2011).
45. See Rozin (1998) for a discussion from an evolutionary theory perspective.
46. Napier & Thomas (2004); Rock & Solodkov (2001).
47. Clark (1996).
48. Lee (1987).
49. Peng (2000).
50. Napier & Thomas (2004).

4
Organizational context of IHRM

CHAPTER LEARNING OBJECTIVES

After reading this chapter you should be able to:

1. Describe the fundamental elements of organizational structure.
2. Outline the ways in national culture influences the structure of organizations.
3. Explain what is meant by the term "organizational culture."
4. Contrast the HRM structures of small and medium enterprises (SMEs) with large organizations.
5. Discuss the implications of different multinational structures for global HRM.

HRM in a high-tech start up

As the new Human Resources Manager for video games developer VG-Arts, Andrew McTavish knew that establishing an HR department in this small technology-oriented company would be a challenge. He had only just taken up his post this week and the week had flown by. "Hard to believe it's Friday already," he thought.

VG-Arts had begun only a few years earlier in Dundee, Scotland, but with the huge success of its now world-famous video game *Champions of Sparta* the firm was growing rapidly. This growth combined with newly formed strategic alliances with game developers in Vancouver, Canada and Mountain View, California had convinced founder and CEO Fergus Macleod that he needed to formalize the human resource management function. A friend from university had recommended Andrew McTavish, the Associate Director of Human Resources for Bank of Scotland.

Andrew was looking for a new opportunity in which he could spread his wings professionally and VG-Arts was located in his home town. When interviewing for the job Andrew discovered that when the company was smaller, Fergus knew every employee well and handled human resource issues very informally as they arose. Now, however, he was not only managing game designers but a whole raft of new positions required for the larger international organization. The task of identifying key positions and planning on how to fill these roles through external recruitment seemed to be overwhelming him. Also the fact that he really didn't have a plan for how to provide a career progression for his most talented developers was one of his biggest concerns.

Andrew liked Fergus immediately and the sense of adventure and excitement that existed at VG-Arts was infectious. "So unlike the formality that had existed in his former organization in Edinburgh," he thought. However, the lack of any formal HR policies and procedures was an issue that he would need to address sooner rather than later. He wondered how much of his previous HR department's policies he could just duplicate in this new organization. For example, VG-Arts certainly needed a talent management system. But it didn't have the infrastructure to support anything like the system at his previous employer, which itself was part of the international conglomerate Lloyds Banking Group. And, he would only have a very small staff to begin with, mostly involved in administrative tasks. The strategic thinking would be up to him.

There were so many things to consider, but right now it was time to go meet some employees at the VG-Arts' traditional Friday afternoon whisky tasting. "There are many things to like about Scotland," he thought. "Not the least of which was single malt whisky." He hoped they had one of the light and grassy Speyside whiskys that he preferred.

INTRODUCTION

The HR function does not operate in a vacuum but is influenced by and influences the larger organization in which it is embedded. As discussed in previous chapters, organizations are not independent of their surroundings, but are open systems that continuously take inputs from the environment (including human resources), transform them, and then return output to the environment in the form of products or services.[1]

All organizations create formal structures to control and coordinate the activities of their members. In addition, the shared perceptions of organizational work practices, the informal organization, is an important influence on the behavior of organization members. Both the formal and informal structures of organizations vary considerably around the world. All international organizations face the challenge of determining the extent to which they should be internally consistent or adapt to the local context in which they operate. As Andrew and Fergus, in the case that opened this chapter discover, the answer to this question is as important for HRM as it is for the organization as a whole.

ORGANIZATIONAL STRUCTURE

Organizations are systems of people that are intentionally structured to achieve goals. This structure consists of a different roles (what jobs need to be done and who does them) and a system of authority (who makes what decisions) to achieve the organizational mission. The structure of any organization can be described in terms of its degree of complexity, formalization, and centralization.[2]

Complexity of an organization is the extent to which it varies along three dimensions: horizontal, vertical, and spatial.

- *The horizontal dimension* refers to the number of different types of jobs that exist in an organization. The greater the number of different occupations in an organization, the greater its horizontal dimension.

- *The vertical dimension* is the number of levels in the hierarchy of the organization. For example, large banks might have as many as eight or nine layers between the teller at the bottom of the hierarchy and the CEO at the top while a small software developer as few as two, consisting of the entrepreneurial founder and employees.
- *The spatial dimension* is the extent to which an organization's physical facilities and personnel are geographically dispersed. Large multinational organizations are often very complex with high levels of all three types of differences.

Formalization is indicated by the extent to which rules and procedures govern the activities of organization members. Formal organizations allow little discretion in the way people do their jobs and often have numerous explicit policies and procedures. The degree of *centralization* is indicated by the extent to which decisions are made at a single point in the organization. In centralized organizations most decisions are made at one location, typically at headquarters by top management, while in decentralized organizations decision-making is dispersed throughout the organization.

There are any numbers of ways that the three elements of organizational structure can be combined, with two fundamental types *organic* and *mechanistic* at the extremes.[3] Mechanistic or bureaucratic organizations are centralized and have high formality and high complexity. In contrast, organic organizations have low formalization and complexity, with decisions being made throughout the organization. Figure 4.1 provides a graphic representation of these two fundamental types of organizational structure.

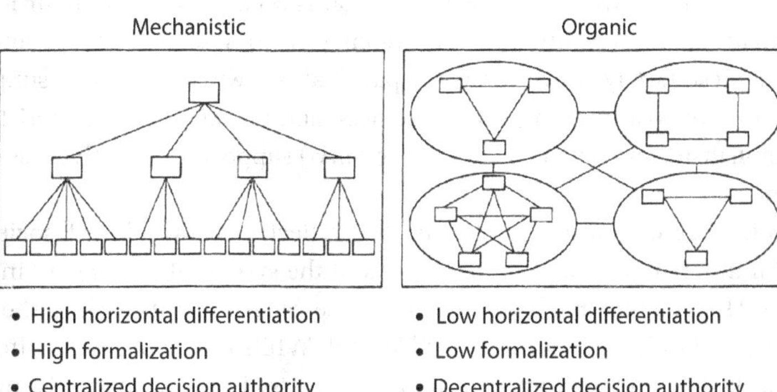

Source: Thomas (2008), p. 193.

Figure 4.1   Fundamental organizational designs

These two general organizational forms are helpful in demonstrating how the various elements of structure might combine. However, the reality for most organizations is that they fall somewhere between these two extremes. For example, the elements of structure may differ depending on the size of the organization, its strategy or technology and the extent of its internationalization and its needs for knowledge exchange.[4] To some extent these factors operate in a similar way to affect organizational structure in any country. For example, large organizations in one country look very much like large organizations in another.[5] However, a number of cross-national differences have been found in structural variables, including the structure of HRM.[6] It is the way in which national culture might influence the organizational context for global HRM that we discuss next.

National culture and organizational structure

As discussed in previous chapters, the institutions of society, that is the political, social and legal ground rules of a society, form a big part of the context in which global HRM must function. These institutions have been influenced by national culture. However, culture may have a more direct effect on the structure of organizations, which in turn influences global HRM.

There are two mechanisms through which culture can influence organizational structure.[7] First, organizational structure can reflect management's cultural values. That is, organizational structures are logical extensions of the specific value orientations of the managers who create them. Managers may not be aware of these subconscious influences and simply make choices about structure that feel right. For example, in a high power distance culture, such as Germany, organizations tend to be more hierarchical and centralized, and the flat organizational structures in Swedish automotive firms are consistent with Sweden's egalitarian cultural values.[8] Second, national culture influences the extent to which different ways of organizing are accepted by members (and the institutions) of society. That is, pressures from the cultural environment dictate the type of structure that is seen as appropriate or legitimate. For example, normative pressures influence the tendency of Chinese firms to stay small and family owned. The Chinese family firm centers on paternalism, which results in simple structures that restrict the focus to a single aspect of business, and the societal characteristics of mutual obligation, familialism, and personal contacts (*guanxi*) support the effectiveness of this organizational form.[9]

Examples of other organizational forms that reflect culturally based societal pressures are the *keiretsu* in Japan, the *chaebol* in Korea, and the system of *putting out* in the knitwear industry in the Modena region of Italy. The Japanese *keiretsu* has its basis in the family-based *zaibatsu* that existed in Japan prior to World War II. While the family name often survived as in Mitsui, Mitsubishi, and Sumitomo, the modern *kieretsu* is no longer family owned but consists of a complex inter-firm network including a trading company (*sogoshosha*), and is usually anchored by a bank. However, the *kieretsu* functions like an extended family with coordination and control facilitated by reciprocal ownership and a focus on long-term success.[10] The Korean *chaebol* are family-dominated multi-industry conglomerates such as Hyundai, Samsung, LG, and Daewoo. They differ from the *kieretsu* in that they are heavily populated by family members, particularly in key positions and are financed by the government. Like other types of family businesses, *chaebols* are paternalistic and highly centralized. Because of a societal preference (supported by government policy) they are also very large. In the Modena region of Italy, a system of production called *putting out* resulted in a unique organizational form that economists considered archaic and inefficient. In this system the manufacturer *puts out* raw material to a network of independent artisanal firms (averaging less than nine workers) who cut, assemble, dye, press, and package knitwear, often in their homes. The success of the system rested on the presence of cohesive family units and cooperative relationships based on centuries of societal engagement in cooperative endeavors, dating back to the straw-hat weaving in the 1600s.[11]

These examples suggest that there may be systematic variation in the structure of organizations based on cultural factors. Not only do these organizational forms dictate the relationship among (hierarchy of authority) and roles of organization members (for example we would expect that most HR decisions would be made by the senior family member in family-oriented business), but they also affect the way in which the organization conveys expectations about appropriate behavior. Consider the situation in Box 4.1 in which a selection policy is interpreted in two different organizational contexts.

BOX 4.1   SELECTION IN TWO CONTEXTS[12]

HR Policy: Attributes of individuals must not be used for differential treatment of individuals unless they are clearly connected to the goals and tasks required.

American MNE Manager: I must hire the best person for the job regardless of class, race, religion, gender or national origin.

Chinese Family Business Manager: I must hire people whom I know or who belong to my network of friends and relatives because I can trust them to be dependable employees.

The interpretation of the formal policy in this case is influenced by factors not represented on the organization chart or in the job descriptions, but by norms for behavior that are informally shared among the organizations members. It is this informal aspect of organization that we discuss next.

INFORMAL ORGANIZATION

The informal organization refers to a set of assumptions shared by organization members that guide their behavior. This set of normative behaviors and relationships is typically referred to as *organizational culture*. Organizational culture can produce both functional behavior that contributes to the goals of the organization, but also dysfunctional behavior that has negative effects. The primary positive effects of organizational culture are to provide:

(a)   a sense of identity for the organization that differentiates it from other organizations, and

(b)   a mechanism for socializing organization members into a way of doing things that are consistent with its goals.

Table 4.1 Characteristics of four organizational culture types

Factor	Family	Eiffel Tower	Guided Missile	Incubator
Relationships	Diffuse, bonded to whole	Specific role in mechanistic system	Specific tasks with shared objectives	Diffuse, spontaneous roles
Authority and status	Parent figures	Superior roles	Contributing members	Achievers
Thinking patterns	Intuitive	Logical, analytical	Problem centered	Creative, ad hoc
Employees	Family members	Human resources	Specialists, experts	Co-creators
Change	By leader	By rules or procedures	As target moves	By improvisation
Reward basis	Intrinsic	Promotion	Performance	Participation
Management	By subjectives	By job description	By objectives	By enthusiasm
Conflict resolution	Turn other cheek, save face	Procedures arbitrate	Constructive, task related	Creative
Preferred in	Singapore, Korea, Japan, France, Belgium, India, Greece, Italy, Spain	Denmark, Germany, Netherlands	United States, Canada, United Kingdom	Silicon Valley, CA; Route 128, Boston; Sweden

This may be particularly important in complex multinationals that have a high degree of geographic differentiation. For example, Johnson & Johnson manufactures and markets consumer and health care products through 250 subsidiary companies in more than 175 different countries. Its strong organizational culture (codified in "The J & J Credo" which is translated into 36 languages) tells managers who and what to care about and in what particular order, regardless of where in the world they are located.[13]

Negative effects of culture result from the fact that organizational culture gives organization members a set of behaviors that have served them well in the past, and can therefore be a barrier to change in the organization or create conflict between merged firms with different cultures. For example, in Chapter 7 we discuss these problems in the merger between Daimler Benz and Chrysler Corporation, which were largely due to a clash of organizational cultures.

While there has been little systematic study of differences in organizational cultures in different countries, some attempts have been made to identify the types of organizational cultures that seem to be most common in different cultural contexts. The categorization of organizational cultures into four types of Family Culture, Eiffel Tower Culture, Guided Missile Culture, and Incubator Culture (shown in Table 4.1) is a useful tool to relate prototypes of organization cultures to their societal context.[14] In reality, of course, organization cultures are influenced by a host of factors in addition to the cultural context in which they are embedded.

Another view of organizational culture in a global context is that the forces of globalization are shaping the cultures of MNEs to be similar, which leads to the emergence of a *global work culture* among members of these organizations that transcend national borders and operate in a global work environment. Global work culture has been defined as "the shared understanding of the visible rules, regulations, and behaviors and the deeper values and ethics of the global work context."[15] Consistent with the demands of the global work environment (e.g., global competitiveness, high dynamism and uncertainty, geographic dispersion and cultural diversity), global work culture reflects global work values such as customer orientation, competitive performance orientation, trust, openness to cultural diversity and organizational social responsibility.

MULTINATIONAL ENTERPRISE STRUCTURE

An organization's choice of structure involves addressing the relationships among individuals and the specification of organizational roles. For multinational enterprises the additional question of where these jobs are located is important. MNEs need to coordinate and control operations across multiple environments and various approaches to placing foreign activity in the organizational structure have been used. The particular approach taken depends on (a) the location and type of foreign subsidiary, (b) the influence of international operations on corporate performance, (c) the way in which international operations have developed over time, and (d) the country of origin of the firm.[16] Five ways of integrating international operations are common. These are the *international division structure*, the *product division structure*, the *functional division structure*, the *geographic division structure*, and the *matrix*.[17]

- *International division*: This structure groups all international activities together in a single organizational unit and is more popular with US than European MNEs. This structure has also been the initial choice of a significant number of firms as they expand internationally. Walmart is a well-known example.
- *Product division*: This structure groups all units involved with like products together around the world. In this case, it is possible for foreign subsidiaries in the same country to have a different relationship to the firm depending on the product line. This is the most popular structure among organizations who market a diverse portfolio of products. For example, in addition to Louis Vuitton luggage, LVMH, the world's largest luxury goods company, markets products as diverse as Tag Heuer watches, Christian Dior perfume, and Moët & Chandon champagne through its five product-based divisions.[18]
- *Functional division*: This structure expands its domestic functional units into its foreign counterparts (e.g., Marketing Europe, Marketing North America, etc.) based on geography. It is popular among companies offering a limited range of related products such as oil and mining companies. One company that uses a functional design is British Airways. The company is focused on providing air transportations services and has company-wide functional operations dedicated to engineering, marketing, HR, and so forth. Lenovo also used this design in the early years of its existence.[19] A weakness of this structure is its inability to respond rapidly to environmental change because of the complexity of supervising value creation of activities in several different business areas.
- *Geographic division*: This structure groups all functional areas into geographic units (e.g., North American Division, European Division, etc.). It is typical in organizations that have large foreign operations and are not dominated by one country or region. Historically this structure was more popular in Europe than in North America. One example here is the Swiss temporary employment company Adecco. A global leader in HR services, Adecco is the world's largest temporary employment agency and is

organized in ten areas. The areas are mostly based on geography (e.g., North America, Northern Europe) with some countries of strategic importance to the organization constituting separate divisions (e.g., France, Switzerland) and two divisions based on mixed criteria: not only geography but also similarity of the markets (Iberia and South America, and Italy, Eastern Europe and India).[20] A limitation of this approach is that it requires an organization to conduct similar activities in several locations rather than combining them into a more cost efficient central location. And, for better or worse, it allows for wide variation in the manner in which subsidiaries in different locations are managed.

- *Matrix structure*: In this structure each subsidiary reports to more than one group (product, geographic, or functional) for the purpose of integrating international operations with functional areas, product areas, or both. The popularity of this type of structure has waxed and waned as the advantages of integration versus the disadvantages of dual reporting were weighed against each other. The Swedish–Swiss company ABB (ASEA Brown Boveri), operating in the power and automation technology sectors, is often given as an example of a matrix organization. The company adopted a matrix structure in the 1980s but has since been reorganized. Some organizations may use a global matrix organization for specific projects. For example, Texas Instruments uses a matrix design for new product development with the respective matrix group dissolving after new product launch.[21]

Few MNEs have structures that exactly match the five ideal types presented here. In reality while a particular organizational form may be preferred, changes in industry conditions, firm capabilities, market trends and so on mean that organizations seldom have all activities corresponding to a single type of organizational structure. In addition, the dynamic and complex nature of the global environment may require a perspective on global organizations that does not focus on trying to find a fit between structure and the environment. One approach involves taking into account the need of these organizations to use human resources more efficiently in order to be more responsive to their environment. A popular and influential categorization considers the configuration of the organization's capabilities, the role of overseas operations, and the development and diffusion of knowledge.[22] This categorization is presented in Table 4.2.

In *international* organizations subunits are loosely aligned and the focus is on transferring technology developed at headquarters throughout the organization. The *multidomestic* is decentralized and it adapts to the local environment. *Global* organizations are centralized with subunits resembling headquarters, while in the *transnational* global standards are shared throughout the organizational network. These four MNE types are described ahead in terms of what they mean for global HRM.

SUBSIDIARY STRUCTURE AND GLOBAL HR

Regardless of the overall form of the organization, the subunits of the MNE operate in distinct local environments. These environments create a unique context for global HRM as discussed in Chapters 2 and 3. In addition, however, the local environment influences how HRM is

Table 4.2 Categorization of MNEs

Organizational Characteristics	Multidomestic	Global	International	Transnational
Configuration of assets and capabilities	Decentralized and nationally self-sufficient	Centralized and globally scaled	Sources of core competencies centralized, others decentralized	Dispersed, interdependent, and specialized
Role of overseas operations	Sensing and exploiting local opportunities	Implementing parent company strategies	Adapting and leveraging parent company competencies	Differentiated contributions by natural units to integrated worldwide operations
Development and diffusion of knowledge	Knowledge developed and retained within each unit	Knowledge developed and retained at the center	Knowledge developed at the center and transferred to overseas units	Knowledge developed jointly and shared worldwide

implemented through its effect on the organization of the foreign subsidiary. An idea helpful in understanding this effect is that the organizational structure and management practices of subsidiaries of MNEs are influenced by the opposing forces toward adaptation to the local environment (*local responsiveness*) and consistency within the organization (*global integration*).[23] The pressures for *global integration* among subsidiaries in the MNE stem from two factors: organizational replication and the imperative for control.[24] Organizational replication is the tendency of organizations to duplicate, in new environments, existing structures and procedures that have been effective. For example, Procter & Gamble initially designed each new foreign subsidiary to be an exact replica of the US organization because of a belief that the same policies and procedures that were successful in the United States would work equally well overseas.[25] The imperative for control means that organizations standardize policies and procedures to try to reduce the complexity and uncertainty involved in controlling international operations. However, in new environments, subunits also face pressures for *local responsiveness* (i.e., adapting to the local environment) because organizations have a tendency to reflect the values, norms, and accepted practices of the societies in which they operate.[26]

The pressures for local responsiveness and global integration can vary from subsidiary to subsidiary resulting in a variety of structures across the organization. Overall HRM policies and practices of foreign subsidiaries often more closely resemble their local competitors than they do their parent company. Also, some HR policies and practices are more susceptible to environmental influence than others. For example, training practices and contingent employment contracts have been found to be easier to adapt to local contexts than compensation practices and wage-bargaining levels.[27] Thus, a complex pattern emerges with elements of foreign subsidiaries having various degrees of conformity to local demands for some practices and not others, and with the subsidiaries in different countries resembling each other to varying degrees. The extent to which subsidiaries' practices reflect the local context as opposed to being consistent with the overall organization is taken up in more detail ahead in Chapter 6.

The four organizational types discussed previously (Table 4.2) are a reflection of the different emphases organizations place on local responsiveness and global integration. Organizations following a *multidomestic* strategy give primary importance to local responsiveness, *global* organizations strive for global efficiency, which requires a focus on consistency and global integration and *transnational* organizations attempt to achieve both local responsiveness and global integration, a goal they accomplish through being highly flexible and continuously adapting to changing circumstances. Finally, *international* organizations do not strive for efficiency as do global companies nor do they pursue local responsiveness to the extent of multidomestic companies, but they pay some attention to both of these goals.[28] International organizations are actually the least internationalized of the four types explored here as they only export a specific business practice or technology that can be exploited in a new market, for example. As a result, integration and responsiveness are less relevant goals for them compared to the other three types of organizations.

CONTROL MECHANISMS IN MNEs

Along with organizational strategy, reporting systems and budgets, organizational structure is a central mechanism for *formal* control and coordination in MNEs. However, as the level of interdependence among different units of the MNE increases, the effectiveness of formal control mechanisms decreases. This creates a vacuum that must be filled by more complex and flexible integrating mechanisms such as organizational culture (discussed previously), informal communication, and networks of personal relationships[29] which are often collectively referred to as means of *informal* control and coordination. Building and maintaining a perfect organizational structure is probably not possible for MNEs. Therefore, these organizations must devote resources to building the capability in individuals to resolve complex and contra-dictory issues or what has been called a "matrix in the mind of managers."[30]

This capability comes from social ties, networks of personal relationships and communi-cation, which are core components of *social capital*.[31] Three types of social capital have been identified: structural, relational, and cognitive. *Structural social capital* consists of the network of relationships that an individual has within the organization. *Relational social capital* involves trust and reciprocity, as well as the willingness of a member of the organization to be flexible and forego individual goals for organizational goals when necessary. Finally, *cognitive social capital* is the shared norms and behaviors of organization members, as well as adherence to common goals and a common approach to accomplishing tasks.[32] Social capital helps infor-mation exchanges and knowledge transfer between individuals and organizational units and thus acts as an informal mechanism of control.

Global HR is central to the development of organizational social capital and other infor-mal control mechanisms in MNEs because of its role in managing the relationships among organization members. For example, the Global HR department manages all forms of inter-national mobility of employees including short-term project work or long-term expatriate assignments. It can manage job assignments of boundary spanners in strategic ways, so that networks among key individuals are created and maintained. Boundary spanners are key in carrying important information from one organizational unit to another and also in creating perceptions of other organizational members or units. For example, if the boundary spanner had a positive experience with an organizational unit in a different country, he or she can convey this to his or her immediate colleagues and build good will between the two units; if the experience was negative, it can taint the broader inter-unit relationship.[33] Global HR can also provide resources to virtual team leaders to ensure that (in addition to accomplishing work-related tasks) personal networks are actively built which can be used even after virtual teams disband. Global HR can also make information sharing and knowledge transfer within the MNEs easier. For example, it can organize corporate events that enable and encourage socializing among employees across organizational units in a way that makes sure that interactions among employees from different units are productive, meaningful and directed toward mutually beneficial work-related goals.[34]

It is important to remember that as the level of interdependence within MNEs increases (from relatively low in the case of multidomestic organizations to very high in transnational organizations), informal control mechanisms become essential. The contribution of Global HR is critical to building these mechanisms in global and transnational MNEs.

GLOBAL HR IN SMEs

Small and medium enterprises (SMEs), the majority of which are family owned are an increasingly important economic player on the international stage. For example, it has been estimated that more than 25% of all exporting firms had fewer than 100 employees,[35] and SMEs may now account for as much as 80% of global economic growth[36] (by some estimates 95% of all firms worldwide could be classified as SMEs[37]). SMEs are particularly important economic contributors in the turbulent contexts of emerging markets (e.g., China, India, Taiwan etc.), transitional economies (e.g., Poland, Hungary, Czech Republic), and economies in crisis (e.g., Greece, Italy, Spain).[38]

Technology makes the entry of small firms into the international business environment easier.[39] As they grow, these firms are increasingly faced with human resource issues. The specific HRM issues vary over the life cycle of the firm, with training issue dominating in high-growth firms, compensation issues dominant in moderate-growth firms and recruiting dominant in no-growth firms.[40] Family-owned SMEs in particular face the problem of attracting and retaining strong nonfamily executives, as well as insufficient and poorly trained personnel at all levels.[41] A skills shortage (along with a decrease in productivity or a specific performance issue) is one of the most important issues in triggering an SME to consider HR practices.[42]

SME performance seems to be positively related to the adoption of effective HRM strategies.[43] This is especially true for practices that promote the sharing of knowledge around discretionary behavior and organizational learning, which positively influence entrepreneurial performance.[44] However, SMEs often lack the capacity to develop formal HRM practices.

It is important to recognize that SMEs face unique HRM challenges. Small firms, regardless of age, face the liabilities of smallness and must often form alliances, purchase opportunities or mimic larger more successful firms in order to gain access to resources. Where resources are limited there may be a small number of HR professionals, increased difficulty in recruiting and retaining employees and a reluctance to engage in costly or restrictive practices. In addition, small firms may face additional challenges such as an ambiguous identity, lack of legitimacy as an employer, and difficulty in maintaining sustainable HR policies.[45] Therefore, it is important to remember that HRM in small business should not be regarded as relying on the same principles as large organizations, only on a smaller scale.

While the majority of SMEs do not have formal HR strategy,[46] the adoption of formal HRM by SMEs is more likely if they employ highly skilled workers, are networked with other organizations,[47] and are unionized.[48] Some research suggests that the selection of HRM practices is best guided by the extent to which the practice facilitates organizational learning.[49] However, the specific HR practices adopted are highly variable among SMEs. Thus, the HRM practices of SMEs are often characterized as ad hoc and informal.

Talent management in SMEs: Planning is a key aspect of any HRM program. However, SMEs exhibit a significant amount of instability as they progress through the organizational life cycle.[50] As SMEs grow in size and complexity it becomes difficult to identify key positions and plan to fill these role either through external recruiting or by developing the internal talent pool.[51] Increasing size leads to an increase in specialized jobs, more hierarchical levels, and divisions among functional areas. While making planning more difficult, it also makes it more important. The lack of strategic HRM planning in SMEs may be linked to a lack of strategic thinking in general, with HR planning taking a variety of forms largely dependent on idiosyncratic aspects of the particular firm.

Recruitment and selection in SMEs: Employee turnover in SMEs can have a huge influence on the survival of the business which makes the recruitment and retention of employees of critical importance.[52] Small firms may not have the financial resources to engage in multiple rounds of a formal recruitment process, so the entire process is often less structured and less bureaucratic than in larger firms.[53] Also, small firms often recruit based on the owner's vision for the company, eschewing the need for formal job descriptions. Recruitment processes include the use of personal networks, word of mouth advertising and walk-ins, which are often perceived as inexpensive and convenient.

Selection in SMEs is similarly informal as less frequent hiring precludes the cost effectiveness of employing HR professionals for this task. SME owners or top managers are unlikely to have HR expertise in employee selection methods.[54] Therefore a common selection method is the so-called trio approach of application, panel interview, and references.[55] An alternative approach used by some SMEs is to outsource the recruitment function in order to gain access to more sophisticated methods.[56]

It is important to note that the informal and ad hoc approach to recruitment and selection in SMEs can lead to discriminatory practices. Failure to monitor equal opportunity in employment, lack of knowledge of employment law, and a pattern of recruiting by word of mouth and personal recommendations can introduce systematic bias into the process.[57]

Training and development in SMEs: SMEs tend to provide less training than larger organizations and the training tends to be informal and short-term oriented. Training is typically provided through direct supervision and/or coaching by another experienced employee.[58]

The content of training tends to be job related as opposed to strategic. Because of financial and resource constraints, management development training is limited in SMEs. Owners and senior managers often have little management training.[59] Organizational size and the ownership characteristics of the SME seem to be an important influence on the level of management development. Larger firms, with their more specialized job functions, obviously do more in this regard. And, family-owned firms are less likely to formalize management development and tend to regard these activities as individual career development.[60]

Employee relations in SMEs: Although somewhat rare, union membership and collective bargaining are not entirely non-existent in SMEs.[61] As with many other HRM functions the extent of formal employee representation tends to increase with firm size and collective representation is not obligatory in many countries. Very small family-owned firms are the least likely to have formal collective employee representation. In non-unionized SMEs employee relations generally involve informal communication between employer and employee.[62] Managers in small firms may engage in a more informational as opposed to a consultative approach in this communication because they see consultation as a threat to their control.[63]

In general, SMEs do not compare favorably with larger firms with regard to salaries and benefits and working conditions.[64] Some of these differences may be the result of a lack of knowledge by SMEs with regard to local employment legislation. As with other HRM functions the lack of formal HR structures, policies and procedures results in informal ad hoc approaches to these issues.

Performance management in SMEs: A minority of SMEs (one fifth according to one study[65]) use some form of performance management procedure – ranging from flexible work arrangements to pay for performance plans. SMEs face five challenges in applying performance management.[66] These are: (1) lack of time required to complete non-operational projects and low commitment of top management, (2) incorrect adaptation of systems designed for larger companies, (3) a focus on only financial aspects in overall planning, (4) planning with a reactive as opposed to proactive focus, and (5) restricted availability of resources required for long-term data management. In fact, introducing performance management systems in SMEs may require a change in the corporate governance structure of the organization. Thus, in most MNEs the performance management system retains the informal and ad hoc nature of HRM functions often using generic simple approaches that are managed by the owners (managers) of the firm.

Some characteristics of SMEs may actually be an advantage in managing HRM. For example, the informality of the SME results in lower levels of internal uncertainty. That is, in small firms the owner/manager is closer to the workforce and thus better able to:

- deliver information and decisions personally and consistently,
- receive immediate feedback from employees, and
- monitor progress with regard to how decisions are being carried out.[67]

However, this reliance on the discretion on the manager and the ad hoc nature of HRM in SMEs can result in a wide variation in HRM practices across countries and firms. Almost certainly differences in culture will influence which practices managers see as important. We should not be surprised to see significant differences in the extent to which particular HRM practices are adopted in SMEs.

The two extremes of HR in SMEs have been described as the *bleak house* model versus the *happy family* model. The bleak house model describes a situation characterized by low wages, numerical flexibility and an exploited workforce, while the happy family model is character-ized by a workforce with reasonable pay, a flexible and informal approach to management and close interpersonal relationships between employees and owners. Of course, the majority of firms probably fall somewhere between these two extremes.[68] The extent to which SMEs adopt a particular model of HRM is highly influenced by the industry in which they operate (with the imitation of the practices of competitors a key factor influencing the HRM approach) along with the values of managers and owners and characteristics of the workforce.[69] However, the willingness of managers to employ innovative and formal HRM systems is constrained by indigenous beliefs about the management of people. For example, in many societies the management of people is not seen as a technical matter necessitating any special expertise,[70] which argues against the adoption of formal HRM systems. In Chinese SMEs for example, the adoption of HRM is strongly influenced by cultural factors (for example, Guanxi) such that the practice that emerges is endowed with Chinese characteristics.[71] This is particularly true with regard to the way in which the HR function is organized in China where HR takes on a very operational role. Furthermore, owners of SMEs often prefer the informal and less structured HRM processes because they believe it minimizes costs and provides flexibility in dealing with employees. The following comment from an Indian entrepreneur provides an illustration:

> Let me tell you a strange incident. A few years ago a senior worker asked me for a loan of 20,000 rupee on the eve of his daughter's marriage. He was an efficient worker. I gave a gift of 25,000 rupee to his daughter as kanyadaan.[72] After his daughter's marriage he did not return to work, so I hired another worker in his place. As a result, he approached the labor department to make a case for reinstatement against my firm. When it was clear that he would not win the case, he begged my pardon by touching my feet (a traditional way of showing respect to elders and people in higher positions). But, I refused to take him back. Does this not illustrate the tyranny of labor law as it encourages workers to file frivolous claims?[73]

This incident illustrates the closer working relationships that management has with employ-ees in SMEs and also the reliance on the cultural norms of society to make decisions about employee relations.

In summary, five factors seem to affect the formalization of HRM practices in SMEs.[74] First, is the degree of internationalization of the firm. The second is the extent to which the SME is linked to larger companies through strategic alliances or other networks. In both these cases the firm may be exposed to more formal HRM approaches. The third, as mentioned previously, is the size of the firm. Larger SMEs tend to have more formal approaches. Fourth, some sectors such as manufacturing tend to have more formalized HRM approaches as growth increases the complexity of the HRM function. Fifth, is the business environment in which the SME has an effect. External pressures and expectations generated by legal requirements, cultural norms, presence of unions, level of technology, life cycle stage and so on can all influence the degree of formalization of HRM practices. The absence of systematic cross cultural/national research on HRM in SMEs means that in practice we must consider how each of these environmental factors might have their influence.

CHAPTER SUMMARY

In this chapter we examine how differences in the structure of organizations influence global HRM. Basic organizational structures can be described in terms of their complexity, formalization, and centralization, which when combined form structures ranging from mechanistic to organic. These structures are influenced by the societal context in which they exist based on what is perceived as legitimate in society and what is consistent with management values. In addition to a formal structure, every organization has an informal structure comprised of a set of normative behaviors and relationships. Global HRM is central to the development of social capital and other informal control mechanisms in the MNE. MNEs have found a variety of ways to integrate their international operations. These different MNE configurations have implications for the extent to which the Global HR department is organized, as we will demonstrate in Chapter 5. Regardless of the overall structure of the organization, the local subsidiaries face conflicting pressures for consistency with the overall organization and adaptation to the local environment. Some HRM activities are more susceptible to the forces for local adaptation than are others. Finally, the extent to which an HRM activity is central to the strategy of the firm and varies across subunits affects how the function is organized and delivered.

QUESTIONS FOR DISCUSSION

1. Describe the three basic dimensions along which an organization's structure can be determined.
2. What are the reasons that an international organization faces the conflicting pressures of internal consistency and local adaptation?
3. Discuss how organizational strategy influences the delivery of different HRM activities.
4. What factors influence the extent to which international SMEs adopt formal HRM practices?

NOTES

1. Katz & Khan (1978).
2. Pugh, Hickson, Hinings, MacDonald, & Turner (1963).
3. Burns & Stalker (1961).
4. Birkinshaw, Nobel, & Ridderstråle (2002); Lawrence & Lorsch (1967).
5. See Hickson & McMillan (1981) and Hickson & Pugh (1995).
6. See for example Azumi & McMillan (1975).

7. See Gibson (1994) and Thomas (2008).

8. Child & Kieser (1979); Ellegard, Jonsson, Enstrom, Johansson, Medbo, & Johansson (1992).

9. Chen (1995); Wu (1999).

10. Ghauri & Prasad (1995).

11. Lazerson (1995); Putnam (1993).

12. Based on Phatak & Habib (1998).

13. From organizing "People, values, and environment" at Johnson & Johnson in Daniels, Radebaugh, & Sullivan (2011).

14. Trompenaars & Hampden-Turner (1998).

15. Erez & Shokef (2008).

16. Leksell (1981); Marschan (1996); Stopford & Wells (1972).

17. Daniels, Radebaugh, & Sullivan (2011).

18. Birkinshaw (2000).

19. Griffin & Pustay (2013).

20. http://www.adecco.com/en-US/About/Organisation/Pages/default.aspx

21. Griffin & Pustay (2013).

22. Bartlett & Ghoshal (1989).

23. Bartlett (1986); Porter (1986).

24. Rosenzweig & Singh (1991).

25. Bartlett & Ghoshal (1989).

26. See Westney (1993).

27. Farndale, Brewster, Ligthart, & Poutsma (2017).

28. Harzing (1995b).

29. Dowling, Festing, Engle, & Gröschl (2009); Kostova & Roth (2003).

30. Bartlett & Ghoshal (1989).

31. Kostova & Roth (2003).

32. Burt (1992); Inkpen & Tsang (2005); Leana & Van Buren (1999); Nahapiet & Ghoshal (1998).

33. Kostova & Roth (2003).

34. Kostova & Roth (2003).

35. Aharoni (1994).

36. Osman, Ho, & Galang (2011).

37. Wong (2010).

38. Prouska & Psychogios (2019).

39. Thomas (2008).

40. Rutherford, Buller, & McMullen (2003).

41. Carlson, Upton, & Seaman (2006).

42. Cassell, Nadin, Gray, & Clegg (2002).

43. Diamantidis & Chatzoglou (2011).

44. Hayton (2003).

45. For a review of HRM in small firms see Cardon & Stevens (2004).

46. Kabst, Wehner, Meifert, & Kötter (2009).

47. Bacon & Hoque (2005).

48. Wagar (1998).

49. Wan Hooi & Sing Ngui (2014).

50. Chandler & Hanks (1994).

51. Krishnan & Scullion (2014).

52. Cameron, Mora, Leutscher, & Calarco (2011).

53. See Leung (2003).

54. Cardon & Stevens (2004).

55. Stavrou-Costea & Manson (2006).

56. Galanaski & Papalexandris (2005).

57. See Forth, Bewley, & Bryson (2006).

58. See Barrett (2015).

59. Smith, Whittaker, Loan Clark, & Boocock (1999).

60. Krishsnan & Scullion (2014).

61. Holten & Crouch (2014).

62. Marlow & Gray (2005).

63. See Dundon & Gollan (2007).

64. See European Commission (2001).

65. See Forth, Bewley, & Bryson (2006).

66. Garengo, Biazzo, Simonetti, & Bernardi (2005).

67. Hill & Stewart (2000).

68. Richbel, Szerb, & Vitai (2010).

69. Tsai (2010).

70. See for example Saini & Budhwar (2008).

71. Cunningham (2011).

72. Kanyadaan is a gift given to a Hindu bride by friends and relatives.

73. Abstracted from a case reported in Saini & Budhwar (2008).

74. See Psychogios, Szamosi, Prouska, & Brewster (2016).

5
The Global HR department

CHAPTER LEARNING OBJECTIVES

After reading this chapter you should be able to:

1. Contrast the various approaches to organizing the HR department and its activities in different countries worldwide.
2. Explain how the HR department can be structured to support an MNE's strategy and structure.
3. Discuss the extent to which the HR department in an MNE must balance both integration and differentiation of HRM activities.
4. Describe the multiple roles of Global HR professionals.

Global HR at Technica[1]

Emma Taylor knew that the executive management team was depending on her to engineer a human resources function that reflected the new reality at Technica. As a result of changes in the external environment, Technica had been paired down to about half its mid-1990s size, but its organization was scattered across six continents. She had recently read *Flight of the Buffalo*[2] and the idea of an organization that was "similar to a flock of geese flying in a 'V' formation" stuck with her. Each goose was responsible for getting itself to wherever the gaggle was going, changing roles whenever necessary, and whenever the task changed the geese would be responsible for changing the structure of the group to accommodate, similar to geese flying in a 'V', but landing in waves. "That's the HR organization I want," she thought; "but how to get it in the context of Technica's strategy, international structure, and cultural differences?"

Technica, founded in the early 1980s in Utah, is now a world leader in the development and marketing of internet networking software. Technica markets its products and support around the world through a partner and leverage model that begins with one-person outposts in widely dispersed, targeted geographic areas. Technica began using local people when country offices were first set up, with anyone who could speak the local language and was willing to sell Technica products recruited to head an international operation. As the market grew additional people were required and initial distributors were replaced with more sophisticated personnel and a more formal structure. Technica delivers uniform products worldwide – only the language differs. That is, the user interface on the screen is in different languages but behind the scenes, the products all operate the same. One of Technica's secret weapons is that it has at its headquarters (because of its location) an arsenal of people from different cultures who speak languages other than English as well as having high levels of technical skill. This had proven a real benefit in the initial communication with foreign markets and in product translation. However, aligning the perspective of Technica's associates around the globe with the organization's vision has been a continuing challenge. Technica's global strategy requires that employees and customers encounter a uniform look and feel when they interact with Technica offices worldwide. However, the balance between headquarters control and local autonomy has been uneven. Local laws, customs, and political events often require Technica to adapt its business model, for example, allowing an exclusive distributorship in Brazil and a joint venture in Japan.

Emma wondered if creating a Global HR function was as feasible as building a global IT product in which everything was identical except the language. What will this HR organization look like? One thing she knew for sure is that she would be expected to work fast. This was an IT company where a one-year plan is long-term.

INTRODUCTION

As described in the opening chapter to this book, the role of the human resources (HR) department has evolved from the welfare secretaries of the 1800s through personnel managers in the 1900s to that of strategic partner in the 21st century; a role in which the HR department must contribute value to the firm. Having a strategic HR department means being able to support organizational goals through people. And now, globalization is changing the HR department once again. The HR department on a global scale has multiple roles as it must deliver basic HRM activities such as building an HR infrastructure and championing employee concerns, while also making the changes required to integrate HRM and business strategy in a dynamic global environment.[3] In seeking to add value to the firm, the HR department faces the challenge of organizing in such a way as to deliver effectively on all its roles simultaneously.

In Chapters 2 and 3, we explored how different cultural and institutional contexts affect the practice of HRM in organizations operating in different countries around the world. But how do these different contexts affect how the HR department operates? In comparing the HR department in the United States of America (USA) with Japan, for example, traditionally HR has held much greater status in Japanese organizations as employees are accepted as critical stakeholders and therefore HR has greater power and legitimacy.[4] There are other country differences that revolve around the extent to which HR is operating in partnership with management and/or with employee representatives such as trade unions, all of which have an impact on the role that HR needs to and can fulfill.

In this chapter, we focus on the structure, role, and activities of the HR department both across different countries and inside MNEs, which are all important aspects to consider when entering an HR role. We first look at the HR department structure from a comparative, cross-national perspective to see how the external context affects what HR can do inside organizations. We then shift the focus from the structure of the HR department to the roles that HR professionals play. We discuss how HR roles differ between countries, questioning, for example, the extent to which HR primarily represents managerial concerns or employee interests, and the extent to which a strategic HR department is valued by organizations. In the second half of the chapter we explore the specific situation of MNEs that operate across multiple country contexts, questioning how they can build an effective HR department structure given the geographical and cultural complexity of their operations. Finally, we explore what it means to be an HR professional in an MNE headquarters or one of the subsidiary locations, including how the global integration–local adaptation paradox affects what activities and roles the Global HR department can fulfill.

HR DEPARTMENTS ACROSS COUNTRIES

In any country, HR departments are support functions and need to be structured to be able to offer the best type and level of support required. There is not one single structure that will suit all organizations, and equally not one type of structure that suits every country context. We highlight the different options that organizations have for structuring their HR department, exploring how and why this varies between countries.

Typically, HR has a "3-legged stool" structure: a corporate HR department supported by centers of excellence, shared services centers, and HR professionals working as business partners with managers in the different organizational units.[5] In more complex organizations, there are also unit-level HR departments that function as conduits for HRM activities to flow from corporate HR through the unit-level HR departments out to HR professionals operating at the heart of the business. In this structure, shared service centers (SSCs) rely heavily on technological capability, providing centralized facilities allowing managers and employees to access most HRM information without needing to contact an HR department member. SSCs are a strong source of centralization of the HR department, as we describe ahead. The centers of excellence (CoEs) are also mechanisms for standardizing HRM practices across an organization. They are either physical or virtual teams that are established to develop best practice across the different HRM areas of activity.[6] CoEs are teams of experts responsible for designing functional HRM practices that are rolled out across the organization.

The balance between these different legs of the HR department "stool" is determined by the extent to which an organization prefers more centralized or decentralized delivery of HRM. As noted, centralization of the HR department often takes the form of SSCs, which are dedicated HR units providing their services across a range of internal clients, rather than different business units having their own dedicated HR department.[7] The SSC uses eHRM technologies to deliver services on demand to clients, allowing managers and employees to access self-service facilities.[8] SSCs typically consolidate transactional activities such as employee records and benefits management,[9] gradually adding more complex activities such as performance management, training, or change management. This centralization leads to greater control and standardization in HRM practice implementation, which is important in countries that value uncertainty avoidance, for example. Having HR professionals deliver practices direct to managers or employees through a more decentralized model can lead to inefficiency and subjectivity in the process, yet at the same time this allows for greater responsiveness to the local business needs.

The three-legged stool has also been expanded with a potential fourth leg: HRM services outsourcing. Outsourcing means paying an external third party to deliver a service rather than employing people inside the organization to provide the same service. There are multiple factors that an organization needs to consider when choosing between insourcing or outsourcing HR, including: the complexity of the HRM activities; the extent to which the outsourcing will be long- or short-term; whether the activities are considered core or peripheral to the organization; and whether third parties and/or technology systems can offer the services required.[10] Outsourcing is generally considered most relevant for administrative, non-core HRM activities provided that a third party offers the desired service (such as payroll, for example) but it is less likely to be used for core HR activities of strategic importance (such as career development, for example). The evidence to date indicates that outsourcing can be a very challenging option, with potentially damaging results for the HR department if not managed appropriately.[11]

These challenges can be exacerbated further when outsourcing to an overseas location, that is, offshoring. HRM activities are complex in that they are embedded at the individual level of employees all the way through to being part of business strategies affecting an entire organization. As such, handing over control to a third party in another country can be complex despite the use of information technology systems that support HRM activities. Decisions to offshore are therefore based around several factors that include cost efficiencies alongside the level of trust in the provider in terms of data and system governance. Firms must balance the strategic importance of activities and the level of interdependence that they require to make critical decisions on whether to offshore their HRM activities.[12]

The extent to which these different "legs" of the HR department are used varies by country. Based on a study involving several well-known MNEs,[13] both outsourcing and the use of HR SSCs were particularly common in Japan and the Americas, while they were used less in Europe. North American firms had made the most use of outsourcing and offshoring HRM activities to low-cost locations, with China being a primary recipient of such work. However, many firms noted that outsourcing was only moderately effective in achieving the organization's goals in any country or region.

HR department roles

In addition to thinking about the way in which HR departments are structured, we can also identify different roles that HR professionals play. Given different institutional and cultural contexts, it is not surprising that the relative importance of these roles differs between countries. Ahead we introduce some commonly accepted role typologies and then illustrate how these typologies are affected by the country in which the HR department is operating.

HR roles can be thought of as both a collection of work tasks as well as a form of identity for the HR department within an organization.[14] The differences between the various roles have been contrasted through a range of typologies:

- HR can be either a *conformist* or *deviant innovator*,[15] depending upon the extent to which HR is reactive, content with towing the company line (conformist), or is more proactive, pushing the company in new directions regarding how people are managed (deviant).
- HR roles can also be divided into those that are strategic ("*architect*"), operational ("*contracts manager*"), or administrative ("*clerk of works*").[16]
- Combining the reactive/proactive and strategic/operational characteristics, HR is described as either a *change-maker* (proactive, strategic), an *adviser* (reactive, strategic), a *regulator* (proactive, operational), or a *handmaiden* (reactive, operational).[17]

Perhaps the most well-known typology was developed by Dave Ulrich[18] and highlights people versus process as well as operational versus strategic dimensions of the activities of HR departments (see also Figure 5.1):

- The *Administrative Expert* is a process-orientated role with a day-to-day, operational focus, such as ensuring appropriate contracts are issued or absence requests are processed.
- The other process-orientated role, *Strategic Partner*, is future-focused, adding value based on aligning HRM strategy and business strategy.
- On the people dimension, *Change Agents* are strategic in that they are responsible for the smooth running of change and culture transformation processes, encouraging the construction of trust relationships, as well as problem identification and solutions.
- Finally, *Employee Champions* are people-focused at an operational level, supporting the daily needs of employees.

This well-known HR role typology was developed in the USA. As shown in Chapters 2 and 3 in this book, we know that the USA has a particular set of cultural values (i.e., high on individualism and masculinity) and institutional infrastructure (based on the neo-liberalist ideology of the liberal market economy). As a result, the typology has been developed with these cultural and ideological values in mind. In countries with different societal values and a different perspective on the balance between shareholder and other stakeholder needs, this US-centric typology may not hold. For example, what happens to the role of HR professionals in a country that is much higher on femininity values and is

Source: Ulrich (1997).

Figure 5.1   Ulrich's HR role typology

embedded in the neo-corporatist ideology of a coordinated market economy, such as in the Netherlands?

This question is answered in a study[19] that tested how well this US typology holds in a survey of HR professionals in the Netherlands. In that context, it was much more difficult to differentiate between people and process roles at the strategic level. That is, the *Strategic Partner* role and the *Change Partner* role looked very similar. Whereas in the USA, strategy development is the exclusive realm of management and generally does not involve the company's employees, in the Netherlands, there is a stronger emphasis on developing and implementing strategy by combining strategic processes with employee reactions to any process changes. Also, in the USA, the *Employee Champion* role is focused on direct communication between the HR department and employees who have issues that need addressing. In the Netherlands, an equally strong *Trade Union Partnership* role emerged, because of the much higher importance of industrial democracy within the Netherlands compared to the USA (see also Chapter 12).

In summary, the relative importance of each of the HR department roles varies according to the cultural and institutional context in which the organization is operating. National level regulations, industry standards, and labor market traditions can affect the way in which HR professionals carry out their tasks. As shown in Chapter 3, there are coercive, normative, and mimetic influences present in any country that restrict the freedom of organizations.[20] For example, employment legislation may mean mandatory approaches to employing certain groups of individuals or having them participate in organizational decisions. The more complex the employment legislation in a country, the more HR professionals may be compelled to spending a great deal of their time on operational tasks as opposed to more strategic activities.[21]

Closely linked to HR department roles is the status that the department holds inside the organization. The professional bodies representing HR professionals have made great progress in increasing the credibility of the profession, and in turn this has increased the status of HR departments. However, this varies across organizations and across countries. A key indicator of the status of HRM in the organization is the extent to which HRM is represented at the board level in organizations. Consistent with their cultural and institutional contexts, coordinated market economies (CMEs) such as France, Spain, and Sweden report the highest percentages of organizations (over 80–90%)[22] that have an HR director on the main decision-making body of the organization (the Board of Directors in publicly held companies). In these countries, HR is an important stakeholder in ensuring employees are well-represented in the organization. In comparison, in more liberal market economies (LMEs), such as Australia, the UK, and USA, the percentage of organizations that have HR representatives at the board level is closer to 70%.[23] However, this CME/LME difference is not the only factor to consider. In Germany, a typical CME, employees have a legal right to be represented on the board. Therefore, there is less need for HR to be represented there with only 50% of German organizations report having HR representatives at board level.[24]

Another indicator of the status of the HR department is the extent to which line managers, versus HR professionals, are directly involved with HRM issues. The trend toward giving line managers more responsibility and reducing the HR department's direct involvement that was prevalent in the 1990s (largely due to HR professionals seeking more strategic roles and hence

Table 5.1a Representation of HR on Board of Directors

	1995	1999/2000	2004/5	2008/9	2014/15
Liberal market economies	52.1%	45.7%	44.1%	64.0%	70.7%
Coordinated market economies	56.0%	58.1%	65.0%	65.6%	64.1%
Mediterranean	63.8%	48.7%	48.1%	59.3%	58.1%
Nordic	63.3%	65.4%	69.0%	75.8%	77.3%
Central and Eastern European	n/a	48.6%	37.4%	61.9%	56.1%

Table 5.1b Mean ratio of HR employees per 100 organizational employees

	1999/2000	2004/5	2008/9	2014/15
Liberal market economies	1.57	1.26	1.48	1.22
Coordinated market economies	1.56	1.47	1.37	1.24
Mediterranean	1.30	1.36	1.43	1.12
Nordic	1.33	1.24	0.97	1.63
Central and Eastern European	1.33	1.20	1.30	1.30

Notes: For all tables, *Liberal Market Economies* include Australia, Canada, Ireland, New Zealand, UK, and USA; *Coordinated Market Economies* include Austria, Belgium, France, Germany, the Netherlands, and Switzerland; *Mediterranean* countries include Cyprus, Greece, Italy, Spain, Portugal, Turkey, and the Turkish Cypriot Community; *Nordic* countries include Denmark, Finland, Iceland, Norway, and Sweden; and *Central and Eastern European Countries* include Bulgaria, Czech Republic, Estonia, Hungary, Lithuania, Russia, Serbia, Slovakia, and Slovenia. Due to data restrictions, country configuration for each cluster varies in each year analyzed.
Source: Cranet study.

pushing more transactional activities out to the line), seems to be reversing. There are variations in this trend around the world. For example, if we look at who is responsible for major pay and benefits policy decisions, in Italy and Belgium this clearly lies with the HR department rather than line management. In contrast, line managers hold most responsibility in this area in the emerging economies of Romania, Latvia, Slovakia, and Hungary.[25] This may be because in these latter countries, the HR department has traditionally had a very limited administrative role and may still be developing their more strategic contribution. Tables 5.1a and 5.1b provide more information on HR representation around the world.

In summary, the roles and status of the HR department in an international context may be influenced by both national culture and institutional factors. The extent of internationalization of the firm, and the range of countries in which the firm operates, may also influence the roles that HR must carry out and on the structure of the HR function. Ahead, we explore these issues in MNEs.

GLOBAL HR DEPARTMENTS IN MNEs

Against the backdrop of substantial country-level differences in how the HR department is structured and the primary roles that HR professionals play, we now turn to how MNEs can build an HR department that is effective across these different contexts. We focus on how MNEs structure their "Global HR" department, that is, the corporate HR department with global responsibilities across the organization. Adopting an appropriate structure for the HR department that can help support the goals of the internationally operating MNE is crucial. In Chapter 4, we presented the typology of MNE internationalization strategies: multidomestic, global, transnational. One implication of this typology is that any combination of structural forms might be effective for an MNE operating in differing contexts. As important, however, is that each of these internationalization strategies may have different implications for the HR department. The limited research on the relationship between organizational structure and the Global HR department[26] allows us to present a conceptual map of internationalization strategies. The Global HR department can be categorized along two dimensions of centralization and interdependence (the extent to which functional activities are coordinated or integrated among units in different countries[27]). These dimensions can be mapped against the internationalization strategies of global, multidomestic, and transnational.[28]

Multidomestic MNEs give rise to a decentralized and independent Global HR department because of their focus on exploiting local opportunities. Local units are largely independent from other subsidiaries. Knowledge is developed within each unit and is generally not well-integrated throughout the organization. Decentralized, independent Global HR departments are typically housed in firms with product-based or geographic based structures. The headquarters HR role is typically limited to dealing with the elite corporate structure, with most functions devolved to the subsidiaries. Corporate HR can sometimes be effective in using informal processes to introduce a degree of corporate integration, for example in influencing operating companies and divisions to support international transfers for development purposes.

Global MNEs are characterized by centralized and dependent HR departments with strategies formulated at headquarters and implemented throughout the organization, with local units having a one-way relationship to headquarters. This type of HR organization is often housed in firms with product-based or matrix organizational structures. The primary role for HR is to establish and maintain control over all high-grade management positions worldwide. Centralized control is established over the careers and mobility of top management positions, and over expatriate transfers. The HR department in these companies is large, well-resourced and responsible for a wide range of functions.

Transnational MNEs foster integrated and interdependent Global HR departments. The headquarters HR department is typically staffed by a relatively small group of corporate HR executives who are primarily engaged in coordination and integration activities. HRM practices from throughout the organization are replicated across the organization both by aligning formal systems and also through the informal mechanisms of instilling shared objectives.[29]

In summary, in centralized/global firms the corporate Global HR department houses a wide range of activities, including management development, succession planning, career planning, strategic staffing, top management rewards and managing the mobility of expatriate managers. In the highly decentralized firms pursuing a multidomestic strategy, Global HR executives are often confined to a more limited range of centralized activities, often related only to HRM pertaining to senior executives. In transnational firms, Global HR has to be able to balance a more centralized approach to HRM practice development while ensuring local subsidiaries feel ownership of such practices. Box 5.1 provides an example of how these different organizational configurations result in different Global HR department structures.

BOX 5.1   CONTRASTING P&G AND IKEA

IKEA is a readily recognized brand across almost 30 countries worldwide. It is recognized because of its distinctive brand, and its offering of home furniture and furnishings, kitchens and appliances. No matter which IKEA store you visit, in whatever country where they operate, their logo will be the same, the atmosphere created in the store will be the same, and most products available to purchase will be identical. This is an extreme of brand and product centralization. However, IKEA has traditionally taken a much less centralized approach to HRM than for its products. Because every store across the globe has unique operating conditions, the supply and demand for employees can vary considerably. In response, store managers have been able to develop their own approach to recruiting, rewarding and retaining employees, provided that these HRM practices were at least in line with IKEA's strong corporate values.[30] As time has passed, however, IKEA has switched to developing a stronger top-down process, as store managers were seeking more guidance from the top as this level of decentralization was said to be resulting in everyone having to reinvent the HRM wheel for themselves.

In contrast, P&G started from a more centralized position regarding its HRM practices. Procter & Gamble (P&G) is a fast-moving consumer goods multinational with multiple global brands, including Head & Shoulders, Olay, Pantene, Gillette, etc.[31] It has some 95,000 employees based in 70 countries. In the past, this US-originated MNE believed in the importance of standardizing its HR delivery worldwide, whereby its HR departments were highly dependent on the headquarters. This is typical of a global organizational configuration leading to very centralized HR departments. Over time however, P&G discovered that it was missing out on the wealth of HRM knowledge that was spread across its operations. As this MNE shifted to a more transnational, networked structure, the level of interdependency among HR professionals across the firm also increased. The result is a strong structure of HR communities of practice[32] that span the globe and support the development and implementation of HRM policies and practices across the organization. This integrated structure allows HR professionals to learn from each other and produce an HRM system that can operate effectively in all parts of the business.[33]

Strategic international human resource management orientation

Both the MNE internationalization strategy (multidomestic, global, transnational) and the degree of centralization or decentralization have implications for adopting an appropriate strategic international human resource management (SIHRM) orientation. SIHRM can take one of three general forms: adaptive, exportive, or integrative:[34]

- *Exportive SIHRM.* In exportive SIHRM, the parent firm attempts to replicate their home HRM practices in all foreign subsidiaries (thus achieving high internal consistency). We would expect to find this approach in firms that believe that their HRM competence is generalizable across contexts (locations). An example would be when a firm decides to implement a standardized performance management process that all managers and employees across all of the firm's operations must follow.
- *Adaptive SIHRM.* An adaptive SIHRM orientation adapts HRM activities to local contexts, creating HRM systems for foreign subsidiaries that reflect the local environment. This results in low internal consistency inside the MNE. This approach is consistent with a multidomestic strategy and a belief that the firm's HRM competence is context (location) specific. For example, rather than an MNE's headquarters stipulating the exact format of performance appraisal meetings in all its operations, each subsidiary location can decide on and implement the appraisal meeting format that will work best in its operating context.
- *Integrative SIHRM.* MNEs with an integrative SIHRM orientation combine characteristics of their overseas subsidiaries with the parent company's HRM system. Transfer of HRM policies and practices occurs but is just as likely to be between subsidiaries or from subsidiaries to parent as they are between the parent and subsidiaries. This SIHRM approach attempts to take "best practices" and use them throughout the organization. It is consistent with a belief that practices can be optimized to fit in more than one context. An example is when an MNE looks for examples of effective performance management practices across the organization and then combines these into an overall best practice for the firm, while allowing some leeway for necessary local adaptations.

These three SIHRM orientations have obvious overlaps with the three internationalization strategies discussed previously. An exportive orientation is focused on central control by the corporate headquarters, as does a global internationalization strategy. The adaptive orientation places greater emphasis on local subsidiaries being able to adapt practices to what is necessary in the local context, which is also the underlying strategy of multidomestic firms. Finally, transnational firms aim to integrate activities across the organization, balancing headquarters and affiliates' contributions and needs, which is also at the heart of the integrative SIHRM orientation. This linking of internationalization strategies to the SIHRM orientations is summarized in Table 5.2.

Another way of thinking about the centralization/decentralization choices within an MNE is to consider the extent to which a firm aims to either integrate or differentiate its *HRM activities.*[35] Corporate integration of HRM practices implies tight control and standardization

Table 5.2   Matching approaches to strategic HRM with internationalization strategies

	Internationalization strategy	SIHRM approach
Home country focus	GLOBAL	EXPORTIVE
Host country focus	MULTIDOMESTIC	ADAPTIVE
Balance between home and host country	TRANSNATIONAL	INTEGRATIVE

as found most commonly in centralized organizations, while differentiation of practices results in activities being adapted to meet the different needs of local contexts as is common in more decentralized operations. The combination of being either low or high on these two dimensions determines the operating context for the HR department and indicates appropriate delivery mechanisms for different types of HRM activity.

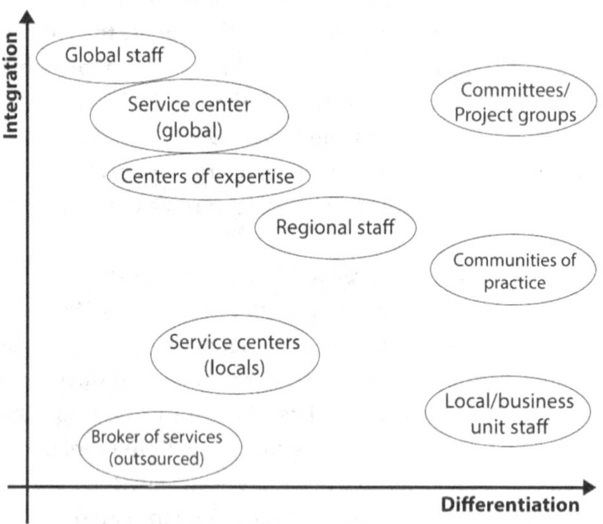

Source: Pucik, Evans, Björkman, & Morris (2016, Figure 14.2 on p. 433).

Figure 5.2   HR structures in MNEs

Figure 5.2 summarizes the ideal elements of the HR department structure (otherwise known as "delivery mechanisms") depending on the extent of integration or differentiation desired. Outsourcing to brokers of services is ideal for low integration–low differentiation activities (e.g., payroll processing). Corporate Global HR should be responsible for activities that are high on integration but low on differentiation (e.g., executive development), while business unit HR departments (either individually or working together in communities of practice) can take responsibility for activities that are high on differentiation but low on integration (e.g., recruitment). For activities that are high on both integration and differentiation (e.g., performance management), this should involve shared responsibility between corporate and business unit HR department members through committees or project groups.

Figure 5.2 also highlights a role for SSCs at the local and the global level. The global SSC focuses on activities that are highly integrated across the MNE. In contrast, the local SSC has less integration but brings together HR practitioners who have the necessary expertise to manage a particular activity or deal with a particular issue, such as diversity management, organizational change consulting, or global knowledge management. Like SSCs, CoEs also involve cross-functional teams that can help develop best practice across the MNE. The middle ground between integration and differentiation is filled by regional HR units that act as a filter between corporate and local activities.

Global HR department competencies in MNEs

Global HR has an important strategic role to play as it is often responsible for overseeing activities related to top talent in MNEs.[36] This means that there are a number of important activities that the department must undertake that can vary depending on the chosen internationalization strategy:

- In *global* firms, the corporate HR department carries out a wide range of activities, including management development, succession planning, career planning, strategic staffing, executive reward, and managing international assignee mobility. The high need for integration of international activities requires centralized control over these managers and high-potential employees.
- In highly decentralized firms that pursue a *multidomestic* internationalization strategy, the corporate HR department focuses only on management development and succession planning for senior executives.[37]

In order to understand the additional areas of competence required in the global context, it is important to go beyond the four basic HR roles we identified earlier (strategic partner, change agent, administrative expert, employee champion). Specifically, Global HR (i.e., the corporate HR department responsible for HRM activities on a global scale) requires four core areas of competence:[38]

- *Champion of processes*: HR polices the HRM activities across the organization, that is, developing HRM practices, strategies, and tools and monitoring their implementation.
- *Guardian of culture*: the HR department contributes to develop an appropriately "international" culture, ensuring values are developed that support global mobility of individuals, and breaking down silo mentalities that can exist between business divisions and geographic regions.
- *Effective political influencer*: an important aspect of this skill is to encourage receptivity among different parts of the business, ensuring that both sending-units and receiving-units are keen to share valuable talent resources to the benefit of the organization, rather than hiding key talent to avoid another business unit "poaching" them.
- *Knowledge management champion*: HR facilitates the development of networks across the organization and with appropriate external bodies to support efficient HRM, while being sensitive to what is happening at both local and global levels.[39]

The relative priority of each of these areas of competence is contingent on the MNE's choice of internationalization strategy and degree of centralization/decentralization.[40] The *champion of processes*, with its focus on monitoring global talent management processes, is very important under a centralized system, but of more limited value due to its difficulty to implement in a decentralized system. The *guardian of culture* is most evident when there is a need for corporate HR support to create a culture of mobility across the firm, especially when there are few formal reporting lines between corporate and subsidiaries as in a decentralized, multidomestic MNE. The *effective political influencer* is similarly strongest in a decentralized structure, whereby encouraging the flow of talent around the organization is closely linked to the credibility and influence of individual HR practitioners in persuading their business units to share. Finally, the *knowledge management champion* is important in both decentralized and centralized models, encouraging the flow of knowledge around the MNE from headquarters to subsidiaries and between subsidiaries (see also "Knowledge flows" ahead).

In MNE subsidiaries, the HR department competencies tend to be more administrative in nature, independent of the level of capability of HR department managers, their background, or degree of international talent flow in the organization.[41] Only larger subsidiaries are more likely to have a stronger strategic role, likely due to the availability of resources.[42] In early stages of internationalization firms are more likely to have corporate HR take control[43] or when a subsidiary is critical to the corporate strategy, headquarters is similarly likely to want to maintain control.[44] Firms originating from the USA[45] or where there is a high degree of similarity between the headquarters and the subsidiary's environment also have a stronger controlling role for headquarters.[46] Finally, the level of control is also related to the internationalization strategy that the firm adopts, whereby subsidiary HR departments are more likely to have a more strategic role either in the networked transnational organization, or when the firm is highly decentralized as in multidomestic MNEs.[47] Table 5.3 summarizes some of the complementarities between the different strategies, structures, roles and competencies.

Knowledge flows

The Global HR department has a role to play as a knowledge management champion, helping knowledge transfer across the organization by developing, maintaining and extending the MNE's structural, cognitive, and relational social capital (see Chapter 4). The HR department is often best positioned to facilitate this transfer. More often than not, the knowledge that can enhance a company's competitive advantage is tacit and thus, difficult to transfer. Transfer of tacit knowledge requires people-based channels, and thus, efforts toward improving communication, building relationships, and reinforcing organizational culture that encourages knowledge sharing, all of which are things the Global HR department can do well.[48]

Global HR departments can help with enhancing knowledge-sharing capabilities by deploying appropriate training and performance management practices. They can also help increase employee motivation for sharing knowledge by introducing promotion and compensation tools that reward this behavior.[49] HR can establish formal mechanisms to help integrate knowledge across the firm, such as liaison personnel, interunit task forces, permanent international committees, and intranets for sharing experiences and accumulated knowledge. They can also

Table 5.3   Linking MNE characteristics and HR department roles

Internationalization strategy	International	Global	Transnational	Multidomestic
Degree of centralization	Decentralized	Centralized	Centralized	Decentralized
Degree of integration	No integration, high differentiation	Maximal integration, minimal differentiation	High integration, medium differentiation	Minimal integration, maximal differentiation
Level of dependence	Independent, except for technology transfer	Highly dependent	Interdependent, based on networking principles of coordination and integration	Independent, often due to a high level of dissimilarity between parent and host country contexts
IHRM approach	Non-existent: loose federation structure (rather than a headquarter/subsidiary relationship) does not require IHRM coordination	Exportive	Integrative	Adaptive
Dominant corporate HR roles	Not applicable	Champion of processes	Guardian of culture Knowledge management champion	Guardian of culture Effective political influencer
Dominant subsidiary HR role	Not applicable	Administrative: implementing headquarters' practices	Administrative & Strategic: implementing corporate practices, but also contributing to the development of these practices	Strategic & Administrative: devising local best practices and implementing at the local level

Source: Based on: Vidović & Farndale (2016).

create informal socialization mechanisms that promote the internalization of MNE goals and mutual understanding through practices like diversity training to decrease negative stereotypes, prejudice, and resistance to knowledge originating elsewhere, corporate mentoring programs, staff transfers between subsidiaries, or cultivating a global mindset among employees.[50]

The HR department can apply these principles of knowledge management to its own activities too, setting up virtual networks of internal experts internationally across the MNE. These international HR networks have multiple goals:[51] developing and implementing global policy; creating and sharing best practice; capturing distributed expertise; building buy-in across the organization; exchanging information; and socializing the network members. All these activities are related to the development, sharing and internalization of knowledge within the HR community inside the MNE. To be effective, the networks benefit from having annual face-to-face meetings to build personal relationships among members and share tacit knowledge,[52] followed up by regular audio and video communications across the geographically dispersed groups. This face-to-face and virtual interaction should then be reinforced through appropriate documentation and data repositories that record the discussions and decisions made.

HR networks can develop strong human capital (with the network members learning from each other as they developed new policy), social capital (as the network members interacted with one another), and organizational capital (as the work of the networks is documented and stored).[53] The most successful networks have a range of strong features, including: clear, shared objectives; strong ties between members with frequent meetings; credibility among individual members; top-down support from the board; and the network members themselves need intercultural competencies that allow them to interact well in a globally diverse group. In contrast, the networks are less effective when there is lack of financial resources to travel for meetings, technological resources to provide appropriate support systems, and/or HR member resources such as time for participation.[54]

Global HR professionals

While the responsibility for managing human resources does not reside exclusively with HR professionals, the competencies of the Global HR manager must be greatly expanded to deal with the multiple countries and cultures with which they must engage. The need for Global HR professionals to have specific competencies is reflected in the criteria that the HR Certification Institution (HRCI) in the USA sets for certification as a *Global Professional in Human Resources*.[55] According to HRCI, a Global Professional in HR's important competencies include:[56]

- The development of global HR strategies to support the organization's short- and long-term goals, objectives, and values.
- The development, implementation, and evaluation of global staffing strategies to support organizational objectives in a culturally appropriate manner.
- The establishment and evaluation of a global compensation and benefits strategy aligned with the business objectives.

- The design, implementation, and evaluation of organizational development programs and processes to effectively develop a global workforce supporting business goals, culture and values.
- The design, implementation, and evaluation of processes and practices that protect or enhance organizational value. This includes managing risk, ensuring compliance, and balancing employer and employee rights and responsibilities on a global basis.

In brief, the Global HR department has additional responsibilities compared to an HR department tasked only with providing support to local operations. In particular, there is an additional HR unit in MNEs not found in domestic operations: the Global Mobility department. Global Mobility's responsibilities include, for example, managing all forms of employee international mobility, including short-term project work through long-term expatriate assignments. Global Mobility professionals manage international assignments strategically, so that networks among key individuals are created and maintained. Developing initially from a more transactional role managing overseas assignments, today there is much greater emphasis on Global Mobility's role as a strategic advisory function supported by an appropriate corporate culture that facilitates employee mobility (see also Chapter 11).[57]

CHAPTER SUMMARY

The organization of the HR department to accomplish its mission creates complex structures and roles for HR professionals that they must keep in balance and in line with corporate strategies to be effective. Variations in national cultural and institutional contexts mean that structures adopted for the HR department and roles conducted by HR professionals can vary considerably between countries. For example, HR work can be organized in terms of delivery through centralized head offices supported by HR business partners, shared service centers, centers of excellence, and outsourced activities. Also, the typical HR roles (strategic partner, change agent, administrative expert, and employee champion) are weighted differently according to the location where organizations are based. An understanding of both the global and local context is critical to becoming a competent Global HR professional.

This complexity of the context for HR is magnified in the multinational operations of MNEs. First, the different internationalization strategies of firms are linked with different strategic international HRM orientations (exportive, adaptive, or integrative). Second, these strategies each require a different area of competence ranging from managing standard processes to developing personal influencing skills, and from protecting the organization's culture to facilitating knowledge sharing throughout the organization. Global HR plays an important role in facilitating strategic HRM within MNEs, ensuring the organization can benefit from its global scope of activities; so much so that there are specific certification routes for Global HR professionals.

QUESTIONS FOR DISCUSSION

1. How applicable is the Ulrich (1997) framework of HR department roles to countries other than the United States, where it was developed?
2. What type of HR department structure best fits with (a) global, (b) multidomestic, and (c) transnational internationalization strategies, and why?
3. How can Global HR help transfer knowledge within MNEs?
4. Based on Table 5.3, discuss how each of the four areas of competence required for Global HR can be effective in multidomestic, global, and transnational MNEs.

NOTES

1. This case is fictional but is based loosely on the development of Novell as described in the case "Novell: Transforming Culture" by Marjorie McEntire in Oddou & Mendenhall (2000).
2. Belasco & Stayer (1994).
3. Ulrich (1997).
4. Jacoby (2005).
5. Reilly, Tamkin, & Broughton (2007).
6. Fischer (2003).
7. Sparrow & Braun (2008).
8. Farndale, Paauwe, & Hoeksema (2009).
9. Adler (2003).
10. Lepak, Bartol, & Erhardt (2005).
11. Patel, Budhwar, Witzemann, & Katou (2019).
12. Paz-Aparicio, Ricart, & Bonache (2017).
13. Based on unpublished research conducted by the author as a member of "Global HR Research Alliance" project in 2004/5.
14. Ulrich & Brockbank (2005).
15. Legge (1978).
16. Tyson & Fell (1986).
17. Storey (1992).
18. Ulrich (1997); later refined by Ulrich & Brockbank (2005).
19. Farndale & Paauwe (2007).
20. DiMaggio & Powell (1983).
21. Sparrow & Hiltrop (1997); for a more extensive treatment of the relationship between HR and institutional context see: Paauwe & Boselie (2003).
22. Cranet International Report (2017).
23. Cranet International Report (2017).
24. Cranet International Report (2017).
25. Cranet International Report (2017).
26. Adler & Ghadar (1990); Farndale, Paauwe, Morris, Stahl, Stiles, Trevor, & Wright (2010); Scullion & Starkey (2000).
27. Roth (1995).

28. "International" is not included here as this type of organizational configuration does not have any need for a Global HR department as it is internationalizing its products or services but does not require any international HRM activity.

29. See Morris, Snell, & Wright (2006).

30. https://seeacareerwithus.com/about-us/our-values/

31. https://us.pg.com/brands/

32. Communities of practice (CoPs) are physical or virtual groups of HR practitioners from inside the firm that are brought together to develop and disseminate HRM policies and practices. (See also Chapter 5.)

33. Based on: Farndale, Paauwe, Morris, Stahl, Stiles, Trevor, & Wright (2010).

34. Taylor, Beechler, & Napier (1996).

35. This discussion draws heavily on Evans, Pucik, & Barsoux (2002).

36. Scullion & Starkey (2000).

37. Vidović & Farndale (2016).

38. Farndale, Paauwe, Morris, Stahl, Stiles, Trevor, & Wright (2010).

39. Farndale, Paauwe, Morris, Stahl, Stiles, Trevor, & Wright (2010).

40. Sparrow, Farndale, & Scullion (2013).

41. Björkman & Lu (2001); Mäkelä, Björkman, & Ehrnrooth (2010); Sumelius, Smale, & Björkman (2009).

42. Sumelius, Smale, & Björkman (2009).

43. Evans, Pucik, & Barsoux (2002).

44. Taylor, Beechler, & Napier (1996).

45. Edwards (2004).

46. Gooderham, Nordhaug, & Ringdal (1999).

47. Farndale, Paauwe, Morris, Stahl, Stiles, Trevor, & Wright (2010).

48. Pucik, Evans, Björkman, & Morris (2016).

49. Minbaeva, Pedersen, Björkman, Fey, & Park (2003).

50. Gooderham, Grøgaard, & Nordhaug (2013); see also Pucik, Evans, Björkman, & Morris (2016).

51. Tregaskis, Glover, & Ferner (2005).

52. Hadjimichael & Tsoukas (2019).

53. Gooderham, Grøgaard, & Nordhaug (2013).

54. Tregaskis, Glover, & Ferner (2005).

55. https://www.hrci.org/our-programs/our-certifications/gphr

56. https://www.hrci.org/docs/default-source/web-files/gphr-exam-content-outline.pdf?sfvrsn=4

57. Valk (2019).

6
Transfer of HRM practices across national boundaries

CHAPTER LEARNING OBJECTIVES

After reading this chapter you should be able to:

1. Explain why MNEs might want to transfer HRM practices globally.
2. Identify the key factors that account for the level and types of HRM practices transferred.
3. Describe the effect of the local cultural, institutional and subsidiary context on the transfer of HRM practices.
4. Discuss the probable causes of the various patterns of diffusion of HRM practices throughout MNEs.

Working for the Mouse[1]

As Jean François prepared to go "on stage" to his "role" (job) at the Euro-Disney Fantasyland shop where he had been a "cast member" (employee) for a week, he wondered how long he would stick it out. Almost all the staff at the shop in which he was working had left and he had heard that about 50% of the entire theme park had quit since it opened just two months ago. "That's almost as bad as the retention rate for students at the French medical school I attended," he thought. The hour-long commute from his flat in Paris to Marne-la-Vallée was bad enough, but when he got to work, he had to put up with all these cast member rules.

At first, he had felt lucky to be selected. The interview process had involved talking with other cast members and then a 45-minute ordeal with a Disney HR manager. And, at the weekend "brain washing" session as he now thought of it, he had been told that Disney cast members must follow the same rules at all the theme parks: Anaheim, Orlando, Paris, and Tokyo. It had sort of made sense at the time… "maintaining services standards" … "delivering a consistent experience" … "exceeding customers' expectations every day" … and so on. But the reality was that he couldn't dress the way he wanted, couldn't take his lunch at the normal time, had to bathe and shave every day, had to be constantly "on stage," and when he asked questions the answer more often than not was "that's not the way we do it at Disney." "Do Disney managers really think all Europeans are alike and that we all think the same way," he wondered.

Some days he just didn't feel like smiling all the time!

INTRODUCTION

A distinctive feature of global HRM is the involvement of operations across several different contexts. In the previous chapters, differences in the cultural, institutional, and organizational contexts affecting global HRM were discussed. In this chapter, we take a more in-depth look at the transfer of HRM practices across contexts. As Disney discovered upon opening its theme park near Paris, just because practices work well in one context is no guarantee that they will transfer effectively to a new one. However, the ability to develop expertise in one country and then implement it in another is one of the key advantages of MNEs.[2] Since, as discussed in previous chapters, the contexts across which global organizations must operate differ significantly, the transfer of practices[3] involves more than the simplistic "think global, act local" mantra that dominates much of the thinking in this regard. Like many processes in MNEs, transfer of practices is subject to the opposing forces of local responsiveness and global integration (see Chapter 4).

WHY FIRMS TRANSFER PRACTICES

The wide variety of contexts across which MNEs must operate along with the inherent pressure for adapting to local conditions, raises the question of why firms would want to engage in the transfer of practices at all. Three basic motives for the transfer of practices have been identified. These are *market, cultural* and *political* motives.[4]

Market motives reflect the view that the transfer of practices can enhance the efficiency of the organization by sharing what are believed to be *best practices* throughout the organization. This is based on the idea that organizations need to develop an integrated network of subunits that share expertise and knowledge with each other in order to survive in an internationally competitive environment.[5] HRM practices are central to developing and sharing the organizational competencies required to enhance the organizations' relative competitive position. For example, a Japanese firm's Singapore subsidiary may develop efficient HRM selection policies to cope with high turnover in the labor market. If the MNE can successfully transfer these policies to other environments that also experience high labor mobility, this can increase the efficiency of the overall organization.[6]

Cultural motives involve the influence that national culture has on the MNE by encouraging it to take aspects of its national culture with it as it expands internationally. The premise is that the organizational culture (discussed in Chapter 4) is influenced by the national culture of the country-of-origin and that this explains the desire to implement home country practices in terms of organizational replication. The transfer of Japanese employment practices to Europe and the United States during the 1980s and 1990s is an often-cited example in which Japanese firms attempted, as they expanded abroad, to employ those practices that had been so successful for them at home.[7]

Political motives refer to organizational actors who, in order to advance their own interest or to gain legitimacy, may initiate – or sabotage – the transfer of practices. Managers throughout the organization may wish to engage in sharing practices to enhance their legitimacy as good corporate citizens and/or as key players in the organizational network.[8] Headquarters personnel, for example, may wish to portray themselves as key agents in controlling the transfer of practices in order to advance their status. And, as shown in Box 6.1, political motives may even obscure the source of an innovative practice.

BOX 6.1   WHOSE IDEA?

Borislav Draganov, HR Manager of the Bulgarian subsidiary of an Austrian industrial goods company, was proud of the practice for socializing new employees he had implemented in the Bulgarian subsidiary. When the regional headquarters HR manager Rudolf (Rudy) Spreckels had visited a few months earlier, he had been skeptical and discouraged Boris from using the practice. Boris, however, had not been discouraged and had decided to present his idea to the Vice President of HR at the company's Vienna headquarters. Imagine his surprise when at the completion of his presentation the VP of HR said, "That's a great idea Boris, but Herr Spreckels is already implementing it here."[9]

While these three broad factors may represent the primary motivation for the transfer of HRM practices, they do not explain the nature and form of this transfer. The specific approach an MNE choose depends on the intersection of a variety of influences as discussed ahead.

FACTORS INFLUENCING TRANSFER OF HRM PRACTICES

The ability of organizations to transfer HRM practices successfully involves both characteristics of the MNE and of the environments in which it is operating. Employment practices are particularly susceptible to the influence of context because these practices are deeply embedded in societal culture and institutions. Factors affecting their successful transfer across contexts include country-of-origin effect, host country effect, characteristics of the MNE and specific subsidiaries, dominance effect, and the type of practice transferred.

Country-of-origin effect

Even the largest MNEs seem to be influenced by the way business is done in the country in which the organization originates. However, this truism applies to MNEs from some countries more than to those from other countries.[10] A key reason for this is that the institutional regime in the MNE's country of origin may allow MNEs a fair amount of strategic freedom. That is, they may operate in very flexible domestic labor markets where they face few legal or institutional constraints with regard to HRM practices. When these MNEs open subsidiaries abroad, they want to hold on to that strategic freedom. They expect to be able to set up the same HRM practices as in their countries of origin and thus tend to resist granting a lot of autonomy to their foreign subsidiaries when it comes to the subsidiaries' HRM practices.[11]

Liberal market economies (see Chapter 3) are an example of one such institutional regime, in which US MNEs are often cited as the prime example of organizations that "hold on" to their home country practices. Research has shown that the subsidiaries of US MNEs have HRM practices that are more similar to US practices, compared to subsidiaries of European MNEs where the practices are less likely to resemble practices in the parent country.[12] Also, US MNEs are often not as *multi*-national as their name implies. General Electric, the second largest multinational in terms of assets, has a ratio of foreign assets to total assets that is only about 40% and Walmart, one of the world's largest employers, has a ratio of only about 32%.[13] What this means is that these large multinational organizations are still dominated by operations and practices that are typical in their country of origin – in this case, the United States. In contrast, large MNEs headquartered in locations with small domestic markets, such as Swiss-based ABB with almost 95% of its assets outside Switzerland,[14] are less likely to have a tradition of replicating home country practices in foreign locations.

Another factor that contributes to the country-of-origin effect is that in organizations in which there is a concentration of activities in the country of origin, home-country nationals tend to dominate senior management positions. Their views on what practices work are, of course, shaped by their home country culture and national business systems. For example, in the 1980s and 1990s, Japanese expatriate managers made attempts to transfer practices associated with lean production, team-work, and functional flexibility, while American managers transferred performance related pay and direct forms of communication to their subsidiaries.[15] Another factor is that the CEOs of the vast majority of MNEs are citizens of the respective country of origin of the MNE and home-country nationals are disproportion- ately represented on management boards.[16] Country-of-origin effects continue to be a factor throughout the life of the firm. However, as might be expected, this effect tends to diminish as firms internationalize.

Consistent with historical patterns of international expansion, most research to-date has focused on MNEs that originate in developed, predominantly Western countries. As FDI from emerging economies has increased, recent research has begun examining the approaches of emerging market MNEs, many of which are rapidly internationalizing and creating new patterns of practice transfer.[17] Compared to Western MNEs, emerging market MNEs are less likely to attempt to transfer their own indigenous practices to their subsidiaries, opting instead to adopt "global practices" or "best practices" that originate in Western counties[18] (see *dominance effect* ahead). The reasons for this may be the relatively modest expertise in HRM of firms from emerging economies, as well as their unique country-of-origin practices, which are not typically associated with generating competitive advantages.

Emerging market MNEs' tendency not to transfer indigenous practices to subsidiaries should not be equated with granting subsidiaries freedom to decide their own HRM practices. A case study of a Brazilian MNE expanding into North America and Europe provides a good example. The MNE imposed a new pay and performance management system on its foreign subsidiaries. The system was not designed at headquarters but rather was heavily influenced by global HRM practices. However, what troubled the Western subsidiaries was the way in which it was introduced: top-down, with no consultation with local constituents, and with no regard for local preferences. The MNE actions were thought to be related to its country of origin, namely the "coercive hierarchal style of management [which is] deeply rooted in Brazilian culture."[19]

Whereas emerging market MNEs tend to adopt best practices in subsidiaries from developed countries, there are occasions when they may want to use country-of-origin practices, namely, in countries with similar institutional conditions or in weaker institutional environments that pose fewer restrictions on them.[20] For example, this is the case with Chinese MNEs in Africa, where countries may have a heavy dependence on Chinese investment and aid, there may be weaker worker protection, and traditional Confucian values such as collectivism and paternalism fit well with dominant values in the host country. There is evidence that in such environments, Chinese MNEs allow implementation of typical Chinese practices such as three-shift production, dormitory labor system, flexible employment and austere work conditions.[21] This example highlights that the transfer of practices within MNEs depends not only on where MNEs come from, but also where they are going – their host country.[22]

Host country effect

As noted in the preceding chapters, the HRM practices used in a country are influenced by the institutional and cultural factors in the local context. An MNE may want to transfer a practice from the headquarters to a subsidiary, but its ability to do so may be constrained by several elements in the subsidiary's national business system (such as legislation or collective bargaining agreements). Research has found that MNEs are more likely to transfer practices to subsidiaries located in *liberal market economies* which tend to have fewer employment regulations than in *coordinated market economies* and *socialist market economies* where labor markets are more tightly regulated[23] (see Chapter 3). MNEs generally have little choice but to abide by the employment laws in a particular country and practices that contravene such legislation are unlikely to be transferred. For example, China restricts what MNEs can do in such core HRM activities such as recruitment, selection, and dismissal.[24] More generally, many aspects related to compensation may be determined at the national (or supra-national) level, for example, minimum wage, overtime, vacation days, and so on, and all companies operating in a particular country must consider all applicable regulations as they design their local compensation programs.

In addition to institutions, host country cultural values exert their influence on practice transfer through differences in individuals' perceptions about whether or not a particular policy or practice is important and/or beneficial. Take, for example, a performance appraisal system that involves subordinate feedback. Commonly used in many low power distance cultures (see Chapter 2), this practice may face resistance in cultures in which it is considered disrespectful to provide feedback on a more senior colleague (see also Chapter 10). Furthermore, practices that are viewed as inconsistent with good management by local managers are unlikely to be implemented. For example, the transfer of high involvement Japanese management practices was resisted by British managers who were not comfortable with giving responsibility of operating decisions to shop floor workers.[25] What is considered good management can be influenced not only by the broad socio-cultural norms but also by local professional norms.[26] The host country context does not necessarily block the transfer of practices, but can alter both the scope of the transfer and the character of the practice being transferred. Some examples of this effect are discussed ahead.

Overall, the extent of transfer of HRM practices from the parent is likely to be negatively associated with institutional distance – how different *overall* the institutional context of the subsidiary is from that of the parent.[27] In terms of cultural differences, research has shown the opposite trend – the larger the cultural distance, the more MNEs tend to transfer home country practices, presumably in an attempt to bring the parent company and the subsidiary closer together. A review of research published on this topic found evidence that, predictably, cultural distance makes the transfer of practices more challenging. In contrast, however, companies that transferred practices in the face of cultural distance benefited from it greatly.[28]

Dominance effect

As suggested, MNEs are not limited to either exporting their own HRM practices or adopting local HRM practices. They may instead choose to adopt what are commonly perceived to be *best practices*, that is, practices believed to work more or less across contexts and credited with increasing organizational competitiveness. Research has suggested that many MNEs, regardless of their countries of origin, are likely to adopt standardized performance appraisal tools and processes.[29] Originating in the United States and more common in liberal market economies, the use of formal performance appraisals is increasingly considered to be best practice critical to leveraging human capital to achieve high organizational performance.[30] The global acceptance of the practice is also legitimized through (global) professional consulting firms leading to its status as standard professional practice and something that is expected of a successful MNE.[31]

More generally, examinations of the HRM practices of MNE subsidiaries across countries have found that there is a high degree of convergence toward best practices.[32] An explanation for this can be found in the concept of *social dominance*.[33] Social dominance is the idea that within every complex society certain groups are dominant over others and thus enjoy a greater amount of privilege. At the global level, there may be a generally accepted hierarchy of nations based on status (for example, status derived from a high level of economic development).[34] The logic is that because a country has a high level of economic development it is assumed that this results from good management practices. Therefore, these practices are more likely to be copied than practices from those countries lower on the economic hierarchy. This would explain the strong influence of US-based practices following World War II in which the United States was the world's dominant economy, and also the high interest in Japanese management practice during the late 1970s and 1980s when Japan was a world leader.[35]

Both the country-of-origin effect and the dominance effect result in the standardization of HRM practices in the MNE, whereas the host country effect results in localization of HRM practices. These ideas are shown graphically in Figure 6.1.

Some research indicates that of the three effects (dominance, country-of-origin, host country), the dominance effect is most important in determining local subsidiary HRM practices. That is, despite HRM often being considered to be the most localized of organizational functions, there is evidence of convergence toward a worldwide best practices model. It may

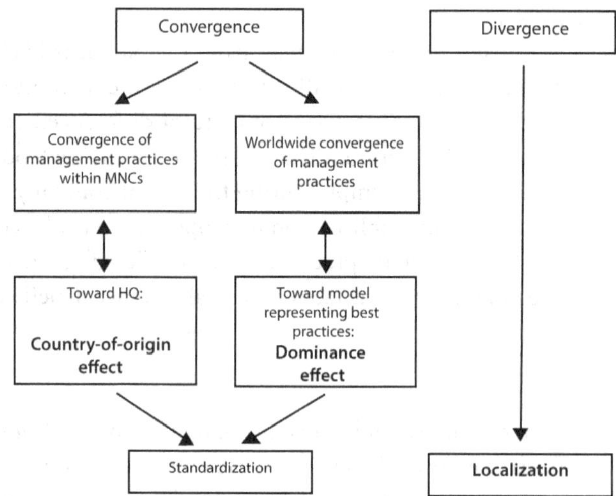

Source: Pudelko & Harzing (2007).

Figure 6.1   Country-of-origin, dominance and host country effects on HRM practices in MNE subsidiaries

be that MNEs limit the export of practices to their core competencies and converge to best practices in other areas.[36] Research has also suggested that many MNEs are powerful actors in any national setting and, aside from ensuring compliance with national legislation, they have substantial leverage when implementing management practices in subsidiaries[37] and may be able to override at least some national institutions.[38]

MNE and subsidiary characteristics

Another important set of determinants of HRM practice transfer stems from the characteristics of the MNE itself and its subsidiaries, including their structure, culture, and mode of entry. As discussed in Chapter 5, the extent to which the structure of the organization is globally integrated affects the organization of the HR department in subsidiaries. Global integration (internal consistency) encourages the tendency of organizations to duplicate practices across new contexts. It also leads to standardization of practices to try to reduce the complexity and uncertainty of operating in multiple environments. Thus, transfer of practices is more likely in MNEs with global and transnational strategies compared to those who pursue multidomestic strategies. Similarly, attempts to transfer practices are most likely in MNEs with an exportive SIHRM orientation, and least likely in MNEs with an adaptive SIHRM orientation, while convergence to "best practices" is likely in MNEs with integrative SIHRM orientation.

Another critical component of global integration is the informal organization, or organizational culture (see Chapter 4). For example, transfer is facilitated if the culture of the receiving unit supports learning, change and innovation.[39] Also relevant here is the extent to which communication flows are largely from the parent to the subsidiary through the use of expatriates and/or frequent communication with the parent, all of which has a negative influence on the degree to which the HRM policies and practices resemble local competitors.[40] Expatriate managers are socialized to have similar ideas about what practices are most effective, and are likely to try to introduce these practices abroad.

Finally, an MNE can take a different approach to HRM practices transfer on a subsidiary-by-subsidiary basis, influenced by factors such as the subsidiaries' mode of entry, local dependence, and subsidiary performance. For example, resistance to transfer is greater for subsidiaries that are embedded in the local environment, such as acquired organizations (which presumably have local practices in place). In contrast, the transfer of standard practices is more likely in subsidiaries that are *greenfield* investments, which are less embedded in the local context,[41] as illustrated in the example in Box 6.2.

BOX 6.2 MORNING CALISTHENICS AT FUJI PHOTO FILM CORPORATION

Fuji Film's operation in Greenwood, South Carolina was a *greenfield* plant built to produce photographic plates for the printing industry. Professor Clarence Ritchie from the University of South Carolina had arranged a visit for his class to see one of the best examples of a continuous process machine that started off with a huge role of aluminum on one end and ended up as plates with many layers of photosensitive emulsion on the other. The class arrived very early before the first shift had started. The receptionist ushered them past the stunning Japanese garden off the reception area into a large conference room saying, "Mr Tokuzawa will be with you shortly."

"Well, this place is certainly different from our previous Japanese plant tour at Showa Denko Carbon," said one of the students. "Yes," replied Clarence, "that company was acquired by the Japanese firm from its British parent." Just then, he thought he heard singing from the door that led from the conference room to the factory floor. By pushing the door open a crack Clarence was presented with a view of the entire local workforce clad in identical company uniforms being led in calisthenics and the company song by the Japanese plant manager. "I wonder how he convinced those rural South Carolinians to do that," thought Clarence.[42]

Types of practices transferred

Not all policies and practices are equally transferable across organizational types and institutional and cultural contexts.[43] Thus, HRM practices that are more institutionally constrained, that is, practices for which there are well-defined local norms or legal mandates (such as compensation and benefits, wage bargaining, time off, etc.), are most likely to reflect the local context, whereas practices that are not legislated, those for which there are ill-defined local norms (e.g., training) or which are central to internal consistency in the MNE are more likely to be transferred. Research has also documented that HRM practices pertaining to rank-and-file employees are more likely to be localized but those that have to do with subsidiary executives (e.g., executive bonuses, expatriate performance appraisal) are likely to be internally consistent throughout the organization.[44]

LOCAL SUBSIDIARY RESPONSE TO TRANSFER

Local subsidiaries do not respond uniformly to the mandate of adopting parent company practices and variation in the level of adoption can occur even on practices that are objectively superior or more efficient. Adoption of a particular practice or process involves not only *implementation* (exhibiting the behaviors required by the practice) but also *internalization* (viewing a practice as valuable for the unit and becoming committed to it).[45] The extent to which practices are adopted (implemented *and* internalized) depends both on institutional/ cultural factors and the relationship of the subsidiary to the parent. The relationship of headquarters to the subsidiary can vary according to the extent to which the subsidiary is dependent on the parent, the extent to which there is trust between these entities and the extent to which the foreign subsidiary identifies with (feels they are a part of) the parent organization.

It is important to point out that implementation does not automatically result in internalization. Rather, four patterns of adoption are possible,[46] as presented in Table 6.1.

Table 6.1   Patterns of practice adoption

	Low Internalization	High Internalization
High Implementation	Ceremonial Adoption	Active Adoption
Low Implementation	Minimal Adoption	Assent Adoption

Source: Based on Kostova & Roth (2002).

In *minimal adoption*, the subsidiary has low levels of implementation and internalization, essentially disavowing the practice. In this case the institutional environment is unfavorable and the relationship with the parent is characterized by low levels of trust and identity, very low dependence. In *assent adoption* there is a perceived value in the practice but there is a low level of implementation of the behaviors indicated by the practice. As in the case of minimal adoption, the institutional context is unfavorable but the level of dependence is high. Given that the value of the practice is recognized, the lack of implementation may reflect insufficient capability in the subsidiary to implement the practice. In *ceremonial adoption*, there is a high level of implementation but a low level of internalization. The subsidiary may formally adopt the practice for legitimacy reasons but not really diffuse it with meaning and may not be truly committed to its implementation in practice. Finally, in *active adoption*, subsidiaries are high on both implementing the practice and on believing in and recognizing the value of the practice. This represents the ideal level of adoption but requires a favorable institutional context as well as high levels of identification with and trust in the parent. Thus, regardless of the effectiveness of a practice, its adoption by a foreign subsidiary depends a great deal on the perceptions of the practice by the subsidiary. Research has also documented that acceptance of a practice may take time, with the subsidiaries rejecting a practice initially but growing used to it as time goes by.[47]

Studies of transfer of practices have also pointed out that the process of transfer can be political (and sometimes contentious). There may be agents in the headquarters or the subsidiaries that can be motivated to either facilitate or sabotage the successful transfer of practices.[48] For example, employees at headquarters may not want to engage in transfer if they believe that doing so will cause them to lose an internal competitive advantage (i.e., they did something special that is now being adopted throughout the organization and will thus no longer be unique). On the other hand, they can also be motivated to advocate strongly for transferring a practice as it may raise their status as key agents in the organization. Further, actors in subsidiaries may refuse to engage in the transfer of a practice if they do not believe the practice is necessary, fitting, or valuable for the local context. Alternatively, they may go along with practice transfer only because doing so will allow them to receive benefits from headquarters which they otherwise might not receive in the absence of cooperation. Studies have also suggested that the success of transfer is dependent on the relationship between employees at the headquarters and in the subsidiaries to which the practice is being transferred (for example, the extent to which there is regular and meaningful interaction between the units or the level of mutual trust that exists between the units) and the extent to which employees at the headquarters are committed to, identify with and trust the parent company.[49]

RECONTEXTUALIZATION

Another perspective on the transfer of HRM practices across the global organization highlights that transfer does not always result in a practice being rejected or accepted "as is." Instead, practices are often modified in some way or given different meaning as they are transferred to a new institutional and cultural context. In some cases, this modification or *hybridization* of the practice is planned and anticipated.[50] For example, Japanese MNEs reduced the requirements for Brazilian workers to rotate across a range of tasks when implementing lean production techniques in Brazil. This was in recognition of the fact that Brazilian workers lacked the breadth of skills required for this rotation among tasks.[51] However, in other cases the policy or practice is reinterpreted in unpredictable ways. In these cases, the policy or practice can be said to be *recontextualized*.

Recontexualization is the idea that when procedures and processes are transferred from one country to another, they take on new meanings in the new socio-cultural context.[52] The concept of recontextualization allows the tracking of meanings attached to procedures

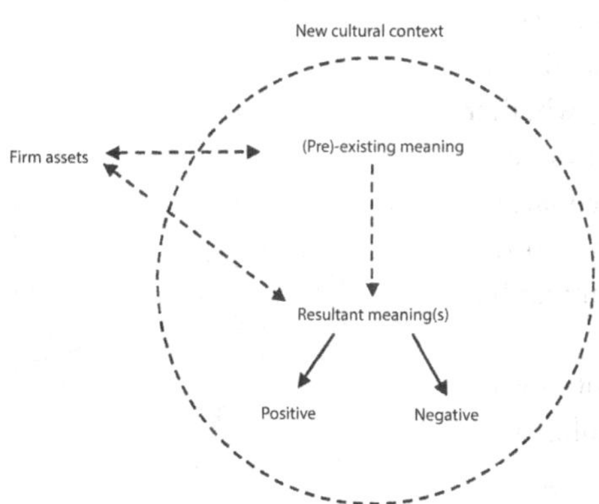

Source: Adapted from Brannen (2004).

Figure 6.2   Process of recontextualization

and processes as they move from one socio-cultural context to another. Figure 6.2 is a graphic representation of the key elements of transnational transfer.

In the first instance, when procedures or policies are transferred across a socio-cultural boundary, new meanings are attached as people make sense of them using their pre-existing frame of reference. An example is the American understanding of sushi as raw fish. In Japan, sushi refers to the pickling agents used in the rice as opposed to the topping.[53] However, in the United States, the strangeness of eating the raw fish that is commonly used as a topping was what received attention. Therefore, sushi was recontextualized as raw fish. A second type of meaning transformation occurs as policies and procedures evolve in the new environment. Continuing with the sushi example, the *California roll* is sushi made with cooked crab and avocado is a further recontextualization that is more palatable for Americans. Finally, a third kind of recontextualization or diffusion can occur if the policy of procedure is repatriated to its country of origin. The example would be finding the California roll offered in sushi bars in Japan.

It is important to note that recontextualization can be either positive or negative (as shown in Figure 6.2). In the vignette that opened this chapter, the attempted transfer of Disney HRM practices that were seen as part of their distinctive competitive advantage had very negative results in France, ultimately resulting in Disney being charged with violating French employment laws.[54] Disney's strategy depends on creating the "Happiest Place on Earth" through well-developed HRM practices that create a clean, safe and friendly environment.[55] For example, in order to achieve what Disney calls *a wholesome American look* it has strict grooming and dress requirements for its employees (cast members) who must deliver "service with a smile." For women this includes the wearing of appropriate undergarments, specifically transparent as opposed to colored or designed pantyhose, skirts no shorter than four centimeters above the knee, fingernails no longer than the fingertips, and naturally colored hair. Men must be clean shaven, with short haircuts, and are not allowed to wear earrings. In France, where freedom of personal expression and dress are highly valued, these *foreign* practices were seen as invasive. No such problems were encountered with the same practices in Tokyo Disney however, where these same HRM practices fit very well with the existing societal context. Thus, whether the foreignness of a practice is seen as a liability or an asset depends on the extent to which it is legitimate or marginalized in the new context. Figure 6.3 provides a humorous look at a practice that worked really well in one context but was ineffective in a different context.

The lesson is that recontextualization does not always conform to strategic intent. Positive recontextualizations may be a source of sustainable competitive advantage, but negative ones can come as an unwelcome shock.[56]

Source: Piraro (2008).

Figure 6.3   HRM practices in a new context

DIFFUSION OF PRACTICES

Thus far in this chapter, the discussion of the transfer of practices has, for the most part, assumed that the transfer was from the parent to the subsidiary. However, the transfer of practices need not originate with the parent and can also involve transfer back to the parent (reverse transfer) or diffusion among foreign operations (i.e., from subsidiary to subsidiary).[57] This process of diffusion can be limited to the flow of practices from a single subsidiary to the MNE home country operations and/or other foreign subsidiaries, or between a group of subsidiaries (for example, within a specific geographic region or industry sector), or any combination thereof. The transfer could be on a voluntary basis, that is, different operations being made aware of the existence of an effective practice that they can request to use, or adoption can be mandated by headquarters. As practices are diffused across the organization, improvements may be made and the "new improved" version of the practice is the one that is consequently shared further, potentially going back to where it was originally conceived. In other words, practice innovations can progress through multiple repeated attempts, in which a practice might be reintroduced after modification to address initial transfer difficulties.[58]

Similar to the case of the transfer of practices from headquarters to subsidiaries, the particular pattern for *diffusion* of HRM practices is dependent on four main factors: the country of origin of the parent firm, the organizational characteristics of the MNE, the organizational conduits through which the practices may be diffused, and the relative influence of each of the national operations.[59] The effect of the *country of origin of the parent firm* on diffusion is consistent with the country of origin and dominance effects discussed previously. For example, some German MNEs have accorded *vanguard* status to their operations in certain foreign countries, enabling them to lead initiatives on which global HRM policies are based.[60] In contrast, evidence suggest that US and French MNEs tend to be more resistant to reverse diffusion.[61]

The second set of factors influencing the pattern of diffusion consists of *the organizational characteristics* of the MNE, including factors like the organizational structure, the similarities among subsidiaries and degree of integration, and how the firm has grown. The network form of organization, with its flexible links among organizational units, is obviously the one in which the subsidiaries have the greatest opportunity to exert influence on the larger organization.[62] The more similar the organization units are to each other and/or the more integrated they are with each other, the more scope there is for them to share practices. Finally, consistent with the transfer of practices, a greenfield start-up or acquisition could influence reverse transfer. Growth though greenfield investment tends to rely on practices that exist in the parent, while in acquisitions there may be more potential for the acquired subsidiary to influence the parent with its pre-existing policies and practices. As discussed ahead in Chapter 7, the distinctive practices of the subsidiary are sometimes part of the motivation for acquisition.[63] That is, firms may see the opportunity to access, absorb, and transfer HRM practices as an attractive aspect of an acquisition.

The third factor affecting diffusion is the *richness of the transmission channels* available among subsidiaries to support diffusion. Explicit, easily codified knowledge concerning HRM practices (see Chapter 5) can be transferred effectively through such mechanisms as international committees, information systems, databases, and management audits. However, these procedural channels are less likely to be effective for tacit knowledge (knowledge that cannot be codified, sometimes called *"in the bones"* expertise) which requires people-based channels, such as cross-national workgroups and international assignments for diffusion.[64] For example, practices in the area of pay and performance management tend to be transferred through procedural channels, while training practices are more likely to be diffused through people-based mechanisms.[65]

A final factor affecting the diffusion of practices is the *relative influence* that a subsidiary has in the MNE. At the outset of this chapter, we noted the importance of the political aspect of the transfer of practices. We should not assume, therefore, that HR managers in foreign operating units will always be willing to share practices that they have developed. However, the more resources and greater the influence of the subsidiary, the more likely it will be a net supplier of practices to the rest of the organization.[66]

The preceding discussion highlights that standardization or the export of practices from the parent to the subsidiaries is not the only way to achieve competitive advantage through integrating best HRM practices throughout the organization. Increasingly, MNEs are recognizing that good practices can originate in foreign subsidiaries. Furthermore, these practices can permeate the organization through a variety of diffusion patterns.

CHAPTER SUMMARY

In this chapter, we have focused on a distinctive aspect of global HRM: the ability of the MNE to develop expertise in HRM in one context and then transfer it to other units or diffuse it throughout the organization. The motives for the transfer of practices may be cultural, political or market driven. There are numerous factors that influence the nature and form of this transfer, which include country-of-origin effects, host country effects, dominance effects, MNE and subsidiary characteristics, and the type of practice that is being transferred. Key factors in the transfer of practices are the extent to which the organization sees HRM practices as a source of competitive advantage, coupled with the extent to which a practice can be used outside of the context in which it was developed.

However, local subsidiaries of an MNE do not respond uniformly to the mandate that parent company practices should be adopted. Adoption of a practice involves both implementation and internalization and is influenced by both the institutional/cultural context of the subsidiary and the relationship that the subsidiary has with the parent. HRM practices do not always transfer across socio-cultural divides in a way that achieves their original strategic intent. Sometimes the practice is given a new meaning through the process of recontextualization, which can have either positive or negative results for the organization.

The transfer of HRM practices occurs not only from the parent to local subsidiaries but practices can be diffused throughout the organization though a variety of different patterns based on the order, direction of transfer, and the number of adopters. The pattern of diffusion is dependent on the country-of-origin of the parent, the configuration of the MNE, the channels available to transfer the practice, and the relative influence of the various national operations. In the following chapter, we move beyond the transfer and diffusion of practices to considering what happens in HRM when whole organizations transfer or merge their operations.

QUESTIONS FOR DISCUSSION

1. Describe how an HRM practice can be a source of competitive advantage in a specific context. Does this mean the practice will be a source of competitive advantage in any organizational setting?
2. Discuss the difference between implementation and internalization of an HRM practice.
3. Explain how the process of recontextualization changes the meaning associated with an HRM practice.
4. Outline the possible patterns of diffusion of an HRM practice. What factors would be likely to generate each pattern?

NOTES

1. This vignette is based on various accounts of the Disneyland Paris case.
2. Bartlett & Ghoshal (1998).
3. In addition to "transfer of practices" research also refers to terms with similar meaning such as "diffusion of practices" or "export of practices." For the sake of simplicity, we use to transfer consistently throughout the chapter, with the exception of the case of reverse practice transfer – to which we refer to as diffusion, consistent with other texts.
4. See Edwards (2011).
5. Bartlett & Ghoshal (1998).
6. Taylor, Beechler, & Napier (1996).
7. Abo (1994).
8. Edwards (2011).
9. Adapted from a case in Lemanski, Björkman, & Stahl (2011).
10. Edwards, Sánchez-Mangas, Jalette, Lavelle, & Minbaeva (2016).
11. Belizon, Gunnigle, & Morley (2013).
12. Gunnigle, Murphy, Cleveland, Heraty, & Morley (2002).
13. http://www.unctad.org/en/docs/gdscsir20041c3_en.pdf
14. http://www.unctad.org/en/docs/gdscsir20041c3_en.pdf
15. See Muller (1998); Oliver & Wilkinson (1992).
16. Edwards (2011).
17. Contrast here findings on Brazilian MNEs: Geary & Aguzzoli (2016); Geary, Aguzzoli, & Lengler (2017); Mellahi, Frynas, & Collings (2016); Chinese MNEs: Cooke (2014); Khan, Wood, Tarba, Rao-Nicholson, & He (2019); Ouyang, Liu, Chen, Li, & Qin (2019); and Indian MNEs: Patel, Sinha, Bhanugopan, Boyle, & Bray (2018).

18. Khan, Wood, Tarba, Rao-Nicholson, & He (2019); Ouyang, Liu, Chen, Li, & Qin (2019); Mellahi, Frynas, & Collings (2016); Patel, Sinha, Bhanugopan, Boyle, & Bray (2018).

19. Geary, Aguzzoli, & Lengler (2017, p. 204); see also Mellahi, Frynas, & Collings (2016).

20. Ouyang, Liu, Chen, Li, & Qin (2019).

21. Cooke (2014); see also Ouyang, Liu, Chen, Li, & Qin (2019).

22. Kostova and Roth (2002).

23. Farndale, Brewster, & Poutsma (2008); Parry, Dickmann, & Morley (2008).

24. Von Glinow & Teagarden (1988).

25. Broad (1994).

26. Björkman (2006).

27. Kostova (1999).

28. Beugelsdijk, Kostova, Kunst, Spadafora, & van Essen (2018); see also Gerhart & Fang (2005).

29. Stahl, Björkman, Farndale, Morris, Paauwe, Stiles, … & Wright (2012); see also Edwards, Sánchez-Mangas, Jalette, Lavelle, & Minbaeva (2016).

30. Boxall & Purcell (2003); Combs, Liu, Hall, & Ketchen (2006); Takeuchi, Lepak, Wang, & Takeuchi (2007).

31. Mellahi, Frynas, & Collings (2016).

32. Pudelko & Harzing (2007).

33. Sidanius (1993).

34. Smith & Meiskins (1995).

35. See Ouchi (1981).

36. Pudelko & Harzing (2007).

37. Kostova, Roth, & Dacin (2008).

38. Edwards & Rees (2006); Edwards, Sánchez-Mangas, Jalette, Lavelle, & Minbaeva (2016).

39. Kostova (1999).

40. Rosenzweig & Nohria (1994).

41. Rosenzweig & Nohria (1994).

42. This case is fictional but based on the experience of the first author.

43. Belizon, Gunnigle, & Morley (2013); Farndale, Brewster, Ligthart, & Poutsma (2017); Jiang (2014); Mellahi, Demirbag, Collings, Tatoglu, & Hughes (2013).

44. Rosenzweig & Nohria (1994); see also Kang & Shen (2016).

45. This section is based on Kostova (1999) and Kostova & Roth (2002).

46. Kostova & Roth (2002).

47. Jiang (2014).

48. Edwards (2011).

49. Björkman & Lervik (2007); Kostova (1999); Kostova & Roth (2002).

50. Zhu & Dowling (2002).

51. Humphrey (1995).

52. See Brannen (2004) for a detailed discussion of this process.

53. What all sushi has in common is *shari* (cooked vinegared rice) which can be combined with a variety of other ingredients.

54. Brannen (2004).

55. See Peters & Waterman, 1982

56. Brannen (2004).

57. Edwards (1998); Edwards, Edwards, Ferner, Marginson, & Tregaskis (2010); Edwards & Tempel (2010).
58. Thory (2008).
59. Edwards, Edwards, Ferner, Marginson, & Tregaskis (2010).
60. Ferner & Varul (2000).
61. Edwards, Almond, Clark, Colling, & Ferner (2005); Thory (2008).
62. Harzing & Nooderhaven (2006).
63. See Schuler, Jackson & Luo (2004).
64. See Tregakis (2003).
65. Edwards, Edwards, Ferner, Marginson, & Tregaskis (2010).
66. See Kristensen & Zeitlin (2005); Minbaeva (2007).

7

HRM in international joint ventures, mergers and acquisitions, and collaborative alliances

CHAPTER LEARNING OBJECTIVES

After reading this chapter you should be able to:

1. Describe the influence of HR at the various stages of the M&A process.
2. Discuss the people and cultural factors important to the success of international M&As.
3. Describe the HR aspects of the "due diligence" process.
4. Outline the HR issues associated with the various stages of IJV formation.
5. Describe and discuss the importance of strategic alliance learning.

Flight UA 7632

Charles W. "Chuck" Wilson accepted the complimentary glass of champagne offered to him as he adjusted his fully reclining business class seat on United Airlines flight 7632. At least I can get some sleep on the overnight flight to Dublin, he thought. It was going to be a stressful day tomorrow!

Chuck was Executive Vice President and Director of Human Resources for US-based New Dominion Bank and he knew what he had to do. The bank could not afford the kind of wholesale departure of personnel that had occurred during its last merger. The takeover of Bancoverde had been a disaster. Called a "merger of equals" by the CEOs of both organizations, Chuck knew at the outset it was going to be anything but. New Dominion, originally headquartered in Charlotte, North Carolina but now based in New York had grown rapidly by acquiring smaller banks in attractive markets. This expansion had now taken it international and the target organizations were much larger. Still, its success depended on introducing competitive lending practices and extremely efficient back room operations. This inevitably meant headcount reductions and staff relocations; and it would be New Dominion policies, procedures and personnel that would prevail.

Bancoverde's international lending division had been headquartered in Miami to take advantage of strong ties to its Latin American base. However, it had always been assumed at New Dominion that this activity would be moved to New York post merger. Chuck remembered vividly that sinking feeling in the pit of his stomach when he had first walked into the Bancoverde International Division offices in Miami. The entire 23rd floor that had been occupied by more than 20 loan officers and their support staff was vacant. Unbelievably, they had left over the long holiday weekend, taking most of their customer base with them and were now working at a competitor institution almost across the street.

This time it had to be different. Tomorrow, when he met with the senior executives of Celtic Shield bank in Dublin, he would outline his plan to give all employees a very clear and realistic picture of what would happen to their job after the merger. He hoped they would agree to let him proceed.

Chuck settled back into his seat and turned on the aircraft entertainment system, hoping that there was at least one movie he hadn't seen.

INTRODUCTION

Mergers and acquisitions (M&As) have become an increasingly popular alternative to greenfield investment for achieving international diversification and growth. In the first half of 2019, cross-border M&As were valued at US$303 billion,[1] a slight drop from the first half of 2018, but still a huge number.[2] The driver of this activity is of course the reduction of boundaries resulting from globalization discussed in Chapter 1 coupled with an increase in global competition. In today's competitive environment, target firms can no longer be acquired and left as independent operations but must be integrated in order capture their added value. However, it is the inability to integrate effectively that is the major cause of the unspectacular performance of the majority of M&As.[3] The failure of M&As can often be attributed to problems of integrating the different cultures and workforces of the combined firms.[4] In this chapter we discuss the HRM challenges associated with international mergers and acquisitions and then go on to discuss the related issues in international joint ventures and other types of international collaborative alliances.

INTERNATIONAL MERGERS AND ACQUISITIONS

Reasons for M&As

From a legal perspective a *merger* occurs when two companies join together to create a new entity, while in an *acquisition* one company acquires sufficient shares to gain control of the other. These ventures may be structured one way or the other for accounting, tax, or public relations purposes. However, there are actually very few mergers among equals. As indicated in the case that opened this chapter, once the agreement is signed most mergers look very much like acquisitions with one organization the dominant partner.

BOX 7.1   M&A STRATEGIES

Market Dominance

Banks and insurance companies in Scandinavia merged across the region to create Nordic financial institutions such as Nordea and SEB in order to achieve economies of scale and control distribution channels.

Geographic Expansion

Brewing companies such as Kirin and Heineken have used acquisitions to extend their geographic reach and global market share.

Leveraging Competence

Foreign companies such as GE and Axa made large-scale acquisitions in the financial industry in Japan to leverage their competence in new product development, credit risk evaluation, and debt management.

Resource Acquisition

In the petroleum industry firms such as BP and Exxon have acquired existing companies with proven oil reserves as a more cost-effective way to grow than through oil exploration.

Capability Acquisition

As the market shifted from voice to data transmission, European wireless makers such as Nokia and Ericsson acquired small start-up companies with competence in emerging data communication technologies.

Adjusting to Competition

Companies are sometimes forced into acquisitions in order to counter the acquisitions strategies of their competitors. For example, in the early 1990s Matsushita (now known by one of its brand names – Panasonic) launched a series of ultimately disastrous acquisitions in Hollywood after Matsushita's competitor Sony acquired Columbia Pictures.

Executive Arrogance

While most companies launch acquisitions for sound strategic reasons there are also cases, regardless of what the press release says, that the logic of an M&A seems to make no sense beyond the CEO's desire to run a bigger company.

Source: Adapted from Evans, Pucik, & Barsoux (2002).

There are a number of reasons why firms engage in international M&As, including response to political or economic conditions, diversifying risk, vertical integration and reducing labor costs. Two of the main reasons for M&As are to achieve competitive size or to increase market share by adding brands or distribution channels.[5] While larger firms aim to gain market power by acquiring companies in areas where they are not represented (as in the case of Bancoverde), smaller firms may try to leverage their niche competencies through cross-border deals. In this way M&As allow a much more rapid response to the pressure of global competition than does a greenfield investment. In some industries, the key motive for an acquisition is access to talented people with the value of the deal calculated accordingly. For example, when the semi-conductor firm Broadcom bought chipmaker SiByte it was reported to have paid $18 million per engineer.[6] Alternatively, the key factor in many M&As is cost cutting and work-force reduction which may be as difficult in some countries as is retaining engineers in Silicon Valley.[7] International mergers and acquisitions occur for both strategic and tactical reasons, while some are the result of corporate egos. Box 7.1 provides some examples.

M&A success and failure

Some M&As are successful, some have little effect on the performance of the acquiring firm and some are spectacular failures such as the much publicized Daimler–Chrysler merger.[8] While estimates of M&A success vary, it has generally been the case that the majority of them do not create value for the acquiring firm, and a significant number actually reduce value.[9] A survey by KPMG found that 17% of deals had added value to the combined company, 30% produced no discernible difference, and 53% actually destroyed value.[10] More recent research has suggested more positive results indicating that companies may be getting better at M&A, but by all accounts failures continue to outnumber successes.[11]

There are many potential causes for the failure of the combined company to achieve its goals, but they fall into four categories. These are *lack of a shared vision, loss of key assets, high transition costs* and *lack of cultural fit*. First, an M&A can fail because there is a difference in the vision of what the two parties want to achieve in the combined firm. Sometimes, for the sake of making the deal, these differences are glossed over and only become a problem in the post-merger integration phase (discussed ahead).

Second, the M&A can fail because assets that were key to achieving the potential value of the combined firm are lost. These assets can be tangible as in the case of the international division employees who left Bancoverde, described in the vignette that opened this chapter. Or they can be intangible such as relationships with suppliers, government, or the local community if the new organization is perceived as insensitive to their concerns. These concerns can be even greater in cross-border M&As because of different legal and regulatory environments, accounting standards, and employment systems.[12]

International differences also contribute to the next general reason for M&A failure, high transition costs. Linking the new entities can be difficult across national contexts and can also incur higher coordination costs because of geographic distance. And, managers can be so consumed with overcoming these coordination problems that they are distracted from the original goals of the M&A.

Finally, the integration of organizational cultures, HRM systems, managerial views, and other aspects of organizational life can lead to severe organizational conflict.[13] The signifi-cant cultural mismatch between Daimler and Chrysler and the inattention to people-related dimensions is often cited as the key reason for the failure of that merger as shown in the news report presented in Box 7.2.

BOX 7.2   DAIMLERCHRYSLER MERGER FIASCO

It was supposed to be a perfect union of carmakers.

When the two companies merged in 1998, Daimler Chairman Juergen Schrempp promised a "merger of equals." But it wasn't long before Chrysler executives complained the bullheaded Germans wouldn't listen to the Americans.

"We don't demand things of people; we seek people's cooperation," says Gerald Meyers, former chairman of American Motors and now a professor at the University of Michigan business school. "These two cultures were therefore bound to collide."

And collide they did.

Americans Feel Deceived

From the beginning, the high command in Stuttgart issued orders to Detroit about everything from where the headquarters would be located (Germany) to what kind of business cards would be used.

The relationship began to fall apart quickly. Since the merger, the company has lost nearly half its value. Somebody had to go, and it was the Americans. Daimler eventually sent in a German management team.

Schrempp's promise of a "merger of equals" had been fiction, and he even admits as much. He told the *Financial Times* that if he had been honest with the Americans about German dominance before the merger, they never would have made a deal.

So what was the reaction at Chrysler?

"One of people who'd been deceived," says Meyers. "People who'd been hoodwinked. This wasn't just a small, a small decision. This was just plain dishonest."

The two cultures had never been compatible. Take the Daimler annual meeting, where stockholders are fed sausages and dumplings. In Germany, there's more attention paid to wining and dining the shareholders than to giving them precise information.

That's the reason Kirk Kerkorian, Chrysler's largest shareholder, sued Daimler for $9 billion, charging fraud. "Apparently in Germany, one can say pretty much whatever one wants to the shareholders of a company," says Terry Christensen, Kerkorian's lawyer. "Here in the United States, what you say to the shareholders has to be true."

Dejected Employees

All of this has demoralized Chrysler's workers. "Most of them are disgusted and frustrated because they seem like they have been shafted," says one.

The rank and file now expects big layoffs, and they worry the company will be sold. Schrempp insists that isn't true, but few of the Americans he has dealt with are willing to take him at his word a second time.

Source: By Bob Jamieson ABC News[14]

Whether or not international M&As are more or less successful than domestic M&As is an especially important question, given that M&A failure often stems from problems related to integrating cultures. The answer to the question is far from straightforward. Cross-border M&As demand a *double-layered acculturation*,[15] as organizations must align both organizational and national cultures, one may conclude that they will be significantly more challenging than domestic M&As. Differences in national culture (see Chapter 2) imply differences in commonly accepted norms, management styles, and prevalent practices, all of which can impede building a sense of shared identity or development of trust between the M&A partners.

While a number of studies provide some support for such negative impact of culture distance between parties in an M&A deal, there are also studies that reach an opposite conclusion and suggest that cultural distance is an asset rather than a liability. A key argument to support this line of reasoning is that in addition to being a potential source of conflict, cultural distance can also be a source of value creation as it provides access to potentially valuable capabilities, resources and learning opportunities. Further, cultural issues (at the level of the organization) are often ignored in domestic M&As and may remain under the radar for far too long. When involved in an international M&A, organizations have increased awareness of the importance of cultural issues for the integration process. They tend to pay much more attention to them and, subsequently, engage in culture integration more purposefully.

While we take note of all these possible ways in which culture can impact M&As, as of now there is no compelling evidence for a relationship (be it positive or negative) between cultural distance between M&A parties and post-M&A performance. Looking for such a direct relationship may be too simplistic. A balanced perspective suggests that the outcomes of cross-border M&A depend not on whether the cultures are different but on the nature and extent of culture differences and, more importantly, on strategic intent, integration approach, and specific interventions chosen to manage the integration of the two entities across borders.[16]

To that end, it seems clear that even in the most well thought out M&As, their ultimate success may depend on the ability to integrate across boundaries effectively.[17] However, what *integration* means may differ depending on the strategic intent underlying the M&A.

Types of M&A integration

One way to understand the implications of the process of combining two firms is to consider the strategic intent behind the acquisition. Most M&A transactions are one of two types, either *traditional* or *transformational*. Traditional M&As leverage existing capabilities through rationalization or transfer, while transformational M&As involve more complex exploration skills so as to create new capabilities or to do things differently.[18] The difference is important because it influences the focus of human resource issues and ultimately the kind of organization that will emerge from the deal.

A useful framework for predicting the character of the organization that results from an M&A is to examine the situation in terms of the amount of cultural change required in both the acquiring and acquired companies in order to achieve the desired goal.[19] Figure 7.1 shows how these factors result in five types of strategies for post-merger outcomes.

High	**ABSORPTION** Acquired Company Conforms to Acquirer – Cultural Assimilation		**TRANSFORMATION** Both Companies find New Ways of Operating – Cultural Transformation
Degree of Change in Aquired Company		**BEST OF BOTH** Additive from Both Sides – Cultural Integration	
Low	**PRESERVATION** Acquired Company Retains its Independence – Cultural Autonomy		**REVERSE MERGER** Unusual Case of Acquired Company Dictating Terms – Cultural Assimilation

Low   High
Degree of Change in Acquiring Company

Source: Mirvis & Marks (1994).

Figure 7.1   Strategies for post-merger outcomes

When no cultural change is required the resulting company is called a *preservation* acquisition, while when large of amounts of change are required in both the acquired and acquiring company the result is a *transformation*. When large change is required in the acquired company, but little change is expected in the acquirer, the result is *absorption*. The rare case of the opposite cultural change requirements, in which the acquiring company is blended into the acquired, is called a *reverse merger*. The case in which the best practices of both sides are integrated is labeled *best of both*. We describe these M&A strategy types in further detail here.

Preservation M&As

In this case, the end goal is that the acquired company will preserve its independence and cultural autonomy. This is often the case when the motive for the merger involves securing talent or other soft skills or when imposing the acquiring company's policies and procedures could harm the company's competitive advantage. However, this independence rarely survives because operational pressures often require some functions to be merged with the rest of the organization.[20]

Transformation M&As

In transformation M&As the goal is that the newly formed entity will break sharply with the past, to do things differently, in effect to reinvent the firm. This type of M&A is difficult to implement and requires a commitment to the vision for the new entity by both parties. An example is Lenovo's acquisition of IBM's PC business.[21]

Absorption M&As

Absorption M&As are common when there are differences in the size or sophistication of the two parties involved in the deal, when the acquired company is performing poorly or when market conditions force consolidation. Often, much of the benefit is derived from cost-cutting and headcount reduction in the acquired company. However, employees of the acquired firm can benefit if they see the new owner as helping them to remain competitive, when the previous management style was unpopular, or when higher pay, benefits or prestige accompany the merger. Cisco Systems is well known for acquiring firms to gain access to technology, but while they are assimilating their acquisitions into the Cisco culture, they try to retain most of the employees including top management.[22]

Reverse merger

The exact opposite of the absorption M&A is the situation in which the acquiring company wants to gain capabilities from the acquired organization. Typically, this takes the form of the acquired company absorbing a parallel unit from the acquiring firms. For example, when Nokia bought a high-tech firm in Silicon Valley, it gave the acquired unit global responsibilities. This meant that part of the business in Finland (Nokia's Headquarters) reported to California.[23]

Best of both

Adopting the best practices from both parties in the merger might seem a painless way of achieving cultural integration. However, in practice this approach almost never occurs. The internal consistency of the organization's culture is lost when practices are adopted piecemeal and the process of deciding which practices are *best* can often become very political. Where this approach has had success the merging organizations were very similar, as in the case of Exxon/Mobile.

Few M&As fit cleanly into any of these categories and cross-border mergers add another complicating factor. That is, in international M&As there may be parts of the organization or units in some countries or regions where a particular approach works well and other parts where it does not.[24]

Critical HRM issues at different stages of M&As

People and cultural issues are key determining factors in the success of M&As. Surveys consistently rank such factors as *retention of key talent, selecting the management team, resolving cultural issues* and *communications* as the key people factors in M&A success.[25] Thus, HRM has an important role to play in all stages of the M&A process. The process is typically divided into three stages – the *initial planning stage* including due diligence, the *closing the deal stage*, and the *post-merger integration* stage. Box 7.3 provides an overview of the HRM activities at each stage. The stages are for illustration only and some HRM activities will occur across stages. For example, communication is a key element of any change process and will cut across all stages.

BOX 7.3   HRM ACTIVITIES IN CROSS-BORDER M&As

Initial Planning Stage

- Participate in selection of M&A targets
- Forming the M&A leadership team
- Determining how success will be measured
- Assuring that the due diligence process deals with HRM considerations

Closing the Deal and Company Integration

- Advising on implementation (staffing plan)
- Integration planning (integration manager and team)
- Deciding on HR policies and procedures
- Planning "how to learn"

Post-Merger Integration

- Communication to alleviate anxiety and stress
- Retaining key talent
- Building the new culture
- Assessing and revising as required

Initial planning stage

In international M&As, HRM strategy cannot be separated from its cultural and social context. Cultural compatibility or incomparability is one of the most discussed issues in cross-border M&As and needs to be assessed at the initial selection of targets.[26] Here, HR can offer an initial assessment of the quality of human assets before committing to a full due diligence assessment (discussed ahead). A second important consideration at this stage is making sure the company has the appropriate leadership team in place to head the M&A process.[27] For example, the success of the Renault acquisition of Nissan is largely attributed to the leadership ability of Carlos Ghosn,[28] while the failed Daimler–Chrysler merger had three different top management teams in its first two years.[29] And, at the planning stage it is important to clearly understand the goals of the M&A and how success will be measured. If, for example, the motive for the acquisition involves talent acquisition, the retention of employees is a key metric perhaps at the cost of efficiency. Finally, the most important contribution that HR can make during this stage is to ensure that the due diligence process covers the critical people issues, which involves a *cultural assessment* and a *human capital audit*.

Due Diligence Process: Due diligence in an M&A of course involves gaining a complete and accurate understanding of the legal, financial and operational issues associated with the deal. However, just as important is learning about the culture and HRM policies and practices of the target organization. As indicated previously, these people issues are often at the core of M&A success or failure and it is therefore important to try to understand them before signing the deal. Box 7.4 outlines the broad list of topics that might be covered in a due diligence audit of a target company.

BOX 7.4   A HUMAN RESOURCE DUE DILIGENCE CHECKLIST

Organization and Management

Organization Charts

- Job Title Hierarchy

Management Committees

Succession Plans

Employment Contracts

Employment Agreements

HR policies

Hiring procedures

Employment Documents

Job Descriptions

Work Rules

- Vacation Policy

- Discipline

Performance Management

Early Retirement

Termination/Severance

Compensation/Benefits

Executive Compensation

General Compensation

Incentive Compensation

- Bonus Eligibility

- Stock Plans

Pension Plan

- Coverage

- Assets and Labilities

Non-monetary Rewards

Labor Relations

Litigations and Claims

Human Resources Information Systems

Employee records

Source: Adapted from Pucik, Evans, Björkman, & Morris (2016), p. 366.

Some of this information is needed in order to protect the company from potential financial exposure, while other information involves the strategy of the M&A. However, HR due diligence is more than just collecting data to avoid financial liability or to assess strategic fit. It means a complete assessment of the HRM environment of the firm including its culture. Before an integration strategy can be developed, the cultures of the two companies must be understood. The *organizational culture assessment* evaluates factors that may influence organizational fit such as core philosophy and values, leadership styles, time orientation, risk tolerance, team versus individual performance and so on, and allows the firm to prepare a plan of how cultural issues should be addressed before the deal is signed. Some information will address the leadership of the target company and their philosophy such as:

- What are their core beliefs about what it takes to succeed?
- Is the company business strategy driven by tradition or innovation?
- Is the company long- or short-term oriented?
- How much risk is the company willing to accept?
- Who are the important stakeholders in the organization?

Other information will examine how the company manages key activities such as:

- Is the company results- or process-oriented?
- Is the power concentrated at the top, in certain functions, or diffused?
- Are decisions made by consensus, by consultation, or by authority?
- Is the information flow in the company wide or narrow?
- Are employees valuable because of their values, skills, and competencies or because of getting results?
- Is the culture oriented toward team-work, individual performance or both?
- Who are the "heroes" in the organization and what are the organization's key "rituals"?[30]

Some companies use the organizational cultural audit to assess fit with the view that it would be difficult to integrate the target if there are large differences in organizational culture. Cisco, for example, avoids acquisitions of companies that are substantially different in the belief that it would be too difficult to retain key staff.[31] However, it may be that the best partner is not always the one with the best cultural fit. For example, while large cultural difference may create difficulties, too small a difference may provide little opportunity to leverage unique competencies. Similarity can in fact lead to redundancies and conflict between the acquirer and the target.[32] A moderate degree of organizational culture difference might be most beneficial in that it prompts discussion about the most appropriate policies and practices for the new organization.[33] What seems to be very important is the complementarity of cultures and managing the integration process (discussed ahead) to build on the unique contributions that each partner brings to the new organization.[34] As noted above, it is also important to remember that the culture of the organization is embedded in the nationality of the country.[35] Therefore, cultural due diligence means evaluating the socio-cultural context in which the company exists as well.

A second aspect of due diligence in HRM is the *human capital audit*. The human capital audit has both a *preventative* dimension (focused on liabilities such as outstanding employee litigation and grievances, labor contracts, and differences in compensation and benefits – any employment-related constraint on the M&A), and a *talent identification* dimension. The talent identification dimension involves understanding if the target company has the talent necessary to execute the acquisition strategy, identifying key individuals, and assessing any weaknesses in the management team. Examples of information required include:

- What unique skills do employees have?
- How does the target company's talent compare to our own?
- What is the background of the management team?

- What are the reporting relationships?
- What effect will losing some of the management team have?
- What is the compensation philosophy?
- How much pay is at risk at various levels of the firm?[36]

The difficulty in gaining access to information about the target's employees causes some firms to ignore this issue in the early stages of the M&A process. However, early talent assessment can identify potential risks and allow time to develop strategies to deal with them. And, this assessment will help with decisions about who to retain in the target organization.[37] Without such an assessment firms run the risk of not having talent with the skills important to the success of the new organization.

Closing the deal

Prior to signing the deal, the HR involvement in the M&A process will likely have been conducted behind the scenes. And, the amount of time from signing the agreement to implementation can be quite long (and in some cases the deal may not go through because of shareholder approval or changes in the market and so on). However, this is an important period because as soon as there is public awareness of the M&A the communication process must kick into gear.[38] This is where first impressions of new *foreign* partners (owners) are formed and communication with all parties including employees and unions begins. Managers from the acquiring company need to become familiar with the organizational culture of the acquired company and also the national culture context in which the firm operates. Because both organizations are unfamiliar with each other there is a tendency for both to display defensive behavior.[39] Additionally, at this pre-closing stage, the firm will now typically have complete access to data to confirm the due diligence assessment. At this stage, the HRM roadmap (organizational structure, reporting relationships and so on) for the post-merger integration phase is finalized. Finally, at this time the integration manager and transition team are identified.[40] Because the new management team is not yet in place, M&As typically turn to a dedicated integration manager and transition team to guide the integration process.

Post-merger integration

The value creation that produces a successful M&A occurs after the acquisition.[41] The integration process required to create new value for the firm involves the separate elements of human and task integration. Both are required to achieve success. However, it is the human integration consisting of activities that foster the participation of the employees of the acquired company that leads to the more comprehensive integration in terms of organizational culture convergence and mutual respect. And then, additional task integration takes place after the human integration process is complete.[42] Figure 7.2 shows graphically these two integration processes.

All M&As require integration to some extent and it is important that the integration be tailored to the goal of the M&A. There are three activities that seem to be critical to the human aspect of effective post-merger integration. These are *communication, retaining key talent*, and *building the new culture*.

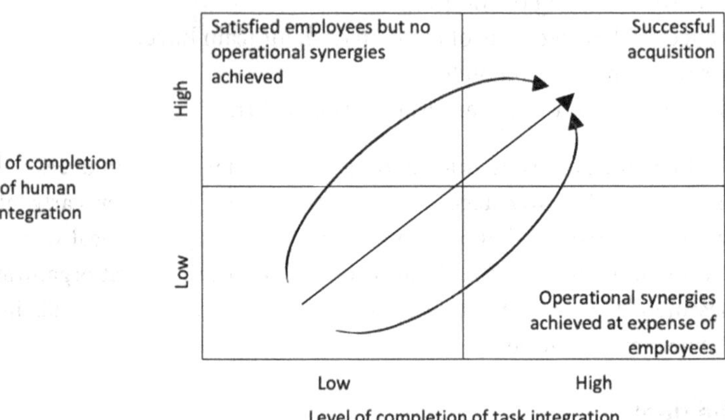

Source: Birkinshaw, Bresman, & Håkanson (2000).

Figure 7.2   Impact of human and task integration on acquisition outcome

Communication: Post-merger integration can be a delicate and complicated process as dysfunctional employee mindsets can lead to numerous HR problems. M&As alter the established order and pattern of activities in the target firm and employee attitudes have been found to decline immediately after the announcement and deteriorate over time. Regardless of the reality of the situation employees fear job loss, question the validity of their skills and knowledge, and generally are uncertain about the future.[43]

Communication is the most basic action that organizations can take to reduce employee anxiety, lack of trust, and other negative feelings following the announcement of an M&A. Communicating the organization's intent increase employee perceptions that the company is trustworthy, honest, and caring and it also helps them understand how they fit in the new company.[44] Communication is also critical to help employees understand the new identity of the merged organization. Additional care must be taken in cross-border M&As where there are language differences. Written documents describing the M&A that are drafted in a foreign language tend to be abstract and limited in scope, which reduces their usefulness.[45] And cross-cultural communication competence does not to receive the attention it should in cross-border M&As.[46]

Communication is necessary but insufficient to reduce employee uncertainty surrounding M&A integration. A related aspect of the process is employee involvement. Employee involvement reduces psychological stress, leads to more successful functional integration, facilitates partnerships and collaborative work environments, and is a key predictor of achieving synergistic outcomes in cross-border M&As.[47] Employee involvement can be achieved through open information exchange, face-to-face personal relationships, by using in-house integration teams consisting of managers from both firms, and by identifying integration entrepreneurs (employees who naturally take on the integration role) and supporting them.[48] In effect employee involvement distributes responsibility for the success of the integration to a wider group of employees across both firms.

Talent retention: Retaining key talent is widely recognized as one of the most (if not *the* most) important element in the success of international M&As.[49] However, as shown in the case that opened this chapter, many acquired firms lose key employees soon after the acquisition. And, there is some evidence (in US acquisitions) that the chance of executives leaving is higher if they are acquired by a foreign firm.[50] Retention of talent is especially important where the value of the M&A lies in the intangible assets such as the knowledge and skills of people in the acquired firm.

The key elements of retaining key talent in an M&A involve, first of all, knowing who the talented people are, then effectively and openly communicating with them, providing financial motivation to stay, and finally integrating these key employees into the leadership development of the organization. Despite the well-known competition for talent there is little evidence that MNEs do talent management in any sort of effective way.[51] But while the basics of identifying high-potential employees are seemingly straightforward, implementing them in practice remains a challenge for many organizations.[52] In an M&A situation obtaining performance information may be even more difficult and complicated by the fact that performance criteria are likely to vary (see Chapter 10). Also, local managers may protect their top people by withholding information about them.[53]

As indicated previously, communication is the most basic intervention and this applies to retaining talent as well. Once top talent is identified, it is important that immediate clear and open communication from the acquiring firm gives them a realistic expectation of their role in the new organization. This communication also involves providing financial motivation to remain. Some employees will be offered financial incentives (stock options, bonuses and so on) to stay until a specific point in time or until merger-related projects are completed. Others will need to be integrated into the longer-term leadership development plans of the company in order to retain them after the initial impact of the financial incentives wears off.

Building the new culture: A final element of the post-merger integration phase that lasts long after the combination of the two firms is building the culture of the new entity. Conflict in M&As is often attributed to a lack of understanding of the partner's organizational culture. The cultural integration problems that arose in the merger between Amazon and Whole Foods were completely predictable based on the differences in the two corporate cultures. Amazon's tight culture (see Chapter 4) was characterized by structure, precision and constant measurement and review, while Whole Foods' loose culture valued openness, creativity and employee empowerment, and was much more disorganized.[54]

Minimizing cultural conflict involves understanding the behavioral norms and routines of both the acquirer and target. Compatibility between M&A partners is achieved through learning within the organization that results in the construction of a shared culture. Identifying cultural differences and learning from them are the only ways in which key elements of both organizations will be valued and preserved in the new organization.[55] A number of interventions have been proposed to accomplish this including collaborative problem solving and intergroup workshops between the merging management teams, and merger workshops that engage employees in determining best practices for the new organization.[56] However, the success of these interventions requires those involved to first have a good understanding of the culture of their own organization.[57] Strong leadership seems to be a key factor in this regard.

For example, for cross-border teams to share knowledge, implementing direct contact among managers to break down stereotypes and extensive training workshops were just some of the measures introduced to break down the "us versus them" mindset in the Renault/Nissan merger.[58]

Cultural differences in integration strategies

We may be seeing the emergence of a set of global "best practices" with regard to the effective integration of firms in an M&A. For example, practices such as performance-related pay, formal planning systems, cost control, and a high level of investment in training have been found across nationalities.[59] However, preferences for certain integration practices in different cultures also exist. For example, among US, British, and French acquirers of Western European targets the French exercised higher formal control consistent with high uncertainty avoidance in French culture. Conversely, American firms were more likely to rely on informal communication.[60] French firms are also more likely to rely on centralizing power at headquarters consistent with French culture's higher power distance.[61] Differences in integration approaches also exist with regard to employment terms, openness of communications, formal versus on-the-job training, performance appraisal, and career development which are consistent with the cultural and institutional context of the acquirer (see Chapters 2 and 3). That is, despite some consistency in HRM practices, there remains the possibility that acquirers may be culturally disposed toward the way they approach integration, and targets may be culturally disposed to the way they respond to integration.[62]

INTERNATIONAL JOINT VENTURES AND COLLABORATIVE ALLIANCES

International collaborative alliances help organizations do things they find difficult or impossible to do on their own such as gain location-specific advantages, overcome legal constraints, diversify geographically, and minimize exposure in risky environments. The types of collaborations engaged in by MNEs vary according to their degree of ownership and control. For example, licenses, management and sales contracts, and franchises do not involve equity ownership and the level of control over foreign operations is relatively low. The terms of the relationship are largely spelled out in the contractual agreement between the parties. While HRM issues do arise in these types of relationships, the level of HR department involvement is much higher in equity-based collaborations such as international joint ventures.

International joint ventures (IJVs) are perhaps the most popular type of international collaborative arrangement.[63] Equity joint ventures occur when at least one of the collaborating companies takes an ownership position in the others.[64] The resulting legally and economically distinct organizational entity is under the joint control of its parent firms. While the majority of IJVs involve only two parent firms they can consist of almost any combination of partners as long as at least one of the partners is foreign.

Reasons for IJVs

Joint ventures are not just a mechanism for cross-border entry but are formed by organizations with all levels of international experience. The reasons typically given for forming an International JV or collaborative alliance are the following:

- Gain and transfer technical and administrative knowledge
- Meet host government conditions for foreign investors
- Gain local knowledge
- Gain rapid market entry, expand market
- Capture increased economies of scale
- Obtain raw materials
- Spread risk
- Improve competitive advantage in the face of global competition
- Support company strategies for internationalization.[65]

Joint ventures are usually formed to achieve a specific objective, as in the case of the Boeing 787 Dreamliner venture, which is a joint effort among numerous companies from eight countries. However, they may operate indefinitely as objectives are redefined. In M&As, discussed previously, the central issue is integrating an existing firm into the parent. However, in IJVs the challenge is to create a new entity with all its related structures, culture, and practices. Unless all the parties in the JV are satisfied with the new entity and its performance, the arrangement may break down.

Reasons for IJV failure

As with M&As, the failure rate of IJVs is high, up to 70% by some estimates.[66] The main tensions in IJVs stem from five factors: the relative importance of the joint venture (JV) to partners, divergent objectives, control problems, comparative contributions and appropriations, and differences in culture.

Relative Importance: It is not uncommon for one company to give more management attention to the JV than does the other. If things go wrong the active partner blames the less active partner for its lack of attention and the less active partner blames the more active partner for making poor decisions. For example, Elders IXL Ltd of Australia surrendered its 50% stake in a JV to grow pineapple in China to its Chinese partner and wrote off its $1 million investment after three years of losses.[67]

Divergent Objectives: Companies may come together to form the JV because of complimentary objectives but over time their objectives may diverge. For example, British Aerospace (BAe) shocked Honda by selling its controlling interest in Rover, which it owned jointly with Honda, to BMW. BAe had decided that the automobile industry was no longer part of its strategic plan.[68]

Control Problems: Sharing assets with another organization can raise issues over control. For example, Sover SPA of Italy alleged that its Chinese partner sold pirated copies of the JV's product (sunglasses) in China and that this constituted a violation of its partnership. However, major decisions required unanimous approval of the board so Sover found itself in a difficult position.[69] And in a proposed JV between US Merrill Lynch and the Japanese firm UFI, one of the key issues was if the person in charge of employees was going to be Japanese or American.[70]

Comparative Contributions and Appropriations: The ability of the partners to contribute assets, technology or capital to the JV may change over time. And the balance of power in a JV can be affected by the teaching and learning in the alliance. For example, a company that is good at learning can access and internalize its partner's capabilities and becomes less dependent on its partner as the alliance evolves. A US producer of industrial coatings was forced to sell out to its Japanese partner after it had learned the production process skills supplied by the US organization. Since the Japanese partner controlled the relationships with customers, the US partner had no choice.[71]

Culture Issues: Both the country culture and the organizational culture of the partners can differ with regard to how the JV is managed and how its success is evaluated. For example, US companies tend to focus on short-term profit and market share while Korean firms tend to view longer term factors such as building strategic capabilities and research and development opportunities as more important. European companies often consider more of a balance between profitability and social objectives, and Chinese state-owned enterprises will be concerned with maximizing employment ahead of efficiency and profit.[72] In contrast to M&As where organizational cultures are integrated, in IJVs the distinct cultures of the partners remain. For example, the highly publicized breakup of AT&T and Olivetti was blamed on differences in culture and management style. "I don't think we or Olivetti spent enough time understanding behavior patterns. We knew that culture was different, but we never really penetrated. We would get angry and they would get upset," said Robert Kravner, an AT&T senior executive.[73] Whether or not cultural differences become dysfunctional of course depends on the ability of the partners to deal with the contradictions that will be present in most alliances.

HRM in IJVs

In IJVs, a number of important issues are related to expertise, policies, and practices in HRM. An overview of the HRM strategy in an alliance is presented in Box 7.5.

As shown in Box 7.5, the HR department has a role to play in all phases of the IJV including partner selection, negotiating the arrangement, implementing the agreement, and management of the venture.[74] Early involvement of the HR department in strategy discussions allows an integration of the HRM strategy with the business logic and long-term objectives of the alliance.

Partner selection

Two main HR issues arise at this stage. They are the extent to which each partner's HRM competencies are expected to contribute to the alliance and the degree to which the HRM policies and procedures of the partners will be linked to the alliance. When the expected contribution of the partner to the JV is high and when the venture is unlikely to be autonomous, it is important to conduct the same type of cultural assessment as you would for an M&A (discussed previously).[75] Differences in HRM policies and procedures are not necessarily a negative factor and in fact may be one of the motivating factors for forming an alliance. However, recognizing and making plans to address these issues is an important step in alliance success.[76]

Negotiating the arrangement

HR can make an operational contribution to the JV by helping to prepare the organization for the negotiation with potential partners. This involves selecting the most appropriate negotiating team for the type of alliance and providing appropriate negotiation training. Different types of alliances require a different mix of entrepreneurial, analytical, and political skills in the negotiation team.[77] Cross-border negotiations require negotiators to restructure their thinking to be effective with potential partners from different cultures.[78] However, organizations tend to underestimate the level of preparation required for these types of complex negotiations.[79]

In addition, HR can influence JV negotiations with regard to both control and senior appointments. While control is often interpreted as the percentage of equity ownership of the venture, it may be a fallacy to assume that equity control means management control. Effective representation on the venture management team and influence over knowledge flows may have more real influence than majority ownership. This type of influence is bound up in key appointments both to the board and senior management of the JV. In most joint ventures senior managers have far more strategic and operational influence than does the board, which may meet very infrequently.[80]

BOX 7.5   THE HR ALLIANCE STRATEGY PLAN

HR issues that may impact partner selection:

- Desired competencies that a partner should possess
- Need for venture HR support from the partner
- Assessment of HR skills and reputation of potential partners
- Assessment of the organizational culture of potential partners

Venture HR issues that need to be resolved in negotiations:

- Management philosophy, notably concerning HRM
- Staffing: sourcing, and criteria
- Compensation and performance management
- Who will provide HR with service support

Desired negotiation outcomes and possible bargaining trade-offs

Specific HR activities that must be implemented early and resources are required:

- Negotiation stage:
  - negotiation team selection, and
  - negotiation training
- Startup stage:
  - staffing decisions, and
  - alliance management training

Estimated timelines for HR actions and allocation of responsibility

Measurements to evaluate the quality of HR support:

- Recruitment target
- Training delivered
- Skill/knowledge transferred

Source: Evans, Pucik, & Barsoux (2002), p. 214.

Implementing the agreement

The implementation phase of the JV involves establishing the vision mission strategy and structure of the new organization.[81] The entire portfolio of HRM policies and procedures need to be created. Appropriate HRM policies and procedures may vary substantially according to the cultural and institutional context of the JV (see Chapters 2 and 3) and they must reflect the partnership objectives and the needs of the parent. The key is aligning the policies and procedures with the parent so they support rather than hinder the joint venture. For example, when Ford entered into a broad cooperative agreement in Japan it recognized the importance of collaboration and made the question "What have you done to support Ford's alliance strategy?" a part of performance appraisal for a large part of the organization.[82] Because joint ventures are inherently unstable, HRM policies and practices must help create trust and an ongoing capacity to cooperate.[83]

Management of the venture

While the whole range of HRM activities requires attention at this stage, the most critical aspect may be staffing. Problems created by poor staffing, repairing the damage done by bad decisions made by individuals unable to cope with the challenges of managing a joint venture, may be difficult or impossible to fix. Differences in the quality of individuals assigned to the joint venture by the different partners is an early warning signal that there may be a lack of commitment on the part of one of the partners to the venture's success, or it may indicate a lack of understanding of the skills required. In either case, once an appointment is made it is difficult to undo. Staffing should reflect a balance of the interests of both partners.[84] In addition to the initial HR decisions made during this stage of the JV process, perhaps the most important aspect of HRM is the process of learning from each other and transferring this knowledge to the JV. Learning and adjustment are the keys to the success of the alliance.[85]

STRATEGIC ALLIANCE LEARNING

While some alliances are created specifically with learning as their objective, all alliances require learning on how to work with partners.[86] This type of learning is difficult because it must occur in a complex context of competition and cultural differences. However, as noted previously, it is required for alliance success and differences in the ability to learn can result in an uneven return for alliance partners. One of the objectives of HR in a strategic alliance is, therefore, to help create a climate that encourages organizational learning and to put in place policies and procedures that guide this activity.[87] One way of understanding this is to look at the obstacles that HR can help to overcome with regard to organizational learning. Table 7.1 outlines the obstacles to organizational learning in JVs and strategic alliances.

Effective organizational learning can be fostered by designing policies and procedures to combat these obstacles. Organizations have many tools to manage the process of learning, but trust between partners is critical because it allows them to concentrate on mutual learning rather than on monitoring and control.

Table 7.1 Obstacles to organizational learning in international strategic alliances

HR Activities	HR Practices
HR Planning	• Strategic intent not communicated • Short-term and static planning horizon • Low priority of learning activities • Lack of involvement by the HR department
Staffing	• Insufficient lead-time for staffing decisions • Resource-poor staffing strategy • Low quality of staff assigned to the JV • Staffing dependence on the partner
Training and Development	• Lack of cross-cultural competence • Unidirectional training programs • Career structure not conductive to learning • Poor culture for transfer of learning
Appraisal and Rewards	• Appraisal focused on short-term goals • No encouragement of learning • Limited incentives for transfer of know-how • Rewards not tied to global strategy
Organizational Design and Control	• Responsibility for learning not clear • Fragmentation of the learning process • Control over the HR department given away • No insight into partner's HR strategy

Source: From Pucik (1988).

CHAPTER SUMMARY

International joint ventures, mergers and acquisitions, and other types of international alliances create unique but increasingly common circumstances for international HRM. While many mergers are advertised as mergers of equals, after the agreement is signed one partner typically dominates. International M&As occur for both strategic and tactical reasons, but only a small percentage achieve their desired results. There are many reasons that M&As fail, but people- and culture-related aspects are prominent in the reasons given. The retention of key talent, selecting the right management team, resolving cultural issues, and communication are key factors in M&A success. An important element of HR department involvement in the M&A process is participation in the due diligence process by conducting a cultural assessment and a human capital audit early on. While what happens before the deal is signed is important, it is increasingly clear that the success of these ventures is largely related to the ability to integrate across boundaries. A key element in the integration process is reducing employee anxiety, lack of trust and other negative feelings through effective communication. While there may be an emerging best practice with regard to post-merger integration, cultural differences in the preference for particular approaches continue to exist.

International joint ventures present their own set of HR challenges. The reasons for entering into an IJV are very similar to an M&A. However, in the IJV, the challenge is in creating a new entity with all its related structures, culture and practices instead of integrating one firm with another. The main tensions in IJVs are the relative importance of the JV to the partners, their divergent objectives, control issues, differences in contributions to the JV, and differences in culture. In IJVs, the whole range of HRM activities requires attention, but two issues stand out: These are staffing and the creation of an environment in which the partners can learn from each other in the context of competition and cultural differences.

QUESTIONS FOR DISCUSSION

1. Why are people and cultural issues the reasons most often give for M&A failure?
2. Compare and contrast the HRM issues associated with different post-merger integration strategies.
3. Discuss the importance of communication in international M&As.
4. What are the essential elements of a cultural assessment and a human capital audit? When should they be conducted? Why?
5. From an HRM perspective, what are the key differences between an international M&A and an IJV?

NOTES

1. Net cross-border M&As are sales of companies in the host economy to foreign transnational corporations excluding sales of foreign affiliates in the host economy.
2. UNCTAD Investment Trends Monitor (2019).
3. Goulet & Schweiger (2006).
4. Marks & Mirvis (2010); Schweiger & Lippert (2005).
5. See Pucik, Evans, Björkman, & Morris (2016).
6. Creswell (2001).
7. Evans, Pucik, & Barsoux (2002).
8. Kühlmann & Dowling (2005).
9. Pucik, Evans, Björkman, & Stahl (2011).
10. See KPMG (1999).
11. Dobbs, Goedhart, & Suonio (2006); http://www.mckinseyquarterly.com/Are_companies_getting_better_at _M_A_1886
12. Shimizu, Hitt, Vaidyanath, & Pisano (2004).
13. Cartwright & Cooper (1996).
14. http://abcnews.go.com/WNT/story?id=131280&page=1#.TtVGnLJCqU8
15. Barkema, Bell, & Pennings (1996).
16. Stahl (2008); Stahl, Pucik, Evans, & Mendenhall (2004); Pucik, Evans, Björkman, & Stahl (2011).
17. Stahl (2008).
18. Evans, Pucik, & Barsoux (2002); Pucik, Evans, Björkman, & Morris (2016).
19. Mirvis & Marks (1994).
20. Killing (2003).
21. Pucik, Evans, Björkman, & Stahl (2011).
22. Pucik, Evans, Björkman, & Stahl (2011).

23. Evans, Pucik, & Barsoux (2002).

24. Evans, Pucik, & Barsoux (2002).

25. KPMG (1999); Kay & Shelton (2000).

26. KPMG (1999).

27. Schuler, Jackson & Luo (2004).

28. Carlos Ghosn was arrested in 2018 for breach of trust and removed as CEO. A year later the merger he orchestrated has started to come apart. See: https://www.wsj.com/articles/without-carlos-ghosn-the-nissan-renault-alliance-has-started-to-crack-11577292916

29. Evans, Pucik, & Barsoux (2002).

30. Adapted from Deal & Kennedy (1982); Pucik, Evans, Björkman, & Morris (2016).

31. http://www.usnews.com/usnews/biztech/articles/060626/26best.htm

32. Krishnan, Miller & Judge (1997).

33. Marks & Mirvis (1998); van Odenhaven & deBoer (1995).

34. Goulet & Schweiger (2006).

35. Thomas (2008).

36. Pucik & Evans (2004); Pucik, Evans, Björkman, & Stahl (2011).

37. Harding & Rouse (2007).

38. Napier (1989).

39. Jemison & Sitkin (1986).

40. Pucik, Evans, Björkman, & Morris (2016).

41. Haspeslagh & Jemison (1991).

42. Birkinshaw, Bresman, & Håkanson (2000).

43. Schweiger & DeNisi (1991); Schweiger & Goulet (2005).

44. Schweiger & DeNisi (1991); Sinetar (1981).

45. Vaara (2003).

46. Gertsen, Söderberg, & Torp (1998).

47. Goulet & Schweiger (2006).

48. For example, see Empson (2000).

49. Kay & Shelton (2000).

50. Krug & Hegarty (1997).

51. Mäkelä, Björkman, & Ehrnrooth (2010).

52. https://hbr.org/2017/10/what-science-says-about-identifying-high-potential-employees; Silzer & Church (2009).

53. Pucik, Evans, Björkman, & Stahl (2011).

54. See Gelfand, Gordon, Li, Choi, & Prokopowicz (2018).

55. Goulet & Schweiger (2006).

56. Blake & Mouton (1984); Leroy & Ramanantsoa (1997).

57. For an example of this process see Vaara, Tienari, & Säntti (2003).

58. Donnelly, Morris, & Donnelly (2005).

59. Faulkner, Pitkethly & Child (2002).

60. Calori, Lubatkin, & Very (1994).

61. Lubatkin, Calori, Very, & Veiga (1998).

62. Goulet & Schweiger (2006).

63. Schuler & Tarique (2006).

64. Daniels, Radebaugh, & Sullivan (2011).

65. Schuler, Jackson, & Luo (2004).

66. Schuler, Jackson, & Luo (2004).

67. Daniels, Radebaugh, & Sullivan (2011).

68. Serapio & Cascio (1996).

69. Serapio & Cascio (1996).

70. Daniels, Radebaugh, & Sullivan (2011).

71. Bleeke & Ernst (1995).

72. See Napier & Thomas (2004); Thomas (2008).

73. Serapio & Cascio (1996, p. 65).

74. Similar four stage models with various stage names have been presented. For example, see Schuler (2001).

75. Evans, Pucik, & Barsoux (2002).

76. Ariño & Reuer (2004).

77. Lorange & Roos (1990).

78. Thomas (2008).

79. Weiss (1993).

80. Evans, Pucik, & Barsoux (2002).

81. Schuler & Tarique (2006).

82. Evans, Pucik, & Barsoux (2002).

83. Child & Faulkner (1998).

84. See Pucik (1988).

85. Doz & Hamel (1998).

86. Barkema, Shenkar, Vermeulen, & Bell (1997).

87. Pucik (1988).

8
Global staffing

After reading this chapter you should be able to:

1. Describe the four strategic approaches to global staffing.
2. Describe the reasons why an organization might choose to fill a position with an expatriate.
3. Outline the criteria used to select expatriates for foreign assignments.
4. Describe important differences in staffing practices across countries.
5. Discuss the issues associated with implementing global staffing programs.

A manager for Russia

Ben Cohen, founder of Ben & Jerry's, had been interested in starting a venture in Russia since he first visited there in 1986. Now, Jeff Furman, long-time friend of Ben and in charge of partnership opportunities, was searching for an American to head up Ben & Jerry's anticipated joint venture in Karelia, Russia. Karelia was a beautiful resort region near the Finnish border and was the sister state of Vermont where Ben & Jerry's started and is still home to its headquarters. Jeff had interviewed numerous business school graduates who spoke Russian, but none of them seemed to fit with Ben & Jerry's culture of social responsibility. So, Jeff posted the job internally. Responding to the ad, Dave Morse, a production supervisor who had worked for Ben & Jerry's for five years encouraged Jeff and Ben to reconsider the type of person they were looking for. Dave had reached the limit of his potential in production and had read about Russia and its history and was ready for an adventure. He argued that it was more diffi-cult to learn how to make super premium ice-cream than anything else the job would require. Anyone else would take at least a year to learn the basics and still would not have Dave's knowledge of the industry, sources of equipment and raw materials, in addition to his technical knowledge of ice cream production. Even though he had no overseas experience, could not speak Russian, and had no formal business training, Dave's energy and can-do attitude impressed Jeff. He was selected to be the first manager of the Russian joint venture.[1]

INTRODUCTION

All organizations face the challenge of finding and keeping the people they need to be competitive. As organizations cross borders and cultures, this task becomes more critical as well as more complex. Two trends make this activity even more challenging today than it was for Ben and Jerry's when they were first internationalizing. First, as discussed in the opening chapter, the number and character of permanent migrants is changing the composition of the workforce in many countries. As boundaries to migration change, patterns of migration resulting from economic, political and social factors fluctuate too. Following World War II, the dominant migration pattern was low-skilled workers from less developed to more developed economies. While economic factors continue to be a major influence on migration, today's migrant (in part because of skills related immigration systems,[2] and the globalization of some professional labor markets[3]) is much more likely to be highly skilled.[4]

Second, regardless of economic swings, the demand for skilled workers is outstripping supply. This ranges from finding skilled expatriates to help organizations expand into emerging markets, through accessing short-term or temporary talent for specific projects, to sourcing cadres of highly mobile elite managers to build global networks and facilitate knowledge transfer.[5] Both developed and emerging economies have recognized human capital as a fundamental means of economic development.[6] In fact, shortages of international management talent have been shown to be a significant constraint on implementation of global strategies.[7] Thus, MNEs are now often competing for the same global talent pool.[8]

APPROACHES TO GLOBAL STAFFING

Global organizations recognize the positive effect of aligning their staffing strategy with the organizational strategy.[9] For MNEs, staffing decisions typically revolve around choices among parent country nationals (PCNs), host country nationals (HCNs) and third country nationals (TCNs, i.e., people from neither the parent nor host country) for filling key positions in their headquarters and subsidiary operations.[10] Managerial attitudes toward staffing with these three categories of employee have resulted in the classification of staffing strategies as ethnocentric, polycentric, geocentric and regiocentric.[11]

- In an *ethnocentric* strategy, key decision-making positions at both headquarters and in the foreign subsidiary are filled by PCNs.
- In a *polycentric* strategy, subsidiaries are more autonomous and key managers are usually HCNs.
- A *geocentric* strategy reflects a more global approach to staffing and is reflected in a mix of PCNs, HCNs, and TCNs both at headquarters and in subsidiaries, with a focus on the unique requirements of each situation.
- And, in a *regiocentric* strategy the staffing of the foreign subsidiary reflects the geographic strategy and structure of the MNE. For example, the organization might be subdivided into regions within which a great deal of mobility occurs, but mobility outside the region would be limited.

While these approaches to staffing strategy may reflect the preferences of management, in many cases organizations may have a somewhat ad hoc policy toward their use of PCNs, HCNs, and TCNs. Also, actual staffing patterns may be based on a variety of contingency factors as we discuss ahead.[12] Regardless, several advantages and disadvantages of staffing with particular employee types have been identified and are presented in Table 8.1.

Staffing contingencies

Table 8.1 The advantages and disadvantages of using PCN, HCN, and TCN

	Advantages	Disadvantages
PCN (parent country national)	• Familiarity with the home office's goals, objectives, policies, and practices • Technical and managerial competence • Effective liaison and communication with home-office personnel • Easier exercise of control over the subsidiary's operation	• Difficulties in adapting to the foreign language and the socio-economic, political, cultural and legal environment • Excessive cost of selecting, training and maintaining expatriate managers and their families abroad • The host countries' insistence on localizing operations and on promoting local nationals in top positions at foreign subsidiaries
HCN (host country national)	• Familiarity with the socio-economic, political and legal environment and with business practices in the host country • Lower cost incurred in hiring HCN as compared to PCN and TCN • Provides opportunities for advancement and promotion to local nationals and, consequently, increases their commitment and motivation	• Family adjustment problems, especially concerning the unemployed partners of managers • Difficulties in exercising effective control over the subsidiary's operation • Communication difficulties in dealing with home-office personnel
TCN (third country national)	• Responds effectively to the host country's demands for localization of the subsidiary's operation • Perhaps the best compromise between securing needed technical and managerial expertise and adapting to a foreign socio economic; and cultural environment • TCN are usually career international business managers • TCN are less expensive to maintain than PCN • TCN may be better informed about the host environment than PCN	• Lack of opportunities for the home country's nationals to gain international and cross-cultural experience • Host countries' sensitivity with respect to nationals of specific countries • Local nationals are impeded in their efforts to upgrade their own ranks and assume responsible positions in the multinational subsidiaries

Source: From Borg & Harzing (1995), p. 186.

While management attitudes may reflect the general strategies outlined previously, it seems that many firms do not have a clearly stated and uniform global staffing policy. It was once thought that the staffing patterns of international organizations followed a pattern consistent with their stage of internationalization.[13] That is, the use of PCNs in overseas posts would predominate in early stages of internationalization, with the use of HCNs increasing as the technology of the firm was disseminated among foreign subsidiaries. However, other factors not related to the stage of internationalization have since been shown to be more important to actual staffing patterns.[14] These include the country of origin of the MNE, the size and task complexity of its foreign affiliates, their performance and strategic importance for the MNE, and the cultural and institutional distance of an affiliate from headquarters.[15] Moreover, linked to our earlier comments on migration patterns, the regulatory environment related to immigration is a substantial factor (along with cost considerations) in organizational choice of the use of local employees (HCNs) versus hiring people who will potentially require work visas (PCNs and TCNs).[16]

Individual staffing decisions reflect the overall staffing strategy of the firm, whether or not this strategy is explicit. Much of what we know about staffing strategy comes from understanding why a company will send a PCN to the foreign operation rather than fill the job locally. An important early study of why organizations might fill an overseas position with a PCN suggested that individuals would be transferred internationally for one of three reasons:

- to fill a technical requirement
- to develop the individual
- to develop the organization.[17]

These three basic reasons for sending an expatriate reflect either demand driven (filling a position) or learning driven (developing the individual or organization) motives on the part of the organization.[18]

Filling a position because of the need for a specific technical requirement seems to be a key reason for staffing with a PCN.[19] The Global Mobility Trends Survey[20] reported that for 54% of expatriate assignments the objective was to fill a managerial or technical skills gap. However, the country of origin of the firm and patterns of national culture values can also be influential.[21] For example, Japanese firms (coming from a societal culture described by high power distance and assertiveness) tend to use more PCNs in their foreign operations than do their US or European counterparts.[22] This may be because Japanese firms rely more heavily on the use of expatriates as a means of management control.[23] In contrast, firms from New Zealand (where society is much lower on power distance and higher on individualism) are more likely to report that the reason for sending expatriates on assignment is for development of the organization or the individual. And, for firms from South Korea (low on assertiveness and high on uncertainty avoidance), the reason most often given for staffing with a local national instead of an expatriate is the lack of local knowledge.[24]

Further, we have evidence that suggests that the importance of the different reasons for staffing with expatriates vary between subsidiaries in MNEs from different home countries and between subsidiaries in different host regions. That is, filling positions is more important for subsidiaries of US and British MNEs located in the Latin American and the Far Eastern regions. In contrast, management development is more important for German, Swiss, and Dutch MNEs and tends to occur more in the Anglo-Saxon region than in the Far Eastern region. Transfers for organizational development appear to be most important for German and Japanese MNEs, in host countries that are culturally distant from headquarters.[25] Thus, these practices suggest an implicit staffing strategy among firms of different national origin.

Several other factors also relate to the use of PCNs (expatriates) including the task complexity found in the foreign operation and the cultural distance of the foreign operations from headquarters. For example, subsidiaries with more complex operations are more likely to be staffed with expatriates.[26] As the cultural distance between headquarters and the foreign subsidiary increases, so does the tendency to use expatriates. However, this tendency decreases over time.[27] The same effect is also evident regarding differences among institutions in home and host countries. That is, firms rely more heavily on expatriates for staffing subsidiaries in institutionally distant environments. This seems to be because of the need and perceived ease of transferring management practices and firm-specific capabilities through the use of PCNs.[28] Finally, the type of industry makes a difference: given the need for knowledge transfer in technology- and knowledge-intensive industries, expatriation is more common there too.[29]

Expatriate roles

The complexity of the global environment in which MNEs operate gives rise to the need for continuous environmental scanning and information exchange, as well as the need for seamless coordination and control of geographically dispersed operations.[30] As we note above, the top reason for sending expatriates remains filling positions for which no local skills are available.[31] However, the strategic importance of using these assignments as a means of organizational development has been recognized.[32] The role expectations that organizations have for expatriates reflect these organizational needs and might vary considerably in the extent to which they emphasize coordination and control or boundary spanning.

Expatriates as agents of control

Control means ensuring that employee behavior conforms to the expectations of the organization. Expatriates can act as agents of control either directly or indirectly.[33] Their assignments may contain formal authority to implement policies and procedures that are mandated from headquarters and are internally consistent throughout the subsidiaries of the organization. Their responsibilities can also include direct surveillance of subsidiaries to ensure that subsidiary activities are consistent with headquarters mandates, norms and expectations. Alternatively, they may exert control indirectly through a more informal mechanism such as transferring corporate values and beliefs throughout the subsidiaries of the organization, sometimes likened to honeybees pollinating flowers.[34]

Another control role available to expatriates is as the disseminator of knowledge from the parent to the subsidiary.[35] This knowledge can be in the form of technical expertise but might also involve work practices in a variety of areas, such as occupational health and safety or quality control. The adoption of uniform practices throughout the organization can be viewed as a form of control. Also, expatriates can establish interpersonal linkages with individuals in the various organizational units with which they have contact. These networks of relationships (like the web of a spider) can also serve as a means of informal control through establishing specific channels of information exchange.[36]

Expatriates as boundary spanners

Expatriates, because of their position in the organization, occupy roles that span both internal and external boundaries.[37] That is, they exist on the boundary between headquarters and the subsidiary and on the boundary between the home and host country cultures. Boundary-spanning roles involve not only information exchange across organizational units, but also roles such as bicultural interpreter, and national advocate that have long been thought to be important to the success of the multinational organization.[38] Expatriates often identify their roles as involving such boundary-spanning activities as representing the organization to customers and the public, transferring information across strategic units and establishing interpersonal bonds with host nations.[39] These activities are obviously beneficial to the organization, but boundary-spanning behavior can also have benefits to the individual including higher job satisfaction and more power in their own organizations.[40] Expatriate boundary spanners can also act as culture brokers to connect groups and resources throughout the organization or as *language nodes* upon return to headquarters by bridging different language groups within the organization.[41] However, not all expatriates operate as effective boundary spanners: the ability to fulfill this role is dependent on whether cross-boundary relationships can be constructed and on the reactions of the local HCNs.[42]

Inpatriates

A variation on the expatriate role occurs when individuals are transferred not from the home country to a foreign subsidiary, but from foreign locations to headquarters. This type of role (called *inpatriate*) involves transfers of both HCNs and TCNs and indicates a particular staffing strategy.[43] The expectation is that inpatriates will transfer knowledge about the local subsidiary to headquarters while also learning headquarters routines and procedures that can be transferred back to the foreign subsidiary.[44] There are four circumstances in which *inpatriation* appears as part of an organization's staffing strategy:[45]

- A desire to create a global core competency, a diversity strategy perspective, or a multicultural frame of reference in the top management team;
- A need to develop emerging markets that are recognized as difficult assignments for expatriates, which reduces the available talent pool;
- A desire to increase the capability of the organization to *think globally but act locally*, which can be achieved by involving inpatriates in decision-making;
- A desire to provide career opportunities for high-potential employees of host countries.

All of these might be considered a more strategic approach to management development in the global business environment. Despite the potentially strategic role of inpatriates, they typically hold only a peripheral status in MNEs and have a rather low level of social influence and credibility. This makes it difficult for them to highlight their unique role and their potential contribution to the MNE and creates substantial barriers to sharing and transferring knowledge. Therefore, inpatriate assignments are probably most valuable in organizational cultures that truly value diversity, are open to accepting knowledge originating in subsidiaries, and create adequate support and integration mechanisms for inpatriates.[46]

The expectations that the organization has for the employees it transfers internationally can involve any combination of these roles. The role expectations, along with the expectations of local employees, influence the entire process of global staffing, beginning with recruitment and selection.

GLOBAL RECRUITMENT AND SELECTION

Recruitment is the process of assembling a pool of potentially qualified applicants for a specific job, while *selection* is the process of evaluating and deciding among these candidates. These staffing issues are more complex in a global environment, with two factors being distinctively different from staffing in a purely domestic context. The first is that individuals must be recruited and selected to take up assignments in foreign locations. The second is that recruitment and selection processes and procedures vary because of the different cultural and institutional context that exists in the different countries in which the MNE operates. In the following we first discuss recruitment and selection for foreign assignments and then present a comparison of recruitment and selection across countries.

Recruitment and selection for foreign assignments

A key challenge for staffing foreign assignments is the supply side issue of availability of individuals to fill the pool of potentially qualified applicants. The willingness and the appropriateness of a candidate for an expatriate assignment can be influenced by the destination. The most challenging host countries for expatriates based on all issues ranging from immigration to housing are China (19%), Brazil and India (7%), Russia (6%), and Saudi Arabia and the United States (5%).[47] Therefore, the availability of potential foreign assignees is limited by the following five factors.

The first factor is a shortage of experienced and competent individuals available to fill these roles on a global basis.[48] That is, demand for individuals with the managerial and/or technical skills required in these managerial roles is outstripping supply at an increasing pace, creating what has been called a *war for global talent*. And, because most expatriates are sourced internally,[49] managers may be reluctant to release their best employees creating competition within the firm for these individuals. In addition to possessing the relevant technical skills, candidates also need to be willing to take on an expatriate assignment. Intrinsic motivation is therefore an important element of candidate availability.[50]

The second factor is the prevalence of dual career couples (i.e., both spouses/partners have their own career). Individuals targeted for overseas assignments were traditionally limited to male sole breadwinners whose spouses were willing and able to follow them on their assignment. The willingness of the spouse to relocate has therefore always been a key factor in an employee's acceptance of overseas assignments, although this has become more challenging as couples try to maintain two careers simultaneously.[51] Moreover, families have generally become less willing to endure the disruption to the spouse's career (and children's education, etc.) that an overseas assignment poses,[52] resulting in a worldwide problem for MNEs.

A third and related factor, is the increased participation of women in the workforce.[53] Interestingly, despite the shortage of management talent, the number of women on overseas assignments remains relatively low. There is an apparent lack of willingness on the part of management to recruit women for overseas assignments based on the myths that they are not interested in taking assignments, of if they are, cannot perform effectively once posted abroad.[54] By ignoring the increasingly large percentage of women in the workforce, this significantly restricts the size of the applicant pool. There is some evidence that the number of women on expatriate assignments is increasing: 25% of expatriates were women in 2016, [55] rising from less than 5% in the early 1980s.[56]

The fourth factor that limits the size of the pool of potential applicants has to do with repatriation and careers. That is, employees typically look to overseas assignments as a way to enhance their career.[57] However, because firms typically do not have programs that integrate the overseas assignment effectively into individuals' career progression, employees are increasingly less willing to accept these postings.[58]

A final factor affecting recruitment for overseas assignments is the limitations of the systems designed to manage global staffing in MNEs. There is little evidence that global organizations practice global staffing in a sufficiently coordinated and efficient way, with many firms unable to identify their high performers or unaware of where their best talent is located.[59] Thus, the pool of potential applicants for an overseas posting is limited by a number of factors, including restrictions imposed by the labor market, by other organizational factors, and by individuals themselves.

Selecting expatriates

Given that firms send expatriates on assignment primarily to fill a managerial or technical need that they cannot staff with a local employee, it is not surprising that technical competency (as in the Ben & Jerry's case that opened this chapter) has traditionally been and continues to be the primary decision criterion used by organizations to select employees for these assignments.[60] Other criteria that can have an important influence on an employee's performance during overseas assignments seem to be generally neglected. This overemphasis on technical competence as a selection criterion may result because selection based on technical competence presents a lower perceived risk of adverse consequences to the selecting manager.[61] That is, it is easier to defend a selection decision based on past performance, which is relatively easy to measure as compared to more subjective criteria.

Effective expatriates: beyond technical competence

Given the challenges in selecting expatriates, adopting a combination of five selection criteria has been suggested as being most effective: technical competence, personal characteristics, spouse and family situation, relational abilities, and organization philosophy.[62]

Personal characteristics: There are certain personality traits that relate to one or more dimensions of effectiveness in international assignments, and hence would help identify potential candidates for expatriation. In particular, some of the Big Five personality characteristics (extraversion, emotional stability, openness to experiences, agreeableness, and conscientiousness) have been shown to be predictive of one dimension or another of expatriate job performance.[63] For example, there is evidence that expatriate adjustment to the local host context and their assignment performance are dependent on emotional stability and openness to experiences.[64] Other personal characteristics include a person's previous international experience and/or their language ability. Both are expected to contribute to an expatriate's adjustment to a new country but also depend on the type of role that a person is expected to undertake. In other words, if the role has minimal interaction with local employees, these characteristics become less important.[65]

Spouse and family situation: The spouse and family situation appears on first sight as an unusual, if not inappropriate, selection criteria. Nevertheless, spousal adjustment to the host location can be just as important as for the expatriate themselves because of the impact of family life outside of work, but is often overlooked.[66] Another perhaps less well considered criterion for expatriate selection is the willingness of the spouse (family) to relocate.[67] If the family are not comfortable in or cannot adjust to the new host location, this puts greater strain on the expatriate's own ability to adjust to the new situation and achieve an appropriate work–life balance. Similarly, for the dual career couples, there is an extra complication because, while many countries have policies that facilitate employment-related immigration, work permits are often available only to the expatriate and not the trailing spouse.

Relational abilities: Relational abilities refer to the ability of expatriates to adapt to working and living in the host location. A critical part of this is the extent to which the candidate possesses cultural agility, which is described as a combination of cross-cultural competencies (such as a tolerance of ambiguity, cultural flexibility, and reduced ethnocentrism) together with sensitivity to a given situation. In other words, cultural agility requires not only having an ability to be open to the unexpected and to see the world through others eyes, but also knowing when each of these abilities is most appropriate to put into action.[68] One group of people that is potentially suitable for expatriate assignments is biculturals, that is, people who live in one culture but are raised in a family from another culture. Biculturals develop cross-cultural effectiveness skills from birth, making them more culturally aware as an employee in their future life.[69]

Organization philosophy: Finally, there is organization philosophy about expatriates, which is an equally important consideration in expatriate selection. Despite evidence that criteria other than technical skills are important to some aspects of expatriate performance they are, as mentioned, typically neglected. One of the key issues is the inability of organizations to assess them. As desirable as it may be to assess personality traits as a criterion, the tests to assess these traits are rarely convincingly validated and most have been developed in the United States making them potentially culture specific.[70] The ability to measure the relationship between an expatriate's skills and abilities and their performance on assignment is also challenging and hence rarely undertaken.[71] This makes it difficult for organizations to establish an appropriate approach to expatriate selection.

Selection process

Despite efforts to make the process of expatriate selection systematic, many expatriate selection decisions probably contain a good deal of subjectivity and serendipity. As demonstrated in the case that opened this chapter, Dave Morse happened to be in the right place at the right time and to have the right attitude to be selected as the manager for Ben & Jerry's new Russian joint venture. A way of categorizing these selection systems is to think of them along the two dimensions of informal–formal and open–closed. As shown in Table 8.2, this results in four selection system types. Actual selection processes might take any of these forms depending on characteristic of the organization (size, industry, level of internationalization and so on) and on the type of expatriate assignment. Formal-open systems would seem to be the most desirable because of their clearly defined criteria and measures, open advertising and so on, but the most prevalent is probably the informal-closed system in which the selectors' individual preferences determine the criteria and measures and nominations are by reputation and networking.[72]

Table 8.2   Typology of selection system types

	Formal	Informal
Open	Clearly defined criteria Clearly defined measures Training for selectors Open advertising of vacancy (internal/external) Panel discussions	Less defined criteria Less defined measures Limited training for selectors No panel discussions Open advertising of vacancy Recommendations
Closed	Clearly defined criteria Clearly defined measures Training for selectors Panel discussions Nominations only (networking/reputation)	Selectors' individual preferences determine criteria and measures No panel discussions Nominations only (networking/reputation)

In the remainder of this chapter, we move on from considering the specific case of expatriates, instead exploring how recruitment and selection activities vary across countries for all different types of employees.

COMPARATIVE RECRUITMENT AND SELECTION

As organizations globalize, they must consider how to implement staffing practices on a worldwide scale. Staffing decisions championed at headquarters also inform and guide staffing decisions about local workforces in the various subsidiaries of the MNE. However, these decisions must also reflect local labor market conditions and consider the extent to which corporate staffing practices will travel well across MNE locations.

Recruitment activities can be classified in numerous ways, one of which being the extent to which the recruitment source is formal and/or active. *Formal sources* include such activities as job postings in newspapers and job fairs, while *informal sources* are ones that use friends and relatives as sources. *Active processes* are those in which the firm initiates the contact with applicants such as the use of search firms, while *passive processes* refer to job postings in newspapers or online.[73]

The use of particular recruitment methods is not determined solely by organizational preference. The institutional context in a country is equally important. For example, many organizations from Central and Eastern Europe tend to use informal recruitment channels, as the labor markets in these countries are not yet well developed. These small labor markets (especially at the level of top managerial positions) allow informal networks to play a much more important role than in larger and more developed labor markets.[74] Countries in which equal employment opportunity laws are strictly enforced also tend to have more formal and structured recruitment processes.[75] Also, more extensive internal labor markets in countries such as Japan mean that organizations focus more on promoting from within than in countries where organizations tend to fill positions through external hires, such as in the US.[76]

The extent to which different recruitment methods are dominant also varies according to national culture characteristics. For example, the cultural value of individualism is positively related to the extent to which organizations use (formal and passive) website recruiting.[77] Recruitment channels and methods that are informal and network-based tend to be more prevalent in cultures that are high on uncertainty avoidance and collectivism, whereas formal channels and methods are more widespread in cultures that are high on universalism and performance orientation.[78] In high power distance cultures, structured interviews are more effective than informal methods, while in feminine cultures, job offers should emphasize fit, culture, and relationships.[79] These examples clearly indicate that organizations can be most successful in hiring if they adjust their staffing practices to different cultural contexts.

The combination of institutional and cultural differences results in a wide variety of recruitment and selection methods across different countries.[80] For example, informal word-of-mouth practices are used widely in the UK and US for all grades of employee, whereas speculative applications (i.e., when someone submits their applicant details to an organization, but not in response to an advertised vacancy) are used only for specific employee types, such as for manual workers in France and professionals in Germany. Similarly, the use of references as a selection tool is common in the US, yet rare in Japan. These different patterns of practice use are likely due to a combination of historical, cultural, and legislative factors.[81]

While a person's ability to perform the technical requirements of a job is ranked as the top selection criterion across the globe, organizations from certain countries may have unique selection criteria. For example, nepotism (i.e., hiring relatives of existing employees) is common in some countries, but condemned in others. Yet even in countries in which nepotism is banned (or associated with corrupt business practices), many organizations readily use employee referrals (recommendations by existing employees) as a recruiting tool.[82] In other countries, such as Mexico, having the right connections (e.g., from school, family friends, in government) is very important. In Japan and Taiwan, it is the person's ability to get along with people already working in the organization that matters. The message that organizations send in trying to generate a pool of potentially qualified applicants reflects the importance of such criteria. The message sent by Ernest Shackleton (see Box 8.1) certainly reflected the desire to attract a certain type of person for his polar expedition.

> ## BOX 8.1   WOULD YOU BE ATTRACTED BY THIS AD?
>
> **MEN WANTED**
> For hazardous journey, small wages,
> bitter cold, constant danger, safe
> return doubtful, honor and recognition
> in case of success.
> Ernest Shackleton 4 Bulington St.
>
> This ad appeared in a London newspaper in 1907 and was effective enough to attract the men from whom Shackleton selected the 28 who would mount his famous expedition to the South Pole.

The evaluation and process of choosing among candidates is also influenced by national culture, leading to considerable variation in selection procedures globally. The Cranet survey, which collects data across almost 40 countries on a regular basis, has captured the similarities and differences in selection procedures.[83] Table 8.3 reports the percentage of organizations across eight countries in terms of the extent to which use a certain selection technique.

These data show the effects of national culture and institutional arrangements on the use of different selection processes. For example, when selecting managers, application forms are used by 26% of organizations in Germany compared to 87% in France, while 31% of organizations in France use interview panels compared to 95% of organizations in the UK. We also know that what job candidates perceive as fair may differ across countries. Compared to college students in the US, French college students assessed personality tests more favorably but thought less favorably of honesty tests (tests that ask about thoughts on theft and experiences related to personal honesty). On the other hand, US students were more likely to say that personality tests were respectful of privacy.[84]

Similarities in the use of selection procedures, as a result of globalization, are also evident. For example, one-to-one interviews are now a common practice across many organizations although this practice was until recently rarely used by Chinese firms. Instead such factors as a person's home province or the institution from which they received their education were more important as selection criteria.[85] Selection decisions can also vary because of the cultural values of the decision-maker. Because managers from different cultures perceive the world differently, the way in which they interpret that reality differs.[86] Therefore, culturally different managers can agree on the same principles but apply them differently. For example, in conducting performance appraisals, the end result can be a written report of how well the employee is doing, but to achieve that, managers in China are more likely to write that report without the input of the individual involved (due to the values of collectivism and power distance), whereas a manager in the Netherlands is more likely to jointly write the report in direct discussion with the individual (due to the lower power distance and greater individualism in that society).

Table 8.3 Percentage of organizations across countries using a range of selection methods (Cranet, 2014/15)

	China n=256	France n=158	Germany n=278	Greece n=188	Sweden n=291	UK n=210	USA n=509
Selecting managers:							
Interview panels	40.2%	31.0%	65.3%	51.6%	39.0%	95.2%	77.8%
One-on-one interviews	60.2%	97.4%	64.5%	74.3%	85.5%	90.8%	76.1%
Application forms	40.2%	87.1%	25.8%	39.0%	53.2%	75.2%	82.4%
Psychometric tests	17.6%	50.0%	17.2%	22.0%	81.2%	75.3%	13.7%
Assessment centres	15.2%	34.7%	27.5%	15.9%	19.9%	53.1%	12.0%
Reference letters	21.5%	79.9%	57.5%	62.1%	95.7%	93.6%	85.8%
Selecting professionals:							
Interview panels	29.3%	15.0%	64.9%	39.7%	28.4%	94.8%	72.8%
One-on-one interviews	27.7%	97.6%	74.4%	66.7%	85.8%	90.9%	76.1%
Application forms	27.3%	84.3%	37.8%	40.7%	55.0%	75.0%	81.9%
Psychometric tests	26.2%	38.5%	11.6%	17.0%	44.7%	73.1%	12.3%
Assessment centres	16.4%	12.1%	22.3%	12.6%	8.2%	60.3%	10.6%
Reference letters	30.1%	71.7%	50.2%	53.8%	93.3%	93.1%	83.4%
Selecting manual staff:							
Interview panels	12.1%	12.1%	48.0%	26.1%	20.2%	92.8%	44.1%
One-on-one interviews	25.8%	97.8%	81.0%	76.5%	83.3%	90.9%	79.3%
Application forms	15.2%	84.5%	52.1%	57.7%	56.7%	76.5%	89.2%
Psychometric tests	14.8%	32.7%	6.3%	16.5%	23.8%	58.1%	8.2%
Assessment centres	12.1%	8.7%	11.0%	11.0%	2.8%	55.8%	14.9%
Reference letters	18.4%	69.4%	31.9%	61.5%	86.5%	92.9%	79.0%

Note: n = number of organizations responding.
Source: Farndale, Panayotopoulou, & Nikandrou (2020), pp. 40–57.

The extent to which individuals are attracted to the characteristics of a job can also vary across cultures because of differences in why they engage in work, what they value in their work and their expectations of their relationship to the organization. For example, when asked to divide 100 points across 11 purposes that work serves, approximately 70% was accounted for by three purposes in all cultures: needed income, an interesting and satisfying experience, and contact with people. But, respondents from different countries prioritized each of these purposes differently. For example, the Japanese gave nearly twice as many points to needed income as did respondents from the Netherlands, while Israelis assigned the most points to an interesting and satisfying experience.[87] In evaluating the goals that people hope to achieve from work, this same research project uncovered some differences across cultures as shown in Table 8.4.

However, it is important to note that the most important goal across cultures was interesting work (work that you really like). Respondents in four countries ranked this goal as most important with the remaining countries ranking it second or third. The importance of interesting work as a work goal across cultures has several implications, not the least of which is for recruitment and selection.

The messages that organizations send when trying to generate a pool of potentially qualified applicants signal what the organization promises and what it expects from employees in return. This understanding of the exchange relationship between the individual and the organization is called the *psychological contract*. Cultural differences exist in the extent to which social cues are important in defining the psychological contract, the extent to which the contract is shared among organizations, and the specific characteristics of the contract.[88] For example, people in France, China, Norway, and Canada describe their relationships to organizations in different terms that are consistent with the national culture. In Canada this relationship is described in terms of equal power relationships that emphasize short-term monetary obligations such as payment for services provided, while at the opposite end of the spectrum, in China, people describe their relationship to their organization as consisting of an unequal power relationship that emphasizes broad, long-term socio-emotional obligations such as commitment and loyalty.[89] Accordingly, cultural differences have also been found in employee perceptions of when psychological contracts have been violated.[90] Thus, culture influences the perceptions and interpretation of the messages that organizations send and determines in part what characteristics of a job individuals find desirable. Recruitment across cultures therefore requires organizations consider how the methods they use and the messages they send will be received across different cultural contexts.

In summary, the form that recruitment and selection processes take and the messages that they convey vary according to societal norms. Global staffing activities need to consider the cultural and institutional context in which this activity is embedded. The methods and processes being used should be evaluated in terms of how individuals in a particular cultural context view why they work, what they value in their work, and the relationship they wish to have with the organization. Global staffing system therefore have the challenge of not only recruiting and selecting individuals for assignments in foreign countries, but also recognizing the cultural and institutional norms for staffing within a variety of national contexts.

Table 8.4 Rank order of work goals across seven countries

	Belgium	Britain	Germany	Israel	Japan	Netherlands	USA
Opportunity to learn	7	8	9	5	7	9	5
Interpersonal relations	5	4	4	2	6	3	7
Opportunity for promotion	10	11	10	8	11	11	10
Convenient work hours	9	5	6	7	8	8	9
Variety	6	7	6	11	9	4	6
Interesting work	1	1	3	1	2	2	1
Job security	3	3	2	10	4	7	3
Match between person & job	8	6	5	6	1	6	4
Pay	2	2	1	3	5	5	2
Working conditions	11	9	11	9	10	10	11
Autonomy	4	10	8	4	3	1	8

Notes: 10 = highest importance; 1 = lowest importance.
Source: Adapted from Harpaz (1990).

GLOBAL STAFFING SYSTEMS

HR managers in MNEs face numerous challenges as they attempt to manage staffing. Given the differences in labor markets as well as cultural and institutional environments around the world, it is understandable that there is often resistance to implementing globally standardized systems. However, there are significant advantages to be gained from having a global system that can be used across multiple countries. An outline of the obstacles and benefits of a global staffing system is presented in Table 8.5.

Table 8.5   Obstacles and benefits of a global staffing system

Obstacles to a Global Staffing System	Benefits of a Global Staffing Systems
• Legal requirements across countries/regions	• Global database of qualified talent
• Educational systems across countries/regions	• Quick identification of candidates to meet needs of a specific location
• Economic conditions across countries/regions	• Provision of a consistent message about the company to candidates worldwide
• Ability to acquire and use technology	• Quality of all hires is ensured
• Labor market variations	• Better understanding of country/regional needs by all HR
• Value differences across cultures	• Global succession planning is enabled
• Availability of off-the-shelf translated tools	• Global HR personnel have access to the latest versions of products/tools
• Level of HR experience varies across regions	• Shared vision of HR globally
• Role of HR in hiring varies across regions	• Comparison of staffing results across locations
• Familiarity with a tool or practice varies	• Global database as an internal benchmark of achievement in different parts of the world
• Misperceptions that something is a cultural difference	
• Limited local resources for implementation	
• Beliefs about whether a global system is UScentric or imposed	

Source: From Wiechmann, Ryan, & Hemingway (2003), p. 82.

Based on the experiences of six MNEs considered leaders in global staffing, best practice in global staffing systems involves:

(a)   acceptability – ensuring employees can see that staffing practices vary between countries based on legitimate differences in cultural and institutional contexts;

(b)   development – receiving input from as many people as possible across the global operations and allowing flexibility of practices to meet local country needs; and

(c)   strong implementation – through communication, careful consideration of how automation meets local cultural needs, and having sufficient global resources assigned to the process.[91]

Many MNEs adopt a global talent pool strategy toward staffing from which they recruit the best people and place them into positions rather than recruiting specifically for a designated position. This approach is central to the identification and development of high potential employees. While many MNEs have systems and mechanisms in place to strategically identify and develop their talent, many more seemingly adopt an ad hoc or haphazard approach. Large organizations, with Global HR functions and standardized products and services are more likely to have standardized systems, as are firms in the low-tech/low-cost sectors.[92] This trend means that organizations need a global template for staffing, but one that allows local subsidiaries to adapt according to their specific circumstances.[93] Figure 8.1 shows how the coordination of talent management systems leads to different talent alignments.

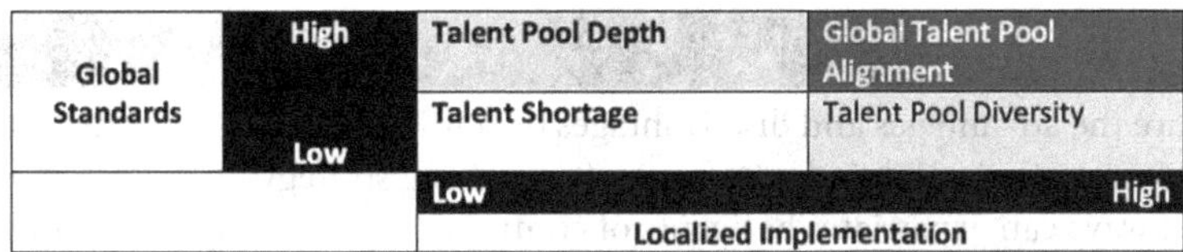

Source: From Stahl, Björkman, Farndale, Morris, Paauwe, Stiles, Trevor, & Wright (2007), p. 24.

Figure 8.1   Global talent management alignment

As shown in Figure 8.1, global standardization with little local differentiation might allow an organization to build a greater talent pool depth, that is, a large pool but one that lacks the diversity needed to adapt to changing environments. Alternatively, a local focus creates opportunities for greater talent diversity but limits the organization's ability to capture economies of scale. Optimally, of course, organizations would be able to balance the talent pool to accommodate both local and global needs (global talent pool alignment). While this balancing act may be difficult to achieve, it is clear that organizations that do not have systems to identify, develop and manage their talent effectively across their span of global operations are likely to be at a strategic disadvantage compared to those with well-developed systems.

CHAPTER SUMMARY

In this chapter we examined global staffing, that is, the recruitment and selection of the employees that organizations need to be effective in a global context. Global operations are concerned both with staffing overseas activities by sending expatriates overseas as well as with local staffing. Four global staffing strategies (ethnocentric, polycentric, geocentric, and regiocentric) based on managerial attitudes toward staffing with PCNs, HCNs, and TCNs were identified.

Much of what we know about global staffing in MNEs has to do with decisions to fill positions with PCNs versus HCNs. The reasons for staffing with PCNs (expatriates) are dominated by the need to fill a particular managerial or technical requirement. This leads to a bias in selection criteria toward technical skills, while neglecting other factors that have a bearing on expatriate effectiveness. In addition to filling a technical requirement, expatriates perform several other roles in the organization, which can be classified as agents of control or boundary spanners.

In addition to the issues associated with sending employees on overseas assignments, MNEs must be aware of and react to the variations in staffing practices that exist around the globe. These practices reflect underlying cultural and institutional differences regarding how people perceive their work and their relationship with the organization. Finally, organizations must find a balance between globally consistent and locally adaptive approaches to staffing as part of their global staffing systems in order to be effective.

QUESTIONS FOR DISCUSSION

1. What are the advantages and disadvantages of staffing with PCNs, HCNs, or TCNs?
2. Discuss why a firm might adopt a geocentric staffing strategy.
3. In what ways can expatriates be agents of control or boundary spanners for MNEs?
4. In what ways are people around the world similar and different in what they want from their work life?
5. Discuss the opposing tensions that must be considered in implementing a global staffing system.

NOTES

1. Material for this vignette was abstracted from the case, "Iceverks: Ben & Jerry's in Russia," by Iris Berdrow and Harry Lane (1993) and from the Ben and Jerry's corporate website.
2. Salt & Millar (2006).
3. Clark, Stewart, & Clark (2006).
4. Cerdin, Diné, & Brewster (2014).
5. See Farndale, Scullion, & Sparrow (2010) for a discussion.
6. Ragazzi (2014).
7. Scullion & Brewster (2001).
8. Sparrow, Schuler, & Collings (2018).
9. Taylor, Beechler, & Napier (1996).
10. See Lazarova (2006) for a discussion.
11. Heenan & Perlmutter (1979); Perlmutter (1969).
12. See Harzing (2001b).
13. See Franko (1973).
14. For example, see Beechler & Iaquinto (1994) and Boyacigiller (1990).
15. Peng & Beamish 2014).
16. Sekiguchi, Froese, & Iguchi (2016).
17. Edstrom & Galbraith (1977).

18. Pucik (1985).

19. See Peterson, Napier, & Won (1995); Scullion (1991).

20. http://globalmobilitytrends.bgrs.com/assets2016/downloads/Full-Report-Brookfield-GRS-2016-Global -Mobility-Trends-Survey.pdf

21. Brock, Shenkar, Shoham, & Siscovick (2008).

22. Beechler (1992); Peterson, Napier & Won (1995).

23. Paik & Sohn (2004).

24. Park, Sun, & David (1993).

25. Harzing (2001a).

26. See Boyacigiller (1990).

27. Gong (2003); Harzing (2001a).

28. Gaur, Delios, & Singh (2007).

29. Harzing, Pudelko, & Sebastian Reiche (2016).

30. Vora (2008).

31. http://globalmobilitytrends.bgrs.com/assets2016/downloads/Full-Report-Brookfield-GRS-2016-Global -Mobility-Trends-Survey.pdf

32. Harzing (2001b).

33. Shortland (2016).

34. Harzing (2001b) refers to the different roles of expatriates as bears, bees or spiders.

35. Harzing, Pudelko, & Sebastian Reiche (2016).

36. See Harzing (2001b); Schweiger, Atamer, & Calori (2003).

37. Thomas (1994).

38. Furusawa & Brewster (2019).

39. Caligiuri (1997).

40. Au & Fukuda (2002).

41. Marschan-Piekkari, Welch, & Welch (1999).

42. Mäkelä, Barner-Rasmussen, Ehrnrooth, & Koveshnikov (2019).

43. Cerdin & Sharma (2014).

44. Moeller & Reiche (2017).

45. Collings & Scullion (2006); see also Reiche (2006).

46. Reiche (2011).

47. http://globalmobilitytrends.bgrs.com/assets2016/downloads/Full-Report-Brookfield-GRS-2016-Global -Mobility-Trends-Survey.pdf

48. Evans, Pucik, & Barsoux (2002).

49. Collings & Sculllion (2006).

50. Caligiuri, Baytalskaya, & Lazarova (2016).

51. Lazarova, McNulty, & Semeniuk (2015).

52. McNulty & Moeller (2018).

53. Fischlmayr & Puchmüller (2016).

54. Adler (2011).

55. http://globalmobilitytrends.bgrs.com/assets2016/downloads/Full-Report-Brookfield-GRS-2016-Global -Mobility-Trends-Survey.pdf

56. Adler (1984).

57. Lazarova (2015).

58. Baruch, Altman, & Tung (2016).

59. For additional information see Evans, Pucik, & Barsoux (2002).

60. Mäkelä, Suutari, Brewster, Dickmann, & Tornikoski (2016).

61. Miller (1975).

62. Ott & Michailova (2016).

63. See Caligiuri (2000); Mol, Born, Willemsen, & Van der Molen (2005).

64. Lauring, Selmer, & Kubovcikova (2019).

65. Caligiuri, Tarique, & Jacobs (2009).

66. Baker & Ciuk (2015); Lauring & Selmer (2010).

67. Baker & Ciuk (2015).

68. Caligiuri & Tarique (2016).

69. Horak, Farndale, Brannen, & Collings (2019).

70. Torbiörn (1982); Willis (1984).

71. Thomas (2010).

72. Harris & Brewster (1999).

73. See Ma & Allen (2009).

74. Svetlik & Alas (2006).

75. Aycan (2005).

76. Aycan (2005); Nikandrou & Panayotopoulou (2012).

77. Puck, Mohr, & Holtbrüggge (2006).

78. Aycan (2005).

79. Ma & Allen (2009).

80. Nikandrou & Panayotopoulou (2018).

81. Ryan, Reeder, Golubovich, Grand, Inceoglu, Bartram, Derous, Nikolaou, & Yao (2017).

82. Vance & Paik (2011).

83. Farndale, Panayotopoulou, & Nikandrou (2020).

84. Steiner & Gilliland (1996).

85. See Huo & Von Glinow (1995); Redding, Norman, & Schlander (1994).

86. See Thomas (2008).

87. Meaning of Work International Research Team (1987).

88. Thomas, Au, & Ravlin (2003).

89. Thomas, Fitzsimmons, Ravlin, Au, Ekelund, & Barzanty (2010).

90. Arshad (2016).

91. Wiechmann, Ryan, & Hemingway (2003).

92. McDonnell, Lamare, Gunnigle, & Lavelle (2010).

93. Evans, Pucik, & Barsoux (2002).

9

Global human resource development

CHAPTER LEARNING OBJECTIVES

After reading this chapter you should be able to:

1. Outline the issues associated with various approaches to training local workforces.
2. Explain the challenges associated with global management development.
3. Describe how international experiences contribute to global management development.
4. Outline different approaches to identifying and developing cross-cultural competencies.
5. Understand the essentials of cross-cultural training and support for international assignees.

Training at Systech

Ayesha Gill had grown up learning to do more with less. But, the impending cuts to her training budget were really going to test her skill. As training and development manager for Palo Alto based Systech she had lobbied long and hard for mandatory cross-cultural training for every employee sent on an overseas assignment. She had never achieved that goal, but at least training was now made available to everyone including their families, and it was up to the employee to decide. That is, that's how it had been until the financial crisis hit. Now, management was questioning the need for such a broad-based approach to training. Some of the top people even suggested doing away with training all together. "These were typically the ones who had never been overseas," Ayesha mused.

"It was no good arguing that training programs shouldn't be cut," she thought.

Cuts were coming! And, she had always had trouble providing hard data on the effectiveness of training, in any case. Employees were sent to so many different cultures and each person responded differently to different situations and types of training. The best evidence she had was from the returning expatriates themselves. She had heard many stories that began, "If only I had known…"

"I have to prioritize," she thought. "If I can only provide pre-departure training to some employees, who should they be? Or should I cut training for families? I don't like the thought of that. Our newest program included in-country mentoring/coaching after the expatriate has been on the assignment for a few months. We don't have much experience with that. Maybe that should be the first to go."

Ayesha though back to her childhood.

She remembered marveling at how her mother could make a meal, planned for their family of four, stretch to accommodate unexpected guests. And, as one of the first Indian families to immigrate to Saskatchewan, Canada, there were frequent visits from newly arrived immigrants. "How did everyone in the Punjab get our phone number?" she once asked. "Mom, I need to know how you did it," she thought.

INTRODUCTION

In order to compete effectively in today's dynamic and complex business environment it is important that organizations develop employees at all levels and in all locations so that they contribute to organizational effectiveness.[1] Organizations do this by implementing a series of training and development activities, with training referring to programs and initiatives that are designed to help employees acquire skills and knowledge needed at the present moment and development referring to activities that prepare employees to meet organizational demands of the future.[2] Training and development have been shown consistently to improve individual and organizational performance and innovation, and are also linked to increased economic national prosperity.[3] Much of what we know about global human resource development is related to the development of international managers and the preparation of individuals for overseas assignments (as discussed in the opening case). However, Global HR managers are also concerned with providing training to local employees. The best way of developing and delivering training and development programs depends largely on the competitiveness and other characteristics of the workforce in specific country locations, which in turn are a product of diverse local educational and vocational training systems.[4]

LOCAL WORKFORCE COMPETITIVENESS

At the most basic level, an assessment of the country's *workforce potential* begins with examining the general level of literacy and educational attainment. Some countries in central Africa have adult literacy rates below 30% while many parts of the industrialized world have rates approaching 100%.[5] Another commonly consulted indicator is provided by the world education rankings of the OECD's Program for International Student Assessment (PISA), which tests 15-year-olds on math, science and reading.[6] The most recent rankings at the time of writing were led by China and Singapore, and the Dominican Republic and the Philippines ranked last among the countries assessed. Also important is the percentage of individuals that have achieved certain educational levels. For example, Figure 9.1 shows the percentage of the population holding a post-secondary (college or university) degree in the OECD.

Comprehensive indices assessing workforce potential are also available. A good example is the Global Talent Competitiveness Index (GTCI). By accounting for how educated the workforce is and also for the country's regulatory, business and market landscape, the index provides an overall assessment of skills, knowledge, and preparedness to meet the volatile

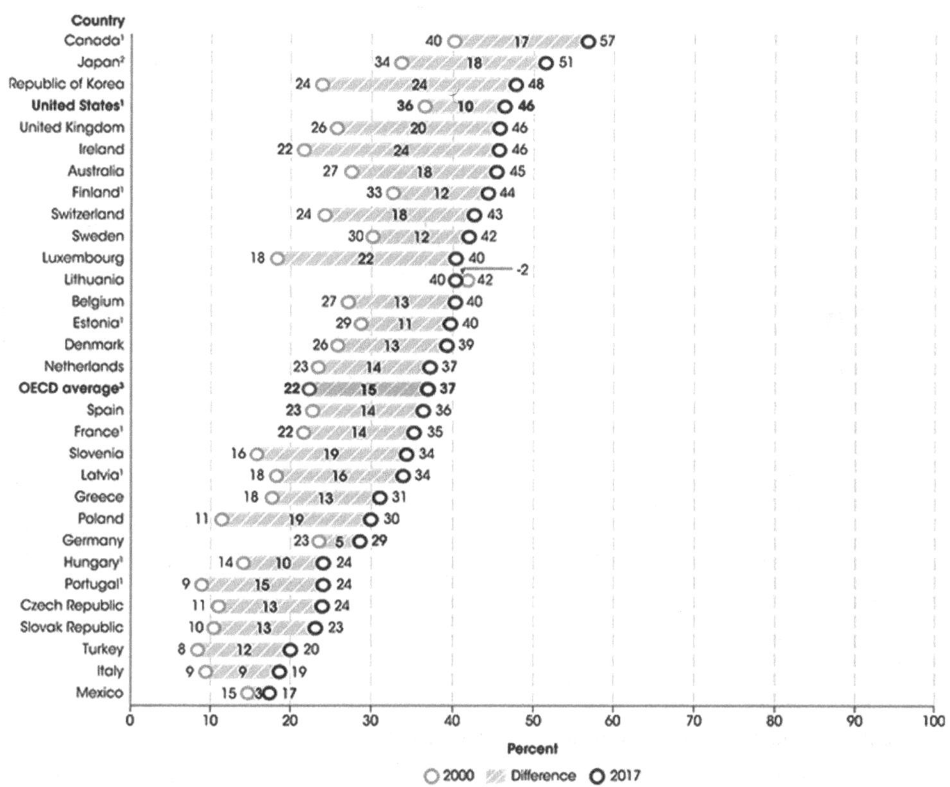

Source: https://nces.ed.gov/programs/coe/indicator_cac.asp.

Figure 9.1   Percentage of the population 25 to 64 years old who had attained any postsecondary degree in OECD countries: 2000 and 2017

demands of work of the future.[7] The report contains specific rankings of countries' vocational and technical skills and higher-level skills associated with the knowledge economy (global knowledge skills). An important observation is the strong correlation between gross domestic product and the country's GTCI ranking, with more prosperous countries also scoring higher on the GTCI, as shown in Figure 9.2.

As indicated in the GTCI rankings, a country's workforce competitiveness is shaped by many factors. Key among them are educational attainment, as discussed previously, and national educational systems. Educational systems (see Chapter 3) differ in their emphasis on *academic* versus *vocational* training. In the former, the emphasis is on more general skills that can be used across a variety of jobs, and in the latter, there is a much closer coordination between educational institutions and industry, and training is more tailored to meeting specific business needs. In systems that emphasize *academic* rather than vocational training (this is the case many liberal market economies, for example, in the UK), it is up to individuals and only occasionally employers, to supplement general skills and knowledge with training for job-related skills and knowledge. External labor markets can be used as a means for upgrad-

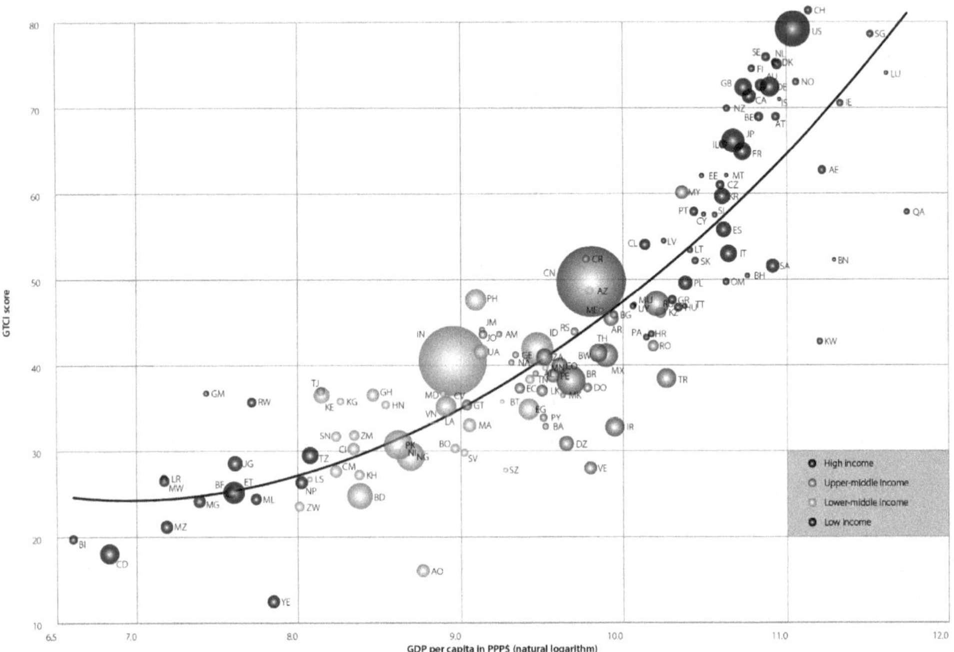

Notes: GDP per capita in PPP$ and population data (represented by the size of the bubbles) are for 2018 or the latest year available. The data are drawn from the World Bank's World Development Indicators database. The trend line is a polynomial of degree two (R^2=0.78).

Figure 9.2   GTCI scores versus GDP per capita

ing organizational skills (e.g., through current workforce downsizing and hiring adequately trained personnel with specific skills from elsewhere).[8] In countries that emphasize *vocational* training (such as Germany, a coordinated market economy) there is a strong collaborative relationship between national educational institutions and employers, and talent development is accomplished through apprenticeships and company-specific training. Such settings are characterized by low external mobility, low use of external labor markets, strong emphasis on succession planning, and lower employee poaching.

TRAINING AND DEVELOPMENT IN MNE OPERATIONS

Referring to indicators and trends such as these can form the basis of the needs analysis, which is at the heart of any training and development program. The comparison between prospective employees' knowledge and skills and what is required by the organization should determine the design and implementation of training and development plans.[9] Because of national differences, training programs will vary widely across national cultural and institutional contexts.[10] Organizational types and industry also influence what programs are emphasized and how much organizations invest in training. For example, firms in low power distance, high future orientation and high uncertainty avoidance cultures tend to invest more in training than firms in high power distance, low future orientation or low uncertainty avoidance cultures. Large high-tech firms tend to invest more in training probably because of their ability to invest in training and the shorter product life cycle in high-tech industries.[11] Further, some countries may have explicit legislation regarding employee training. For example, French companies above a certain size are required to invest a certain percentage of their payroll in training and development activities.[12] Similar legislation has also been adopted by the Canadian province of Quebec (but not in any of the other Canadian provinces).[13]

Regardless of scope, all training programs should involve a needs assessment based on the competencies required for a particular job or set of jobs. Based on the needs assessment, program objectives are set and content and methods for delivering the training are established. Training evaluation should be conducted at all training stages. Figure 9.3 shows a simplified diagram of a typical training cycle.[14]

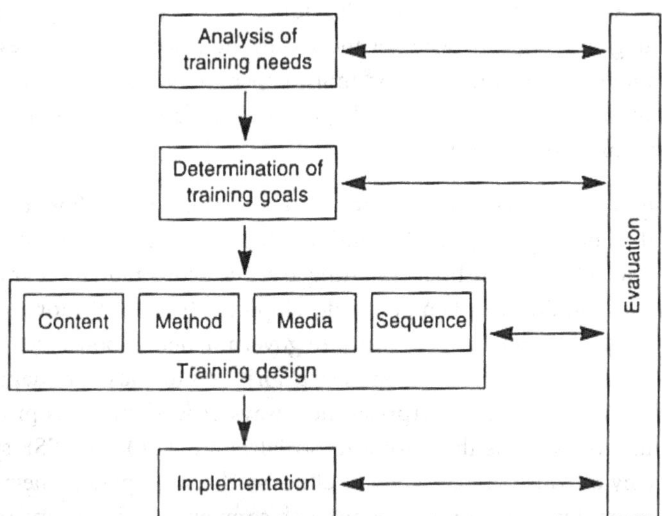

Source: Baumgarten (1995), p. 209.

Figure 9.3   Basic training cycle

The approaches MNEs take to train local workforces range from complete localization, with all training designed and delivered at the subsidiary level to total standardization with all training directed from headquarters. As companies choose their approach, they have to consider a number of questions about the who, what, where, and how of training.[15] For example:

- Who should deliver training in the foreign subsidiary or joint ventures? Trainers from headquarters? Local trainers? Independent trainers?
- What are the effects of language differences? Although there may be a tendency to conduct training in the main corporate language (or in a *lingua franca* like English), recent research suggests that imposing a language on local employees may lead to a number of non-trivial frustrations and resistance among them.[16]
- Where should training programs be developed? If developed at headquarters, will they need to be adapted? Where should they be delivered? Should overseas employees be brought to headquarters or regional training facilities? Can training be developed in various locations and delivered across the organization?
- How should training be delivered? A key consideration is that training methods need to be based on an understanding of the differences in learning styles that exist in different cultures.[17] Culture differences, and particularly the extent to which power differences are present in and accepted by a society and the extent to which people are comfortable with uncertainty, may impact the training process, including the relationship and interactions between the instructor and the trainees, as well as among trainees; how formal the training should be; or whether more didactic (formal approaches such as lectures, presentations, demonstrations) or more experiential training (focusing the learning process on the individual such as role plays or simulations) would be more appropriate for a particular group of trainees.[18]

And, of course, all these questions must be answered within the confines of a training budget. As shown in the opening case, training and development activities are often one of the first HRM activities to fall under the budget-cutting axe. Such constraints recognized, many organizations do an outstanding job of employee development (see Box 9.1 for an example). And in some parts of the globe, employers can turn to governmentally sponsored training programs. For example, one of the European Union's key priorities is to boost the adaptability of workers with new skills and encourage enterprises' new ways of working. This priority is supported by various initiatives such as the European Social Fund (ESF). The ESF sponsors a variety of projects, many of which are designed to allow workers to upgrade their skills and sustain their long-term employability, in accordance with company needs and any relevant regulatory requirements.[19]

BOX 9.1   WORLD CLASS TRAINING AT BEST BUY

Best Buy Co., Inc. is an American multinational consumer electronics retailer headquartered in Richfield, Minnesota that operates internationally in Canada and Mexico. In 2019 Best Buy ranked No. 3 on *Training* magazine's 2019 Training Top 125 list of the world's most successful training programs. This was its third straight year in the top 10. Best Buy also won an Outstanding Initiative award for its Best Buy Certified program, which requires store employees to go through extensive training and be approved by their manager before they're allowed to start helping customers on the sales floor.

Training is crucially important to Best Buy because of the changing nature of the retail landscape. Technology is changing so fast that customers want to talk to someone whose expertise they can trust to help them find solutions that satisfy their needs. According to Alistair Dobbie, senior director of Enterprise Learning and Development, training at Best Buy receives strong financial support because of its direct effect on sales and better customer service. Top managers willingly participate in sales training strategy, planning and content creation.

The effect of the Best Buy Certified program is clear. Since the program launched more than 94% of retail employees completed on board certification and participation in ongoing training has increased from 88% to 93.8%. The company's overall engagement score increased dramatically, turnover decreased, and the company-wide Customer Satisfaction Score increased.

While the Best Buy Certified program is winning awards, it is far from the only training innovation to be found at Best Buy. For example, because the main employee population is composed of hourly employees in a retail environment it is difficult to schedule long and uninterrupted training time. So Best Buy has created "bite-sized" training modules in its Learning Management System that can be consumed in a few minutes or less. This bite sized design was recently incorporated into Best Buy's Code of Business Ethics required e-learning. The result was a 98% company-wide completion in the first month after the launch as compared to 80% in the six months prior.

Best Buy continues to invest in training through enhancements to its Learning Management System (LMS), while reducing costs of traditional classroom-based, instructor-led training. By increasing virtual classes and other quick and easy to use tools Best Buy continues its efforts to create a culture of continuous learning.

Source: https://trainingmag.com/trgmag-article/best-buy%E2%80%99s-training-evolution/ ; https://corporate.bestbuy.com/why-best-buys-employee-training-program-is-world -class/.

GLOBAL MANAGEMENT DEVELOPMENT

In addition to training their rank-and-file employees, MNEs also invest a lot of effort and resources in developing people that occupy or are expected to occupy managerial and leadership roles. The jobs of managers and leaders in MNEs often involve crossing national boundaries and working with people from all corners of the world.[20]

An important clarification is in order when talking about the development of "global" managers and leaders is whether or not there is a common set of skills and behaviors that work across *all* national and cultural settings that should be taught to *all* leaders? Research on leadership has long suggested that while some universals exist (for example, few would doubt the benefits of having business acumen), there are also important differences in what are considered appropriate or desirable traits and behaviors in leaders around the world.[21] For example, US employees and managers value highly transformational and participative leadership styles but there are many places in the world, especially in Asia, in which it is authoritative, decisive, and forceful leaders that are more effective.[22] Across countries managers also rate certain skills as more important than others. For example, managing networks is a key competency for navigating the French environment but is not considered critical in Germany, Italy, Korea, or the UK.[23] Finally, the larger national context is important. For example, managers who operate in countries where the environment is less stable or predictable or in which political connections are just as important as the right organizational strategy (e.g., many countries in Africa) may not benefit as much from extensive training about long-term strategic planning as would managers who operate in (relatively) more stable environments (e.g., most developed countries).[24]

Having said this, it is easy to understand that, at the level of the MNE, the goal of global management development cannot be (and should not be) developing leaders who know *everything* about leading in *every* country around the globe. Instead, what global management development ought to accomplish is to provide the skills and competencies managers and leaders need so that they can conduct their work across borders effectively. Reflecting this complexity, the content of management development programs needs to be carefully calibrated, even within the same MNE. Global management programs must not only equip people with the knowledge, skills and competencies that are specific to their own job and position, but must also help them develop broad understanding that contexts differ, that an approach that works in one country may not work in another, and awareness of their own assumptions and blind-spots. Rather than delivering fixed knowledge, global management development should be focused on training people to keep an open mind in cross-cultural situations and withhold judgment in the absence of appropriate information.[25] Accomplishing this involves the development of a wide range of *cross-cultural knowledge, skills, abilities and competencies*[26] that can improve one's effectiveness across diverse cultures and contexts. This is the topic of the reminder of this chapter.

Developing global management competencies

Global management development tends to be a long-term effort that involves assessing the company's strategic needs and implementing programs to develop individuals that can meet this need. A starting point is mapping the skills, abilities and characteristics (or competencies) required to be effective in the context of the global organization. Given the variety of environments in which global managers must operate it is difficult to come up with a generic job description. However, a number of activities associated with the global management context have been identified. These are listed in Box 9.2.

BOX 9.2 GLOBAL MANAGEMENT ACTIVITIES[27]

- Work with colleagues from different countries
- Interact with both internal and external clients from different countries
- May need to speak a language other than their mother tongue
- Supervise employees who are of different nationalities
- Develop strategic business plans on a global basis
- Manage a budget on a global basis
- Negotiate in other countries and with people from other countries
- Manage foreign suppliers or vendors
- Manage risk on a global basis

Even a casual look at the job requirements outlined in Box 9.2 suggests that working in a cross-border managerial role requires the development of numerous distinctive competencies. In fact, some multinational organizations have identified as many as 250 such competencies.[28] A number of different typologies of competencies on which management development programs could be based have been proposed.[29] The ability of these typologies to predict success overseas or success as a global leader is not well established and the range of competencies is quite large. However, they tend to cluster around six broad dimensions as shown in Table 9.1.

These competencies include elements that are relatively stable and difficult to influence, such as traits, as well as those that can be more readily developed. The challenge, of course, is to identify and foster those qualities in individuals that make them better global managers. Given the complexity involved in even defining the necessary global management competencies, HR managers often get bogged down in the tools and techniques of training, which can become ends in themselves.[30] Yet, as noted previously, the crux of preparing managers for the global business environment is perhaps best captured by the idea that the core requirement of successful development is to expand the manager's mind past domestic borders and create a mental map of the world.[31]

Development of this type could be achieved by a wide variety of different techniques, such as informational training, area briefings, cultural awareness seminars, or cross-cultural skills training. Training methods that demand that the trainee be more mentally engaged are relatively more rigorous that methods that allow passive engagement.[32] For example, trainees are more cognitively involved when they must participate as opposed to just observe, and are more involved when they physically model the behaviors being taught as opposed to only participate in a training session verbally. Having to rehearse the activity in order to perform correctly requires even more involvement. Figure 9.4 presents several common training methods arranged by rigor and feedback received by the trainee.

As shown in Figure 9.4, *formal classroom* approaches involve factual training, such as books, lectures, seminars and briefings, and trainees are passive recipients for information. *International exchanges with others* provide more analytical training, such as case studies or cultural assimilators,[33] and requires more active engagement. Finally, with the highest level

Table 9.1 Mapping global leadership competencies

Cross-cultural relationship skills	Traits	Global business expertise	Global organizing expertise	Cognitive orientation	Visioning
Close personal relationships	Inquisitiveness	Global business savvy	Team building	Environmental sense-making	Articulating a tangible vision and strategy
Cross-cultural communication skills			Community building	Global mindset	Envisioning
Ability to connect emotionally inspire, motivate	Continual learner	Business acumen	Organizational and global networking	Thinking agility	Entrepreneurial spirit
		Total organizational astuteness/savvy	Creating learning systems	Improvisation	Catalyst for cultural change
Conflict management	Accountability	Stakeholder orientation	Strong operational codes	Pattern recognition	Change agentry
Negotiation expertise	Integrity	Results orientation	Global networking	Cognitive complexity	Catalyst for strategic change
Empowering others	Courage		Strong customer orientation	Cosmopolitanism	
Managing CC ethical issues	Commitment			Managing uncertainty	
Social literacy	Hardiness			Local versus global paradoxes	
Cultural literacy	Maturity Tenacity Personal literacy Behavioral flexibility				

Source: Based on Mendenhall & Osland (2002).

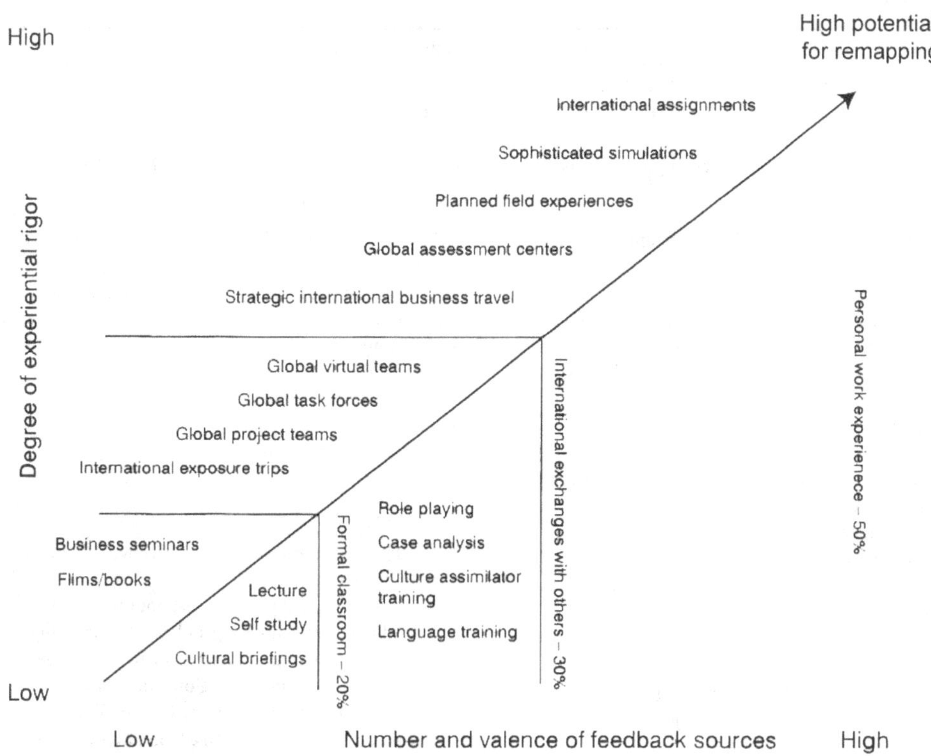

Source: From Mendenhall & Oddou (2012), p. 230.

Figure 9.4   Relationship of experiential rigor and number of feedback sources on mental remapping potential in global leadership development programs

of cognitive involvement, there are *experiential training* experiences, such as participation in sophisticated simulations or international business travel. All things being equal, the more rigorous training methods give the best results.[34]

The developmental role of personal experiences

Considering all these diverse approaches, the key to managerial development may lie in the simple principle that people learn most by doing things they have not done before.[35] The implication of this idea for global management development is that people develop best through situations, experiences and assignments that challenge them. Yet it is important to strike just the right balance. If an assignment is too challenging, there is a high risk of failure. This risk must be managed. But, if the risk of failure is minimized to negligible and success is guaranteed, people are unlikely to learn how deal with situations that are outside their comfort zone. Therefore, the three basic elements of management development can be categorized as challenging assignments, risk management, and hardship testing.[36] Table 9.2 provides a summary of these elements.

Table 9.2 Elements of management development

Management Development Summary

People develop through **CHALLENGING assignments**…

…this requires **RISK MANAGEMENT (coaching)** so as to avoid failure that the enterprise naturally wishes to avoid…

…but not so much that success is guaranteed and that people will never learn **to deal with HARDSHIP**.

Assignments

- Scope: Increase in numbers of people, dollars and functions to manage (traditional vertical development in responsibility).
- Project/task force assignments (integrative skills): Working with other experts, negotiating and defining objectives, and working collectively so as to deliver a result that meets the often unclear needs of sponsors.
- Cross-functional assignments (integrative skills): Moving to a job where one has no expertise, and learning how to lead in the sense of getting results through people who have more expertise than oneself.
- International assignments (integrative skills).
- Starting from scratch: Building something from nothing.
- Change projects: Fixing or stabilizing a failing operation.
- Entrepreneurial projects: Being given the go-ahead and resources to test out a project initiative that the person has been fighting for.

Risk Management

- Assessment of the skills, motives and attitudes of the individual.
- Clarification of the goals and targets in the new assignment.
- Coaching (supervision or informal).
- Mentoring.
- Exposure to role models.
- Training.
- Access to people with experience.
- Feedback.

Hardship Testing

- Business failure and mistakes: Ideas that fail, deals that fall apart.
- Demotions, missed promotions, poor jobs.
- Subordinate performance problems: Confronting a subordinate with a serious performance problem.
- Breaking out of a rut: Taking on a new career in response to discontent with the current job.
- Personal trauma: Crisis such a being fired, divorce, illness, or death.

Source: McCall (1998).

The role of experience-based learning is confirmed in the training literature[37] and by research on leadership development.[38] Studies have shown that various personal experiences (such as involvement in global teams, or global travel that encourages learning from colleagues in different countries), can provide opportunities for global management development.[39]

Recent research suggests that so-called "error management training" should supplement any cross-cultural training activity. Error management training refers to training that views errors as informative signals to enhance learning. It does not try to minimize or avoid errors but rather frames errors positively, as opportunities to foster learning and transfer. If a trainee makes an error, they are made aware of it and asked to think through what brought up the error and how such an error can be avoided in the future. Rather than being taught what the "right" behavior is, managers must intentionally monitor and adjust their behavior to a changing environment. Learning is supported by timely and appropriate culture-based feedback.[40] Personal international experiences are ideally suited for the application of error management training.

Not all training experiences are created equal when it comes to development of cross-cultural competencies. First, it has been found that *high contact* cross-cultural leadership development experiences (e.g., structured rotational leadership development program, short-term or long-term expatriate assignment, participation in global meetings in various international locations, being a member on a global team, or being mentored by someone from another culture) are more effective than *low-contact* cross-cultural leadership development experiences (e.g., university coursework, cross-cultural training, psychological assessments, assessment center for leadership development, diversity training programs, and language training programs).[41]

Second, as *longer* experiences provide more opportunities for exposure to foreign environments, they are more influential for leadership competency development. Different learning and cognitive processing occur at various stages of one's experience. Early on, individuals amass varied knowledge about their new context and it is only as time passes that they are able to synthesize, filter, and apply this knowledge to formulate more strategic responses to the issues at hand.[42]

Third, experiences trigger more learning and development if they happen in more *culturally distant settings*. Spending time in cultures that are very different than one's own is much more likely to challenge one's knowledge and implicit assumptions about people, their habits and motivations, or require them to consider and accommodate different viewpoints on various issues.[43]

Finally, compared to work experiences, *non-work experiences* (e.g., traveling, volunteering or studying abroad, being born in a country different than one's parent(s)) can be just as useful, if not more useful, for development of cross-cultural competencies (e.g., cultural flexibility, adaptability) which in turn are related to global leadership effectiveness.[44]

EXPATRIATE ASSIGNMENTS AND GLOBAL MANAGEMENT DEVELOPMENT

Expatriate assignments provide opportunities to work in a different country for an extended period of time and can be an excellent tool for developing the "global mindset"[45] thought to be important for global managers.[46] During the process of adjustment to a new cultural context, people may develop not only knowledge of another culture and the opportunity to practice different behaviors, but also higher order mental structures and processes because they must be more systematic and careful in processing the cues they receive from cultural situations.[47] That is, as individuals deal with new and conflicting information they must acknowledge the legitimacy of competing perspectives on the same issue and must integrate these multiple perspectives in their mind. For this development to take place individuals need to be prepared for the international assignment.

Preparation for expatriate assignments

An important initial step in integrating international assignments into the management development plan is anticipating and providing training for the international assignment itself. However, providing cross-cultural training is not as extensive as we might assume. A recent survey on mobility practices suggested that while 82% of MNEs provide training, it is a core policy benefit only in 44% of MNEs. In the remainder of cases cross-cultural training was provided for select assignees only, in the case of certain home-host country combinations, or at the discretion of the organization.[48] Two common reasons for why not all organizations provide cross-cultural training are the belief that since expatriate assignments are temporary, they do not warrant training expenditures, and reservations regarding the effectiveness of such training programs.[49] Without doubt, another reason is the cost of providing training (most MNEs contract third-party training experts)[50] at a time when most global mobility functions are under pressure to reduce costs.[51] Training for international assignments might involve activities ranging from formal university programs in international management to cross-cultural coaching and mentoring. However, the most common programs by far are cross-cultural and foreign language training.[52]

Cross-cultural training

The general goal of cross-cultural training is to improve the chances of success for the international assignee and their family on the foreign assignment. Success is a somewhat vague term and has often been equated with simply staying on assignment the agreed upon length of time. A broader view of success consists of the following the components:[53]

- *Good personal adjustment*, indicated by feelings of contentment and well-being.
- Development and maintenance of *good interpersonal relationships with culturally different others.*
- The effective *completion of task-related goals.*

That is, an overseas assignment can be called a success if the expatriate feels happy and satisfied with the situation abroad, is effective in interacting with host nationals, and performs his/her duties and responsibilities in a competent manner.

There is general endorsement for the idea that cross-cultural training is helpful to expatriates.[54] However, there are very few studies that furnish solid evidence on its benefits. Research has found that it has positive – but inconsistent – effects on expatriate adjustment and performance.[55] The lack of convincing evidence may be due primarily to the many methodological challenges of conducting longitudinal studies in which expatriates are studied before training, after training, and during various points of their assignment and are then compared to colleagues who did not receive training.[56] Another thing to consider is that not all country contexts are the same and different expatriate assignments have different demands. Thus, the effectiveness of cross-cultural programs would depend on factors such as the timing of the program (when is it offered, i.e., before or during an assignment), the attributes of the expatriate's job, and the distance between the home and the host cultures.[57] In other words, there is no such thing as a universally effective cross-cultural training program.

Three contextual factors can help determine the most appropriate training for a particular expatriate assignment. They are the degree of novelty of the host culture, the level of interaction required with the host culture, and the novelty of the assignment.[58]

- *Culture novelty:* Attending to and retaining various models of appropriate behavior for cultures that are very different to the expatriate's home culture will require more rigorous training. However, individuals with frequent and involved experiences of similar cultures may require somewhat less rigorous training.
- *Degree of interaction:* The degree of interaction with the host culture involves both the frequency of the interaction and its importance. If the expectation is for few and relatively trivial interactions the level of training rigor can be lower than for frequent and important interactions.
- *Job novelty:* The arguments for the effect of job novelty on the need for training rigor are the same as for cultural novelty. While sometimes the novelty of the culture influences how different a job is, there are instances in which the new job overseas is very different from the previous job. Different performance standards, tasks, procedures, resources, legal restrictions, technology and so on can all contribute to job novelty.

Integrating these three factors determines the need for training rigor as shown in Figure 9.5.

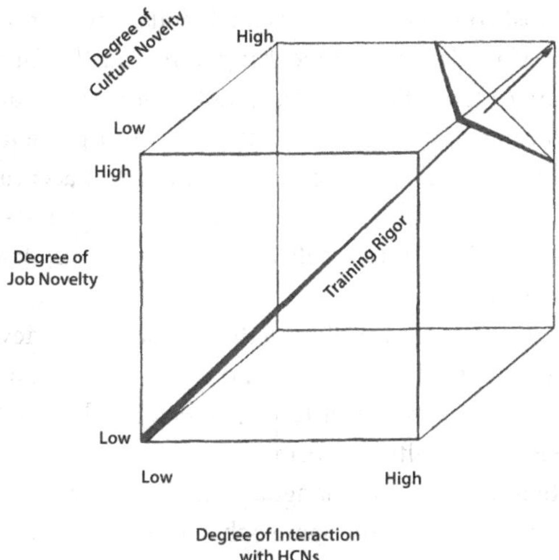

Source: Black & Mendenhall (1989), p. 528.

Figure 9.5   Integration training contingency factors

As shown in Figure 9.5, the vertical axis represents job novelty, the horizontal axis the degree of interaction with the host culture, and the front to back axis the degree of cultural novelty. Since each of the context dimensions may not have an equal effect on training rigor the degree of rigor required is represented as a plane, the shape of which is determined by where it intersects each axis. The rationale for the model is that as the requirements of the situation become more demanding, the cross-cultural training provided should move from more passive to more participative modes. That is, while fact-oriented training might suffice in situations with low job novelty, low cultural novelty, and low interaction requirements, more analytical and experiential elements are required at the other end of the spectrum. Use of rules of thumb such as this one depends on adequate time to design and deliver training.

One interesting recent development is the notion of providing training at multiple points of time rather than only pre-departure when training is typically offered.[59] This has been referred to as *sequential*[60] or *real time*[61] training. While pre-departure training can support one's transition to the assignment country, there are added benefits to continuing the training post-arrival through individualized coaching or mentoring programs, occurring after the employee has had some experience and has a higher learning readiness.[62] Such an approach is consistent with the idea that training is (or should be) a process and not an event.[63]

Foreign language training

While English may be becoming the lingua franca of international business,[64] the importance of foreign language training for expatriates and their families cannot be overemphasized. The fact that English dominates business transactions is largely a by-product of Anglo-American economic dominance in the 20th century and the unwillingness of many British and American people to learn languages other than their own.[65] This ethnocentrism is reflected in surveys of overseas executives. When asked if speaking a foreign language was important to their success, executives from Australia, Canada, the United Kingdom, and the United States said it was unimportant, while executives from Europe, Asia, and South American said it was critical.[66] Broad-based research indicates that foreign language skill is a prerequisite for intercultural adjustment and is related to the ability of the expatriate to form accurate expectations of the new cultural environment.[67] In addition, the lack of foreign language skills can have a negative effect on the strategic and operational ability of the manager in that it can limit access to important business information.

One caveat about foreign language training is that it should be viewed as only one component of cross-cultural training. That is, it is important to understand that higher degrees of fluency can lead the second language user to be perceived as having higher competency in other areas such as knowledge of cultural norms.[68] For example, cultural blunders by a foreigner who is not competent in the foreign language might be forgiven consistent with his or her level of language fluency. However, the same behavior by a fluent speaker of the language can be perceived negatively, because the person should know better based on his or her level of language fluency.

Training for family members

As discussed ahead in Chapter 11, one of the main reasons that expatriate assignments do not achieve their desired results is that family members (in particular the accompanying spouse or partner) have difficulty adapting to the foreign cultural environment. Surveys of global mobility experts in MNEs suggest that not all organizations offer training for the entire family.[69] This is unfortunate as the expatriate's partner may have the most difficult role during an international relocation, because they may have a greater exposure to the host culture but lack the continuity that membership in the organization provides to the expatriate.[70] Equipping them appropriately by providing training contributes not only to their own adjustment but to the expatriate's success as well.

Limits of international assignments as a development tool

International assignments are considered a key tool for leadership development,[71] but their limitations should be acknowledged too. First, as noted previously, assignments character-ized by novelty and challenges are most likely to lead to global management development. Organizations often shelter their expatriates by creating cultural bubbles that isolate them from having to engage with the local culture. If they are met by a chauffeur at the airport, pro-vided accommodation very similar to what they have at home regardless of the context of the local country, provided with staff that essentially prevents them from figuring out anything on their own, they will be unlikely to experience much change in their mental maps of how things are done differently in different parts of the world.[72]

Second, assignments can develop some competencies but not others. For example, one study[73] asked three groups of employees (potential expatriates not yet on assignment, current expatriates, and repatriates) to rate themselves on global competencies. There were no differ-ences in how the groups assessed their *personality traits*; those who had been on assignment reported having more *knowledge* compared to potential expatriates; and, intriguingly, employ-ees who had been on overseas assignments rated themselves *lower* on some *cross-cultural abil-ities* as compared to their colleagues who had not yet worked internationally. It was not that their abilities had diminished after their assignments but rather they were humbled by their international experience. Their assignments had helped them develop an acute sensitivity to the challenges of working in another context and they "knew what they did not know." Thus, it appears that the most valuable developmental aspect of international assignments might be the development of an appreciation for the complexities of transacting business across national borders and the related cognitive complexity that stems from this understanding.

Third, assignments are not equally beneficial for everyone. Instead, they provide more opportunities for learning for individuals that are more open to the foreign experience (e.g., those that possess certain personality characteristics, like conscientiousness, extraversion, or openness, or higher motivation to learn).[74] Related to this, while many assume that one can learn the most in environments that are very different and distinct from one's home country, studies have shown that people with lower initial cross-cultural competencies learn more in settings with *lower* rather than cultural novelty, as settings that are too different may provide too large of a stretch, which may limit the lessons learned from their experience.[75] In summary, the effectiveness of international assignments and other global management developmental initiatives is not guaranteed but rather depends both on the characteristics of the assignment and the individual characteristics of the assignee.

Training for non-traditional assignments

In recent years, short-term and other non-traditional international assignments have become a popular alternative to long-term postings (see Chapter 11). However, formal training for these employees who make up a large proportion of the international workforce, seems to get little if any attention. Box 9.3 provides an example of the life of the frequent business traveler.

BOX 9.3   SENIOR EXECUTIVE, AUSTRALIAN MULTINATIONAL

On average, I would go to Asia for two weeks and come back, go to the US for two weeks and come back, go to Europe for two weeks and come back. The next time I went to Asia probably go to a different part of it. I guess I was away – if you accumulated it – for 8 to 9 months of the year.

Source: Welch & Worm (2006).

Working in non-traditional assignments such as international short-term/project work or frequent business travel poses considerable pressures such as:[76]

- Intense pace of work
- Being accountable for one's work to more than one supervisor
- Difficulties adjusting to any one location given the limited time spent there
- Stress related to intensive travel and associated health concerns
- Unpredictability of work schedules and employees' limited ability to exercise control over them
- Insufficient support from the organization.

HR departments (particularly global mobility departments) tend to have more limited involvement with non-traditional international assignments. Their activities are largely confined to expatriate management and international relocation. However, non-traditional assignees may have significant training needs. In addition to enduring the obvious stress of frequent travel and family separation, these employees often have critical business interactions in a variety of different local contexts on a very regular basis. However, their training seems to be primarily of the "on the job" variety with little if any involvement of HR. The support of these employees where "the job is the travel and travel is the job" is a current challenge for Global HR.[77]

Company-sponsored volunteering assignments: an example of novel approaches to global management development

The global competitive environment has changed the way organizations handle global mobility (see Chapter11). There is a general trend for decreasing the number of long-term expatriates in favor of alternative work arrangements of much shorter duration. Among other issues, this also poses a challenge for leadership development. Given the value of personal experience and the diminishing number of long-term assignments, forward-thinking organizations need novel approaches to continue to cultivate global leaders.

One example is a very different type of "expatriate" program: company-sponsored volunteering assignments or service-learning assignments in which participants are sent abroad for a shorter period of time to tackle important community issues. The programs are designed to provide rich experiences that serve as fertile ground for learning.[78] Early results suggest that these programs have great potential for global leadership development.[79] Table 9.3 provides

Table 9.3 Volunteerism programs

	PricewaterhouseCoopers' The Ulysses Program (Ulysses)	*Pfizer's Global Fellows Program (GHF)*	*EY's Americas Corporate Responsibility Fellows Program (ACRFP)*	*IBM's Corporate Service Corps (CSC)*	*Intel Education Service Corps Program (IESC*	*The Novartis Entrepreneurial Leadership Program (ELP)*
Program description	A highly structured leadership-development program in which multicultural teams work in developing countries in collaboration with social organizations	A global skills-based volunteer program that places Pfizer employees in short-term assignments with leading international development organizations in developing and emerging markets	A skill-based volunteering program helping to improve the success of high impact entrepreneurs operating within emerging markets in Latin America	An international community service assignment and leadership development program for high- potential IBM employees inspired by the US Peace Corps	An International Corporate Volunteering program enabling talented employees to work with NGOs in developing countries to support the deployment of Intel classmate PCs including teaching and training	An action-based leadership development program sending global teams of talent to emerging markets to develop a solution to country-specific health challenges
Key focus area	Various: Economic and social development, health, education, environment, etc.	Social: Health	Economic: SME development	Various: Social, economic, business, environment, education, health, etc.	A skill-based volunteering program helping to improve the success of high impact entrepreneurs operating within emerging markets in Latin America	Social: Health
Length of program	8 weeks	3-6 months	7 weeks	4 weeks	2 weeks	4 weeks

Table 9.3 continued

	PricewaterhouseCoopers' The Ulysses Program (Ulysses)	Pfizer's Global Fellows Program (GHF)	EY's Americas Corporate Responsibility Fellows Program (ACRFP)	IBM's Corporate Service Corps (CSC)	Intel Education Service Corps Program (IESC	The Novartis Entrepreneurial Leadership Program (ELP)
Examples of activities in which participants engage	E.g., creating framework for good governance, anticorruption and poverty reduction	E.g., optimizing supply chains and business functions Scaling up promising health prevention approaches	Utilizing the workplace skills and knowledge (in accounting, tax, audit, IT and project management): Improving a range of business processes	Increasing the competitiveness of SMEs by, e.g., Strategy development, Marketing, HR Management; Organizational design: Special projects (websites, feasibility studies etc.)	Primarily technical installation, setting up and troubleshooting of hardware and software; Training of teachers, students and school leaders on the effective use of technology	E.g. stakeholder dialogue/ engagement, esp. in low-income settings; Analyzing market conditions and patient journey; Developing business models or improved service delivery opportunities
Examples of claimed benefits for participants	Leadership capabilities and other soft skills; Team-work skills; Position-related outcomes	Leadership capabilities and other soft skills; Experience from developing and emerging markets; Hard and technical skills	Leadership capabilities and other soft skills	Leadership capabilities and other soft skills; Team-work skills; Experience from developing and emerging markets	Leadership capabilities and other soft skills; Team-work skills; Experience from developing and emerging markets; Hard and technical skills	Leadership capabilities and other soft skills; Team-work skills; Experience from developing and emerging markets

Source: Pless & Borecká (2014).

examples of six programs launched by large MNEs in collaboration with local or international organizations.

These programs vary in their design, length of placement, number of participants, composition of volunteering teams, and how the pre-assignment, field, and post assignment phases are managed. Typically they are targeted only to current and future leaders and are not broadly offered. Not all of them are formally part of the global management initiatives, but regardless of their stated objectives, such programs are proving to have beneficial outcomes not only for the individual participants but also for the broader organization and the broader community.[80]

Company-sponsored volunteering assignments develop awareness and appreciation of differences across contexts and raise cultural empathy and sensitivity.[81] Participants are often pushed outside their comfort zones, are exposed to very different conditions of living and working and are placed in situations in which they face ambiguity and cultural and ethical paradoxes. The exposure to many pressing issues stemming from poverty, hardship, and inequality can challenge long-held views and can enhance leaders' ethical mindsets and socially responsible behavior.[82] Such assignments also create skills that can be applied to one's present work. Participants can gain a better understanding of emerging markets, service delivery under challenging circumstances, working with multiple stakeholders, working in teams, or enhanced project management or technical skills. Such gains can spill over to the larger organization through process improvement, knowledge building, and capacity building.[83]

As is the case for other global management development initiatives, these programs must be well designed. Volunteer assignments are more valuable when they happen in a novel context, when volunteers perceive that their projects make a meaningful contribution, when volunteers receive adequate social support and when they can use their professional skills.[84] An important aspect of such programs is debrief and individual reflection, during which participants analyze their experiences and extract key lessons learned.[85]

CHAPTER SUMMARY

The challenge for global organizations is to develop individuals at all levels and in a variety of locations. Until recently Global HR has been primarily concerned with the training of expatriates for international assignments. Their focus has shifted to the development of global managers. The Global HR department is concerned with the training and development needs of employees in all the locations in which it does business. Training and development should be based on needs analysis of the competencies required for a particular job or set of jobs. A key competency required from international managers is working with individuals from different cultures and countries and conducting operations on a global basis. An important way of developing these abilities is to provide employees with challenging assignments that expand their thinking beyond domestic borders.

An effective way to provide challenging assignments that develop managers is an international posting. For international assignments to be successful developmental experiences, managers must be suitably prepared, which commonly involves cross-cultural and language training. However, different types of overseas assignments need different types and levels of cross-cultural training. The required level of training can be determined by the degree of cultural novelty, degree of interaction with local nationals, and the novelty of the assignment job. Cross-cultural training can range from fact-oriented training though analytical to experiential types of training. Over the years, as MNEs have gained experience in expatriating employees, many firms have also recognized the importance of training for the assignee's spouse and family. As patterns of global mobility in recent years have shifted away from long-term expatriation, Global HR departments have also had to consider training and support for short-term and non-traditional assignments. MNEs are also beginning to experiment with innovative approaches to global leadership development such as international volunteer assignments.

QUESTIONS FOR DISCUSSION

1. Why should the global organization be concerned with the educational system in countries in which it does business?
2. What are the most important competencies for global managers? Why?
3. What is considered to be the most effective approach to developing global managers?
4. If cross-cultural training is so effective, why don't all firms make it mandatory?
5. Should fluency in a foreign language be a requirement for global managers? Why or why not?
6. Why are company-sponsored volunteering assignments gaining popularity as a way to develop global leadership skills?

NOTES

1. Thomas, Lazarova, & Inkson (2005).
2. Fitzgerald (1992).
3. Aguinis & Kraiger (2009).
4. Tregaskis & Heraty (2018).
5. http://www.nationmaster.com/graph/edu_lit_tot_pop-education-literacy-total-population
6. https://www.oecd.org/pisa/PISA-results_ENGLISH.png
7. https://www.insead.edu/sites/default/files/assets/dept/globalindices/docs/GTCI-2020-report.pdf
8. Mabey & Ramirez (2012) and Van der Klink & Mulder (1995).
9. Dessler (2011).
10. Lazarova, Mayrhofer, Briscoe, Dickmann, Hall, & Parry (2018).
11. Peretz & Rosenblatt (2011).
12. https://www.eurofound.europa.eu/observatories/emcc/erm/legislation/france-employers-obligation-to-provide-skill-development-plans-or-training
13. http://legisquebec.gouv.qc.ca/enr/showdoc/cs/D-8.3
14. Baumgarten (1995).
15. Briscoe, Schuler, & Tarique (2012).
16. Neeley, Hinds & Cramton (2012); Piekkari & Tietze (2012).
17. Yamazaki (2005).

18. Briscoe, Schuler, & Tarique (2012).

19. https://ec.europa.eu/esf/main.jsp?catId=35&langId=en

20. We note here that many make an important distinction between *managers* and *leaders*, but examining this issue in detail is well beyond the scope of this book. Also, *global management development programs* can be referred to as *international management development programs, global leadership development programs,* or *executive development programs,* and the like. In practice, there is little difference.

21. House, Dorfman, Javidan, Hanges, & Sully de Luque (2014); House, Hanges, Javidan, Dorfman, & Gupta (2004).

22. Woodall (2011).

23. Woodall (2011).

24. Jones (1986).

25. Ran & Huang (2019).

26. Similarly, cross-cultural competencies are known by many names, such as global competencies, global leadership competencies, and international competencies, global executive competencies. We use these terms synonymously in this chapter.

27. Adapted from Caligiuri (2006).

28. Morrison (2000).

29. See for example Kets de Vries, Vrinaud, & Florent-Treacy (2004); Mendenhall & Osland (2002); Vijayakumar, Morley, Heraty, Mendenhall, & Osland (2018).

30. Evans, Pucik, & Barsoux (2002).

31. Black & Gregerson (2000).

32. This section based on Black & Mendenhall (1989) and Mendenhall & Oddou (2012).

33. The cultural assimilator uses a series of critical incidents that involve some sort of culture clash or misunderstanding. The trainee reads the incident and selects one of several explanations (attributions) and then receives feedback on the appropriateness of his or her choice. Through repeated exposure trainees learn to make attributions similar to those made by the culture involved.

34. Brislin, MacNab, & Nayani (2008).

35. McCall (1998).

36. Evans, Pucik, & Barsoux (2002); McCall (1998).

37. Bell, Tannenbaum, Ford, Noe, & Kraiger (2017).

38. Wilson & Yip (2010).

39. Caligiuri & Tarique (2012b).

40. Ran and Huang (2019).

41. Caligiuri & Tarique (2009).

42. Dragoni, Oh, Tesluk, Moore, VanKatwyk, & Hazucha (2014).

43. Dragoni, Oh, Tesluk, Moore, VanKatwyk, & Hazucha (2014).

44. Caligiuri & Tarique (2012b).

45. See Levy, Beechler, Taylor, & Boyacigiller (2007).

46. Evans, Pucik, & Björkman (2011).

47. See Tadmor & Tetlock (2006).

48. KPMG (2018).

49. Mendenhall & Oddou (1985).

50. KPMG (2018).

51. http://globalmobilitytrends.bgrs.com/#/insights

52. Caligiuri & Tarique (2006); KPMG (2018).

53. Caligiuri (1997).

54. Morris & Robie (2001).

55. Ran & Huang (2019).

56. Caligiuri & Tarique (2012a).

57. Littrell, Salas, Hess, Paley, & Riedel (2006).

58. Based on Black & Mendenhall (1989); Tung (1981, 1998).

59. KPMG (2018).

60. Selmer, Torbiörn, & de Leon (1998).

61. Mendenhall & Stahl (2000).

62. Mendenhall & Stahl (2000).

63. Baumgarten (1995).

64. Naisbett & Aburdene (1990); Neeley (2012).

65. Thomas & Inkson (2009).

66. Tung (1998).

67. Caligiuri, Phillips, Lazarova, Tarique, & Bürgi (2001); Puck, Kittler & Wright (2008).

68. Hui & Cheng (1987).

69. Brookfield Global Relocation Services (2012).

70. Briody & Chrisman (1991).

71. Evans, Pucik, & Björkman (2011).

72. Mendenhall, Osland, Bird, Oddou, & Maznevski (2008).

73. Caligiuri & DiSanto (2001).

74. Caligiuri & Dragoni (2015); Caligiuri & Tarique (2012a).

75. Caligiuri, Mencin, Jayne, & Traylor (2019).

76. Baker & Ciuk (2015); Suutari, Brewster, Riusala, & Syrjäkari (2013).

77. See Welch & Worm (2006).

78. Pless & Borecká (2014).

79. Caligiuri, Mencin, Jayne, & Traylor (2019).

80. Pless & Borecká (2014).

81. Pless, Maak, & Stahl (2011, 2012); Caligiuri, Mencin, & Jiang (2013).

82. Pless, Maak, & Stahl (2011); Pless & Borecká (2014).

83. Caligiuri, Mencin, Jayne, & Traylor (2019); Pless & Borecká (2014).

84. Caligiuri, Mencin, & Jiang (2013); Caligiuri, Mencin, Jayne, & Traylor (2019).

85. Pless, Maak, & Stahl (2012).

10
Global performance management and compensation

After reading this chapter you should be able to:

1. Describe the objectives of a global performance management system.
2. Explain how and why performance management systems are different in different countries.
3. Identify the issues in performance appraisal of expatriates.
4. Explain the influence of national differences on compensation systems.
5. Outline best practices in compensation programs for expatriates.

Home on the Bosphorus

It had been three years since Maya Trudeau had visited her old university friend Yasemin Önal in Istanbul. They had both received their MBA from McGill University in Canada five years ago and Maya had jumped at the chance to visit Yasemin in Istanbul. She remembered being a little surprised when Yasemin had offered to "have Mustafa, her driver, pick her up from the airport." She knew that as an area manager for one of the world's largest pharmaceutical companies that her compensation would be pretty good. However, nothing had quite prepared her for the fabulous apartment in the up market Bebek neighborhood, with its panoramic view of the brightly lit Bebek Mosque and the fishing boats on the Bosphorus. Plus the car and driver, and Dugyu her housekeeper.

Shortly after receiving her degree, Yasemin had been offered the position in Istanbul. She was already a senior product manager, and the opportunity to work in Turkey where she could use the language she learned as a child but never used in Canada had been a big attraction. Compensation hadn't really been on the top of her list of issues to discuss, so she was very pleased that Pharmaceutico had a clear policy about salary and benefits for foreign assignments. Her base salary was 120% of what it would be in Canada, health care was taken care of and she was protected from double taxation in Turkey. The company had paid for the apartment, car and driver and so on and deducted 7% from her salary to cover. And, overall the cost of living in Istanbul was just about the same as Montreal.

However, the days of having a housekeeper and a driver were over, at least for now. The political situation in Turkey coupled with the COVID-19 pandemic had caused Pharmaceutico to recall Yasemin to Montreal to run the Middle East operations from there. Of course Yasemin would miss the perks associated with an expatriate assignment, but more important to her was that now the evaluation of her performance might no longer include factors such as the ability to develop and maintain good relationships with foreign nationals that had allowed her to be so successful in Turkey. Pharmaceutico was learning how productive and effective managers could be using the latest in online collaborative tools. She wondered how much thought had been given to how the performance of area managers was going to be evaluated in this new environment.

But, right now it was time to visit her old friend Maya. And, Maya had done her best to make Yasemin's favorite dish, Imam bayildi[1] for a welcome home dinner.

INTRODUCTION

The "care and feeding" of expatriate executives such as Yasemin is only one aspect of global performance management and compensation. Global organizations need performance management systems that achieve the best return on the investment made in all their employees, and the global environment requires a consideration of both cultural differences in performance management and institutional differences in compensation practices. Organizations with strong performance management systems are much more likely to outperform their competitors both on financial and non-financial (e.g., customer satisfaction, employee retention, product and service quality) indicators of performance.[2] Performance management systems are increasingly used for identifying organizational talent, leadership development and succession planning and they tie with compensation strategy. Performance management is increasingly seen as a critical tool that allows an organization to achieve high-performance culture[3] and is an extremely important aspect of global HRM.

PERFORMANCE MANAGEMENT

Performance management consists of a range of activities designed to enhance the performance of employees and/or groups so that organizational effectiveness is improved.[4] Performance management systems have components that can be evaluative (providing feedback and making pay and future job decisions) and/or developmental (helping employees improve their performance and enhancing engagement through recognition of achievements).[5] A performance management system might include a broad set of performance management interventions. However, the central component of most performance management systems is the performance appraisal process.

Performance appraisal process

To provide employees with effective feedback about their performance against goals, performance appraisal processes need to address the following elements:[6]

- *How will the evaluation be conducted?* The process for conducting the evaluation includes the responsibilities of the employee and the evaluator(s), specific steps, dates, venue and so on. The specific steps will vary considerably among organizations, but the critical factor is the communication of the process to everyone involved.
- *Who will conduct the evaluation?* While it may seem obvious that all employees need to be aware who is ultimately responsible for evaluating their performance, the complex structures of global organizations make this less than straightforward. For example, expatriates may often find themselves reporting to both a headquarters and a local supervisor for various aspects of their role.
- *When will the evaluation be conducted?* Many traditional systems rely on annual performance appraisals, but numerous options are available, including quarterly or biennial reviews, end of project evaluations and so on. Ad hoc (when the supervisor has time) evaluations often seem to substitute for a carefully scheduled process but have the potential of undermining the process.
- *What will be evaluated?* Options for what should be evaluated include traits, behavior, and outcomes. The merits of evaluations based on each of these measures have long been debated.[7] Their use depends on the organization's culture, objectives, management philosophy and the extent to which the criteria are perceived as legitimate in the broader socio-cultural context.
- *What are the potential consequences of the evaluation?* The effectiveness of performance appraisals in meeting the objectives of the organization rests on making the connection between the performance appraisal and these outcomes clear. Tying rewards to the results of performance reviews makes them more effective for two reasons: (a) when rewards (pay, bonuses, stock options) are involved, all parties are likely to take them seriously, (b) when significant financial rewards (and continued employment) are on the line, it is more likely that organizations will spend more time developing and training individuals to use their performance management systems properly.[8]

PERFORMANCE MANAGEMENT IN A GLOBAL CONTEXT

The challenges in implementing global performance management systems result from the differences in cultural and institutional contexts associated with international operations. Even the purpose of performance appraisal itself may vary across cultures ranging from determining individual rewards, to developing long-term potential, or maintaining group harmony.[9]

Cultural and institutional factors

Culture and institutional factors can have wide-ranging influence on performance management systems in terms of performance criteria or standards, supervisor–subordinate relationships, and the consequences of the appraisal.[10] One of the most significant issues in performance evaluation is called the "criterion problem" – what constitutes good performance? In the global context the problem is heightened because what is considered good performance can be culture-bound. For example, in individualist cultures evaluation systems tend to be based on individual employee productivity, timeliness, quality of output, and job-specific knowledge and proficiency. In these cases, performance measures are objective, quantifiable and observable. In contrast, in collectivist cultures where the in-group can be valued more than individual productivity, high-performing employees who stand out may disturb group harmony. While work outcomes are important, social and relational criteria such as trustworthiness, a respectful attitude, awareness of duties and obligations, gratitude, and conformity carry more weight.[11]

Even off-the-job behavior has been traditionally considered a legitimate criterion in some cultures.[12] Recently, even in countries where off-the-job behavior was largely hidden to employers (and therefore not considered in any performance management decisions) advances in technology have caused a noticeable change. Employees are being disciplined over posting personal opinions on social media platforms or on the basis of digitally recorded instances of inappropriate (off-the-job) behavior, sometimes resulting in severe consequences such as losing their jobs.[13]

Culture also influences the appropriateness of performance appraisal processes and how feedback is given. For example, the popular multi-source (360 degree) feedback method is only appropriate in low power distance cultures in which high levels of participation is the norm, such as in the United States. Self-appraisals are more likely to be used in individualistic than in collectivistic countries.[14] For example, in Japan only 10% of employees contributed to their own evaluation, compared to 61% in Spain and 94% in the UK (the most individualistic country of these three).[15] In high power distance cultures, performance appraisal is more likely to be a top-down one-way process,[16] initiated by a trusted or expert superior.[17] A directive and autocratic style of delivering feedback is common while open discussions between supervisor and employee are not expected. Feedback in collectivist cultures is likely to be:

- indirect and subtle,
- non-confrontational,
- delivered to the workgroup as opposed to individuals,[18]
- and not challenged as it comes from a powerful authority figure.[19]

Even positive feedback delivered to individuals in these cultures can be seen as disturbing group harmony.[20]

Institutional factors such as the legal and employee relations system operating in a country influence how performance appraisals are conducted and the extent to which information is shared. In countries where performance appraisals are potentially open to external scrutiny, such as the United States, they may be very detailed and well documented.[21] In contrast, EU regulations considered much of performance evaluation to be private data and as such, organizations are limited in how these data can be used and transferred.[22] In countries with a strong tradition of collective bargaining, such as Germany, performance management systems have a high level of worker involvement through works councils and similar groups, and the focus is on long-term career, job security and technical development.[23] And, while the strict labor laws in France dictate many aspects of performance management systems, the hierarchical French culture accepts that such factors as the university a person attended and their position in the organization will influence performance appraisal.[24]

Although it is impossible to outline all of the variation in performance management systems that exist across the world, these examples should alert us to the importance of designing systems that align with local realities, while serving organizational objectives.

Organizational factors

Since the overriding goal of performance management strategies is to encourage behavior that helps the organization meet its goals, performance management systems will reflect the industry in which the firm operates as well as firm strategy. For example, compared to service organizations, those in advanced manufacturing industries have performance criteria that are narrow and task-related. And private sector firms tend to use more specific and outcome-based criteria than public sector organizations. Organizations that require innovation and creativity will likely use performance criteria that are broadly defined and process- rather than outcome-oriented.[25] Finally, large organizations tend to have more formal performance management systems, consistent with a more formal HRM structure overall (as discussed in Chapter 4).

The fact that MNEs operate subsidiaries across a variety of locations creates an additional set of issues for the performance management of subsidiaries and their employees. These issues include: the importance of firm versus subsidiary goals, differences in performance criteria and data across country contexts, and the additional difficulties imposed by time and distance between organizational units.

Firm versus subsidiary goals: Global firms often make strategic decisions based on the overall long-term impact on the organization, as opposed to the short-term effect on a particular subsidiary. For example, a firm might decide to withhold needed investment in a particular subsidiary in order to focus activity, and ultimately move production to another market, thus negatively affecting the short-term performance of the subsidiary. Or an organization might establish a joint venture in a particular geographic location simply as a temporary measure without the intent of supporting it long-term. In cases such as these, performance of the affected subsidiary and its management should take into account organizational-level strategy.

Consistency of criteria and data: The volatility of the global environment, as well as national differences in the availability of data, increase the difficulty in specifying performance criteria that apply across the organization. For example, managers of a foreign subsidiary may have less control over profit levels because of exchange rate fluctuations, price controls, and differences in accounting standards, making profit an unfair standard appraisal criterion. In addition, in the global environment subsidiaries are affected differently by issues such as natural disasters, political and labor unrest, or terrorism, making the use of standard performance criteria based on subsidiary performance questionable. For example, imagine the manager of a mine in Chile who single handedly averted a strike that would have shut down production for months (considered a major accomplishment by his Chilean colleagues), but who received only an average performance rating based on mine productivity.[26]

Geographic separation of organizational units: A third factor that constrains global performance management is the geographic and time differences among far-flung organizational units that result in low levels of contact between individuals in headquarters and subsidiaries. The infrequency of contact forces MNEs to design performance management systems that rely less on face-to-face interactions.[27] Advances in communications technology can provide solutions to geographic separation. However, these sophisticated performance management systems are not perfect substitutes for clearly specifying roles, processes, and procedures[28] and cannot always account for country-specific factors.

Technology can drive the content of performance management systems, by focusing attention on those aspects of performance that can be easily captured. For example, it is easier to record the number of calls a customer service representative handles than it is to assess the satisfaction of the customer with the service. However, increasingly affordable web-based systems allow for gathering more information from a variety of sources, including monitoring employees that work remotely.[29] Advances in technology have also enhanced HR information systems, which have allowed for corporate-wide standardization of key elements of the performance management system and for central control in many MNEs.[30] Many MNEs use single performance management systems for all employees and differences among MNEs are harder to detect as, regardless of their country of origin, global organizations tend to adopt similar performance management practices and benchmark against each other.[31]

In addition to managing performance of employees across subsidiaries, MNEs face the additional challenge of assessing the performance of expatriate employees sent to a foreign country for both long and short-term assignments. It is the special situation of performance appraisal for these employees that we discuss next.

PERFORMANCE MANAGEMENT OF EXPATRIATES

Assessing expatriate performance is not always straightforward. Beyond their *task performance* (i.e., completion of tasks formally recognized to be part of their jobs and meeting organizational objectives), one must also account for their *contextual performance* (i.e., establishing and maintaining relationships and effectively interacting with host-country colleagues, representing the MNE to the local customers and the broader community, following ethical standards, mentoring and coaching local employees).[32] In addition, developing and transferring knowledge and skills to others in the organization is also important to consider.[33] Such knowledge and skills can pertain either to the local market or may involve more general lessons related to doing business globally. Finally, there are aspects of performance unique to the expatriate experience such as handling emergencies or crises, handling work stress, and solving problems creatively.[34] Such factors are rarely visible to those who do not work closely with the expatriate.

Expatriate performance can also be viewed through different lenses by local nationals and home country supervisors.[35] This complexity makes performance management of expatriates challenging even under the best of circumstances. A systematic approach to designing appropriate expatriate performance appraisal begins with asking the fundamental questions of: (a) who conducts the appraisal, (b) what criteria are assessed, (c) when and how often appraisals are they conducted, and (d) what format is used?[36]

Who conducts expatriate appraisal?

The issue of who conducts expatriate appraisal is complicated by the differing expectations that host country stakeholders and the home country management have for expatriates. Performance appraisal from these different sources runs the risk of offering different judgments of an expatriate's performance. Because the overseas context varies widely and can be a major determinant of expatriate performance,[37] appraisers need to understand the foreign context in which the expatriate must perform. While host country stakeholders may be more aware of the contextual issues surrounding expatriate performance,[38] home country superiors may have a clearer picture of the goals of the expatriate assignment. Often, performance appraisals are conducted by the expatriate's immediate supervisor as opposed to HR professionals, under the assumption that the immediate supervisor is in the best position to evaluate a subordinate's performance.[39] However, as discussed previously, if the expatriate's performance is tied to that of the local subsidiary, the remoteness of a headquarters superior could influence the effectiveness of the evaluation.

Alternatives to immediate supervisor appraisals include peer appraisals, rating committees, self-ratings, subordinate ratings and multiple (360 degree) rater feedback.[40] Each of these has its advantages and disadvantages and the extent to which they are considered legitimate in various societies will vary widely. However, many firms recognize the advantage of using more than one rater in assessing expatriate performance to achieve a more balanced view of expatriate performance. Perhaps not surprisingly, organizations often use more than one rater to evaluate expatriates[41] and nearly five times as many organizations have reported conducting performance reviews in the host versus the home country (45% and 9% respectively), with some organizations conducting performance reviews in both countries (26%).[42] Assignment goals are more likely to be aligned with the host-country goal-setting process (25%) than the home-country goal-setting process (18%). It is also common (22%) to establish specific assignment-related goals for individual assignees.[43]

What expatriate performance criteria are assessed?

Deciding what is to be measured and evaluated in expatriate appraisal is more complicated than in domestic situations. Assignments differ in what expatriates are expected to accomplish, with some assignments being very technical while others are more strategic.[44] However, certain aspects of performance criteria apply across situations.

Performance criteria can be *objective* (hard) or *subjective* (soft). Specific *contextual* criteria are also considered.[45] *Objective* criteria are used to assess task performance and tend to be outcome-based (profits, market share, etc.). They are typically easy to interpret and can be more easily defended legally.[46] Such hard criteria might appear to be comparable across employees and organizational units, but the complexity of expatriate performance context can create inconsistent data. In addition, objective measurable criteria are often not available.[47] *Subjective* criteria typically relate to relationship or trait-based goals (for example, how good the expatriate is at establishing relationships with host-country national constituents). Soft criteria reflect critical aspects of the expatriate role that are difficult to capture but they are just as important as hard criteria for comprehensive evaluation of expatriate performance.[48] However, their subjective nature makes them susceptible to an almost limitless list of biases.[49]

Contextual criteria assess factors that reflect the specific expatriate positing and the specific subsidiary context (for example, how successful the expatriate is in terms of developing a local successor or transferring the corporate culture to a subsidiary that was obtained through a local acquisition). Given that by definition such criteria reflect the situation in unique contexts, comparisons across subunits can be difficult. They can also be challenging to interpret, particularly for assessors who do not have experience as expatriates themselves.

When and how often should expatriate appraisals be conducted?

While the *annual* performance appraisal is enshrined in many organizations, conducting performance appraisal once or even twice year may be insufficient.[50] Not only is it difficult for raters to recall information over the previous six to twelve months, but the more recent information is likely to be given more weight in the evaluation.[51] Also, frequent performance appraisals are more likely to have a developmental component.[52] In addition, the international context of the expatriate assignment suggests more frequent appraisals given that business and environmental conditions change quickly. More frequent check-ins also create an opportunity for the raters to become more familiar with the expatriate, the job, and the required performance.[53]

What format should be used in expatriate appraisal?

Many organizations develop standardized formats for particular job categories. The use of standard performance appraisal formats is based on maintaining a system that has been validated, has identified baselines, and minimizes future development costs.[54] This makes sense if the context of employee performance is relatively stable. However, the context of an expatriate assignment is very fluid and can change greatly. Standardized formats can rarely capture the complexity of international assignments and should be customized to specific country contexts and expatriate roles.[55] Yet, many firms use the same standardized appraisal forms for expatriate appraisal.[56]

In summary, expatriate assignments have a number of unique elements that should be considered when designing a performance management system. Despite these unique aspects of expatriate performance management, many firms, regardless of where their overseas subsidiaries are based, treat the performance appraisal of expatriates as extensions of domestic evaluation systems.[57] Appropriately evaluating expatriate performance is important not only to the expatriate, but also for creating competitive advantage for the organization. Therefore, the performance management system for expatriates should be modified to fit the overseas position and the particular country context. This may entail creating a development cycle that involves continuously re-evaluating expatriates and including input from returned expatriates and/or outside experts who specialize in these areas.[58] Organizations are also introducing new forms of global mobility such as short-term or project work, which make it difficult to isolate the international and the domestic aspects of the job, in turn making it more difficult to assess individual performance.[59]

Performance management is integral to other aspects of global HRM such as training and development and international mobility and careers. However, one of the key linkages with the evaluative component of performance management is the relationship to organizational rewards. Therefore, the remainder of this chapter is concerned with compensation in a global business environment

COMPENSATION IN A GLOBAL CONTEXT

Compensation refers to all forms of pay to employees as a result of their employment and consists of direct financial compensation (wages, salaries, incentives, commissions, and bonuses) and indirect financial compensation (benefits such as employer-paid insurance and vacations).[60] Certain principles of compensation hold across countries. For example, time-based pay (paying someone hourly, weekly, monthly) and performance-based pay (e.g., pay based on commission, incentives for achieving and exceeding goals) form the foundation of most organizational direct compensation plans.

Pay levels (the amount employees receive from their employers) and pay mixes (how different direct compensation elements are mixed to shape employees total compensation packages) differ widely from country to country. For example, levels of total executive compensation in the United States far exceed levels in other countries; and variable compensation of executives can vary from 5% in Mexico to 55% in the USA.[61] Compared to other HRM practices, there is probably most variation in compensation approaches across countries.[62] This variability can be traced to differences in institutional, economic, organizational and cultural environments, differences in social norms, as well as the historical development of compensation practices.[63]

National variation in compensation systems

The large number of factors that affect differences in compensations systems can be reduced to a small number of broad elements: national culture, institutions in the form of social contracts, employee relations, ownership structures, management autonomy, and common practices.[64]

National culture

As discussed in Chapter 2, societal level culture influences HRM policies and practices through the extent to which members of society see the practice as important, beneficial and legitimate. Therefore, we would expect preferences for compensation policies and practices to be consistent with culturally based values. For example, hierarchical compensation systems would be prevalent in high power distance cultures, fixed salary programs in high uncertainty avoidance cultures, individual-based pay for performance systems in individualistic cultures, differential pay policies that allow inequalities in pay in more masculine cultures, and social benefits in more feminine cultures, and so on.[65] Some research has also suggested that compensation approaches that match the culture may result in higher organizational performance. For example, high use of merit-based awards was associated with superior performance in masculine cultures and inferior performance in feminine cultures.[66]

However, others have pointed out that the view that culture determines the effectiveness of compensation practices is somewhat simplistic and the evidence supporting this link is not entirely convincing.[67] While it makes sense to implement compensation practices that fit with the dominant cultural norms in a country, a more complete explanation of national variation in compensation systems is that it stems from the combined influence of culture and a number of institutional factors.

Institutions: social contracts

The social contract refers to the expectations and obligations of all relevant parties (government, unions, employees, employers, and business organizations) with regard to compensation. Differences exist among countries in the extent to which compensation frameworks are centralized and influenced by social legislation. For example, the United States, Canada and the United Kingdom have highly decentralized compensation systems with minimal government intervention, while Sweden, Denmark, and Belgium have highly centralized national wage systems.[68] And, France and Germany have highly regulated social welfare systems that have a direct bearing on compensation systems.[69] Different social contracts also influence the extent to which wage inequality is present and accepted in a society. For example, in Costa Rica, the top 10% of people earn nearly ten times as much as the bottom 10%; in Canada, they earn nearly four times as much, and in Nordic countries (the countries with lowest income inequality), about three times as much.[70]

The influence of government regulations and social welfare systems is strongest for employee benefits.[71] There is wide country-to-country variation in the proportion of social insurance expenditures (including health insurance, retirement and disability pensions, pay for sick leave, unemployment insurance) as a percentage of total compensation. For example, these expenditures represent around 33% of pay in Sweden, France, Italy, and Mexico but about 24% in the United States, and in the Philippines social insurance is less than 10%.[72] A big reason for these differences lies in institutional arrangements over who is responsible for funding health care. While in many countries health care insurance is provided entirely by the government, in others – the United States being a notable example here – it is funded largely as an employee benefit by employers or by individuals themselves; or for some groups (e.g., elderly and lower-income individuals) by government programs.

Employee relations: Related to the overarching social contract is the employee relations system and the presence of collective bargaining. Trade union involvement and collective bargaining agreements reduce the freedom that organizations have to unilaterally establish compensation systems. In Belgium, for example, employee compensation is established through a collective agreement with employees (through a "National Labour Council") and even employees that are not union members are covered by the agreement.[73] There is a national minimum wage, which rises in line with a government-determined price index.[74] In another example, while employment law in Germany mandates that employees receive 24 paid vacation days per year, the norm, as a direct result of collective bargaining agreements, is to provide 30 paid vacation days.[75] And, of course, employee relations influences compensation rates and income inequality, especially at the lower end of the income distribution.[76] For example, in 2016 the average hourly compensation costs in manufacturing was US$2.06 per hour in the Philippines compared to US$60.36 per hour in Switzerland.[77]

Ownership structures: Financial and ownership structures differ around the world and these differences can affect compensation structures. For example, ownership and access to capital in the United States is very dispersed, while at the opposite end of the continuum the economic structure in South Korea depends on a small number of huge family-dominated *chaebol* with strong reliance on government funding.[78] Another example of the influence of ownership structure is provided by Chinese private sector enterprises which are more likely to have performance-based compensation programs than their state-owned counterparts.[79] Ownership structures also influence the appeal of stock option plans, equity participation or equity compensation programs and profit-sharing, with clear differences in the occurrence and character of financial participation practices in companies located in different countries.[80]

Management autonomy: Managers do not have unlimited discretion in designing compensation systems and implementing reward practices, and the extent of managerial discretion varies by country. Managerial autonomy is constrained not only by law but also by the influence of trade unions and government regulations, especially as they relate to social security and tax systems. For example, employee financial participation (i.e., profit sharing, share ownership plans) varies widely across the world, mostly due to differences in tax incentives.[81] Under the US tax law, a salary (fixed component of pay) that exceeds one million dollars is not tax deductible for a firm. As a result, executive compensation in US firms tends to emphasize instead financial incentives such as bonuses and stock awards. In contrast, stock options were prohibited by the government regulations in some countries (e.g., Germany, Japan) until relatively recently.[82] Finally, within subsidiaries of MNEs, managers must align their compensation decisions with the corporate strategy of their parent organization, even if this sometimes results in practices that would not have been implemented locally, had the subsidiary managers had unrestricted autonomy.[83]

Common practices: Firms face pressure to implement practices that are commonly used by other companies in the country. As with other HRM practices, compensation is influenced by the extent to which these practices are considered legitimate and acceptable in a society. That is, organizations are influenced to be similar to each other not only because of regulation requiring particular practices, but also by mimicking other successful organizations and by adopting the best practices (norms) for compensation as established by professional organizations, consultants and the like.[84] For example, if an organization is overgenerous in compensating its executives, it may lose social support and its reputation may suffer,[85] or the use of incentive systems based on stock options may be used not only to align the interests of management with that of the organization but also to gain legitimacy by imitating the practices of other firms in the same sector. The existing practices in a country can sometimes be disrupted by outsiders: for example, US MNEs tend to transfer their financial participation practices to subsidiaries in countries where such practices were previously unknown.

Designing compensation systems within MNEs

Given the patchwork of diverse institutional and cultural factors, designing a global compensation system can be difficult even for experienced MNEs. The key challenge stems from the need to align vastly different national level factors while creating a consistent approach to compensation that is aligned with the organization's strategy.

Consider performance-based pay, commonly used around the world, as an example. A well-designed performance-based approach will be characterized by two key features, effectiveness and acceptance.[86] To be *effective* performance-based pay must reward those behaviors and outcomes that are related to the strategy of the firm. That means determining correct reward criteria that can be measured in a valid way. To be *accepted*, performance-based pay must be consistent with the institutional and organizational framework in which it exists and must motivate employees. That is, not everyone reacts to rewards in the same way and not all rewards are appropriate for all situations. Failure to recognize the motivational basis for incentive pay plans in a global context may be an important reason for a lack of success.

Another issue to consider within an MNE context is that of perceived fairness. As interconnectedness between organizational units increases, it becomes far more likely that employees will compare their compensation (not only in terms of direct pay but also in terms of benefits such as vacation days or medical insurance coverage) with that of colleagues in similar roles in other subsidiaries in the MNE. Often, such comparisons reveal specific compensation practices across countries and may bring about perceptions that employees in certain countries are better rewarded in other countries. In such cases, MNEs are best advised to ensure there is organization-wide equity in terms of "total rewards" (including all direct and indirect, extrinsic and intrinsic rewards) rather than attempt to standardize compensation practices.[87]

Strategic flexibility approach: In order to achieve strategic organizational priorities worldwide, MNEs can also adopt a *strategic flexibility approach* to compensation, whereby compensation packages consist of three related components: core, crafted, and choice. The *core* section includes compensation forms that signal the corporate global mindset (that is, whatever is of strategic importance to the MNE). The *crafted* set of compensation elements should reflect conditions at the national business unit (i.e., offer compensation deemed desirable by local employees that is culturally influenced and mandated by law). The *choice* components allow individual employees to select among various forms of total compensation that are important to them and meet their individual needs (e.g., education leave versus dental insurance), thus providing customization at the individual level. Such an approach allows MNEs to achieve both global strategic integration and local responsiveness in their compensation practices.[88]

COMPENSATION OF INTERNATIONAL ASSIGNEES

A problem particular to global compensation is designing effective systems that reward adequately individuals sent on international assignments. Managing expatriate compensation is a task that occupies a lot of the time of global mobility managers – but it is also an area that rarely meets assignee expectations.[89] A well-designed expatriate compensation system should make expatriation attractive to employees, foster the expatriate behaviors required to implement the MNE's strategy, and facilitate the transfers to and from the host country. It is equally important that it be cost effective and fair with respect to all employees, including host country nationals and expatriates across locations globally.[90] The factors that influence compensation of international assignees include:

- their nationality,
- their family situation (number and ages of children, work situation of their spouse),
- differences in exchange rates and rates of inflation,
- cost of living differences,
- host country laws regarding compensation and benefits, and
- taxes.

Traditional components of expatriate compensation

The complexity of expatriate compensation stems from the fact that working abroad temporarily gives rise to unique issues such as having to procure temporary housing, owing taxes to two – or more – countries, having to relocate one's family, meaning that one's partner may lose their income and one's children may need to be educated at an (expensive) international school. Given that most people would not take a job, international or domestic, that would put them at a financial disadvantage, organizations strive to offer carefully calibrated total rewards packages to those posted abroad. While the specific components of an expatriate's compensation can vary widely, they fall into four main categories. These are base salary, foreign service premium, allowances, and benefits.

Base salary

Base salary is the pay employees posted overseas would receive for performing their job. As discussed ahead, it can be set based on the going rate at the expatriate home office or at the host country labor market. Base pay serves as the benchmark for other forms of discretionary compensation such as merit pay bonuses and incentives and can vary substantially depending on where a company's headquarters is located. However, an example of logistical challenges faced by MNEs is protecting expatriates' net salaries from variations in tax rates. For example, the US maximum marginal tax rate is 31%, compared to 45% in Spain, 53% in Germany, and 65% in Japan. Thus, to maintain the same base salary, US expatriates must receive higher gross salaries in these host locations.[91]

Table 10.1 Hardship differential (selected locations) (percentage of base compensation)

Country (City)	Rate
Afghanistan (Kabul)	35%
Azerbaijan(Baku)	35%
Belize (Belize City)	15%
Brazil (Rio de Janeiro)	10%
Cameroon (Yaounde)	30%
China (Beijing)	20%
Ghana (Accra)	25%
India (Mumbai)	25%
Iraq (Baghdad)	30%
Kuwait (Kuwait City)	15%
Malaysia (Kuala Lampur)	15%
Mexico (Mexico City)	15%
Nigeria (Lagos)	30%
Pakistan (Islamabad)	25%
Russia (Moscow)	20%
Saudi Arabia (Jeddah)	25%
South Africa (Johannesburg)	10%
Turkey (Istanbul)	5%
Vietnam (Hanoi)	20%

Source: US Department of State, Office of Allowances, 2020 https://aoprals.state.gov/web920/location.asp?menu_id=95.

International mobility inducements

There are three types of such inducements, each with a different goal.[92]

- *Foreign service premiums* encourage employees to accept assignments in a foreign country and vary depending on base salary, typically ranging from 10% to 30% of base.
- *Mobility premiums* are lump sum bonuses made to employees for their willingness to relocate between international posts.
- *Hardship premiums* are lump sum cash bonuses paid for the adversity encountered in living in locations where conditions are difficult, unhealthy or where physical hardships are extreme (e.g., where there is threat of physical harm due to civil disobedience, civil war, terrorism, and war). Depending on the level of danger, differentials range from 5% to 35% of base salary (see Table 10.1).

For a long time, international mobility inducements were a core component of expatriate compensation. Since the early 2000s, other than the case of hardship premiums, which are still routinely offered, waves of cost cutting have caused most MNEs to offer fewer international mobility inducements, with some organizations now referring to them as "legacy" benefits.[93]

Allowances

Allowances are discretionary payments made to employees to promote a sense of well-being in expatriates and their families, to maintain their standard of living and to protect their purchasing power.[94] They can include cost of living allowances, exchange rate protection, housing allowance, home leave allowance, rest, relaxation and rehabilitation allowance, education allowance for children, relocation allowance, and spouse support allowance. As in the case of international mobility inducements, the use of allowances has been decreasing steadily.[95]

Cost of living allowances (COLAs) remain the most widely used discretionary allowance and compensate expatriates for difference in living expense between the home and host country. (As of 2019, roughly two thirds of assignees received a COLA.[96]) COLAs are calculated based on the cost of a typical market basket of goods and services in different locations. Figure 10.1 illustrates the differences in cost of living across several major cities. The last few years have seen the steady increase of organizations using limited (capped) COLA amounts, aimed at reducing program costs while still providing some allowance to the assignees. Only a few organizations (12% in 2019) have "negative" COLA practices in cases where the cost of living in the host country are significantly lower than that in the home country.[97]

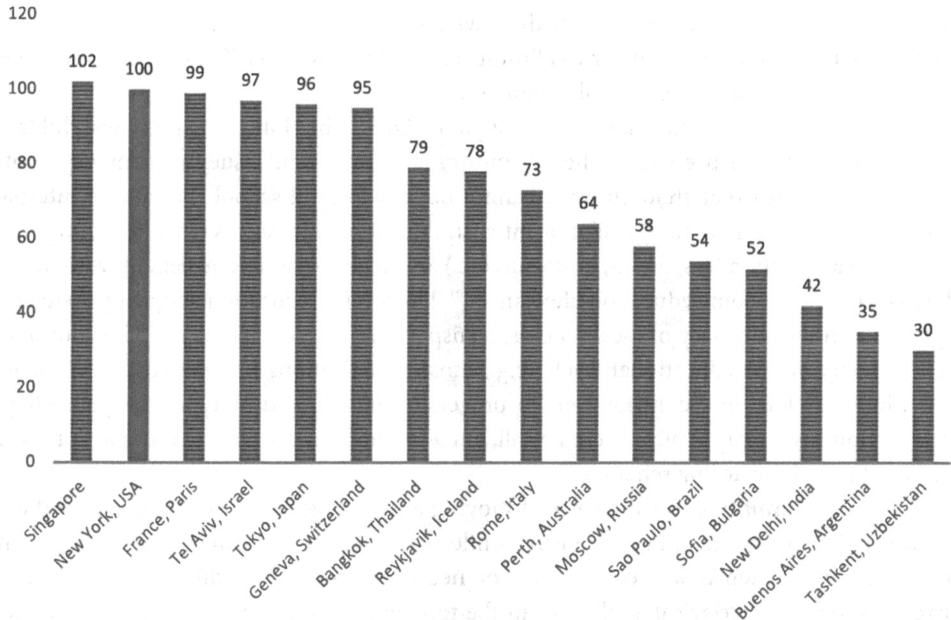

Source: Figure created by authors based in data reported in The Economist Intelligence Unit, 2020. Worldwide Cost of Living 2020: Which global cities have the highest cost of living? A report by The Economist Intelligence Unit.

Figure 10.1   Cost of living in select major global cities in 2020 (compared to New York = 100)

Because of price volatility and different spending patterns among expatriates from different countries, calculating comparative cost of living indices can be complicated and needs to be updated regularly. Several global relocation firms provide cost of living calculations. In addition to COLAs, *exchange rate protection* may be offered to protect expatriates from the volatility in the foreign exchange markets. Exchange rate protection allows for periodic adjustments for rate fluctuations to be made to pay (e.g., if the exchange rate changes by more than 10% within three months, an adjustment is made). Other organizations use a *split pay method* where some pay is made in the home country currency, and the remainder in the host country currency (the mix of home–host currency can vary).[98]

Housing allowances are provided in order that employees can maintain their home country living standards or in some cases receive accommodation that is equivalent to local employees and peers. A core benefit for most, only 5% of companies do not provide any housing allowances.[99] Housing issues are typically dealt with on a case-by-case basis. These allowances are either paid on an actual or assessed basis. Alternatives to allowances such as company-provided housing, fixed housing allowances or a deduction of a fixed percentage of income with actual costs paid for by the firm are also common. *Home leave allowance*, and *rest, relaxation and rehabilitation allowance* are designed to allow expatriates to make trips home to maintain business or family ties. For those in hardship or danger areas, they may need time away to recover from the rigors of the environment. Home leave allowance is typically restricted to trips home, but some firms allow its use for foreign travel. These benefits typically apply to both the expatriate and family members.[100]

Another issue involves *education allowances for children*. The ability of expatriates' children to keep pace with their peers in the home country is an important issue for many expatriate families. This means that children often cannot be sent to local schools but attend international schools, which may carry a significant cost. Education allowances (covering things like registration and tuition fees, books, uniforms, etc.) are an almost universal benefit, with nearly all MNEs providing some education allowance.[101] The level of education support provided is dependent on the adequacy of local schools, transportation issues, and so on. The allowance itself can vary across educational levels (e.g., most organizations pay the costs of primary school but very few offer contributions to university tuition) and by type of expense (e.g., direct tuition costs are typically covered by all, but less than 20% of organizations pay for room and board costs in boarding schools).[102]

Relocation allowances cover the costs of moving and storage of household goods and can also cover the costs of temporary housing while searching for permanent accommodation. In addition, it is often more cost effective or necessary (because of differences in electric current) to buy new electrical appliances in the foreign location. Finally, travel expenses for the expatriate and family to the new location are covered in this category. The increase in dual career couples has created the need to add *spouse assistance* to many expatriate compensation plans. Spousal careers are often disrupted, and income lost as a result of overseas assignments. Spousal assistance is a relatively new benefit that has become necessary as more and more expatriate families are dual career couples. Almost two thirds of organizations offer some sort of spousal assistance, most commonly in the form of work visa assistance, or allowances that must be used for designated expenses such as job search or education. In very rare cases, MNEs may also offer financial compensation for lost spousal salary.[103] Spousal assistance is a benefit particularly relevant for female assignees as they are still more likely to face dual-career dilemmas stemming from expatriation.[104]

Benefits

The ability to transport pension plans, medical coverage, and social security programs between countries is very limited and national practices vary considerably. Some countries do not allow individuals to opt out of local plans even if they are on temporary assignment. While expatriates from headquarters are typically well looked after by their MNE employers, the issues for expatriates from countries other than the MNE home country are more complicated. The basic decisions for MNEs regarding global benefits plans are:

- Should home country plans be maintained?
- What are the tax implications of this decision?
- Must or should the expatriate enroll in local benefits programs?
- Is making up any difference in local versus home benefits an option?
- What options for social security benefits are available/best for the expatriate?

Balance sheet approaches to expatriate compensation

Traditionally, expatriate compensation has been based on the *balance sheet approach* in which the central idea is to keep expatriates "whole" so that they neither lose nor gain financially from their assignment.[105] The balance sheet approach begins with the employee's base salary and uses that as a reference point for calculating various adjustments and allowances, such as those described previously, to arrive at a fair net disposable income.[106] Although companies are gradually reducing various allowances, the balance sheet approach still dominates expatriate compensation models.[107] There are three options in terms of what is chosen as a base (reference) salary.

Home country approach: Taking the expatriate's home country salary as a reference point is the most common balance sheet approach.[108] It provides expatriates equivalent purchasing power in the host country in order to maintain an equivalent standard of living to that of their home country. The advantage of the home-based approach is that expatriates from the same nationality are treated equally around the world and are kept in line with home country structures so they can more easily be reintegrated when they return. While this approach is most likely to attract people to expatriate positions, it is very expensive, with expatriates costing two to five times as much as their counterparts at home.[109]

Critics of this approach have also pointed out that in certain settings the home country balance sheet approach may act as an obstacle to cross-cultural integration.[110] Expatriates may receive substantially higher compensation than their local colleagues, especially in host countries where salaries are generally lower. They may end up living in "expatriate bubbles," where they socialize primarily with other well-paid expatriates and may neither fully experience nor adjust to the host country. Pay inequality between expatriates and local nationals has been highlighted as having a generally negative impact on the perceived fairness of compensation differentials. Such pay inequality has been linked to negative attitudes and behaviors of host country nationals toward expatriates, which negatively influences expatriate adjustment and performance.[111] Compensation gaps between expatriates and locals are also related to lower creativity[112] and even workplace deviance by local employees (i.e., engaging in behavior that can hurt the organization such as theft, fraud, taking long breaks, absenteeism, working inefficiently).[113]

Host country approach: The second most popular approach has been the *host country* approach, which fits expatriate compensation into the local salary structure. This approach is more cost effective and creates a sense of equity with local nationals. However, it is limited in its ability to attract individuals to international assignments except in cases where the local salary is attractive on a comparative basis or when individuals have a personal interest in living in the country. Worldwide variation and inconsistencies in compensation structures limit the use of this approach.

Global approach: The third traditional approach bases compensation on an international scale that is applied to expatriates regardless of country of origin, with allowances calculated based on this "global" scale.[114] While most appropriate in cases where expatriates from different nationalities move to more than one foreign country and lose contact with home country pay structures, it carries a high cost and can create problems upon the return home.[115]

Cost-cutting and "localization" of expatriate compensation

While the balance sheet approach is still most commonly utilized, expatriate compensation is currently undergoing an important transformation, spurred by two related trends – the continuous cost-cutting efforts in MNEs and the increased use of alternatives to long-term expatriation such as short-term assignments, project work, increased international busines travel, or one-way transfers.[116] As we discuss in Chapter 11, there are many reasons for introducing such alternatives, but keeping assignment costs down is certainly one of the most significant. Global mobility managers report that controlling the costs of assignments is by far the most important metric for which they are held accountable by internal stakeholders.[117] Compensation programs for short-term international assignments, for example, involve considerably fewer elements than expatriate compensation and few MNEs have well-established policies for what type of expenses are covered or not.[118]

Beyond rethinking patterns of mobility, MNEs are also rethinking the components of a traditional expatriation package. One increasingly noticeable trend is *localizing* expatriate salaries.[119] In its pure form localization means that after their international transfer, expatriates are compensated exactly as local employees. Full localization is still uncommon with most MNEs taking a *local-plus* approach, whereby the expatriate has a local salary but is still provided with certain allowances. Localization can also be immediate (less common) or gradual, in which case the expatriate may have a *local-plus* compensation with allowances only continuing for a certain amount of time. In this case it is important that employees are informed initially that their compensation will be localized rather than be told mid-way through their assignment.[120] Compensation localization is not a new idea (indeed, it is a stripped down version of the host-country approach discussed previously) but historically, full localization is still rather rare. Even among MNEs that have embraced localization, it is still more common for certain types of assignees and for certain assignment destinations with high income levels and low tax obligations.[121]

Global tax issues

The final piece of expatriate compensation involves tax issues. The nature of expatriate assignments makes many expatriates subject to tax regimes in more than one jurisdiction. Countries differ in the determination of tax obligations in that some countries tax the income of residents while others, such as the United States, tax their citizens, regardless of where they reside. Tax treaties or conventions between governments allow certain credits, deductions, exemptions, and reduced foreign tax rates. However, depending on tax rates, expatriates may be obligated for more tax than at home and in some cases double taxation cannot be avoided. The complexity of global tax issues requires a significant amount of country-specific expertise and means that tax consultation and tax preparation activities are commonly outsourced to professional accounting companies.[122]

Other than a laissez-faire (the MNE does not provide assistance with tax issues) or ad hoc (every case is handled individually and no common policy exists) method, there are two basic approaches to expatriate tax issues, *tax equalization* and *tax protection*. *Tax equalization* programs provide that expatriates neither gain nor lose as a result of taxation while on assignment. MNEs withhold taxes in an amount approximate to what the expatriate would pay at home (commonly referred to as "hypothetical tax") and the company pays the actual taxes owed in both the home and host country. If the overall tax obligation is higher than the tax obligation had the expatriate stayed in his/her home country, the employer covers the difference. If the tax obligation is lower, the employer collects the difference. This approach is by far the most common among MNEs.[123] Under *tax protection* plans, employees pay their taxes based on the home and host country tax laws. As with the tax equalization approach, if their overall tax obligation exceeds the taxes they would have owed in their home country, the employer reimburses them for the excess amount. In contrast to tax equalization, employees with lower tax obligations get to pocket the resulting tax benefit. Thus employees are "protected" against higher taxes. Only a very small portion of MNEs adopt this approach.[124]

CHAPTER SUMMARY

In this chapter we examined performance management and compensation in a global context. Performance management involves the evaluation and continuous improvement of individuals and has both evaluative and developmental components. Central to performance management systems is the performance appraisal process. Both institutional and cultural factors influence the implementation of performance management systems on a global basis. In addition, the fact that MNEs operate in a variety of locations creates an additional set of performance management issues such as differences in firm versus subsidiary goals, consistency of criteria and data, and the geographic separation of organizational units. The unique role of expatriates affects the ability of organizations to design an effective performance management system for them. Key issues are who conducts the performance appraisal, what criteria are assessed, and how the appraisal should be conducted.

One of the key linkages between performance management and other aspects of global HRM is the relationship to organizational rewards in the form of compensation systems. National compensation systems are influenced by factors such as social contracts, employee relations, ownership structures, and the degree of management autonomy. Also, the institutional and cultural context influences the extent to which compensation systems are seen to be legitimate and acceptable in society. The compensation of expatriates presents an additional set of issues. Expatriate compensation traditionally involved taking one's host country, global or home country base salary and integrating it in a balance sheet approach that offers many adjustments and allowances. Such allowances are becoming less frequent and expatriate compensation is increasingly being localized due to cost issues. A myriad of factors are involved in expatriate compensation, but benefits and tax issues are potentially the most difficult to manage.

QUESTIONS FOR DISCUSSION

1. Compare and contrast the evaluative and development components of performance management systems.
2. Explain the effect of cultural and institutional factors on performance management.
3. Outline the key issues in the performance evaluation of expatriates.
4. Describe the key factors affecting compensation practices in various countries.
5. Compare the advantages and disadvantages of the main approaches to expatriate compensation.
6. What is salary localization? What could be some benefits and downsides for MNEs that localize expatriate salaries?

NOTES

1. *Imam bayildi* (translated from Turkish as the "imam (priest) fainted," presumably because the dish was so good) consists of braised aubergine (eggplant) stuffed with onion, garlic, and tomatoes, then simmered in olive oil.
2. Bernthal, Rogers, & Smith (2003).
3. Boselie, Farndale, & Pauuwe (2018).
4. DeNisi (2000).
5. Beer (1981).
6. Varma & Budhwar (2011).
7. See DeNisi (1996) for a discussion.
8. Cascio (2006).
9. Varma, Budhwar, & DeNisi (2008); Varma, & Budhwar (2011).
10. Varma & Budhwar (2011).
11. Aycan (2005).
12. Seddon (1987).

13. https://www.hrreporter.com/employment-law/news/angry-off-duty-tweets-challenge-employers/326985; https://www.nbcnews.com/news/us-news/i-feel-threatened-unmasked-florida-man-s-viral-costco-outburst-n1233161; https://www.cnn.com/2020/05/26/us/central-park-video-dog-video-african-american-trnd/index.html

14. Cascio (2012).

15. Boselie, Farndale, & Paauwe (2012).

16. Fletcher & Perry (2001).

17. Huo & Von Glinow (1995).

18. Bailey, Chen, & Dou (1997); Flecther & Perry (2001).

19. Mendonca & Kanungo (1996).

20. Triandis (1994).

21. Murphy & DeNisi (2008).

22. https://www.hrtechnologist.com/articles/hr-compliance/gdpr-series-part-2-steps-to-compliance/

23. Festing & Barzantny (2008).

24. Festing & Barzantny (2008).

25. Aycan (2005).

26. Oddou & Mendenhall (2000).

27. See Pucik (1985).

28. See Varma & Budhwar (2011).

29. Murphy & DeNisi (2008).

30. Boselie, Farndale, & Pauuwe (2012).

31. Boselie, Farndale, & Pauuwe (2018).

32. Care & Donohue (2017).

33. Brewster, Bonache, Cerdin, & Suutari (2014); Downes & Thomas (1999).

34. Mol, Born, Willemsen, & Van der Molen (2005).

35. Toh & DeNisi (2007).

36. See Claus & Briscoe (2009) for a discussion.

37. See Chapter 9 this volume.

38. See Murphy and Cleveland (1995) for an in-depth discussion of performance appraisal issues.

39. Dessler (2011).

40. Dessler (2011).

41. Gregersen, Hite, & Black (1996).

42. Global Relocation Trends (2011).

43. KPMG (2019).

44. Caligiuri (2006).

45. Care & Donahue (2017); Dessler (2011).

46. Bernardin & Cascio (1984).

47. Gregersen, Hite, & Black (1996).

48. Thomas & Lazarova (2008).

49. For a discussion of reducing bias in performance appraisal see Wilson & Jones (2008).

50. Cardy & Dobbins (1994).

51. Dessler (2011).

52. Murphy & Cleveland (1995).

53. Gregersen, Hite, & Black (1996).

54. Dessler (2011).

55. Oddou & Mendenhall (2000).

56. Gregersen, Hite, & Black (1996).

57. Shih, Chiang, & Kim (2005).

58. Oddou & Mendenhall (2000).

59. Fenwick (2004).

60. Dessler (2011).

61. Yanadori (2014).

62. Farndale, Brewster, Ligthart, & Poutsma (2017).

63. Festing & Sahakiants (2013).

64. Adapted from Milkovich & Newman (2008).

65. Schuler & Rogowsky (1998); Gomez-Mejia and Welbourne (1991).

66. Newman and Nollen (1996).

67. Sahakiants, Festing, Engle, & Dowling (2018).

68. Freeman & Katz (1994).

69. Marín (2008).

70. https://data.oecd.org/inequality/income-inequality.htm

71. Yanadori (2014).

72. https://www.conference-board.org/ilcprogram/index.cfm?id=38269

73. Milkovich & Newman (2008).

74. Fulton (2020).

75. Festing, Engle, Dowling, & Sahakiants (2012); Sahakiants, Festing, Engle, & Dowling (2018).

76. Vernon (2011).

77. https://www.conference-board.org/ilcprogram/index.cfm?id=38269

78. Steers, Shin, & Ungson (1989).

79. Zhou & Martocchio (2001).

80. Pendleton & Poutsma (2012).

81. Ligthart, Pendleton, & Poutsma (2018).

82. Yanadori (2014).

83. Roth & O'Donnell (1996).

84. See DiMaggio & Powell (1983).

85. Gomez-Mejia & Wiseman (1997).

86. Salimäki & Heneman (2008).

87. Sahakiants, Festing, Engle, & Dowling (2018).

88. Milkovich & Bloom (1998).

89. KPMG (2019); McNulty, Rason, & Lockwood (2014).

90. Bonache (2006); Bonache & Zárraga-Oberty (2017).

91. Bonache & Stripe (2012).

92. Burnett & Von Glinow (2011).

93. KPMG (2019).

94. Burnett & Von Glinow (2011).

95. KPMG (2019).

96. KPMG (2019).

97. KPMG (2019).

98. Global Relocation Trends (2011); Mercer (n.d.).

99. KPMG (2019).

100. Burnett & Von Glinow (2011); KPMG (2019).

101. KPMG (2019).

102. KPMG (2019).

103. KPMG (2019).

104. Shortland (2018b).

105. Shortland and Perkins (2016).

106. Bonache & Zárraga-Oberty (2017); Shortland and Perkins (2016).

107. KPMG (2019).

108. KPMG (2019).

109. BGRS (2020); Bonache & Stripe (2012); Reynolds (1997).

110. Bonache & Zárraga-Oberty (2017).

111. Kang & Shen (2018); Leung, Lin, & Lu (2014); Toh & DeNisi (2003); Toh & DeNisi (2007).

112. Hon & Lu (2015).

113. Hon, Lu & Chan (2015).

114. Freeman & Kane (1995).

115. Bonache & Stripe (2012); O'Reilly (1996).

116. KPMG (2019); Santa Fe Relocation (2019).

117. KPMG (2019).

118. BGRS (2020); Bonache & Stripe (2012); Meyskens, Von Glinow, Werther, & Clarke (2009).

119. KPMG (2019); Santa Fe Relocation (2019).

120. McNulty, Rason, & Lockwood (2014); Tornikoski, Suutari, & Festing (2014).

121. McNulty, Rason, & Lockwood (2014).

122. KPMG (2019).

123. KPMG (2019); Latta & Danielson (2003).

124. KMPG (2019).

11

International mobility and global careers

After reading this chapter you should be able to:

1. Describe the impact of a global assignment on an individual's career.
2. Outline the types of global mobility assignments.
3. Discuss the factors associated with adjusting to a foreign environment.
4. Describe the special issues associated with women expatriates, dual career couples, and self-initiated expatriates.
5. Outline the elements of an effective global mobility program.

The Cantonese lunch

As Mike Faraday walked toward the Tsim Sha Tsui MTR Station from the Golden Pearl Seafood Restaurant he recalled having attended his first "Cantonese Lunch." It had sounded like a good idea when he read on the expat website about the opportunity to learn Cantonese, while having lunch at a different Hong Kong restaurant each week. The food had been fabulous, that is when he could snag some of it using his novice chopstick skills. An amazing variety of dishes had whizzed around in front of him on the turntable (which he had learned to call a "lazy Susan" as a kid in the US) in the center of the table of ten. He knew that the other *spouses* of expatriate managers were most likely to be wives. However, he was surprised at how quickly the language lesson had been dispensed with. Despite the organizer's protest that they should introduce Cantonese words, the conversation quickly turned to where to buy favorite foods from "back home"

and how to deal with the Filipina maid. Now, well into his third year as a "trailing spouse" he had learned to enjoy the weekly outing but wondered just how long he and his wife Meredith would be in Hong Kong. The recent demonstrations in Hong Kong had sent shock waves through the expat community and the rumor was that some firms were considering relocating significant aspects of their Asia operations to Singapore.

As he changed to the Island Line at Admiralty, he reflected on the decision for Meredith to take the job as Senior Vice President for Asia for Financebank. It had hardly required any discussion at all, he remembered. At the time, he had not really recovered from losing his job as a securities trader in the Wall Street meltdown. However, Meredith, unlike many of her colleagues, had not only survived the banking crisis, but she would also be one of the most senior women in the firm.

The opportunity was just too good to pass up and within a month they were in Hong Kong.

Mike got off the train at Sheung Wan, the heat and humidity pressed down on him unmercifully as he began the hike up to their apartment in the mid-levels. "We've been here almost four years now, Meredith is so busy I rarely see her, I've settled in, but I still haven't any idea what I'm doing here, and the political situation in Hong Kong is a worry. This trailing spouse business isn't fun anymore. I hope there is still some vodka in the fridge!"

INTRODUCTION

A period of time living and working in a foreign country can be exciting, but also challenging for the individual, for his or her family and also for the employer. Whether or not an overseas work experience has a positive effect on an employee's career, benefits his or her family and also achieves the desired organizational outcomes depends on a wide variety of factors. These include the characteristics of the overseas work, organizational differences and also factors associated with the employee and his or her family.[1] In addition, how a person views his or her career is an important consideration. The way in which people view their career has been changing from an upward progression of job experiences to a more subjective sense of where one is going in one's work life.[2] The characteristics of a career in the age of globalization require that we consider global mobility from the perspective of both the individual and the organization.[3]

GLOBAL CAREERS

Traditionally a global career involved one or several long-term expatriate assignments, each of which might last a few years and included relocation of the expatriate's family. There was a fairly standard expatriation support package in terms of relocation assistance and compensation. As most of these assignments were not truly integrated into employees' career progression, the returnees were often rather dissatisfied with their positions upon returning home because these positions rarely offered the opportunity to use their newly acquired international management skills. This led to higher-than-expected turnover among expatriates.[4]

As the global economic and political landscape evolved toward deepening globalization, more companies started doing more business in more countries, some of which had been previously inaccessible.[5] Perhaps inevitably, today there are more people than ever before that have undertaken global mobility for work-related reasons. This trend has held even in times of economic uncertainty (such as the global financial crisis of 2008) and, until recently, was expected to continue for years to come.[6] Having said this, global mobility has been changing in significant ways. Many organizations are reconsidering long-term expatriation because of the cost involved and are experimenting with other more flexible mobility types such as the short-term assignments, commuting, frequent travelers, and virtual assignments.[7] Organizations are also introducing more mobility across organizational units, including mobility from host locations to the head office (called inpatriates, see Chapter 8).[8] In addition we are seeing an increase in individually initiated mobility (self-initiated assignments) as the global marketplace puts greater value on international experience and as restrictions on mobility and migration are lifted or eased around the world.[9] Finally, there are now "global" careers that do not even include physical international mobility. For example, some employees have international responsibilities without relocating, as they interact with clients or partners internationally and work on global projects in virtual teams.[10] Of course, at the time of writing, there is great uncertainty surrounding global mobility of all kinds, brought about by the COVID-19 pandemic and a shared expectation of inevitable changes to mobility, in ways we cannot even anticipate yet.[11] It's worth noting that despite such concerns, most organizations still think that business-related global mobility will not disappear any time soon.[12]

GLOBAL ASSIGNMENT TYPES

Despite changes in the international business environment, traditional expatriation is still the dominant type of global mobility. While there have been noticeable changes in the ratio of long-term and short-term expatriate postings, long-term expatriate positions remain strategically important for MNCs as they remain an important way of transferring expertise and controlling and coordinating their networks of subsidiaries.

Traditional long-term expatriation

As discussed in Chapter 8 the key reasons for corporate expatriation include filling a skills gap and organizational and managerial development. Traditionally, most expatriates sent on assignments were male, married, and accompanied by their spouse or children. Their postings typically lasted for three to five years. Expatriates were well supported logistically before and during their assignments and many earned significantly more during assignment than in their domestic positions, receiving standard expatriate supplements such as housing allowances and cost-of-living adjustments.[13] Over the last couple of decades, however, expatriation has been undergoing several important changes. First, there have been marked changes in the demographic profile of expatriates, with a notable increase of younger expatriates, increasing numbers of female expatriates and single expatriates, with more dual career couples, and more non-traditional families.[14] A 2019 report indicated that the majority of organizations recognize unmarried partners of the opposite or the same sex as a "family" for assignment purposes.[15] Second, as discussed in the previous chapter, expatriate compensation and benefits are continuously being reduced, and more and more positions are being "localized."[16] Finally, since the turn of the millennium many have predicted that advances in transportation and technology combined with increasing costs of managing long-term assignments would lead to an overall decline of long-term expatriation. Evidence is mounting that these predictions are gradually coming to fruition. While there are still plenty of traditional expatriates being sent around the world, long-term expatriation is indeed decreasing in relative importance[17] and the growth of mobility is now due to the use of alternative assignment types (described in the next section).

As an example, a recent report indicated that 28% of organizations anticipated that long-term assignments would decrease, while there were increases expected in short-term assignments (41%) and business travel (39%).[18] Such options appear to be widely shared among mobility experts.[19] We now turn to describing this alternative types of global mobility

Alternate forms of corporate global assignments

- *Short-term Assignments*: Definitions of short-term assignments vary but they typically last from three months to a year and rarely involve relocation of family members. These postings typically involve project work, skill/technology transfer, or problem solving but are sometimes simply a shorter-term posting. The employee salary, pension, and social security as well as career aspects are handled in the home country.
- *Commuter Assignments*: A commuter assignment involves a person living in one country but doing most of his/her work in another, which involves regular travel between home and host destination, usually weekly or bi-weekly.[20] These assignments typically involve weekdays working abroad and home for the weekend.
- *International Business Travelers* are employees who take multiple short international business trips to various international locations. While international commuting is more structured, there is no regular rhythm to international business travel.[21] The most common reasons for these assignments are knowledge transfer, negotiations, meetings, conferences or discussions. Trips may last for up to three weeks and may involve multiple countries.[22]
- *Flexpatriates and Other Arrangements*: *Flexpatriate* is a catch-all term sometimes used to indicate employees with domestically based jobs but who also travel extensively and work in alternating locations (i.e., frequent travelers, commuters, and short-term assignments).[23] Another example of expatriation is *rotational* assignments, or short-term relocation to take up a post in a foreign location followed by time off in the home location.[24] Another type of work that has been added to the group of global experiences is that of *virtual work*. Most frequently this refers to being actively engaged in cross-border virtual teams but it can mean any domestic job with substantial international responsibilities. These assignments do not involve relocation nor do they involve extensive (or even any) international travel. Employees (who are sometimes referred to as *virtual assignees*, or as *global domestics*) work from their home office but have to collaborate with (or sometimes manage) colleagues from different national locations, across (several) time zones, language and cultural barriers.[25]

Although the number of people that are undertaking such alternate types of global mobility is increasing and, as just noted, is expected to increase even further, organizations know very little about how to best manage these assignments and often treat them as an extension of one's domestic job responsibilities,[26] despite evidence that they pose many unique challenges to employees, as discussed ahead in the chapter.

Self-initiated global mobility

Another category of global mobility involves *self-initiated expatriates*, or individuals who "make their own way" and choose to undertake an overseas assignment for personal or professional development by themselves.[27] They simply go to a foreign country without a pre-set contract or posting, in search for better professional opportunities or move due to personal reasons and find a job as a consequence. Their move is not supported nor orchestrated by anyone else. These self-initiated expatriates (SIEs) are not migrants as they intend this *assignment* to be temporary.[28] The skills they gain are for their own benefit but may ultimately be used to advantage by an organization when they return.[29]

There has been a lot of interest in SIEs in the last two decades. One important topic is what motivates SIEs to move abroad. Whereas expatriates tend to be driven mostly by career considerations and they are sent to accomplish company objectives, SIEs follow their own agenda, and their reasons for moving are far more varied: some do move to advance their careers, just like company expatriates do, but there are also those who move for adventure, more travel opportunities, or lifestyle reasons – simply to live in a country that they love. Some move for relationship reasons such as joining a loved one abroad. There are also those who move after a life change (e.g., divorce), to escape unpleasant circumstances at home or simply to earn more money.[30]

Compared to corporate expatriates, SIEs tend to be more embedded in local communities, more likely to speak the local language and more likely to interact with – and learn from – host country nationals. Partly as a result of such factors, SIEs are believed to have higher interaction adjustment.[31] At the same time, SIEs tend to have less challenging jobs, be at lower hierarchical positions,[32] more likely to be working under local supervisors and may report lower job satisfaction.[33] In terms of career development, it has been pointed out that SIE careers resemble rivers rather than ladders. Whilst ladders imply continued upward mobility (this is still the expected career pattern in many MNCs), rivers move through varied terrains, widening and deepening in some places, narrowing and becoming shallower in others but ultimately following their own natural course, whatever it may be.[34]

ADJUSTMENT TO THE FOREIGN CULTURE

An important consideration in global assignments is the ability of the individual to adjust, not only to their new job but also to the new and often very different cultural environment.[35] Adjustment is a condition consisting of a person's relationship with their environment in which their needs are satisfied and the ability to meet physical and social demands exists.[36] That is, adjustment can include psychological and emotional well-being and satisfaction as well as the ability to fit in, to acquire culturally appropriate skills, and to interact effectively in the host culture.[37] In addition to this general adjustment expatriates must adjust to new work roles and family role demands.[38]

The challenges faced by individuals in adjusting to a new cultural context are complex and different individuals might employ very different coping mechanisms. However, it has been suggested that for many people adjusting to a new cultural context progresses through a cycle of adjustment that follows a U-shaped pattern,[39] which is extended to a W shape when repatriation is considered.[40] This adjustment cycle is presented in Figure 11.1.

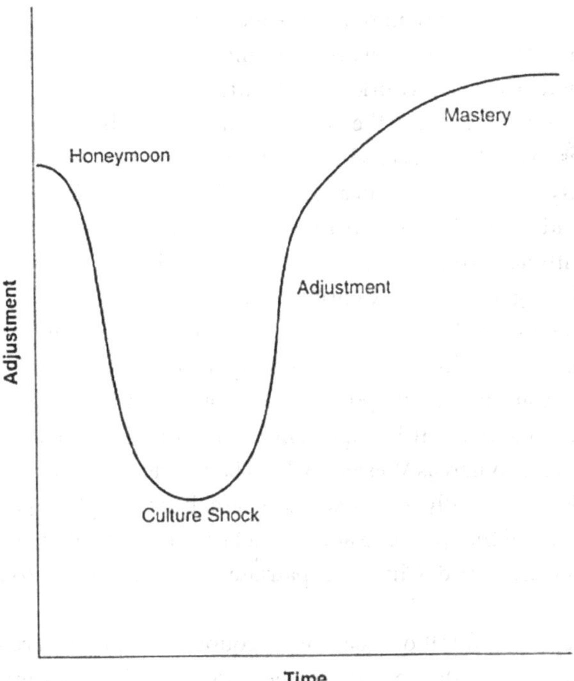

Figure 11.1   The U-curve of cross-cultural adjustment

According to the model shown in Figure 11.1 expatriates (and their family members) progress through the four phases of honeymoon, culture shock, adjustment and finally mastery. In the *honeymoon* stage, everything is new and interesting, and the environment intrigues the expatriate and family in much the same way as if they were a tourists. There is a sense of adventure and excitement. At the *culture shock* stage individuals become frustrated and confused because the environment is not providing familiar cues. The realities of everyday life have become apparent and the novelty has worn off. At the *adjustment* stage, the expatriate and family begin to understand cultural differences, learn the ways to get things done, and begin to settle into the rhythm of daily living in the foreign country. Eventually, people can achieve the *mastery* stage and become able to function in the new culture almost as well as at home. Not all individuals achieve mastery in their new culture. Some return home early, whereas others complete their assignment but without really adjusting. While this model is useful as guide to possible phases of adjustment neither the various phases nor the time parameters have been supported by research.[41] In addition, different patterns of adjustment have been found for work and non-work environments and for expatriates and their spouses.[42] And of course it does not explain how and why people adjust.

Family considerations

The strongest predictor of expatriate adjustment is the extent to which their partner adjusts.[43] And, the partner, particularly if he or she is not working, often has a more difficult time making the transition to the new environment than the expatriate.[44] There are several reasons for this. First, while the expatriate may have a work environment that is somewhat similar to that in the parent country with a social network of host nationals and other expatriates, other family members are completely immersed in the new surroundings in their day-to-day life with more limited opportunities to establish a social network. In moving, children may lose friends and ties to the community that may be critical to their identity formulation, thus affecting their feelings of security and well-being and creating stress.[45] And, just when the partner needs the expatriate to help with adjustment issues at home he or she is faced with the challenges of a new job, often with long hours and extensive travel requirements.

The most critical family challenges on assignment have traditionally been adjustment and spouse/partner resistance to relocation and spouse/partner dissatisfaction during the assignment. Family concerns are frequently pointed out as a reason for assignment refusal and as a cause for assignment failures.[46] It is important to note that how MNCs think of expatriate families varies by context. Whereas Western MNCs have long identified family issues as problematic, the issue is less frequently discussed elsewhere. For example, Japanese expatriates are less likely to list inability of the spouse to adjust as a factor because of the role and status of the spouse in Japanese society.[47] And, Chinese expatriates are far less likely to bring their families along on assignment.[48]

Assignments place a special toll on dual career couples (couples where both partners have careers), especially in circumstances where the accompanying partner wishes to pursue a career in the host country but cannot. Partners who want a job but cannot find one (or are prevented from working because of visa restrictions) may experience various issues such as changes in identity, decreased financial independence, and lower self-worth. They may feel like they are contributing little to the family, they may miss working and may feel unable to fulfill their own career ambitions. This can happen even in couples where the accompanying partner willingly gave up their own job before the relocation. Over time, the situation may lead to frustration and resignation and may build tension in the couple.[49] This is a non-trivial issue in a world where more and more expatriates are in dual-career couples and is thus a point of increasing concern for organizations.[50]

With the increased number of women taking global assignments it is now more probable that the trailing spouse will be male. However, expatriate enclaves, social support networks and the like have been established around the fact that most accompanying partners were female. As shown in the case that opened this chapter, this can make male trailing spouses feel uncomfortable or disinterested in the activities of these groups,[51] and appropriate support activities for them may be difficult to find.[52] Research indicates that while 70% of female accompanying partners feel included in socializing that takes place with other global assignees, less that 40% of male accompanying partners feel that way.[53] Some male trailing spouses feel uncomfortable when being put in a position that does not allow them to contribute to the household income. And, male accompanying partners report being perceived as atypical by others in the host country which can cause them to re-examine their identity, even if they themselves have no gender-role concerns.[54]

Individual factors

In an effort to provide appropriate expatriate selection and training recommendations numerous individual factors related to adjustment have been studied. This search for an *expatriate type* of person has been inconclusive. Some personality characteristics such as openness to new experience seem to be important predictors, but others do not.[55] And, while it is generally believed that cross-cultural skills and abilities such as adaptability or relational ability or cultural intelligence are important for adjustment, there is no consensus with regard to which ones are most important.[56] We do know that certain demographic characteristics such as age, tenure and education level are positively related to adjustment, but the reasons for this relationship are unclear.[57] However, as indicators of life stage, career stage or family situation, and in combination with organizational and environmental factors these individual differences can be useful in understanding adjustment. That is, it may be possible to create a profile of an individual based on their characteristics and match that profile to the specific overseas assignment to understand and predict adjustment issues.

Both ability in the foreign language and previous international experience would seem to be logical predictors of adjustment. It turns out however that this intuitively appealing idea does not hold up in all situations. It seems clear that the individuals highly fluent in the foreign language are more likely to interact with host nationals[58] and in some cases are better adjusted.[59] However, it is probably not fluency in the foreign language itself, but the willingness to interact with and seek support from local nationals (helped along by language fluency) that is the critical factor in adjustment.[60]

Another consideration is previous overseas experience that individuals may have.[61] Some research has found that the amount of previous overseas experience helps with adjustment,[62] but other research indicates it can have a negative effect on job attitudes.[63] It is probably the type and the quality of the overseas experience as opposed to the mere quantity that is important.[64] In order for previous experience in another culture to have a positive effect that carries over to a new situation, individuals must undergo self-development in the way they think about and act toward other cultures.[65] This development requires a significant amount of engagement with the foreign culture.[66] For some people this could occur in a small amount of time in another culture, but others may never really engage despite having spent a long time overseas. For both language fluency and previous international experience, the effect on adjustment is likely influenced by environmental and organizational factors such as how different the foreign culture is, the organizational level of the expatriate and the amount of interaction with locals that is required by the assignment.[67]

Contextual factors

The environment of the assignment is also important, notably how different one's home and the host country's are. It has long been suggested that the more different a new culture is, the more challenging adjustment to this country will be. Although this argument is quite intuitive, the actual evidence regarding this can be best described as mixed,[68] with several studies finding that it may be just as difficult to adjust in similar countries than to dissimilar ones.[69] One explanation for this finding is that when a person is posted in a country that is similar to their own, they tend to assume similarities and underestimate the challenges involved to moving to a new country.

Research has also shown that certain differences between cultures may be positively related to adjustment[70] and that some differences (even large ones) between home and host settings may be perceived quite positively by expatriates[71] (for example, a female expatriate from a culture low on gender egalitarianism may be pleased to be posted in a country with higher gender egalitarianism). Research has also shown that the direction of transfer matters – that is, it is important where one comes from and where they are going. Thus, one study found that German expatriates in the US were better adjusted than American expatriates in Germany.[72] Along similar lines, another study showed expatriates from individualistic countries on assignments in more collectivist locations adjusted better compared to expatriates from collectivistic countries traveling to individualistic ones.[73] Finally, some have noted that it may not be the culture distance per se that matters but how accepting to differences and to foreigners a host society is.[74]

CHALLENGES IN ALTERNATE ASSIGNMENT TYPES

Alternate assignment types such as commuter assignments, frequent travelers, virtual assignments and the like, although typically motivated by cost savings to the organization, would seem to solve many of the problems associated with the typical expatriate assignment such as expatriate adjustment, family relocation, and dual career couples and so on. However, neither managers nor researchers have enough experience with these kinds of assignments to know with any sense of certainty if they offer an improvement over traditional expatriation.[75] That is, while many of the challenges of traditional expatriation associated with relocation are eliminated, these global road warriors face a whole new set of challenges.[76] Just because one's family does not move, does not in any way imply that such assignments do not affect the family.[77] Such assignments mean frequent absences from home and family, which can have negative effects on their relationship with their partner and with children. For example, familial separation is often associated with stress and higher divorce rates, as well as higher incidence of alcoholism.[78] Additionally, their work roles often have domestic aspects that cannot be neglected while they travel. Research among international business travelers has shown high levels of work–family conflict among parents, more so among mothers.[79] A recent study[80] showed that despite their intensive travel schedules, female international business travelers stay very engaged in their family lives. They still take up a big share of childcare and household responsibilities, while their male partners take only specific caring responsibilities that are traditionally associated with fatherhood, such as sports education. Female travelers also reported that they remain primarily responsible for household tasks such as shopping and cleaning between trips, pre-arranging activities as much as possible before their trips (freezing meals, pre-arranging playdates and organizing daycare or school picks ups) and frequently calling home from abroad to make sure everything was running smoothly. Meanwhile, their male partners tended to take up roles they were comfortable with and enjoyed such as gardening and cooking.

In addition to family tensions, all the negative aspects of frequent travel such as waiting at airports, lack of sleep and exercise, poor diet, time zone differences and so on can take a heavy toll.[81] Even the idea that adjustment issues are minimized might be challenged. That is, in these types of mobility assignments the employee is often confronted with multiple foreign environments to which he or she is expected to adapt. Adapting one's perspective and behavior on each occasion may be a very different skill set from that required of the traditional expatriate.[82] And, it is unlikely that shorter assignments, with limited involvement in different cultural contexts, will be particularly helpful in terms of developing an international perspective, which is a key positive outcome of traditional overseas postings.[83] Short-term assignments tend to involve weaker integration with the local setting, which may result in strained relationships and possibly conflict with local colleagues.[84]

Unlike expatriation, alternate assignment types are rarely supported by the organization and HR departments are less consistently involved in managing them. For example, there is little in the way of formal selection[85] and despite having to work with employees from different cultures, these assignees are rarely offered any form of cross-cultural training.[86] They are typically offered limited destination services, may have to stay in hotels for extended periods of time, and the financial terms and taxation-related terms of their assignments may be decided at hoc and so on.[87] Perhaps because of their newness few MNEs have developed formal policies for alternate assignments. Most attention is paid to short-term assignments but international business travel and work in virtual teams are much less likely to be the subject of targeted policies and practices.[88] Performance management of these assignments is also an emerging challenge given their often simultaneous responsibilities in multiple MNE locations. It appears that while organizations embrace the flexibility such assignments provide, they are not entirely clear about their real value or cost.[89] An important issue for organizations is managing extended business travel and short reassignments in a way to avoid incurring tax obligations in the host country. Although this has long been identified as an area in need of urgent attention, the majority of organizations do not approach it in any systematic way.[90]

WOMEN ON OVERSEAS ASSIGNMENTS

Women have always been under-represented in expatriate positions, with research from the early 1980s suggesting that less than 5% of assignees were women. Over the years, many have predicted that the number of women expatriates would increase because of a shortage of qualified men, legal and social pressure for equal opportunity, the increasing familiarity with women in management positions, and the increasing ability (because of changing company attitudes) of women to self-select for an overseas assignment.[91] While the proportion of women has indeed been rising, they are still less than a third of all corporate expatriates.[92] They also tend to hold fewer of the highest international postings despite having similar socio-economic backgrounds and equal, if not higher, educational qualifications than their male counterparts.[93] There are also differences by industry with women severely under-represented in industries such as oil and gas.[94] On a more positive note, there are considerably more women among self-initiated expatriates.[95]

The low percentage of women on company-initiated overseas assignments seems to have little to do with how well they do on assignments compared to men. Women perform as well as their male counterparts even in environments considered unfriendly to female managers.[96] And in some cases their uniqueness may actually be an advantage.[97] A recent study explored the role of gender for expatriate effectiveness using different groups of measures: adjustment, premature return, performance, commitment and job satisfaction. The analyses did not uncover any significant differences on effectiveness between female and male expatriates.[98] What then may be at the heart of the low percentage of female expatriates? The explanations fall into four major categories: perceptions regarding their willingness to accept an overseas assignment, family factors, host country national attitudes, and organizational factors.

The *perceptions* that women are unwilling to take up international postings is fairly common,[99] although there is no convincing evidence that supports that.[100] Indeed, we know that women have a similar desire to have an international career compared to their male counterparts.[101] The first explanation is often related to the second: the assumption that women in dual-career relationships and/or with children would not accept global assignments because of their families and the various family challenges an assignment may pose. While work–life balance issues are equally relevant to men and women, societal norms often cast women as the primary care givers for children and thus female expatriates may feel pressure to take on a greater share of the work associated with children's relocation, education and so on. And, male trailing spouses are typically more concerned with continuing their careers in the host country than are their female counterparts.[102] However, it may be that the importance of career can outweigh gender-based family issues. A recent study found that the more important a woman's career role was to her, the more likely she was to accept an international assignment. In contrast, there was no relationship between the importance to her of her roles as partner and parent and willingness for assignment.[103] Research has also shown that, given sufficient incentives, there are women that are more than willing to undertake assignments, with their family support, even in industries traditionally considered "challenging" such as oil and gas.[104] But another point has also been made recently: assignment type may be an important consideration for women, with long-term assignments on which they can be accompanied by their family being preferred to alternative assignment types. As discussed in the previous section, the "flexibility" these assignments provide to MNEs also create a lot of work–family challenges,[105] while not providing women with great potential for developing their careers.[106]

Another core issue for female expatriates is the extent to which women actually face greater difficulty overseas than men. While it is true that negative attitudes toward women expatriates, discrimination against them and preferences for dealing with male executives do exist in some countries,[107] women expatriates seem to find ways to overcome these issues over time.[108] Overcoming this resistance may have its costs, with women in countries with low female workforce participation and a low percentage of women managers reporting being less adjusted to the non-work aspects of their life.[109] A recent study on Chinese female expats indicated that host country prejudices were associated with decreased performance but much less so in cases where the expatriates felt supported by their organizations and their families.[110] But research has also shown that even in culturally tough countries, the longer female expatriates spend on assignment, the less likely they are to think that local prejudices inhibit their effectiveness. While women can overcome the additional challenges associated with an overseas assignment, the *perception* of these additional difficulties may nevertheless influence decisions by both organizations and potential assignees as to whether to undertake the assignment in the first place.[111]

Finally, women may have low expectations of their opportunity for being selected and therefore fail to actively pursue opportunities for overseas placement.[112] There are two factors that may be relevant here: the quality of the relationship between female subordinates and predominantly male supervisors, and negative attitudes of senior managers with regard to the participation of women on international assignment. First, individual characteristics such as gender, age, race, educational background and so on can be related to the quality of the relationship between a subordinate and his/her supervisor. It is certainly possible that this informal relationship is important in selecting overseas assignees and that women are disadvantaged as a result.[113] Second, senior managers in the home country are often responsible for selecting overseas assignees. Surveys of these managers continue to show that they mistakenly believe that women are not interested in international assignments, will not be accepted by local nationals, or are not as qualified as their male counterparts. Supervisors are also more likely to think that women in dual-career relationships are less likely to accept a foreign posting. It may be that these senior management attitudes are the factor that is the most resistant to change.

REPATRIATION

Once an assignment is completed, assignees "repatriate," or return home (another way of saying this is that after the assignment is complete, "expatriates" become "repatriates"). Returning home from a long period abroad involves a transition similar to the initial transfer yet different from other types of geographic-related job transfers. In a traditional repatriation situation, the individual is returning to his/her home country after a period of absence of two to five years (or longer for German or Japanese expatriates).[114] During this time, the individual, the country, and the organization have undergone gradual changes largely independent of each other. However, the expatriate is very likely confronted with these changes simultaneously upon return. And the repatriation experience is qualitatively different in that most repatriates (80% by some estimates)[115] are returning home from an assignment in a country of which they had little or no prior experience. Therefore, their knowledge and expectations about moving *home* are likely very different to the initial move to a foreign country. Also, the same sorts of things that help expatriates adjust to their expatriate assignment can in turn inhibit repatriation.[116] For example, the improved housing conditions that most expatriates experience might help them cope while on assignment, but the drop in housing conditions on repatriation has a negative effect.

The factors that make the transition back to the home country and socio-cultural environment so difficult include both job-related and personal and family issues. Job-related issues involve concerns about career, adjustment to the new work role, and compensation and status changes. Family issues include the adjustment of the family to the home environment including re-establishing social networks and the effect on the partner's career.

Career concerns

Perhaps the most important re-entry issue is the uncertainty about their career that many expatriates face. Only a minority of repatriates have clearly assigned duties on return and there seems to be a trend away from post assignment job guarantees.[117] Typically, the repatriate's role back home is at best a lateral move that does not take advantage of their development on assignment. Given that many expatriates take up the overseas assignment with the expectation of career advancement upon return, these unmet expectations are clearly a source of concern with regard to adjustment. In addition, many expatriates will experience the *out of sight, out of mind* effect as a result of being absent from the home office environment where constant exposure to informal communication and mentors is possible. Lack of information can increase anxiety about the type of re-entry position that is available, about details of the repatriation process, and generally what to expect upon return. Career concerns can also be heighted by organizational changes at home. Organizational reorganizations create anxiety for all employees, but this effect can be even more stressful for the repatriate who is already wondering how he or she will fit back into the organizational structure.[118] Inadequate career advancement upon repatriation is related to perceptions of underemployment among repatriates, which in turn lead to higher turnover intentions.[119] We now know that career-related support is linked to repatriate intentions to leave their companies, such that career prospects after repatriation are positively related to retaining repatriates two and four years after their assignments have ended.[120] Unfortunately, evidence suggests that very few organizations appear to engage in any advance planning regarding post-repatriation postings, have formal repatriation strategies or programs linked to career management and retention,[121] with 70% saying they do not even track repatriate retention.[122]

Work role adjustment

The role that expatriates assume upon return is highly variable. Many are put in *holding patterns* until an appropriate job is found, and some are promoted, but in all cases their role back home has different characteristics from their job overseas. In their overseas post expatriates often have a very high level of overall responsibility in challenging jobs with a high level of status. They may have even adjusted their behavior to be more consistent with what was expected of them overseas. Some of the behavior that was appropriate in their expatriate role may not conform to home office expectations. The mismatch between the expectations that returnees have about their role and what is expected of them by the organization is a significant cause of stress.[123]

Many employees develop what is called *an international employee identity* during their assignments. That is, they think of themselves as international employees and identify strongly with their international assignment experience. If they perceive that their situation (job autonomy, job responsibility, compensation, status, and promotional opportunity) compares negatively to that of their peers who have not been on international assignments they develop a sense of conflict, tension. and misfit between their sense of self and their current organizational roles. This identity strain is in turn related to turnover.[124]

Compensation and status changes

In many cases an expatriate assignment is a promotion granting greater responsibility and autonomy, and even a prominent role in the local community. On return, the expatriates resume their position in the organization resulting in a loss of this status and autonomy. Decisions that were the responsibility of the expatriate while on overseas assignment must now be cleared with a superior or taken to a committee. While most expatriates report being financially better off after their overseas assignment their overall compensation is usually lower in absolute terms.[125] That is, many expatriates are able to increase their savings while on assignment. However, they lose such factors as cost-of-living allowances (COLA) and other perks upon return. Often the absence of these financial considerations has a negative influence on the ability of the expatriate and his/her family to reintegrate into the home environment.[126]

Family adjustment

The experience of living overseas can distance the expatriate's family both socially and psychologically from their friends and family back home. Many of us can recall returning from a particularly exciting or interesting holiday only to find they when we try to recount the experience our friends have little if any interest. Returning from many years in a foreign country only enhances this effect. Without a frame of reference our friends and family are unlikely to understand the significant influence that life in a foreign environment has had.[127] This, along with economic factors, can often make the home environment, that we may have glamorized while overseas, dull and unexciting by comparison. Expatriates often return from a very tight knit community of fellow expatriates to a home environment in which everyone seems consumed by their own lives making reestablishing social networks difficult.[128] Children can also have a difficult time reintegrating into peer groups and the education system.[129] Although not well studied, it seems likely that being out of touch with home country changes in fashion, music slang, sports and the like will make it difficult for children to reestablish their own social networks. While advancements in technology and the rise of social media in particular make keeping up with various trends around the world much easier than it was even 20 years ago, technology is (still) a rather poor substitute for peer-to-peer contact and gathering with one's friends, as evidenced during the COVID-19 pandemic that restricted youth to communicating with each other primarily online.[130]

Partner's career

The ability of the trailing partner to re-enter the workforce upon return is affected by the trailing partner's occupation, length of time abroad, unemployment levels in the home country, and individual factors such as age and gender.[131] Even with the rise in dual career couples we know surprisingly little about this issue. According to the global mobility surveys, about a third of firms provided some sort of career assistance to spouses, but it is not clear if this extended to repatriation.[132] Given that so few organizations implement any career management programs for their repatriates, it is highly unlikely that they do so for repatriate spouses.

Repatriation of self-initiated expatriates

While our knowledge on this is still somewhat limited, it appears that there are unique aspects to the repatriation of SIEs. Given that they control their work situation abroad, they have far more agency than corporate expatriates as to whether to go back to their home country. Thus, unless prompted by an unexpected shock or a crisis (e.g., sudden illness of a loved one), they rarely undertake repatriation without at least some career planning. Whilst SIEs are in control of their return, they also bear all the costs of transferring back: it is they themselves that have to find new jobs and pay the costs of moving their belongings. But on balance, given that SIEs set their own repatriation expectations, these expectations are far more likely to be met than the expectations of corporate expatriates.[133] Research has shown that SIEs repatriation decisions are driven by both "push" and "pull" factors.[134] Push factors typically reflect dissatisfaction with the host country that makes the SIE unable or unwilling to stay in the host country (e.g., losing one's job, expiring visa, deteriorating economic outlook, social unrest) and pull factors are anything that draws a person back home, for example, deepening sense of national identity, desire for a certain lifestyle, having stronger support networks, wanting to educate one's children in the host country, and so on.[135]

IMPACT OF OVERSEAS ASSIGNMENTS

Overseas assignments have important outcomes for the expatriate, his or her family and for the organization. But to the extent that organizations monitor impact at all,[136] they tend to focus on a narrow set of outcomes related to the expatriate only (notable examples are expatriate satisfaction and repatriate retention). But research on the impact of assignments has been growing steadily, and organizations are increasingly advised to provide a more comprehensive assessment of assignment outcomes.

Impact on assignees

The effect of an overseas assignment on the longer-term career of managers may depend in part on how one defines career success. It is widely accepted that there are two major components of career success: objective and subjective. The former reflects measurable results such as promotions, hierarchical position, or salary, and the second taps into subjective indicators such as career satisfaction.[137]

Early research presented a somewhat negative view in terms of objective career outcomes. It was commonly reported that instead of moving up the career ladder expatriates are often neglected on their return, put in a holding pattern, and not valued for their international experience by their firms.[138] More recently, a more (cautiously) optimistic picture has emerged. Evidence is accumulating that international experience is related to promotions[139] and higher pay.[140] Research has also pointed out that in terms of career development, not all assignments are created equal, with developmental assignments having more positive impact on careers. Finally, there is some evidence that career advancement may be best for those either with a single assignment or with many assignments (above four), but not for those in between.[141] It is important to point out that one's objective career may develop as a result of a global assignment – but not necessarily in the company with which the person expatriated initially. In other words, in order to be able to capitalize on international experience, one may need to move to another employer. And indeed, there is evidence that those with expatriate experience report increased marketability and most receive one or more job offer(s) after their assignments.[142]

In terms of subjective career, expatriates have long reported high levels of personal enrichment and skills development, which they can leverage in new roles.[143] For example, research has shown that assignments build career capital among both organizational expats and SIEs. There are three main components to career capital: *knowing how* (the skills, knowledge, insights and abilities that individuals possess), *knowing whom* (all relationships that can be beneficial to one's work and career), and *knowing why* (reflecting what motivates people in their careers). Evidence is emerging that knowing whom and knowing why increase more among OEs.[144]

Impact on family members

While the failure of family members to adjust to the foreign environment is a key factor in the failure of expatriates to remain on assignment for the agreed upon length of time, families who do adjust to the overseas experience can gain huge benefits. For example, if expatriation occurs during the critical developmental stages, expatriate children's maturity can be enhanced, as they develop an international perspective.[145] Many of these children may become what have been called *third culture kids* (exposed to more than one culture for a significant period of time) who develop differently and exhibit different characteristics than their single culture peers. In particular, in addition to foreign language skills and preference for international careers, they have a greater open-mindedness, respect and tolerance toward other cultures, as well as flexibility with regard to their own cultural identity.[146] Clearly, for some families, a global assignment can have far-reaching implications.

Impact on host country nationals

It is only recently that research has suggested that assignments may also affect local colleagues with whom the expatriate works. Studies have mostly focused on the compensation disparity host country nationals perceive when they compare their pay to that of their expatriate counterparts, and its negative consequences. Host country nationals may report lower satisfaction and lower commitment but they may also spill into developing negative stereotypes about assignees and withdrawal behaviors (i.e., HCNs choosing not to support or help expatriates perform their jobs), which can not only strain relationships between expatriates and HCNs but may have larger organizational consequences.[147] Research has also highlighted that the need to support expatriate colleagues creates a wide range of extra-role demands for host-country nationals, which in turn make their working lives more complex and stressful, much to their chagrin.[148]

Impact on the organization

From an organizational standpoint, all overseas assignments require a substantial investment, which includes direct costs such as increased compensation, relocation expenses and so on and also indirect costs such as the cost of premature return, underperformance, and the opportunity cost of not using a local national.[149] However, knowing if an adequate return on this investment (ROI) is achieved is difficult. In the most recent global relocation trends survey, 89% of firms rated their ROI on expatriate assignments (defined as accomplishing the assignment objectives at the expected cost) as good or very good. However, only 8% actually made an effort to measure ROI, reflecting the difficulty in actually calculating the costs and benefits of an expatriate assignment.[150] While costs of assignments are easy to calculate, benefits such as knowledge and skills transfer, management development, and developing relationships with host nationals that have potentially positive long-term benefits to the firm are particularly difficult to quantify.[151] Reflecting this, a recent report indicates that while 71% of organizations track assignment costs, 39% track employee satisfaction and only 16% track career progression of assignee.[152]

As noted above, retention upon repatriation is a key concern to MNEs.[153] While the overall turnover rates among repatriates may not be significantly higher than general turnover, repatriates are a unique group in that that their assignment usually equips them with specialized knowledge, skills and abilities, such as country-specific knowledge, interpersonal skills, job-related management skills, knowledge of business networks, and general management knowledge, that can create competitive advantage for their organization.[154] To actually gain the benefits from this knowledge, it must be effectively transferred to the organization. However, much of this knowledge is *tacit*, or contained within the person and difficult to codify and thus harder to transfer. Skills and abilities developed overseas are also, of course, within the individual. Therefore, the knowledge, skills, and abilities of repatriates can best be leveraged to the organization's benefit if they are retained following the overseas experience.[155] Beyond merely keeping repatriates, it is also in the organization's best interest to create conditions that facilitate repatriate knowledge transfer.[156] Research has shown that organizational support practices can be very helpful, particularly initiatives that open channels of communication and provide opportunities for the repatriate to share knowledge with their colleagues (e.g., knowledge-sharing debriefing sessions, targeted internal communication mechanisms).

Programs supporting repatriate career development have also been suggested to motivate repatriates to share knowledge.

Additional considerations

Ideally, various indicators of success will be well-aligned across all stakeholders (expatriates, family members, colleagues, the organization overall) but the reality is that there are situations that may create a good outcome for one but not all parties.[157] For example, what is desirable for organizations may not always be desirable for individuals and meeting individual needs does not always accomplish organizational goals. Indeed, retention in itself does not equal success for either party. Consider the frustrated repatriate who is put on a holding pattern and never uses the knowledge or skills obtained abroad: not only is s/he unhappy, but the organization is not actually gaining the benefit of its investment in the overseas assignment. Even if an organization handles repatriation well, some individuals with overseas experience may receive competitive offers from other employers and leave (a good career outcome for them but a bad financial investment of their expatriating organization).

Another consideration is that an outcome that appears to be "bad" in the short term, may be beneficial in the larger scale of things. A good example here is maybe a person who returns from assignment prematurely. Although technically a "failure," returning may be far better than staying on the assignment – which may end up being more costly for both parties, with a miserable expatriate that fails to meet his/her performance targets and whose family disintegrates amidst adjustment challenges.[158] On the same train of thought, a long-term perspective to assessing the impact of assignments is necessary. For example, one can have a short-term outcome that appears good but ends up having negative long-term consequences (imagine a keen short-term assignee posted to a subsidiary that manages to report positive outcomes as a result of a managerial intervention, but that same intervention is imposed without the collaboration of the subsidiary and in the long run ends up creating more problems than it solves).[159]

DESIGNING A GLOBAL MOBILITY PROGRAM

If MNEs are to capitalize on the knowledge and competencies gained by their expatriates, they need global mobility programs that are not only systematic but also aligned to the strategy of the organization.[160] Yet most organizations report that the way they manage mobility is not meaningfully integrated with organizational talent management.[161] There are several key areas that must be considered in designing a global mobility program:

- *Strategic alignment*: It is important to understand how the expatriation/repatriation program fits with the staffing strategy of the organizations. Further, understanding the overall strategy of the firm allows time for mobility programs to be developed in advance as opposed to as a response to problems.
- *Understanding different strategic demands*: The support requirements for an organization that operates in a few relatively similar host countries are dramatically different to that of an organization that relocates employees to dozens of culturally different loca-

tions around the world. Assignments are also likely to vary on the degree of intercultural interaction required and expatriate roles vary with regard to the extent to which they contain a developmental component. These factors influence the appropriateness of specific support activities. A key area to consider here is alternative mobility forms for which very little organizational support appears to exist.[162]

- *Defining the expatriation–repatriation cycle*: Consistent with the staffing strategy of the firm, the most likely mix of assignment types, their sequence and duration needs to be determined. This provides the organization and the employee with a road map of the type, length and possible countries of assignments that would be likely and how this would relate to career development.

- *Developing support practices for the entire assignment*: Support is needed before, during and after the assignment. While practices should be customized to fit specific circumstances, the best practices that have been identified center around proving career support, greater opportunity to use the international experience, greater choices of post-assignment positions, greater recognition during and after assignment, logistical help, and support for the family.

- *Monitoring programs*: Practices must be carefully monitored to ensure the desired effects are being achieved. For example, programs designed to encourage long-term loyalty may succeed only in improving short-term retention.[163] Organizations must consider the career aspirations of their employees as well as how global mobility fits with the organization's strategic staffing plan.

CHAPTER SUMMARY

This chapter examines global mobility issues both from the perspective of the employee and the employer. Employers are interested in deploying individuals according to their global staffing strategy to positions where they can perform effectively. Employees are also interested in accomplishing the job at hand, but typically take on a foreign assignment with a goal of advancing their career. A changing perspective on what constitutes a career is an important consideration in how both the individual and the organization view a global assignment. A key factor in the success of an overseas assignment is the extent to which the employee and his or her family adjust to the overseas environment. Individual, job, and organizational factors all contribute to the ability of expatriates and their family to adjust. In addition to traditional expatriate postings many organizations, often in order to reduce costs, employ different mobility options such as short-term assignments, commuter assignments and flexpatriates. Another source of globally mobile talent is self-initiated expatriates. Each type of mobility has its own advantages and disadvantages for individuals, their families, and organizations. While most employees on overseas assignment are men, there is a growing number of female expatriates. Along with the increase in dual career couples, this presents additional challenges to organizations to provide appropriate support for international assignees. In order for firms to capitalize on the knowledge and experience gained by employees on overseas assignments they try to retain repatriates in the organization. But retention is only one possible way of measuring whether assignments are successful or not.

QUESTIONS FOR DISCUSSION

1. What are the advantages and disadvantages of the different types of global assignments?
2. Why is family adjustment the reason most often given for expatriates failing to meet the terms of the global assignment?
3. Are women just as effective in global assignments as men? Why or why not?
4. Are global assignments good for your career? Why or why not?
5. Why is repatriation adjustment often more difficult than the initial adjustment to the foreign country?
6. Are there any differences between corporate and self-initiated expatriation?

NOTES

1. Shaffer, Kraimer, Chen, & Bolino (2012); Takeuchi (2010).
2. Briscoe and Hall (2006); Schein (1996).
3. Thomas, Lazarova, & Inkson (2005).
4. GMAC, NFTC, & SHRM Global Forum (2004); Reiche & Harzing (2011).
5. World Trade Organization (2012).
6. KPMG (2019).
7. Deloitte (2018); KPMG (2019); Santa Fe Relocation (2019); Shaffer, Kraimer, Chen, & Bolino (2012).
8. Reiche (2006); Reiche (2011).
9. Inkson, Arthur, Pringle, & Barry (1997); Suutari, Brewster, Mäkelä, Dickmann, & Tornikoski (2018).
10. See Peiperl & Jonsen (2007) for a discussion; Shaffer, Kraimer, Chen, & Bolino (2012).
11. Deloitte (2020).
12. PwC Global (2020).
13. Briscoe, Schuler, & Tarique (2012); Caligiuri & Bonache (2016); Dowling, Festing, Engle, & Gröschl (2009); Global Relocation Trends (2012); GMAC, NFTC, & SHRM Global Forum (2004).
14. Global Relocation Trends (2010, 2011, 2012); GMAC, NFTC, & SHRM Global Forum (2004); Caligiuri & Bonache (2016).
15. KPMG (2019).
16. Global Relocation Trends (2012); Santa Fe Relocation (2019).
17. Collings & Isichei (2018).
18. Santa Fe Relocation (2019).
19. See BGRS (2020); Deloitte (2018); KPMG (2019).
20. Mayrhofer, Reichel, & Sparrow (2012).
21. Mayrhofer, Reichel, & Sparrow (2012).
22. Shaffer, Kraimer, Chen, & Bolino (2012).
23. Mayrhofer, Hartmann, Michelitsch-Rield, & Kollinger (2004); Shaffer, Kraimer, Chen, & Bolino (2012).
24. Collings & Isichei (2018).

25. Shaffer, Kraimer, Chen, & Bolino (2012).

26. Bücker, Poutsma, Schouteten, & Nies (2020).

27. Suutari & Brewster (2000).

28. McNulty & Brewster (2017).

29. For more on self-initiated overseas experience see Inkson, Arthur, Pringle, & Barry (1997) and Suutari & Brewster (2000).

30. Doherty, Dickmann, & Mills (2011); Glassock & Fee (2015).

31. Froese & Peltokorpi (2013).

32. Dickmann, Suutari, Brewster, Mäkelä, Tanskanen, & Tornikoski (2018).

33. Froese & Petlokorpi (2013).

34. Crowley-Henry (2012).

35. Hippler, Haslberger, & Brewster (2017).

36. English (1958).

37. Ward & Kennedy (1993).

38. Lazarova, Westman. & Shaffer (2010).

39. Lysgaard (1955).

40. Gullahorn & Gullahorn (1963).

41. Church (1982); see also related work on the complex ways in which types of international experience relate to expatriate performance in Takeuchi, Li, & Wang (2019).

42. See Briody & Chrisman (1991); Nicholson & Imaizumi (1993).

43. Bhaskar-Shrinivas, Harrison, Shaffer, & Luk (2005); Hechanova, Beehr, & Christiansen (2003); Takeuchi, Yun, & Tesluk (2002).

44. Cole (2011); Shaffer & Harrison (2001).

45. De Leon & McPartlin (1995).

46. Brookfield Global Relocation Services (2016); Global Relocation Trends (2012).

47. See Tung (1981).

48. He, An, & Berry (2019); Selmer, Ebrahimi, & Mingtao (2002).

49. Kierner (2018).

50. Santa Fe Relocation (2019).

51. See Harris (2004); Punnett, Crocker, & Stevens (1992).

52. Cole (2012); Linehan & Walsh (2001).

53. Moore (2002).

54. For additional discussion see Cole (2012); Harris (2004); Harris (2006); Linehan & Walsh (2001); Punnett (1997); Punnet, Crocker, & Stevens (1992).

55. See Caliguiri (2000); Mol, Born, Willemsen, & Van der Molen (2005).

56. See Thomas & Fitzsimmons (2008).

57. Thomas (1998).

58. Church (1982).

59. Thomas & Fitzsimmons (2008).

60. See Benson (1978); Thomas (2008).

61. Takeuchi, Tesluk, Yun, & Lepak (2005); see also Takeuchi, Li, & Wang (2019).

62. See for example, Naumann (1993); Takeuchi & Hannon (1996); Takeuchi, Li, & Wang (2019).

63. Black & Gregersen (1991).

64. Takeuchi, Li, & Wang (2019).

65. See Thomas, Elron, Stahl, Ekelund, Ravlin, Cerdin, et al. (2008).

66. Tadmor & Tetlock (2006).

67. See Taylor & Napier (1996).

68. Hemmasi & Downes (2013).

69. Selmer & Lauring (2009); see another example in Furusawa & Brewster (2016).

70. Hemmasi & Downes (2013).

71. Hippler, Caligiuri, Johnson, & Baytalskaya (2014).

72. Selmer, Chiu, & Shenkar (2007).

73. Hemmasi & Downes (2013).

74. Florkowski & Fogel (1999).

75. Mayrhofer, Reichel, & Sparrow (2012); Meyskens, Von Glinow, Werther, & Clarke (2009).

76. Collings & Isichei (2018).

77. Crowley-Henry, Heaslip, & Martin (2014).

78. Tahvanainen, Welch, & Worm (2005).

79. Mäkelä, Bergbom, Saarenpää, & Suutari (2015).

80. Fischlmayr & Puchmüller (2016).

81. Mayrhofer, Hartmann, Michelitsch-Rield, & Kollinger (2004); Starr & Currie (2009); Welch, Welch, & Worm (2007).

82. See Thomas & Fitzsimmons (2008) for a discussion of cross-cultural skills.

83. Thomas (2008).

84. Tahvanainen, Welch, & Worm (2005).

85. Kang, Shen, & Benson (2017); Tahvanainen, Welch, & Worm (2005).

86. Global Relocation Trends (2012).

87. Mayrhofer, Hartmann, Michelitsch-Rield, & Kollinger (2004); Welch, Welch, & Worm (2007).

88. Global Relocation Trends (2010, 2011, 2012).

89. Mayrhofer, Reichel, & Sparrow (2012).

90. BGRS (2020).

91. Antal & Izraeli (1993).

92. Brookfield Global Relocation Services (2016); Santa Fe Relocation (2019).

93. Berry & Bell (2012) cited in Shortland (2018a).

94. Shortland (2018b).

95. Doherty, Dickmann, & Mills (2011); Froese & Peltokorpi (2013).

96. Caligiuri & Tung (1999); Sinangil & Ones (2003).

97. For example, see Taylor & Napier (1996).

98. Bastida (2018).

99. Stroh, Varma, & Valy-Durbin (2000).

100. Adler (1984); Stroh, Varma, & Valy-Durbin (2000).

101. Adler (1984); Lowe, Downes, & Kroeck (1999).

102. Punnett (1997).

103. van der Velde, Bossink, & Jansen (2005).

104. Shortland (2018b).

105. Fischlmayr & Puchmüller (2016).

106. Shortland (2018a).

107. See Thomas (2008).

108. Napier & Taylor (2002).

109. See Caligiuri & Tung (1999); Napier & Taylor (2002).

110. Shen & Jiang (2015).

111. Stroh, Varma, & Valy-Durbin (2000).

112. Chusmir & Frontczak (1990).

113. Varma & Stroh (2001).

114. See Black & Gregerson (1991); Peterson, Napier, & Won (1995).

115. Black & Gregerson (1991).

116. See Poe (2000).

117. Global Relocation Trends (2010).

118. Lazarova & Cerdin (2007).

119. Kraimer, Shaffer, & Bolino (2009).

120. Reiche, Kraimer, & Harzing (2011); for a recent review, see Chiang, van Esch, Birtch, & Shaffer (2018).

121. Brookfield Global Relocation Services (2016).

122. AIRINC (2019).

123. For a discussion see Torbiörn (1985) and also Black & Gregersen (1991).

124. Kraimer, Shaffer, Harrison, & Ren (2012).

125. Napier & Peterson (1991).

126. Harvey (1989).

127. See Harvey (1982) for additional information on this topic.

128. See De Cieri, Dowling, & Taylor (1991).

129. Enloe & Lewin (1987).

130. Rogers, Ha, & Ockey (2020).

131. Black & Gregersen (1991).

132. Global Relocation Trends (2010, 2012).

133. Ellis, Thorn, & Yao (in press).

134. Tharenou & Caulfield (2010).

135. Lindsay, Sharma, & Rashad (2019); Tharenou & Caufield (2010).

136. AIRINC (2019).

137. Spurk, Hirschi, & Dries (2019).

138. For example, see Feldman & Thomas (1992); Stahl & Cerdin (2004).

139. Benson & Pattie (2008); Biemann & Braakmann (2013); Doherty & Dickmann (2012); Zhu, Wanberg, Harrison, & Diehn (2016).

140. Carpenter, Sanders, & Gregersen (2001); Conyon, Haß, Vergauwe, & Zhang (2018).

141. Kraimer, Shaffer, & Bolino (2009).

142. Suutari, Brewster, Mäkelä, Dickmann, & Tornikoski (2018).

143. Inkson, Arthur, Pringle, & Barry (1997); Shaffer, Kraimer, Chen, & Bolino (2012).

144. Dickmann, Suutari, Brewster, Mäkelä, Tanskanen, & Tornikoski (2018).

145. De Leon & McPartlin (1995); see also Weeks, Weeks, & Willis-Muller (2009).

146. See Selmar & Lam (2004).

147. Hon & Lu (2010); Peltokorpi (in press); Toh & DeNisi (2003); van Bakel (2019).

148. Fee (2020).

149. McNulty & Tharenou (2004).

150. Global Relocation Trends (2010).

151. McNulty, De Cieri, & Hutchings (2013).

152. KPMG (2019).

153. Global Relocation Trends (2012); Lazarova & Caligiuri (2001).

154. Fink, Meierewert, & Rohr (2005).

155. See Lazarova & Tarique (2005) for a discussion of knowledge transfer upon repatriation.

156. Burmeister & Deller (2016); Burmeister, Lazarova, & Deller (2018); Lazarova & Cerdin (2007); Sanchez-Vidal, Sanz-Valle, & Barba-Aragon (2018).

157. Brewster, Bonache, Cerdin, & Suutari (2014); Inkson, Arthur, Pringle, & Barry (1997); Lazarova & Cerdin (2007).

158. Harzing (1995a).

159. Brewster, Bonache, Cerdin, & Suutari (2014).

160. Collings & Isichei (2018).

161. AIRINC (2019); KPMG (2018, 2019).

162. Bücker, Poutsma, Schouteten, & Nies (2020).

163. Bücker, Poutsma, Schouteten, & Nies (2020).

12
International employment relations

CHAPTER LEARNING OBJECTIVES

After reading this chapter, you should be able to:

1. Compare and contrast the elements of national employment relations systems.
2. Identify how national cultures, institutions, and MNEs influence approaches to industrial/employment relations globally.
3. Describe how MNEs handle country variations in employee communication and participation.
4. Recognize the impact of international organizations and supranational bodies on employment relations systems.

Social dumping within the European Union[1]

Jan de Vries, director of HR at Digital Device Corporation's (DDC) Rotterdam production facility, stared in disbelief at the email he had just received from DDC's headquarters in San Jose, California. It seemed that the company had decided to make the production facility in Limerick, Ireland, its lead operation in Europe. Two production lines in the Rotterdam plant were to be shut down making several hundred employees redundant, while the Limerick facility would be greatly expanded. Besides, once the transition was complete his own responsibilities would be handled from the Limerick facility and it was suggested that he should take early retirement.

DDC was a leading manufacturer of signal processing devices. Increased competition from Asia had caused it to restructure worldwide to reduce manufacturing costs. Two days previous all employees at the Limerick facility had attended a video presentation in which the CEO of DDC had (based on an EU grant) described DDC's intention to invest almost €75 million in the plant, resulting in the gain of hundreds of jobs. However, in return for the additional investment DDC wanted employees at the Limerick plant to take a 12% pay reduction. The following day each employee received a letter saying that the CDC was not convinced that Limerick was the best location for their European headquarters and that the question of location was still open. Attached to the letter was a ballot asking for acceptance of the pay cut. Only a dozen employees voted No.

Jan de Vries wasn't sure about the labor laws in Ireland, but he felt sure the company's action was a clear violation of the Works Councils Act in the Netherlands and similar EU legislation that required consultation on such matters. "This will all be settled in court," he thought to himself. "But how long will that take and what will be the end result? Can our local works council actually win in a battle with a large multinational company like DDC?"

INTRODUCTION

Different economic, political, legal, and socio-cultural environments have resulted in very different employment relations (ER) systems (aka industrial relations or labor relations systems) around the world. For many years, MNEs have had to consider how the ER systems function locally within each individual country where they operate. In the early 21st century, however, global organizations, such as DDC in the opening vignette, must consider the increasing profile of international employee representation. Major campaigns by international trade union federations bolstered by regional regulation such as in the European Union (EU) are increasing the level of cross-border communication on ER issues. Moreover, in many countries, ER is an integrated aspect of HRM activities and cannot be dismissed as a separate field of study or activity. We explore further here what ER means for managing people globally.

EMPLOYMENT RELATIONS

Contemporary international employment relations has at its core the trade union movement that evolved in many countries during the Industrial Revolution. Trade unions (called labor unions in the United States, and hence also the term "labor relations") originate from large numbers of workers who were drawn into the workforce by the Industrial Revolution and took up unfamiliar roles in industrial firms. These unskilled and semi-skilled workers lacked individual bargaining power with their employer and thus banded together to improve their employment conditions. While similar to the guilds of medieval Europe in some ways, these unions lacked control over the artisanship of a craft because of the changing nature of work.

In general, a trade union, through its leadership, bargains with the employer on behalf of union members and negotiates contracts regarding wages and working conditions. Some unions may provide benefits to members such as unemployment insurance, professional training, or legal advice. Unions can also try to further their goals through industrial action (strikes and resistance to lockouts) and by promoting favorable legislation.[2] Several types of unions are common today across many countries:[3]

- *General unions* may be open to membership of almost everyone in a country, irrespective of the organization or industry in which they work, such as the Transport and General Workers' Union in the United Kingdom and the Australian Workers' Union in Australia.
- *Industry unions* represent all levels of employees in an industry, such as the Utility Workers Union of America (UWUA) in the United States.
- *Craft unions* are based on occupations and represent employees across industries, such as plumbers, carpenters, or musicians.
- *Conglomerate unions* are a more recent phenomenon that has emerged from unions merging to increase their membership and power (such as the *Vereinte Dienstleistungsgewerkschaft* [United Services Union] in Germany).[4]
- *Enterprise unions* limit their membership to employees of a single firm, which has been common practice in Japan.

- Other types of union include *professional unions* such as the Department for Professional Employees in the United States, or *public sector* unions such as UNISON in the United Kingdom.

Trade unions are one mechanism through which employees are given *voice* in an organization. Other employee voice mechanisms range from informal opportunities for employees to share their ideas or concerns directly with management, through formal activities put in place by the organization such as suggestion schemes or quality circles.[5]

Regardless of the employee voice mechanism in place, how employees can be involved in organizational decision-making related to the employment relationship can take three forms:

- *Information*: management shares with employees (or their representatives) information about strategic or financial matters such as how well the company is performing or any planned changes that might affect the workforce.
- *Consultation*: management seeks the opinion of employees (or their representatives) in planned strategic or operational changes that might in some way affect the employment relationship or aspects of the workplace.
- *Negotiation*: management must reach a deal with employees (or their representatives) regarding a planned change that affects them, such as the closing of an operating unit or the introduction of a new work from home policy.

Whether employees are entitled to either information, consultation, or negotiation rights depends on (a) what the topic is, and (b) the regulations or agreements in place that provide employees with such rights. We discuss how this varies between countries here.

National ER systems

National ER[6] systems reflect the society in which they operate. They can be thought of as a sub-system of society, not unlike political or economic systems.[7] An ER system consists of *actors*, *rules*, *environmental context*, and *ideology* which is represented graphically in Figure 12.1. The *actors* are organizations, employees, and governments who maintain relations with each other through three tightly interconnected *environmental contexts*. The technological features of the work situation (technological context), the market opportunities or limitations (economic context), and the relative power distribution between actors (political context) are dynamic forces that result in the interactions among actors. The products of this interaction are the substantive and procedural *rules* regarding ER that occupy the center of Figure 12.1. Finally, the system includes an *ideology* that helps to bind the system together as an entity.

This framework represents a generic model of ER that exists within a nation. However, the precise structure of the ER system in different countries is distinctive because of its historical development.

Studies of ER across countries have highlighted that there are systematic differences in approaches across institutional contexts. In *liberal market economies*, companies have a lot of autonomy when they bargain with labor market participants. This leads to either corporatist or voluntarist ER systems. Corporatist systems take a unilateral approach, whereby firms make

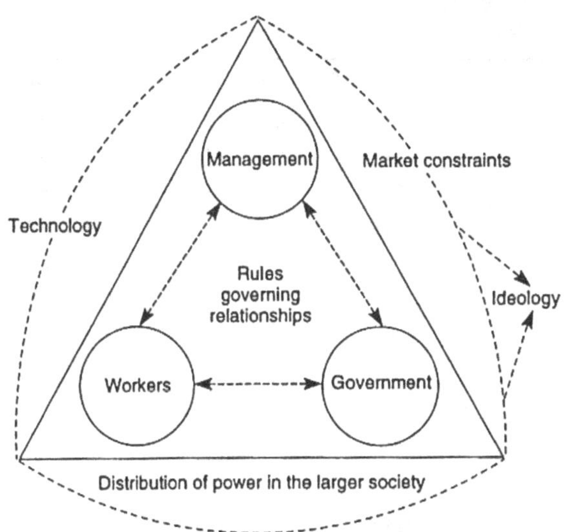

Source: Dunlop (1958).

Figure 12.1 Industrial relations system

their own decision whether to recognize employee representatives. Voluntarist systems also allow firms to make their own decisions, but employers are encouraged to enter voluntarily into agreements with employee representative bodies such as trade unions.[8] *Coordinated market economies*, in contrast, have statutory ER systems characterized by dense networks of institutions, sustained by law, customs, and values, that constrain individual actors to broader collective priorities.[9] Finally, *socialist market economies* are marked by centralized government control, which also extends to all union activities.

The union structure in a society is the result of many factors including how the unions have evolved historically.[10] For example, the new skills of the Industrial Revolution led to craft and professional unions, while mass production favored industrial and general unions. And white-collar employees tend to see their interests as different from those of other workers and hence prefer separate unions. In some countries, unions and management are considered adversaries (e.g., India, United States, United Kingdom), while in others (e.g., the Netherlands) there is extensive employee voice in corporate decision-making through works councils, and in some (e.g., Germany) employees are represented on supervisory boards and other decision-making bodies where they have codetermination rights on major employment-related strategic decisions, as we discuss further below.[11]

While unions continue to be influential around the world, trade union membership as a percentage of the workforce (union membership density) has been in decline in most industrialized countries for some time. Table 12.1 shows a comparison of the union density in several OECD countries between 2008 and 2018, also indicating the peak of union participation. Only three countries (France, Iceland, Italy) show a slight increase in union density over this time. The highest level of union membership in 2018 was in Iceland at 90.7% followed by Denmark

Table 12.1 Trade union density in a range of OECD Countries 2008–2018 (peak trade union density since 1960)

Country	Density 2018	Density 2008	Peak Density	Date of Peak
Australia	13.7	18.8	50.2	1976
Austria	26.3	29.6	67.9	1960**
Belgium	50.3	54.5	55.7	1995
Canada	25.9	27.0	35.9	1984
Czech Republic	11.5	16.9	46.3	1995**
Denmark	66.5	67.6	80.8	1983
Finland	60.3	69.9	80.7	1993
France	8.8	8.5	22.1	1973
Germany	16.5	19.0	36.0	1991
Hungary	7.9	14.4	49.1	1995**
Iceland	90.7	84.7	94.3	2004
Ireland	24.1	30.9	54.8	1978
Italy	34.4	33.4	50.4	1978
Japan	17.0	18.0	35.2	1969
Luxembourg	31.8	36.5	53.0	1984
Mexico	12.0	15.6	24.3	1992**
Netherlands	16.4	20.0	40.0	1960**
New Zealand	18.8	21.4	69.1	1980
Norway	49.2	49.4	60.8	1961
South Korea	10.5*	10.2	18.6	1989
Spain	13.6	17.5	18.0	1993
Sweden	64.9	68.3	83.9	1993
Turkey	9.2	10.7	23.0	1987
United Kingdom	23.4	27.5	50.0	1981
United States	10.1	11.9	30.9	1960

Notes: *2017, ** First year data available.
Source: OECD (2019).

at 66.5% and Sweden at 64.9%. The lowest union membership was in Hungary at 7.9% followed by France at 8.8% and Turkey at 9.2%.[12]

However, it is very important to recognize that union density tells only part of the story. In some countries, unions may represent the majority of workers even though only a small percentage are members (e.g., Austria, Germany, France, the Netherlands), while in other countries they only represent their actual members (e.g., Canada, United States).[13] To illustrate this point further, although France has one of the lowest levels of trade union density (as noted earlier), it has one of the highest levels of collective bargaining coverage in the OECD, last recorded at 98.9% in 2014.[14] In other words, employees do not necessarily have to be a member of a trade union to be recipients of the agreements that the relevant trade union has reached with their employer or the industry in which they work. Figure 12.2 compares several nations in terms of trade union density versus collective bargaining coverage. We can see that there is a clear divide between countries where trade union density figures are very similar to the level of collective bargaining coverage, and those where there are substantial differences between the two.

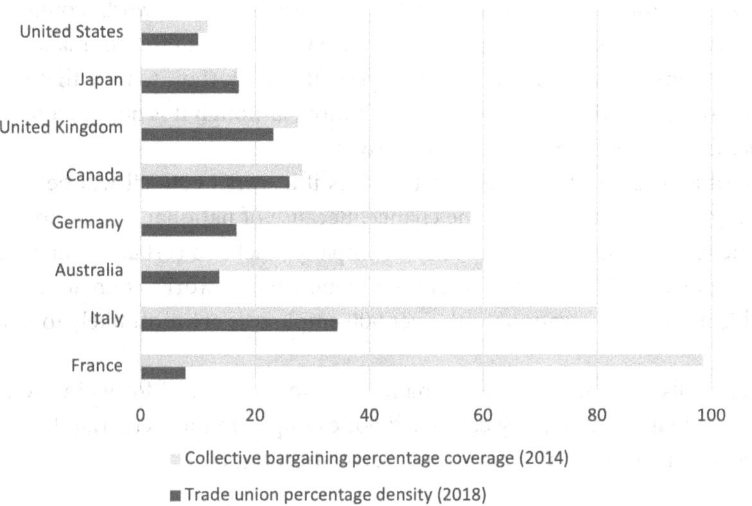

Source: Trade union percentage density data from https://stats.oecd.org/Index.aspx?DataSetCode =TUD; Collective bargaining percentage coverage data from https://stats.oecd.org/Index.aspx ?DataSetCode=CBC.

Figure 12.2   Comparison of trade union density and collective bargaining coverage across nations

Overall, the trend that we can see is of union representation decline, both in terms of union density and collective bargaining coverage.[15] Much of the numerical decline can be attributed to economic factors such as reduced public sector employment, heightened price competition, and a reduction in the percentage of employment accounted for by manufacturing industries. However, a dramatic rise or fall in trade union membership is often linked to systematic changes in governance or major legislative changes in countries or regions. For example, in the early 1990s, a huge increase in unionization rates accompanied the end of the apartheid era in South Africa and a large decrease followed the introduction of the Employment Contracts Act in New Zealand.[16]

The diverse strategies of labor, management, and the government are related to variations in union density. For example, the low union density in the United States is likely due to the limited extent of collective bargaining in the public sector and among white-collar workers. In contrast, the depth of collective bargaining and union security, combined with favorable public policy, explains Sweden's high union density.[17]

Works councils and codetermination

An alternative form of employee representation to trade unions that exists primarily across many European countries is works councils.[18] A works council is a firm-level elected body representing the interests of all workers in an organization. As such, it facilitates management–labor communication on a wide range of employment-related issues (aka employee voice), functioning as a complement to national collective bargaining. The works council has the right to receive information and to be consulted relative to decisions the firm makes that will have social and economic consequences for employees. It is important to note that works councils are not synonymous with trade union representation, although it is not uncommon for works council members to also be union representatives.

The size of an organization largely determines if a works council will be established: the larger the organization, the greater the chance. Because of national legislation or regulations, works councils only come into effect once a company reaches a certain number of employees. It is then employees who need to initiate the request that a works council be established. In practice, this means organizations with over 500 employees are most likely to establish works councils.[19]

Works councils exist under different names and in a variety of forms in several European countries, and their rights vary by country.[20] For example, in the Netherlands, works councils legally have information, consultation, and negotiation rights.

- Information facilitates the works council monitoring the organization's compliance with relevant laws or agreements related to employee well-being, health, and safety.
- Consultation rights relate to decisions with major economic consequences such as corporate downsizing or expansion, or financial loans or investments.
- Negotiation rights are more specifically tied to decisions related directly to employees, including vacation allowances, working hours, selection and promotion policies, training opportunities, and health and safety in the workplace.[21]

Unlike a trade union, works councils do not have the right to call a strike.

The extensive right of employees to voice their views in organizations is referred to as *codetermination*. Codetermination is the legal requirement that employees participate on supervisory boards or boards of directors requiring management to obtain their agreement when major strategic decisions are to be made.[22] Germany has a well-established system of codetermination that is reinforced through national legislation. The Works Constitution Act (*Betriebsverfassungsgesetz*) applies to companies with five or more permanent employees and provides employees extensive voice rights (through works councils) depending on the topic under consideration. In Germany, there is also a two-tier board system for organizations: a supervisory board representing owners and stakeholders, and a smaller board of the company's managers. Under codetermination, employee representatives (either works councilors or trade union officials) make up one-third to one-half of the supervisory board (depending on the relevant piece of legislation for the company).[23]

EMPLOYMENT RELATIONS POLICIES IN MNEs

Because of the significant variation that exists around the world in regulations and traditions by which employers interact with trade unions and other employee representative bodies, MNEs often rely heavily on managers in local subsidiaries for direction.[24] The extent to which MNE headquarters exercise control over ER in the subsidiary depends on several factors including: (a) the location of the firm headquarters and the importance of its international operations, (b) the characteristics and degree of integration of subsidiaries, and (c) the experience of the MNE in ER and the attitude of its managers toward unions.[25] This implies that MNEs can consider the operating conditions and then choose their overall strategy toward handling ER. This can take one of three approaches:

- *Unitarist*: In the United States, the traditionally unitarist (anti-union) stance of firms (based on a history of violence and intimidation) means that employees have little opportunity for formal, independent representation. Instead, employers who are known for looking after their employees adopt a system of welfare capitalism, whereby enlightened employer initiatives are introduced to prevent unionization (such as high involvement or high commitment work systems). US-headquartered firms also tend to exercise greater control over ER in their subsidiaries than do their European counterparts. Perhaps due to the success of the US economy operating under this model, there has been significant impact of US MNEs spreading this unitarist model of ER best practice worldwide.[26]
- *Partnership*: Partnership means creating a balance between employer and employee interests for mutual benefit, whereby both parties (management and employees) have common goals and believe in working together for the betterment of both.[27] European firms have a long history of dealing with industrial unions as compared to the United States where firm-level ER is more prevalent.[28] Partnership approaches that include a "win–win" attitude are therefore not uncommon (see Box 12.1 for an example).
- *Contingent*: Taking a contingent approach means adopting the local host-country practices as opposed to having an overall strategic approach to ER. Each subsidiary conducts its ER in a manner that meets local legislative and regulatory requirements (either unitarist or partnership), allowing the MNE to be compliant across its operating locations.

BOX 12.1 PARTNERSHIP IN UNILEVER

In research conducted in the early 2000s, Unilever describe their approach to ER as proactively and deliberately involving trade unions in management decisions that influence employee working life. This partnership approach emphasized the importance of developing a cooperative relationship with unions, in which the key to success is the creation of trust relationships between management and employee representatives.

In Netherlands-based Unilever, trust is reinforced by the company providing union and works council member training to ensure the negotiating partners have the skills that they need to be effective. In this country, collective agreements negotiated with trade unions apply to all employees covered by the agreement regardless of whether they are trade union members. This means that there is little motivation for employees to become members of the union. Consequently, Unilever provided funds to the primary trade union to help increase membership levels to ensure the representativeness of this compulsory negotiating body.[29]

A key factor in determining the extent to which headquarters attempts to exercise control over subsidiary ER policies is the extent to which the activities of subsidiaries are integrated. The development of an integrated network among subsidiaries requires a high level of coordination and control, not only of investment and production policies but also for the transfer of technology. The combination of the need for consistency in technology transfer, the importance of the integrated subsidiary to overall operations, and the high degree of labor mobility that this causes encourages the involvement of headquarters in ER.[30] Other subsidiary characteristics are influential as well. Not surprisingly, for example, subsidiaries that are formed through greenfield activities tend to be more influenced by headquarters than those acquired from established local organizations. In the greenfield case, organizations are likely to replicate policies and practices that have worked well elsewhere. There also tends to be more headquarters involvement in ER in younger, strategically important, and poorly performing subsidiaries or those highly dependent on headquarters.[31]

An MNE's country of origin also influences its ER approach. Given the importance of shareholder value in liberal market economies (LMEs) (the United States or United Kingdom are common examples), firms in these economies focus on short-term maximization of the value of assets and minimal employee voice. In contrast, in coordinated market economies (CME), such as Germany and the Netherlands, firms adopt a long-term perspective to meet a range of stakeholders' needs, including providing employees with voice. Consequently, the MNE's country of origin affects the employees' ability to influence management decisions.[32]

When MNEs from LME or CME countries encounter the socialist market economies of Asia, the ER systems can look very different. In China, for example, traditionally, trade unions were mandatory at firm level but controlled by the state. Strikes were illegal and worker rights generally suppressed. Over recent years, however, underground independent union activity has been increasing, as has the number of labor disputes. The essence of the unrest is that while unions want better employment conditions, the state wants to keep employment costs low to support the growing economy.[33] To address the unrest, the Chinese government has implemented various steps to improve the ER climate, including the Labor Contract Law of 2008, which was designed to improve employment conditions.[34]

In many socialist market economies, the story is similar to that of China. The state plays a dominant role, the economy is built on the principles of low cost, and worker rights remain constrained. This is not a situation of employees not having rights protected by law but rather that those laws are not uniformly applied. Many socialist market economies use the law to severely restrict trade union activity, collective bargaining rights, and the right to strike. As markets in these economies slowly started to open to increasing MNE penetration, the pressure for more pluralistic ER systems has been increasing and strikes and other forms of labor activism have become somewhat more common.[35] Globalization is slowly weakening some restrictions on collective ER activities, increasing employer autonomy, but overall, the labor movement remains underdeveloped.

EMPLOYMENT RELATIONS IN MNEs

The previous discussion outlined the variation in ER policies and procedures that exist in MNEs. However, it is not only the multi-nationality of the organization that is important but also the strategy of the particular MNE in combination with the ER systems in the countries in which it operates that should be considered. In the following, we examine how the MNE upsets the balance in an ER system and also how trade unions influence the strategy of the MNE.

MNEs and national ER systems

MNEs may upset the balance of national ER systems (as shown in Figure 12.1) because (a) the decision-making process and strategy of the MNE lie outside national boundaries, making it difficult for local actors to know about or understand, and (b) the MNE can reorganize its factors of production internationally.[36] As such, they are not bound by the constraints of a single national ER system and thus have far more leverage than enterprises that operate strictly within national boundaries. This raises concerns for trade unions in at least the following three areas.[37]

Ability to relocate factors of production: MNEs can find alternate sources of supply to reduce exposure to an unfavorable ER climate. Multiple sources of supply can be used to reduce vulnerability to industrial action and production can be temporarily shifted between subsidiaries in various countries. According to the International Confederation of Free Trade Unions, it is the "ever-present threat of relocation to countries with low wages, low standards and a low degree of organization" that puts MNEs in a strong position to put pressure on trade unions and their workers, as well as on their governments, to accept whatever they are proposing.[38]

Remote location of authority: The decision-making structure of the MNE is not tied to location and the exact locus of power may be difficult for unions to decipher. Local management may claim that they are simply following orders from headquarters, while at the same time headquarters may claim that local management is entirely responsible for the issue at hand. Contributing to this problem is that the exact strategy of the MNE is difficult for unions to understand. And, because of obscure financial reporting, internal transfers among subsidiaries, and so on, it may even be difficult to know exactly what activities are carried out by the organization in what countries. This severely limits the union's bargaining position because they find it difficult to determine if a particular subsidiary can meet bargaining demands.

Substantial resources: The broad financial resources of the MNE can limit the union's bargaining power. Large multinationals can absorb losses as a result of industrial action in one location and, as indicated previously, compensate with operations in another location. The ability of unions to have an economic impact on these organizations is therefore limited. In addition to financial resources, large MNEs have significant expertise in ER at their disposal which may be far superior to the knowledge held by local unions.

Despite the many advantages that accrue to the MNE because of its border-spanning activities, trade unions are a significant consideration in the formation and implementation of MNE strategy. In fact, the characteristics of the ER system are a key consideration in making strategic location decisions.[39]

Influence of trade unions on MNEs

While labor does not have the enforcement tools of government, it can still influence the strategy of the MNE. From the perspective of the MNE, organized labor limits strategic choice by preventing the optimum degree of global integration, constraining the ability of MNEs to vary employment levels, and by affecting wage rates.[40]

Barriers to Global Integration: Plans to increase efficiency by rationalizing and integrating operations can be prevented or delayed in countries, under pressure from national unions that have enacted restrictive legislation. For example, in some European countries, to carry out layoff plans, MNEs must demonstrate substantial losses resulting from structural conditions that make the proposed changes necessary. As shown in the opening vignette, unilateral action by MNEs can sometimes create serious repercussions. As a result, some MNEs have bought labor peace by committing not to integrate their operations to the most efficient degree.[41]

Constraints on Employment Levels: The inability to adjust staffing levels at will can have broad implications, especially in countries where reductions in staffing levels are particularly difficult. For example, a strike at one General Motors plant in the United States prevented GM's Mexican operations from getting the parts it needed. However, Mexican labor law prevented GM from laying off workers thus adding to the pressure on GM to settle.[42]

Influencing Wage Rates: Labor costs, while decreasing in comparison to other costs, still play a major role in determining organizational competitiveness. The influence of labor negotiations on wage rates within different countries can significantly limit the strategic options available to firms.

In this way, labor unions may exert influence more by quietly limiting strategic decisions than by open conflict where they often are at a disadvantage to the superior power of MNEs. MNEs, while delegating much of their ER activity to local subsidiaries, must take this into account when making strategic decisions, especially those involving integration, rationalization, and divestment of activities.

Trade union response to MNEs

Although MNEs are not uniformly anti-union, they have generally been regarded as a threat to the bargaining power of labor.[43] The response of trade unions to try to restore a balance of power in the ER system has taken two basic forms. First is the exchange of information and coordination of activities through the formation of international trade secretariats. Second, is lobbying for favorable national legislation and trying to influence MNEs through international organizations.[44]

Coordination and International Trade Secretariats: Perhaps the most common way in which trade unions try to counter the MNE's bargaining power is through sharing information on the MNE's policies and activities. Additionally, labor groups in one country may support their counterparts in other countries by such activities as refusing to work overtime to supply a market served by striking workers, sending aid to workers in other countries, or disrupting work in their own country.

More formal coordination, primarily information exchange, occurs through global union federations. Global union federations represent workers in a specific industry such as the International Trade Union Confederation (ITUC) and the World Federation of Trade Unions (WFTU). These organizations engage in several information exchange activities (such as research, conferences, company councils, and union–management discussions) with a long-term goal of achieving transnational collective bargaining in the industry they represent.[45]

Influencing through Transnational Organizations and Regulation: Another way in which organized labor can influence MNEs is by lobbying national governments directly. Trade unions in the United States and Europe have been engaged in this activity for many years. However, the conflicting economic interest of both governments and unions has limited the effectiveness of this strategy.[46] That is, it is important to recognize that countries are in competition with each other for the economic benefits that MNEs can bring. Trade union federations have had more success exerting influence over MNEs through transnational organizations such as the International Labour Organization (ILO), the United Nations Council on Trade and Development (UNCTAD), and the Organisation for Economic Co-operation and Development (OECD), as we discuss in the next chapter. However, the guidelines produced by these bodies remain largely voluntary in nature, and hence at the discretion of MNEs if they wish to adopt the recommended principles and practices.

Overall, organized labor has met with only limited success in influencing national and international bodies to regulate MNEs. Additionally, several factors hamper the ability of unions to cooperate internationally. These include that unions in different countries have different goals, different union structures, and collective bargaining methods, and operate in very different legal environments concerning ER.[47] The goal of transnational collective bargaining may in fact be too ambitious[48] and unions might better focus their activities on strengthening national union involvement through company-based bargaining, supporting research on the vulnerability of selected MNEs (such as Walmart[49]), and consolidating the activities of global union federations.

The role of the European Union

What has had a more direct impact than transnational organization guidelines is the European Union (EU), which is a rare example of a supranational governmental entity. The EU can make rules with the force of law, such as the Social Charter (1961; revised 1996) of the Council of Europe and the European Community Charter of Fundamental Social Rights (1989).[50] The EU is a union of 27 member countries across Europe as of 2021, as the United Kingdom exited at the end of 2020 in the widely debated "Brexit" (see Box 12.2).[51] the Social Charter sets out human rights across a range of social situations, including work and employment. Specifically, it lays out the principles of workers' fundamental rights that apply to all member countries. A primary motivation for adoption of the Social Charter is to set a baseline of employment standards that all member countries must incorporate into national legislation so that MNEs locating their operations in European countries cannot play one country off against another in pursuit of "softer" employment standards.

BOX 12.2 BREXIT AND EMPLOYMENT IN THE UNITED KINGDOM

In June 2016, voters in a referendum in the United Kingdom voted by a small majority that the country should leave the EU. The vote was controversial as there were strong feelings on both the "leave" and "remain" sides of the debate. The "leave" voters believed that the control of the EU over the United Kingdom had become too intrusive. The "remain" voters saw value in the regulations imposed by the EU in strengthening the economy and relations with other European countries and beyond. The reality is that, at the time of writing, we do not know for sure what impact Brexit will have on work and employment both in the UK and across Europe in the years ahead when the United Kingdom leaves the union at the end of 2020.

By way of an example, the EU Directive 2004/38/EC allows the free movement of workers between member countries. Once Brexit is complete, this is likely to be one of the most influential changes on the UK economy. Questions are being raised regarding how many lower-paid jobs will be filled in the future. The UK has for several years relied on the influx of employees from less developed Central and Eastern European countries who were prepared to work for lower wages than local workers. Similarly, the UK economy relied to some extent on foreign hires in high-skilled areas where there was insufficient supply within the local labor market. In brief, the lack of freedom of movement of workers is likely to reduce the talent pool open to UK companies and will force greater focus on finding and training local employees.

The EU influences national-level employment legislation in its member countries by issuing Directives. For those Directives that relate to working environments, working conditions, worker protection, employee representation, discrimination, and equality, the EU usually consults with unions and employers. There are many EU Directives that influence the employment relationship, including those that affect collective layoffs, the transfer of undertakings, data protection, discrimination, employer insolvency, information and consultation rights, equal pay, health and safety, a-typical workers, pregnant workers, young workers, posted workers, temporary agency workers, and working time. The Charter of Fundamental Rights does not, however, legislate in pay, right of association, right to strike, or right to impose lockouts.[52]

The Working Time Directive (1993, revised 2003), for example, was highly influential as it introduced a maximum 48-hour workweek, annual paid vacation of at least four weeks, and eleven hours of rest in every 24-hour period. All Directives can be supplemented by legislation or collective bargaining agreements at the national level that surpasses the baseline requirements. In France, for example, the Working Time Directive was improved, in order to increase employment opportunities and reduce work–life imbalance, by restricting the maximum workweek to 35 hours.[53]

European Works Councils: In 1994, the European Union passed a Directive on establishing European Works Councils (EWC) – with functions similar to those of the local works councils, but which operate at the EU level. The EWC Directive applies to companies with at least 1,000 employees within the EU and at least 150 employees in each of at least two Member States. EWCs affect about 60% of the workers in the EU. European Works Councils were created to give representatives of workers from all European countries in large MNEs a direct line of communication to top management.[54] They also ensure that workers in different countries receive the same information about transnational policies and plans (see the vignette that opened this chapter). They give workers' representatives in unions and national works councils the opportunity to consult with each other and to develop a common European response to employers' transnational plans, which management must then consider before those plans are implemented.[55] While there is some speculation that EWCs could become instruments for collective bargaining at the European level, so far this does not seem to be the case. Most sectors seem to use the EWCs as a means to gain information to be used in domestic negotiations rather than across countries.[56]

The effectiveness of EWCs on management decision-making has been traced to six factors that relate to the company's business operations and the organization and policy approaches of the parties involved.[57] Three sets of structural factors are expected to facilitate or constrain the effectiveness of EWCs. These are:

- Business alignment – the focus and integration of the firm's business activities;
- Management structure – the characteristics of the European management structure, if any;
- ER structure – the existence of an ER system.

Three additional sets of factors relate to the parties involved. These are:

- Management policy – the levels and functions of management that are routinely involved in the EWC (minimalist compliance versus enthusiastic embrace);
- Employee organization – the extent to which the employees involved are a cohesive unit and can draw on trade union resources to support its activity;
- EWC interaction – open constructive and ongoing versus adversarial interaction between management and employees.

In general, it has been found that while EWCs affect the *process* of decision-making on ER issues, it is less common for the *outcomes* of decisions to be affected.[58]

MNE interest in employee representation

The growth both in number and significance of MNEs has created the need for a countervailing force to restore balance to the ER system. International employee representation in the form of EWCs or the like has seemed likely to increase in significance. There are two reasons why MNEs might want to embrace, even take the initiative in establishing international employee representation. These result from a concern for maintaining employee cooperation and commitment and a concern for social responsibility.[59]

Given the intense competition for scarce human resources, management must reconcile two potentially conflicting pressures. On the one hand, there is pressure to reduce costs (often through restructuring) and, on the other, to promote the conditions that result in security, teamwork, and innovation among employees. Employee representation that legitimates management decisions can help to ensure the kind of cooperation and commitment necessary to implement organizational structures that give management the flexibility it needs while also providing security for workers.

In addition to the usefulness of employee representation to maintain internal legitimacy is the increasing concern that organizations have for their image in the larger society. The negotiation of global frameworks that require employee representation is an important way in which MNEs can demonstrate their corporate social responsibility.

CHAPTER SUMMARY

In this chapter, we discuss contemporary international employment relations, which is based on the ER systems that exist in the various societies in which MNEs operate. These systems are composed of organizations, employees, and governments who maintain a balanced relationship with each other within society. However, the transnational capabilities of the MNE such as the ability to relocate factors of production, their remote location of authority, and their significant resources upset the balance of these systems. Typical features of societies with strong employee voice include systems of works councils and/or codetermination to ensure employees have representation in decisions affecting issues related to work and employment. Other factors affecting employee rights to representation in organizational decision-making include the role of transnational organizations (such as the OECD, ILO, and UNCTAD) and supranational bodies, such as the European Union.

QUESTIONS FOR DISCUSSION

1. Describe how the MNE upsets the balance of national employment relations systems.
2. Why is there a decline in union density around the world? What is the likely cause of dramatic rises and falls in unionization?
3. Describe the different approaches that an MNE can take to manage its international employment relations.
4. What is a works council and why might MNEs be interested in them?
5. How is the European Union able to influence the employment relationship in member countries?

NOTES

1. This case is fictional but based on an incident that occurred with Hyster Co. as reported in the *Wall Street Journal*, November 30, 1983.
2. Croucher & Cotton (2009).
3. Poole (1986).
4. Thomas (2017).
5. Kwon & Farndale (2020).
6. While recognizing newer terms such as employment relations we use the more traditional term industrial relations here.
7. Dunlop (1958).
8. Inversi, Buckley, & Dundon (2017).
9. Andersen, Kaine, & Lansbury (2017); Hyman (2004).
10. Clegg (1976).
11. Hannon (2011); Rogers & Streeck (1995).
12. OECD (2019).
13. Briscoe, Schuler & Tarique (2012); Schmitt & Mitukiewicz (2012).
14. https://stats.oecd.org/Index.aspx?DataSetCode=TUD
15. Croucher & Rizov (2012); Schmitt & Mitukiewicz (2012).
16. ILO Press Release November 4, 1997.
17. Poole (1986).
18. Nienhüser 2020).
19. Nienhüser (2020).
20. See https://www.worker-participation.eu/National-Industrial-Relations/Countries for detailed country information.
21. Van den Berg, Grift, & Van Witteloostuijn (2011).
22. Keller & Kirsch (2020).
23. Keller & Kirsch (2020).
24. McDonald, Tüselmann, & Heise (2003).
25. Enderwick (1982); Hamill (1984); Rosenzweig & Nohria (1994).
26. Lamare, Ryan, Farndale, & Gunnigle (2014).
27. Xi, Xu, Wang, & Zhao (2017).
28. Cooke (2001).
29. Lamare, Ryan, Farndale, & Gunnigle (2014).
30. Hamill (1984).
31. Hamill (1984).
32. Lamare, Ryan, Farndale, & Gunnigle (2014).
33. Liu (2013).
34. Chung (2016).
35. Chung (2016).
36. de Nijs (1995).
37. Bean (1985); http://www.icftu.org/pubs/globalisation/EN/report.pdf
38. http://www.icftu.org/pubs/globalisation/EN/report.pdf

39. Cooke & Noble (1998); Radulescu & Robson (2013).

40. Prahalad & Doz (1999).

41. Prahalad & Doz (1999).

42. Templin (1996).

43. de Nijs (1995).

44. See Kosterlitz (1998).

45. Ales & Dufresne (2012).

46. de Nijs (1995).

47. Daniels, Radebaugh, & Sullivan (2011).

48. Ales & Dufresne (2012).

49. See *Wal-Mart: The high cost of low price*, http://www.imdb.com/title/tt0473107/

50. See Addison & Siebert (1994); http://www.europarl.europa.eu/charter/pdf/text_en.pdf

51. Teague & Donaghey (2018).

52. Kaminska (2013).

53. Fagnani & Letablier (2004).

54. http://www.etuc.org/r/57

55. See Sisson (2006) for a discussion of various forms of employee representation.

56. Hann, Hauptmeier, & Waddington (2017).

57. Marginson, Hall, Hoffmann, & Müller (2004).

58. Marginson, Hall, Hoffmann, & Müller (2004).

59. Sisson (2006).

13
Global corporate social responsibility

After reading this chapter you should be able to:

1. Describe how different institutional environments relate to different forms of corporate social responsibility.
2. Identify the ethical issues facing MNEs in the process of the globalization of business.
3. Discuss the elements and usefulness of corporate codes of conduct.
4. Describe the different types of sustainable HRM.
5. Interpret the implications of socially responsible data protection regulations for MNEs.

Tension in Indonesia

Ian McKinstry, General Manager, Global Human Resources for Sydney-based AusBank had been enjoying watching Australia demolish Italy in the Rugby World Cup, when a news bulletin caused him to switch to Sky News Australia. The screen was filled with images of water cannons spraying rioters and protestors beating an unconscious police officer. Most disturbing for Ian was the travel advisory from the Australian Government that Australian citizens should consider leaving Indonesia. AusBank had 150 employees in Indonesia and this was his cue to initiate the bank's Crisis Management Plan.

The riots began over an apparent misunderstanding about the fate of the tomb of Habib Hasan bin Muhammed Al Hadad, a revered 18th-century Arab cleric known to Indonesians as Mbah Priok. Shortly after dawn members of the public order branch of the police, called Satpol, arrived to evict squatters and remove illegal buildings on the land surrounding the tomb. But residents of Tanjung Priok port, where the tomb is located, believed the police and city officials were there to tear it down and attacked them. The violence spread rapidly, and ethnic Chinese businesses quickly became the new targets of the rioters. While ethnic Chinese people make up only about 3% of Indonesia's population, they control a substantial part of the economic wealth of the country. Some Prebunis (native Indonesians) felt that this economic power was a result of a close association with and patronage from the previous Suharto government and thus ethnic Chinese people are often scapegoats regardless of the issue.

Ian's first call was to Bill Witherspoon at Braveheart Security, with whom AusBank had contracted for global security. Bill had already contacted his Jakarta office and plans were being made to move all expatriates and their families to foreign hotels where they would be more secure and could be evacuated more easily if it came to that. "But that's only about 15 employees," thought Ian. "What about the rest of the staff? We don't have an automatic protocol for local nationals. Should I offer emergency assistance to them, especially the ethnic Chinese employees? The cost of that would be huge and what would be the reaction if I only provided security to some local employees and not others."

Ian turned back to the television, the final score of the rugby was Australia 32–Italy 6, but there were fires burning on the streets of Jakarta. "Maybe this will all just blow over," he hoped.

INTRODUCTION

The concept of corporate social responsibility (CSR) is not understood in the same way around the world and affects global corporations in different ways than domestic operations.[1] In the case of AusBank in the opening vignette, Ian had some critical decisions to make regarding his firm's responsibility for employees potentially in danger. But not all MNEs will see their responsibilities in the same way. Social responsibility is defined as companies voluntarily integrating social and environmental concerns in their business operations and their interaction with their stakeholders.[2] This social performance by firms can be thought of as occurring on a continuum from narrow self-interest to broader social interests resulting in three stages of development:

- *Social obligation* – in which responsibility is limited to reactive compliance with local laws attending to shareholder interests.
- *Social responsibility* – in which the firm reacts to the needs of all organizational stakeholders including employees, customers, and suppliers.
- *Social responsiveness* – in which the firm is proactive in determining the needs of external social interests including the environment.[3]

Whether reactive or proactive, CSR is often considered to be acting beyond legal obligations to ensure that the interests of stakeholders and the wider environment are considered. For global corporations, this means considering not only their social impact in the city or region where they are headquartered (which is usually the point of focus for CSR activities), but also understanding how they are impacting on lives and the environment on a global scale.[4] CSR positioning is related to the overall strategic orientation of the MNE. For example, while all types of MNE may place importance on global CSR issues such as preservation of the environment, multidomestic and transnational MNEs are most likely to place significant importance on local CSR issues, such as creating employment in developing countries.[5]

NATIONAL DIFFERENCES IN CSR

National differences in the concept of and motives for CSR can be traced to different institutional environments (discussed in Chapter 3), such as *liberal market economies* (in which competitive markets dominate interactions), *coordinated market economies* (in which organizations interact more directly with the institutional environment), and *socialist market economies* (in which the state controls all interactions). These different institutional environments give rise to two distinct approaches to CSR:

- Explicit CSR,
- Implicit CSR.

A comparison of these two approaches is presented in Table 13.1.[6]

Table 13.1 Comparison of explicit and implicit CSR

Explicit CSR	Implicit CSR
• Describes corporate activities that assume responsibility for the interests of society • Consists of voluntary corporate policies, programs, and strategies • Incentives and opportunities are motivated by the perceived expectations of different stakeholders of the corporation	• Describes corporations' role within the wider formal and informal institutions for society's interests and concerns • Consists of values, norms, and rules that result in (often codified and mandatory) requirements for corporations • Motivated by the expectations on the legitimate expectations of the roles and contributions of all major groups in society, including corporations

Explicit CSR refers to corporate policies that create a sense of responsibility for some societal interest and typically involve voluntary programs by organizations that address issues perceived as being the social responsibility of the company. These often combine social and business interests, such as the response of US firms to working conditions in Asian supply chains. Explicit CSR, while it may reflect governmental or broader institutional views, is at the discretion of the organization, and is typical of US organizations. For example, explicit CSR practices concerning customers and community stakeholders are more prevalent in the US than in China.[7]

Implicit CSR consists of mandatory or customary requirements for organizations to address stakeholder issues within the wider framework of formal and informal institutions of society. In other words, implicit CSR is more intuitive and seen as the normal way of doing things, compared to explicit CSR, which is documented in corporate policies. Implicit approaches are more consistent with the European (and to some extent Asian) context. Representative business associations, as opposed to individual firms, are directly involved in the definition and legitimization of these activities. However, there may be a worldwide trend toward more explicit CSR, especially in larger firms, as local governments and industry associations change their focus, and as locally important CSR issues (such as genetic engineering in Europe) emerge.[8]

GLOBAL HR AND CSR

Controversy regarding the proper role of business in society[9] has fueled debate about the necessity of CSR activities. Today, however, whether management sees value in CSR activities may be largely irrelevant as there is a rapidly growing interest in the social dimension of business. The pressures for a greater concern for the environment, work practices, and human rights come from:

- increased regulation by a diverse set of international institutions such as the United Nations (UN), the International Labour Organization (ILO), and the Organisation for Economic Co-operation and Development (OECD);
- consumers who are increasingly making purchases following CSR criteria;
- and financial markets where a growing number of investors are looking for socially responsible investments.[10]

CSR involves many dimensions that affect almost all facets of an organization. Table 13.2 presents a list of the variety of issues that have been included under the CSR concept.

Table 13.2 Issues covered by CSR

• Environmental	• Concern for human rights
• Fair trade	• Philanthropic history
• Organic produce	• Cooperative principles
• Not tested on animals	• Support for education
• Community involvement	• Participates in local business initiatives
• Cause related marketing	• Supports national business initiatives
• Charitable giving	• Commitment to reporting
• Religious foundation	• Employee schemes
• Support for social cause	• Refusal to trade in certain markets

Source: Howard & Willmott (2001).

While labor issues are often at the core of the ethical questions that arise under this umbrella concept, many of the issues seem unconnected. However, HR is often at the forefront in all manner of CSR activities. There are at least four reasons for this:[11]

- First, many CSR principles are directly related to employees as a key stakeholder group. Issues of discrimination, working conditions, health and safety, harassment, pay, child labor, forced labor, freedom of association, and collective bargaining are prominent among CSR issues.
- Second, the social and ethical dimensions of CSR involve people and their relationships, which relate to the values of the organization. The link between an organization's values (its culture) and the human resources of the company is often made through HR decisions. CSR can be driven from the top, by the values of leaders or from the bottom by

employees who have direct knowledge of the influence of their work. In either case, HR plays a critical role. Consequently, HR departments are second only to legal departments in developing corporate codes of conduct (discussed ahead).[12]

- Third, CSR often requires a significant change in the philosophy and behavior of organizational units. HR is well-positioned to act as a change agent through its roles in organizational socialization, training and development, and management of reward systems. For example, some organizations use appraisal and pay systems to encourage socially responsible behavior by making bonus payments partly dependent on health and safety, environmental, and employee satisfaction outcomes.[13]

- Fourth, CSR is becoming central to being perceived as a good employer. A poor reputation in this regard can hurt recruitment and retention of staff in an increasingly competitive labor market. Employees also need to understand the point of CSR initiatives for them to be effective. HR is a central player in communicating with and engaging employees and is therefore a focal point for CSR activities.

The pressures for businesses to respond to the greater needs of society have existed for centuries. The specific issues may have shifted, and the intensity of these pressures may have grown, but at the core of these issues is a concern for the ethical dimension of decisions and actions of organizations. Nowhere are these issues more apparent than in MNEs that operate in countries with very different values, attitudes, and beliefs about appropriate behavior.

ETHICAL GLOBAL HR DECISIONS

CSR and business ethics are distinct concepts in that business ethics involves who benefits, or should benefit, from decisions, while CSR refers to the broader integration of social and environmental concerns into business operations. Increasingly, however, a focus on CSR requires organizations around the world to recognize the ethical dimension involved in their decisions. Although organizational leaders generally agree that sound ethics is good for business, they are very skeptical in their views about the existence of unethical practices in their industry.[14]

MORAL PHILOSOPHIES

The decisions that global managers make cross cultural as well as geographic boundaries. In crossing these boundaries, the consensus about what is morally correct erodes in the face of differing values and norms. For example, discrimination in employment against women that is reprehensible in one culture is a normal expression of gender-based roles in another. The study of ethical decision-making in organizations has resulted in normative or prescriptive approaches (what you should do) as well as descriptive approaches (what is actually done). Because managers and organizations are reluctant to have their ethics directly observed or measured, we know much more about what should be done than we do about what organizations and managers actually do.

A moral philosophy as used in decision-making is a set of principles used to distinguish between what is right or wrong.[15] Organizations and managers can be guided by one of several moral philosophies when making decisions or designing a policy that presents an ethical dilemma. The main categories of moral philosophies that are relevant to global HRM decisions are (a) consequential models (teleology), (b) rule-based models (deontology), and (c) cultural relativism.

Consequential models

Consequential models focus on the outcomes or consequences of a decision to determine if the decision is ethical. A key aspect of this principle as a guide for decision-making is utilitarianism.[16] Utilitarianism is the moral doctrine that we should always act to produce the greatest possible balance of good over harm for everyone affected by our decision.[17] In reality, making a decision that considers the interests and maximizes the utility for all individuals and groups affected by the decision is extremely difficult. It becomes even more difficult when those stakeholders affected by a decision have culturally different values and attitudes. Sometimes it is suggested that if general rules (religious norms, for example) are followed, the benefits to all will be maximized. Therefore, these rules can be used as a shortcut to the complexity of evaluating the utility of each decision or policy. This approach is guided by the belief that some types of behavior (e.g., refraining from excess profits) will always maximize the utility of everyone involved.

Rule-based models

Deontological principles hold that human beings have certain fundamental rights and that a sense of duty to uphold these rights is the basis of ethical decision-making rather than a concern for consequences.[18] One of the best-known rule-based approaches is the categorical imperative of Immanuel Kant (1724–1804). Essentially, the categorical imperative asserts that individuals have the right to be treated as an entity unto themselves and not simply as a means to an end. Unlike utilitarianism, deontology argues that some behaviors exist that are never moral even though they maximize utility. An obvious difficulty with rule-based normative approaches to decision-making is achieving a wide consensus on which rules (whose values) to base fundamental rights.[19]

Despite this difficulty, some transnational corporate codes have been constructed that attempt to specify a set of universal guides for international managers.[20] The ILO is the international organization responsible for drawing up and overseeing international labor standards. It is the only *tripartite* UN agency that brings together representatives of governments, employers, and workers to jointly shape policies and programs promoting humane labor conditions. The goals of the ILO are to promote rights at work, encourage decent employment opportunities, enhance social protection, and strengthen dialogue on work-related issues.[21] The ILO adopted a code of conduct for MNEs, which was in turn influential in developing OECD guidelines. The OECD Guidelines note that "Enterprises should take fully into account established policies in the countries in which they operate and consider the views of other stakeholders."[22] Box 13.1 presents the General Policies section of the guidelines.

BOX 13.1 OECD GUIDELINES FOR MNES: GENERAL POLICIES

A. Enterprises should:

1. Contribute to economic, environmental and social progress with a view to achieving sustainable development.
2. Respect the internationally recognized human rights of those affected by their activities.
3. Encourage local capacity building through close co-operation with the local community, including business interests, as well as developing the enterprise's activities in domestic and foreign markets, consistent with the need for sound commercial practice.
4. Encourage human capital formation, in particular by creating employment opportunities and facilitating training opportunities for employees.
5. Refrain from seeking or accepting exemptions not contemplated in the statutory or regulatory framework related to human rights, environmental, health, safety, labor, taxation, financial incentives, or other issues.
6. Support and uphold good corporate governance principles and develop and apply good corporate governance practices, including throughout enterprise groups.
7. Develop and apply effective self-regulatory practices and management systems that foster a relationship of confidence and mutual trust between enterprises and the societies in which they operate.
8. Promote awareness of and compliance by workers employed by multinational enterprises with respect to company policies through appropriate dissemination of these policies, including through training programs.
9. Refrain from discriminatory or disciplinary action against workers who make bona fide reports to management or, as appropriate, to the competent public authorities, on practices that contravene the law, the Guidelines or the enterprise's policies.
10. Carry out risk-based due diligence, for example by incorporating it into their enterprise risk management systems, to identify, prevent and mitigate actual and potential adverse impacts as described in paragraphs 11 and 12, and account for how these impacts are addressed. The nature and extent of due diligence depend on the circumstances of a particular situation.
11. Avoid causing or contributing to adverse impacts on matters covered by the Guidelines, through their own activities, and address such impacts when they occur.
12. Seek to prevent or mitigate an adverse impact where they have not contributed to that impact, when the impact is nevertheless directly linked to their operations, products or services by a business relationship. This is not intended to shift responsibility from

the entity causing an adverse impact to the enterprise with which it has a business relationship.

13. In addition to addressing adverse impacts in relation to matters covered by the Guidelines, encourage, where practicable, business partners, including suppliers and sub-contractors, to apply principles of responsible business conduct compatible with the Guidelines.

14. Engage with relevant stakeholders in order to provide meaningful opportunities for their views to be taken into account in relation to planning and decision-making for projects or other activities that may significantly impact local communities.

15. Abstain from any improper involvement in local political activities.

B. Enterprises are encouraged to:

1. Support, as appropriate to their circumstances, cooperative efforts in the appropriate fora to promote Internet Freedom through respect of freedom of expression, assembly and association online.

2. Engage in or support, where appropriate, private or multi-stakeholder initiatives and social dialogue on responsible supply chain management while ensuring that these initiatives take due account of their social and economic effects on developing countries and of existing internationally recognized standards.

Source: https://www.oecd.org/daf/inv/mne/48004323.pdf.

As shown in Box 13.1 the OECD guidelines are wide-ranging. As significant as the establishment of these guidelines has been, it is important to note that compliance with them is entirely voluntary. Organizations can also choose to sign up to other external entities that help to reinforce internal CSR initiatives. One example is an international standard for Social Accountability (SA 8000) along the lines of the ISO 9000 quality standard. SA8000 is based on the principles of international human rights norms as described in ILO conventions, the UN Convention on the Rights of the Child and the Universal Declaration of Human Rights. SA8000 measures the performance of companies in eight key areas: child labor, forced labor, health and safety, free association and collective bargaining, discrimination, disciplinary practices, working hours, and compensation. SA8000 also provides for a social accountability management system to demonstrate ongoing conformance with the standard.[23]

Another example is the Global Reporting Initiative (GRI), established in 1997. The GRI is an independent international organization, based out of the Netherlands, that focuses on sustainability reporting. By having a global common language that all member organizations use to report their sustainability initiatives, this enables better monitoring of progress in this area and informed discussions across national boundaries. In 2016, the GRI Standards were developed, which include three universal standards (GRI 101: Using the GRI Standards; GRI 102: About the Organization; and GRI 103: Material Topics), supported by many detailed topic-specific standards ranging from diversity management and tax reporting, through health and safety and training and education.[24] The standards are designed to facilitate organizations assessing the effect they may have on the economy, environment, or people, including on human rights, as a result of their activities or business relationships.

We highlight a final example of a set of voluntary guidelines in this area: ISO 26000.[25] ISO 26000 was established in 2010 as social responsibility guidance that organizations can use to assess their commitment to contributing to sustainable development. The guidelines cover human rights, labor practices, the environment, fair operating practices, consumer fairness, and community involvement and development. ISO 26000 is not (yet) a certification (as is SA8000) but rather a set of guidelines aimed at spreading best practice in sustainability efforts of organizations.

It might be possible to gain universal acceptance for these codes of conduct or frameworks of fundamental rights if they protect something of great importance in all cultures, if they are under continuous threat, and if all cultures can absorb the cost of protecting them.[26] However, national culture affects the preference of individuals for consequential versus rule-based principles in ethical decision-making. For example, consequential principles are preferred in China but ruled-based approaches are preferred in the United States, Mexico, and, to some extent, South Korea. More important, perhaps, is that managers in different cultures can subscribe to the same moral philosophy but still choose to behave in ways that are very different.[27] This is the problem of cultural relativism.

Cultural relativism

In cultural relativism, moral concepts are legitimate only to the extent that they reflect the habits and attitudes of a given culture.[28] That is, ethical standards are specific to a particular culture and any cross-cultural comparison is meaningless. What is considered unethical in one culture might be quite acceptable in another even though the same moral principle is being followed. Cultural relativism implies that one should not impose one's own ethical or moral standards on others and that international decisions should be evaluated in the context of differences in legal, political, and cultural systems. However, it also leaves open the opportunity to attribute a wide range of behavior to cultural norms. The use of child labor in Myanmar and China[29] and discrimination against women in Japan and Saudi Arabia[30] are just two examples of conduct that is attributed to cultural relativism. To adopt the concept of cultural relativism in its entirety declares the global business decisions an arena where anything goes.[31] For cultural relativism to hold up as a useful model for global business decisions, we must declare that even the most hideous or reprehensible acts are not objectively wrong but depend on how a culture defines *wrong*. However, most of us can imagine acts that we cannot defend in terms of variation in cultural practice.

CORPORATE CODES OF CONDUCT

The problems associated with ethical relativism become clear to Global HR managers when faced with the common dilemma of an employment practice that is viewed as wrong in the home country but acceptable in the host country. The occurrence of these situations has caused many MNEs to develop written codes of conduct for their organization. While there are sources (mostly trade or employment legislation) that mandate that certain issues are addressed by businesses,[32] corporate codes of conduct are largely voluntary initiatives. Often developed in response to a particular crisis in their supply chain, these codes have been widely criticized as "corporate gloss" and a public relations exercise to preempt accusations of unacceptable practices.[33] Indeed, a PricewaterhouseCoopers survey found that nearly 30% of CEOs regard corporate social responsibility mainly as a PR issue.[34] Interestingly, it has been noted that the process of establishing an MNE code of conduct involved negotiations with an international union federation or works council in less than 20% of the cases, with US MNEs being much less likely to conduct such negotiations compared to their Nordic and German counterparts.[35]

Even when they are well-intentioned, several issues have been raised about corporate codes of conduct. These include failure to translate the code in languages other than that of the headquarters (often English), the lack of availability of the code throughout the organization, and failure to monitor and enforce the code. Even the monitoring of codes by large accounting firms came into question in the wake of conflicts of interest brought to light by the disastrous Enron crisis in the early 2000s. While many organizations file corporate social responsibility reports, only a minority include hard data about what CSR has accomplished, even in cases where it would have been relatively easy to obtain.[36]

There are also significant differences in the content of these codes according to a review of 215 codes of conduct conducted by the ILO. The most frequently addressed issues are occupational health and safety (75%), followed by discrimination in hiring or terms and conditions of employment (66%). Approximately 45% of the codes reviewed contained a clause relating to the elimination of child labor or refusing to work with companies that employ children, why only 25% spoke to forced labor. Issues around wage levels appeared in about 40% of codes. Interestingly only about 15% of codes dealt with freedom of association and collective bargaining. The selectivity in the areas covered by these codes is probably the result of the concern for particular issues by the firm, the extent to which various stakeholders are involved in the process of the creation of the code, and the degree to which a particular policy or practice is acceptable to the firm.[37]

THE ROLE OF MNEs IN UPHOLDING ETHICAL STANDARDS

Issues of MNE social accountability are likely to remain prominent, given a neo-liberal trend for governments to withdraw increasingly from economic activities, with businesses left to fill in the gaps and play a major role in providing services that were once the domain of the state. Some have argued that MNEs have risen in prominence in a way that has diminished national political institutions.[38] For example, MNEs have significant resources available to them to influence host locations, especially in less well-developed economies. MNEs also have the ability to relocate their factors of production internationally, weighing one host country against another. This makes it necessary that MNEs become more socially accountable. But there is also the opinion that CSR activities in many MNEs are mostly financially driven, with the utmost objectives to uphold the reputation of corporate brands rather than address social inequalities. As to whether investment in CSR pays off, researchers have produced somewhat conflicting accounts. Some studies suggest negative financial outcomes, but more studies appear to find positive outcomes in terms of increased corporate reputation and improved financial returns, with some differences across industries.[39]

CSR AND THE GLOBAL SUPPLY CHAIN

A major challenge facing MNEs results from global supply chains and the conditions of workers in countries in which its downstream suppliers operate. These challenges are particularly acute in textiles, apparel, footwear, and agriculture, where very large percentages of production are outsourced to independent companies in foreign countries. These suppliers are often located in the developing world where working conditions are well below that of the firm's home country. For MNEs, the challenge is not only navigating the legal, cultural, political context on its own behalf but recognizing that the overseas supplier faces its own local pressures. Responding to this challenge requires MNEs to seek creative solutions to the ethical dilemmas these situations create.

For example, Levi Strauss discovered that the issue of two of its Bangladesh suppliers employing workers under the minimum working age of 15 was not as simple as it first seemed. In Bangladesh, it is not uncommon for children this young to be the sole support for the family. Rather than just instruct its suppliers to fire the underage workers or terminate their contracts, Levi Strauss negotiated an agreement in which the factories agreed to pay the underage workers their salaries and benefits while they attended school and then offer them full-time jobs when they reached legal working age.[40] It is important to note that Levi Strauss discovered the underage workers in an assessment of their suppliers' compliance with what the company calls their Terms of Engagement. These guidelines specify the requirements by which all their contract factories and licensees must abide – including ethical standards, legal requirements, environmental requirements, and community involvement. They also set out employment standards and specifically address issues of child labor, forced labor, disciplinary practices, working hours, wages and benefits, freedom of association, discrimination, and health and safety.[41]

Similar creative solutions have been found by IKEA for suppliers of carpets in India, even though carpets make up a very small percent of IKEA's sales and it would have been very easy to sidestep the issue.[42] Sometimes, however, there are few short-term alternatives to just leaving the market and advocating for change, as shown in Box 13.2.

BOX 13.2 GOVERNMENT-APPROVED CHILD LABOR

My 9-year-old son's list of daily tasks is pretty brief. Make your bed. Feed the dog. Do your homework. Pick up after yourself. Simple stuff. If we lived in Uzbekistan, it could be a different story.

Each fall, the Uzbekistan government closes schools and forces more than one million children to work in the country's cotton fields. This is child labor, driven not by poverty, but by government policy. And why? It earns the government more than $1 billion annually.

Tomorrow, June 12, is World Day Against Child Labor. If you're a citizen of the developed world, it may seem like a distant problem. But remember what's happening in Uzbekistan … and think about what happens with cotton once harvested. It's often made into clothing – like khakis, shirts and jeans.

That brief list of products should tell you why Levi Strauss & Co. cares about what's happening in Uzbekistan: We don't want cotton textiles made with child labor used in our products. That's why we've prohibited the use of cotton from Uzbekistan since 2008, when credible sources brought this issue to our attention. We were the first U.S. apparel brand and/or retailer to prohibit the use of Uzbek cotton in its supply chain, and we're proud that others have joined us.

But the fact is, prohibiting the use of Uzbek cotton in our products is difficult to verify. As a commodity, cotton is challenging to trace as it moves from farm to textile mill to garment factory. We're working closely with experts in supply chain traceability to address this challenge. It's important to us as a company, to those of us who work here, and to our customers.

My uncle was a cotton farmer in West Texas. It's difficult, backbreaking work – for an adult. From my perspective, forcing children to do this kind of hard labor is cruel, especially when you're depriving them of an education in the process.

Our hope at Levi Strauss & Co. is that, with mounting international awareness and advocacy, we will see real change by the Uzbek government to end the practice of forced child labor in Uzbekistan. As my son grows, his daily chores will change. Still, he and I can both be thankful that his tasks will never be anything like those currently faced by the children in the cotton fields of Uzbekistan.

Source: https://www.levistrauss.com/2010/06/09/government-approved-child-labor/.

Global HR has a significant role to play in shaping and implementing policies related to the broader social interests of the organization. Whether acting as the champion of employee interests, as guardian of the corporate culture, or as an organizational change agent, Global HR is a central player in the ethical behavior of the organization. In a global context, this behavior should be guided by respect for core human values that establish the moral threshold for business decisions, combined with a respect for local traditions and a belief that context matters in determining an appropriate course of action.[43] This approach will often lead to creative solutions to ethical dilemmas in international business operations that transcend the simple enforcement of corporate codes of conduct.

SUSTAINABLE HRM

Sustainability is a broad ranging topic, inherently linked with the concept of CSR. On a global scale, the UN highlights 17 sustainable development goals that are closely related to the actions of organizations (see Figure 13.1).

Source: United Nations: https://www.un.org/development/desa/disabilities/about-us/sustainable
-development-goals-sdgs-and-disability.html.

Figure 13.1   The United Nations Sustainable Development Goals

There is increasing interest as to how the HR department can contribute to an organization's sustainability goals. Sustainability is about a combination of finding ways to do good as well as avoiding doing harm in economic, environmental, and social domains.[44] HRM sustainability means adding a long-term dimension to the activities of the HR department (such as dealing with climate change, workforce demographics, and urbanization) alongside shorter-term goals such as productivity and turnover figures. Sustainable HRM has four types:[45]

- *Socially responsible HRM*: ensuring awareness beyond the immediate organizational context of the impact of HRM policies, practices, and actions.
- *Green HRM*: using HRM policies, practices, and actions to encourage environmentally friendly attitudes and behaviors of employees and managers.
- *Triple bottom line HRM*: adding social and environmental goals to HRM policies, practices, and actions beyond economic goals.
- *Common good HRM*: exploring how HRM can be used to address the "grand challenges" often related to human rights, such as decent working conditions in supply chains (as discussed in Box 13.2).

Given this emerging perspective, Global HR professionals need to develop a set of competencies that allows them to consider the broader impact of their activities. This can also be reinforced by relying on resources such as the GRI, SA8000, or ISO 26000 that were mentioned previously, in order to demonstrate how an organization is addressing sustainability issues.

Overall, the HR function is in a strong position to influence employee behavior (through employee socialization, performance management, and reward practices) that can help an MNE achieve its sustainability goals.[46] However, it is important to note that by increasing the range of goals toward which employees are working (as per the triple bottom line, simultaneously accounting for economic, social and environmental impact), this can lead to tension, ambiguity, and conflict between goals that can create additional stress for employees.[47] Figure 13.2 shows the wide range of roles that HR can undertake to try to help organizations achieve their sustainability goals at the same time as helping employees navigate through potential uncertainty.

Another area of sustainability directly linked to HRM is how human (employee) sustainability can be enhanced in organizations through the principles of lifetime employability and sustainable careers.[48] The term "sustainable careers" refers to the range of work experiences that a person will have over their lifetime, each one providing:

- opportunities for growth and renewal,
- the ability to match work and income to evolving life circumstances,
- an overall increase in well-being.[49]

To create sustainable careers within the global context requires addressing challenges such as income inequalities within and between countries, as well as precarious working conditions, both of which run counter to the principles of sustainability. Overall, we have seen how closely global economic and social forces affect MNEs, which in turn have a direct effect on individual careers.

DATA PROTECTION

A relatively new area of corporate social responsibility, increasingly important to HRM, is the emergence of big data and artificial intelligence as part of MNE activities. These developments raise questions about the socially responsible way to protect employee data. Going beyond voluntary acts of CSR, the General Data Protection Regulation (GDPR) became law across the EU in May 2018 but it has important consequences for organizations globally. Following its 1995 predecessor, the Data Protection Directive, GDPR was designed to harmonize the protection of personal data, ultimately resulting in citizens (including employees) rather than companies having control over their own data. The regulation applies to any organization offering goods and/or services to citizens in the EU. Therefore, it can be as relevant to a US or Chinese MNE with operations in the EU, as to firms headquartered in Germany, the UK, or Spain, for example.

Personal data is defined as "any information relating to an individual, whether it relates to his or her private, professional or public life. It can be anything from a name, a photo, an email address, bank details, [your] posts on social networking websites, [your] medical information, or [your] computer's IP address."[50] The regulation affects how organizations manage, use, store, secure, and otherwise process personal data, which includes data on employees, ranging from their personal details through to their performance evaluations. This has far-reaching

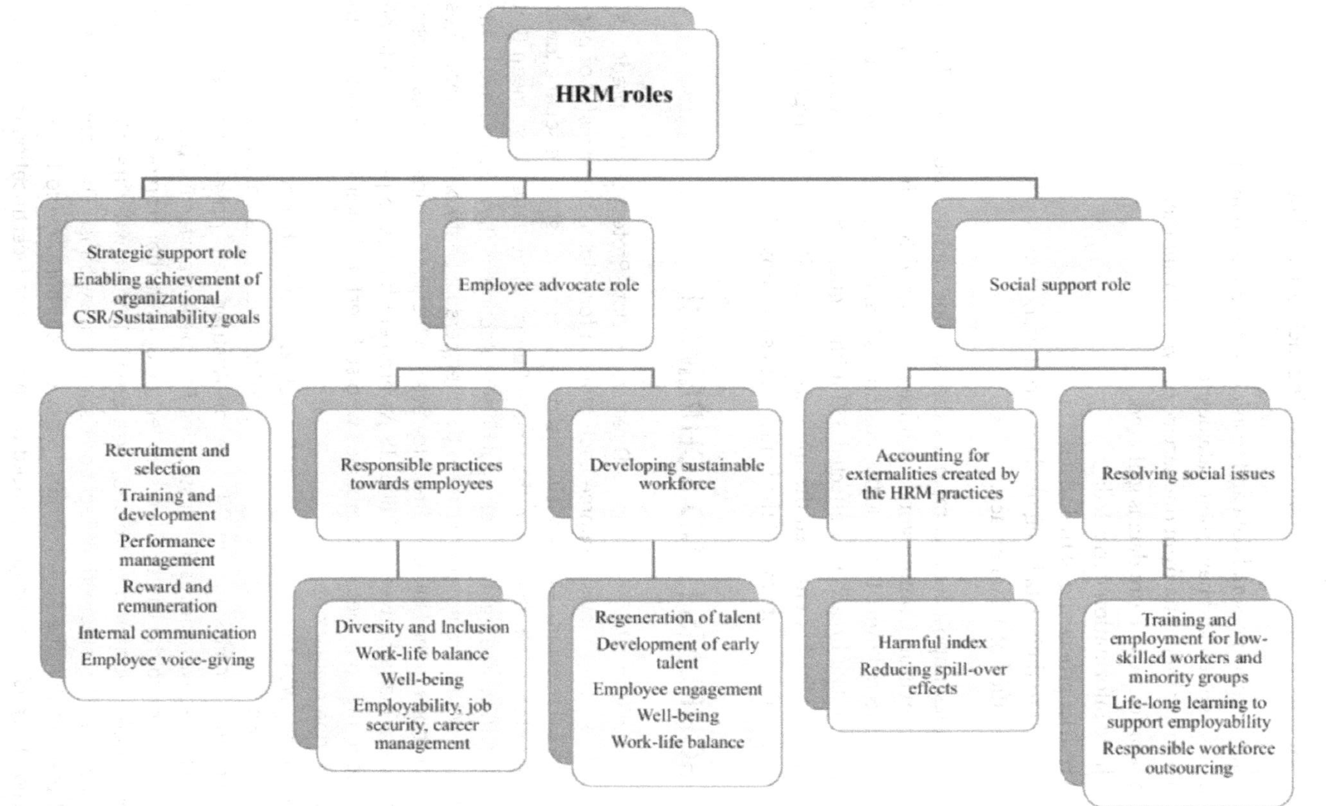

Source: Podgorodnichenko, Edgar, & McAndrew (2020).

Figure 13.2 HRM roles in developing sustainable and responsible organizations

implications for the Global HR function. How can the corporate headquarters based in the United States locate future senior leadership if the performance data of its managers across Europe cannot be transferred to the HQ?

GDPR gives EU citizens the following rights regarding their personal data:

- The right to access their personal data and to ask how their data is used;
- The right to be forgotten and have their data deleted;
- The right to transfer their data from one service provider to another;
- The right to be informed before data is gathered;
- The right to have information corrected;
- The right to restrict processing of their data;
- The right to object to their data being used for direct marketing;
- The right to be notified of a data breach.

There are extensive fines imposed on companies that do not comply with the GDPR: in October 2020, the Information Commissioner's Office (ICO) fined British Airways US$26m for a data breach that affected more than 400,000 customers,[51] and Marriott International Inc. was fined US$24m for a data breach that affected 339 million guests.[52] There have also been legal challenges that have further enforced the application of GDPR, especially regarding the transfer of data between EU countries and the United States (see Box 13.3).

BOX 13.3 SCHREMS I AND SCHREMS II

In 1995, the European Commission issued its Directive on Data Protection, the predecessor to the 2018 GDPR. These laws reinforce each other in forbidding the transfer of personal data from the EU to countries where citizens' data protection rights are set at a lower level than those granted within the EU. In the United States, surveillance laws mean that citizens do not have the same rights to personal data protection as they would have in the EU. This means that MNEs are not permitted to transfer personal data on their employees from their EU operations to the United States. However, to facilitate business transactions, two agreements were made between EU and US government bodies to permit data to be transferred between the countries by companies who self-certified their compliance with certain data protection regulations.

The first agreement was the EU–U.S. Data Protection Safe Harbor framework, introduced in 2000.[53] However, this was brought into question following a case brought to the Irish Data Protection Commissioner in 2015 by an Austrian data privacy activist, Max Schrems. Schrems' case was successful in stopping Facebook transferring protected data belonging to EU citizens to the United States under the Safe Harbor framework. Schrems argued that Facebook, registered in Ireland, was breaking the law by transferring data about him to the United States within Facebook's internal systems. The complaint was based around the fact that the Safe Harbor framework did not provide the same rights to data protection because the system is based on company self-certification rather than legal requirements. This case was known as Schrems I.

Following the failure of the Safe Harbor framework, in 2016, the EU–U.S. Privacy Shield was introduced,[54] which permitted companies to transfer personal data across the Atlantic. However, in a second case in 2020, Schrems II, the Privacy Shield was contested as illegally infringing on EU resident's data protection and privacy rights, also because it relied on self-certification by US companies. The Privacy Shield has therefore been invalidated, preventing the transfer of data between the EU and the United States.

What does data protection have to do with HR? The answer is "a lot"! Increasingly, HR is a data-driven function. In addition to standard personal data that all HR departments hold (such as employee address details or tax information), there has been an increase in employee (electronic) monitoring (especially during the COVID-19 pandemic) across organizations as they aim to cut costs to be competitive. Electronic monitoring of productivity or compliance with relevant regulations or procedures generates large amounts of data that the HR department must then manage. Moreover, companies collect data on their employees to varying extents through many routes, including tracking access to websites, reading employee emails, tracking time spent on activities, and capturing video surveillance and images. In addition to the GDPR requirements laid out above regarding the transfer of personal data, there are also broader issues that emerge regarding the transparency and legitimacy, and hence socially responsible handling, of employee data. For example, based on the principles of cultural relativism, the interpretation of what data might be appropriate to collect and analyze in MNEs may also vary considerably across nations.

Global HRM plays a crucial role in both the formulation and implementation of policies and procedures related to CSR. At the core of many CSR activities is the ethical dimension of business decision-making as MNEs consider their responsibilities to the societies in which they are embedded. A common ethical dilemma that confronts MNEs occurs when employment practices considered appropriate in one location are unacceptable in another location. Global HR has a key role to play in finding creative solutions to these difficult problems, considering the cultural relativism of appropriate employer behavior. Following mandated regulations (such as those related to personal data protection) as well as adopting voluntary codes of conduct can help support Global HR's activities but ultimately, appropriate roles need to be adopted to help the organization achieve its sustainability goals.

CHAPTER SUMMARY

CSR is understood differently in organizations across the globe. The responsibilities are largely voluntary, and as such, this creates leeway for management interpretation of what might be "the right thing to do" with respect to an organization's various stakeholders and the environment. CSR can either be made explicit through corporate policies and/or be implicit in the day-to-day values and deeds of all organizational members.

Organizations such as the UN, ILO, and OECD provide frameworks for MNEs to guide their CSR activities, but ultimately, Global HR has a substantial role to play in encouraging socially responsible employee behaviors. Firms can adopt different moral philosophies that underpin their approach to CSR, either with a focus on considering the ethical outcomes of individual decisions, or on following rule-based guidelines (such as those offered by the OECD, the Global Reporting Initiative, or the International Organization for Standardization). Such decisions or guidelines will, however, always be interpreted relative to the cultural values of the society in which they are being applied.

MNEs can also play a role in CSR by developing their own in-house codes of conduct. Again, these are voluntary initiatives that may or may not be implemented to their full extent as can be witnessed when exploring global supply chains. In helping such initiatives, Global HR can adopt a range of roles to encourage socially responsible and sustainable practices within an MNE, including being proactive in managing data protection in an increasingly data-driven digital age.

QUESTIONS FOR DISCUSSION

1. How can explicit and implicit approaches to CSR complement each other in helping an MNE to achieve its CSR goals?
2. Describe and give examples of key ethical dilemmas that confront most MNEs related to their employees.
3. Do you believe consequential models or rule-based models are more effective for making ethical decisions in organizations? Explain your reasoning and why opinions may vary.
4. To what extent are corporate codes of conduct effective in helping achieve global CSR goals?
5. What are the implications of the General Data Protection Regulation (GDPR) for MNEs headquartered outside the European Union?

NOTES

1. Davis, Whitman, & Zald (2006).
2. Cooke (2011).
3. Sethi (1975) for a discussion of social responsiveness.
4. Davis, Whitman, & Zald (2006).
5. Husted & Allen (2006).
6. Matten & Moon (2008).
7. Lo, Egri, & Ralston (2008).
8. Lo, Egri, & Ralston (2008).
9. For example, see Friedman (2002) for a discussion.
10. Fuentes-García, Núñez-Tabales, & Herrandón (2008).
11. Lam & Khare (2010).
12. Sajdev (2006).
13. Maitland (2003).
14. Brenner & Molander (1977).
15. Ferrell & Fraedrich (1994).

16. Mill (1863).

17. Shaw (1996).

18. Borchert & Stewart (1986).

19. Donaldson (1989).

20. See Frederick (1991) for more on this topic.

21. http://www.ilo.org/global/lang--en/index.htm

22. https://www.oecd.org/daf/inv/mne/48004323.pdf

23. https://sa-intl.org/programs/sa8000/

24. https://www.globalreporting.org/standards/

25. https://www.iso.org/iso-26000-social-responsibility.html

26. Donaldson (1989).

27. Phatak & Habib (1998).

28. Donaldson (1989).

29. Beaver (1995).

30. Mayer & Cava (1993).

31. Donaldson (1989).

32. Sajdev (2011).

33. Klein (2000).

34. Sajdev (2006).

35. Sajdey (2011).

36. Sajdev (2006).

37. Diller (2008).

38. See Sajdev (2011).

39. Baird, Geyliani & Roberts (2012); Aguinis & Glavas (2012).

40. http://www.levistrauss.com/sites/default/files/librarydocument/2010/4/Case_Study_Child_Labor_Bangladesh.pdf

41. http://www.levistrauss.com/sustainability/people/worker-rights

42. Luce (2004).

43. Donaldson (1996).

44. Stahl, Brewster, Collings, & Hajro (2020).

45. Aust (Ehnert), Matthews, & Muller-Camen (2020).

46. Podgorodnichenko, Edgar, & McAndrew (2020).

47. Bush (2020).

48. Lopez-Cabrales & Valle-Cabrera (2020).

49. McDonald & Hite (2018).

50. European Commission: https://ec.europa.eu/commission/presscorner/detail/en/IP_12_46

51. https://www.bbc.com/news/technology-54568784

52. https://ico.org.uk/about-the-ico/news-and-events/news-and-blogs/2020/10/ico-fines-marriott-international-inc-184million-for-failing-to-keep-customers-personal-data-secure/

53. https://2016.export.gov/safeharbor/

54. https://www.privacyshield.gov/Program-Overview

14

Postscript – Global HR in a post COVID-19 world

The arrival of COVID-19

In late February 2020, an international manager unknowingly catches COVID-19 during a business trip to China. On his return to Toronto he sneezes several times as he passes through customs at Pearson International airport. A few days later the international manager, a customs official, and several other airline passengers are suffering at home from the potentially deadly effects of the virus, having no doubt passed it on to other contacts in the interim. Globalization was thus a major culprit in the spread of the disease.

There is little doubt that had the initial outbreak in China occurred 50 years previously, when international travel was confined to small numbers of people, the spread would have been much slower, and the disease might have been confined to China.

Was international travel a major contributor to the pandemic? Probably. Did the Global HR department have policies and procedures in place to deal with the effects of a pandemic in their organizations? Probably not. Will the world return to "normal" after a cure or a vaccine is discovered? Probably not, but what will the "new normal" be like? And what role does Global HR have to play?

GLOBAL HR THROUGH THE PRISM OF A GLOBAL PANDEMIC

In the opening chapter of this book we suggested that there were several environmental trends that were influencing global HRM, including:

- the uneven economic development that is occurring around the globe,
- the influence that transition/emerging economies have as they grow in importance on the global stage,
- the exponential rate of change in information and communications technology,
- the increased pressure on and concern for the natural environment, and
- changes in the profile of global organizations.

However, as we write this book, the world is still in the grips of an international crisis that has caused some to suggest that life will never be the same again. In early 2020 it became apparent that the virus called COVID-19 was a worldwide pandemic.[1] Governments around the world struggled to find the right strategies to control the spread of the virus. Cities were locked down, socializing with others was discouraged, international borders closed, and many businesses suddenly found they had no customers. Millions of workers found themselves out of work. The economic crisis that ensued created a balancing act that pitted the economic effect of the crisis against "flattening the curve," the catchphrase referring to slowing down the rate of infection to allow time for treatments and a vaccine to be developed. By the autumn of 2020, more than a million people had died around the world and a second wave of increased infections was predicted.

Exactly how the world will be affected by COVID-19 is speculation, given that at the time of completing this book, the pandemic is far from over. However, we can draw some conclusions based on the global response to previous crises. For example, when terrorists flew hijacked airlines into the World Trade Center in New York on September 11, 2001, and when the global financial crisis gripped the world in 2007–2008, similar dire predictions of global change were heard. Certainly, there were changes following these events. For example, airline security procedures became dramatically more thorough (and intrusive), and more stringent lending requirements were placed on the home loan policies of banks. However, the economic, political, legal, and cultural systems of the world did not change in any fundamental way. We suspect the effects of globalization following the COVID-19 pandemic will not change course but will accelerate in the direction of changes already underway.[2]

At the time of this writing, we note that although there had been a stabilization of the steady growth in corporate globalization since World War II,[3] some may think that we are at the dawn of a new era. The intercountry dependencies created previously are being diminished by increased political nationalism and protectionism.[4] The result is a period described as "globalization on pause" or "deglobalization."[5] Events such as Brexit, a growing trade war between the United States and China, the failed Transatlantic Trade and Investment Partnership negotiations, and travel bans as a consequence of the COVID-19 pandemic are breaking down the infrastructure that supports global trade.[6] Consequently, the global supply of talent through migration is being curtailed.[7] This globalization pause has substantial implications for global HRM given the increase in business uncertainty in line with new emerging talent shortages.[8]

Any notion of deglobalization must, however, be kept in perspective. The pace of uneven economic development around world is continuing to show signs of acceleration. In the second quarter of 2020 the distribution of growth rates across 50 economies was wider than it had been for at least 40 years.[9] The heavy toll that the COVID-19 pandemic is taking on the developing world is devastating countries like Peru because of inadequate health care, lack of protective benefits such as unemployment insurance, and the predominance of an informal economy.[10] The lack of resilience of these economies will likely mean a larger and longer lasting effect of the pandemic. In contrast, forecasts suggest by the end of 2021 the US economy will be about the same size it was in 2019, while China's will be 10% larger.[11]

The best example of the increased influence of transition and emerging economies is perhaps found in China as it envisions itself as a superpower in the face of the extreme consequences of the COVID-19 pandemic in the United States.[12] China's ability to fulfill her ambition, as well as that of other emerging economies, such as Brazil, India, and Russia will depend on their ability to rebound from the economic toll taken by the pandemic. So far, China seems to be emerging from the pandemic strongest.[13]

The influence of the pandemic is clearly apparent in the technology sector. As millions of people work remotely, the need for increased levels and sophistication of technological solutions has been a boon to this industry sector. An example is provided by the video conferencing company, Zoom Video Communications. Prior to the pandemic Zoom had 10 million users, by the first of April 2020, daily users topped 200 million and at the end of April its user base was 300 million and growing.[14]

The natural environment has actually benefited from the pandemic, with carbon emissions dramatically reduced because of drastic reductions in travel, at least in the short term.[15] The relationship of humans with the earth's environment is complicated. However, the pandemic has caused increased scrutiny on the effect of human activity on the planet, with some suggesting new strategies to create "peaceful coexistence" with Mother Nature.[16]

That the profile of organizations will be affected by the pandemic is undeniable. Organizations have always adapted their structures to changes in the global business environment. The pressures being placed on many industries by the pandemic are now requiring an unprecedented pace of change. For example, a recent survey revealed that one-third of surveyed companies had accelerated the digitization of their supply chains, half had sped up the digitization of their customer channels, and two-thirds have moved faster to adopt artificial intelligence and automation. Managers will need to process these changes, and many others, in order to thrive in the future.

The response of organizations to the COVID-19 pandemic has made the role of the HR manager much more noticeable. While chief financial officers may have been the heroes of the 2007–2008 financial crisis, it is the HR manager's role that is critical in the current crisis.[17] Their challenges include maintaining the health of employees and their morale, as well as managing the sudden shift to remote working. Three future trends in the development of the Global HR function seem clear:[18]

- First, the management of health and safety will continue to be a key challenge in global HRM in the future. It will be important to remember that the relationship between the well-being of employees and the well-being of the organization is tightly interwoven.[19]
- Second, facilitating the new global work environment will be key and will involve the increased use of virtual collaboration as well as rethinking international assignments. The change management skills of Global HR can be vital in helping the leadership of the organization make the most balanced and empathetic decisions for both the employee and the organization.
- Finally, the roles of the employees of MNEs will likely undergo significant change. Therefore, performance management may take center stage, as organizations redefine what is meant by performance. For the Global HR department to make the best of the unprecedented situation presented by the pandemic, good people metrics will be more important than ever before.

CONCLUSION

In this postscript we highlight some of the challenges that the Global HR department will face in the future as a result of the increased complexity, interconnectedness, growing diversity, and rapid change that is the result of globalization of business. We suggest that the COVID-19 pandemic will accelerate this effect in the direction of changes already underway. The changing environment for global HRM is influenced by uneven economic development around the world that influences the characteristics of the global workforce, the increased influence of emerging and transition economies, the exponential growth and change in information and communications technology, and a deepening concern for the natural environment. In addition, global HRM is influenced by broader organizational response to changes in the external environment. Taken together, these trends and the upheaval created by the pandemic pose numerous challenges for the future of global HRM.

QUESTIONS FOR DISCUSSION

1. What changes in your life have resulted from the COVID-19 pandemic? If you are employed, how did your work environment change? If in school, how did that environment change?
2. Did the COVID-19 pandemic cause you to be more concerned about your own health and safety as an employee or student? How did your school or work organization respond to this concern?
3. What role will the Global HR department have in reinforcing the core values of organizations as they respond to the challenges and opportunities presented by the "new normal"? How might they do this?
4. Is "deglobalization" really happening? What effect could an extended period of deglobalization have on the work of the Global HR department?

NOTES

1. For a summary of the economic effects of the pandemic see https://fas.org/sgp/crs/row/R46270.pdf
2. Bonciu (2020).
3. Sparrow, Vaiman, Schuler & Collings (2018).
4. Evenett (2019).
5. Petricevic & Teece (2019).
6. Verbeke, Coeurderoy, & Matt (2018).
7. Horak, Farndale, Brannen & Collings (2019).
8. Allen & Raynor (2004).
9. https://www.economist.com/leaders/2020/10/08/the-pandemic-has-caused-the-worlds-economies-to-diverge
10. https://www.weforum.org/agenda/2020/06/the-plight-of-peru-illustrates-the-danger-of-covid-19-to-developing-countries/

11. https://www.economist.com/leaders/2020/10/08/the-pandemic-has-caused-the-worlds-economies-to-diverge

12. https://isreview.org/issue/112/chinas-rise-world-power

13. https://www.economist.com/leaders/2020/10/08/the-pandemic-has-caused-the-worlds-economies-to-diverge

14. https://www.theverge.com/2020/4/23/21232401/zoom-300-million-users-growth-coronavirus-pandemic-security-privacy-concerns-response

15. https://www.bbc.com/news/science-environment-52485712

16. https://www.thenation.com/article/environment/coronavirus-nature-humans/

17. https://www.economist.com/business/2020/03/24/the-coronavirus-crisis-thrusts-corporate-hr-chiefs-into-the-spotlight

18. For a review of international HRM trends see Caligiuri, De Cieri, Minbaeva, Verbeke, & Zimmerman (2020).

19. De Cieri and Lazarova (2020).

Case 1: Importing diversity management to Finland[1]

Adam Smale and Ingmar Björkman[2]

LOCAL HR GETS THE CALL FROM CORPORATE

Maria, the HR Manager of Petrocom Finland, had been both excited and anxious when news came through from corporate headquarters that Finland had been selected as one of the first to implement the new "Global Workforce Diversity Management and Inclusiveness Initiative" (hereafter D&I Initiative). The mission of the D&I Initiative was to integrate better into the workforce employees from a variety of backgrounds such as gender, race, sexual orientation, age, family status, values, beliefs, physical and mental abilities, income, education, and work experience. Maria had known that it was going to mean a lot of work and that getting local buy-in to a corporate initiative of this kind would be a huge challenge. Although she knew that there had been very few cases of harassment or discrimination, she had felt for some time now that Finland and the people at Petrocom Finland had limited experience in addressing certain areas of workforce diversity management in comparison with some of their European counterparts. Maria just hoped that her personal convictions about the business case for diversity management would be shared by others.

IMPLEMENTING THE GLOBAL D&I INITIATIVE IN PETROCOM FINLAND

Petrocom Group, a well-known European energy firm, operates in nearly 100 countries employing more than 100,000 people. In the early 2000s the Petrocom Group initiated a significant restructuring. The restructuring included the launch of its "Global Organisation" program, which for HR strategy meant, among other things, greater standardization of its HRM policies, practices and processes.

As a by-product of this, Petrocom headquarters unveiled its new D&I Initiative that was presented as being an extension of their global business principles, a reinforcement of their existing core values, and a means of reaffirming Petrocom Group's commitment to sustainable development by enhancing social performance and strengthening engagement with external stakeholders. Based on the successful model of managing workforce diversity in Petrocom Group's USA subsidiary, and in accordance with the "Global Organisation" vision, Petrocom developed a five-year implementation plan, which sought to integrate the principles of diversity and inclusiveness into key business and HRM practices throughout their worldwide operations. In doing so, Petrocom HQ aimed to attract and retain key global talent, to increase productivity through improved employee engagement, and to strengthen their reputation within the global community.

Representing one of the smallest of their foreign operations, Petrocom Finland was established before World War I and employed approximately 1,700 people across 400 service outlets at the time the D&I Initiative began. After several years of planning and development, Petrocom HQ began to launch the D&I Initiative in waves. Along with several other select European operations, Petrocom Finland was included in the first wave.

Since "Diversity and Inclusiveness" was adopted as one of Petrocom Group's formal, "Global Standards," it was clear from the beginning that there was to be very little scope for country deviations in implementation, which was evident in the kick-off memo from the Global Head of the D&I Initiative:

> We start from the point that it must be followed. Naturally, there will be some legal limitations to its application that will be considered, but otherwise we assume that the D&I Standard is translated directly and that there are no local modifications. This is necessary to create truly a global D&I Standard for Petrocom and to ensure the implementation of one of our key business principles. During implementation the D&I Initiative was perceived as an external and largely Anglo-Saxon intervention concerned only with the narrower issues of gender, nationality and the staffing of senior country positions with host-country nationals (i.e., not expatriates). Subsequently, Petrocom HQ began to emphasize the inclusiveness component of the initiative to make employees and managers realize that discrimination can occur in the workplace either due to visible differences between individuals (e.g., physical ability, age, language) or invisible differences (e.g., beliefs, sexual orientation, family status).

ENTHUSIASM GLOBALLY RECEIVES MIXED REACTION LOCALLY

The implementation of the D&I Initiative did not encounter any significant legal obstacles in Finland as Petrocom Finland was cautious from the outset not to violate any local laws and to allow legally obliged modifications. This was also reflected in the responses of local union representatives (who are typically quite influential in the highly unionized Finnish business environment), who remained relatively silent throughout the implementation process, despite some short-lived defensive reactions at the beginning when discussions turned to the employment of immigrants (e.g., the effect of low-cost labor on employee wage levels and rights). Instead, the biggest challenges were associated with the level of priority given to diversity management and how to introduce the issue of diversity sensitively into the workplace.

Getting priorities straight

From the outset, people within Petrocom Finland disagreed about the level of priority that should be given to diversity management issues. Some of these arguments were based on whether diversity management represents a critical business issue, some were based on its relevance in a workplace setting, and others were based on its relevance given Finland's and the Finnish unit's demographics. The newly appointed Finnish Diversity Coordinator believed the D&I Initiative was an important business issue and had come at the right time due to increasing diversity challenges:

> Our local unit faces more and more challenges related to personnel. We are increasingly talking about different groups that are formed based around certain minority status. Well, not only have these groups now become a very important target for recruitment in Finland, but we also have to understand that such a variety of individuals can't be managed in the same way, so we need to adapt. I think we need to pay more attention to these groups, and consider the special needs of women, ethnic minorities and other groups that face obstacles to inclusion.

Petrocom Finland's CEO was more diplomatic, but still believed that diversity management issues were premature. However, several employees in the Finnish unit generally described the D&I Initiative as an overreaction and "like using a sledgehammer to crack a nut," as one disgruntled employee explains:

> We have been told that diversity is just about anything that distinguishes individuals from each other, like religion, culture and ethnicity, language and so on. But I still think that here in my work it is a question of males and females being equal. We haven't got any immigrants, for example. In my work, everybody speaks largely Finnish and some English. Religion isn't visible here, why would it be? It is work, after all. I guess the guys at headquarters have a point generally, and I understand that the main issues are important at that level. A small office in Finland doesn't count for much there and thus it has to go with the flow, regardless of the local importance of these matters. Suddenly we have all kinds of promotional events and trainings going on. I'll be retired before those things become important here.

Maria the HR Manager faced ongoing challenges about how to strike the right balance between raising awareness, educating and supporting individuals to focus on the unfamiliar aspects of work and behaviors presented by the principles of D&I, and on the other hand, bringing the level of attention to a level that didn't overshadow key business issues since employees started to view it with scepticism and as a passing fad. At times, she herself questioned what their role as a local subsidiary was supposed to be:

> We are not here to change society. That's not our prime reason for being in Finland. We are here to do business. But we have to do it as a good Finnish company, as a good Finnish

citizen, so that everyone who works for Petrocom can be proud of what we are doing. But I don't feel that our task is to be the one who comes and breaks the walls down.

Cultural sensitivities

At a relatively early stage in the implementation process it became apparent that the magnitude of cultural adjustments required to openly discuss diversity meant that the Finnish subsidiary considered itself insufficiently prepared to embrace everything that was being suggested by headquarters. For example, the suggested use of affinity groups was regarded as inappropriate and not used by the Finnish subsidiary. It was argued that they represented a culture-specific tool reflecting Anglo-Saxon assumptions that everybody is ready and willing to "open up" and discuss issues such as religion and homosexuality with others in a group.

For employees, the introduction of sensitive and personal issues in discussions of D&I made typically reserved Finnish people feel noticeably uncomfortable. Middle managers started to voice concerns about whether these types of discussions would require them to "reveal who we really are" to their colleagues and subordinates. The questioning of people's values and norms regarding diversity and inequality was also shown to be a painful experience for some. Maria recalls a certain landmark team meeting a year into the implementation process in which they discussed issues of inequality and were asked to share personal experiences:

> The atmosphere was unique. The subjects of discussion were unique. The inner dynamics of that team were discussed openly. It had people crying. And that was certainly unique in that department!

The perceived Anglo-Saxon approach of discussing diversity-related issues in the open in order to raise awareness and provide evidence of "progress" did not sit comfortably with the much more modest, reserved and private nature of the Finns. Although Maria suspected possible traces of denial in people's attitudes to diversity, even fairly open-minded employees voiced their preferences to keep such personal matters separate from the workplace and were certainly opposed to confronting them in intimate, face-to-face settings. Maria tried to explain this is an informal email to corporate headquarters:

> It may just be the Finnish way. People feel uncomfortable when, for example, sexual orientation is brought up as a topic of discussion, and then you are given the instruction to change your mindset, your behavior, to be more open towards this. I think most people think that the best way to approach diversity is to be pragmatic – just focus on the work at hand. To do that, you have to cooperate and get along with everybody.

LESSONS LEARNED, AND WHAT NEXT?

While putting the final touches on the latest official diversity and inclusiveness progress report for the corporate D&I Board, Maria reflected back on how she felt when she heard about

Finland's inclusion in the global D&I Initiative. She was right to have felt excited and anxious since the D&I Initiative had proven to be rewarding yet very challenging. Reflecting Finland's national standing and changing demographics, Maria knew that Petrocom Finland had started off in a strong position in certain areas such as gender diversity, and that position had not changed. Some progress had been made in recruiting ethnic minorities and supporting their inclusion in the workplace. However, Maria knew intuitively that the D&I Initiative had been much less effective culturally in influencing people's attitudes and behaviors concerning the more "invisible" aspects of diversity such as individuals' beliefs and sexual orientation. Maria felt she was at a crossroads.

With many corporate expectations met, was Finnish society and the employees at Petrocom Finland ready for further progress in these difficult areas, and what was the best way to do it? Maria felt positive she could make a real difference, but where should the line be drawn?

Case study questions

1. In your opinion, how well was the implementation of Petrocom's global D&I Initiative handled?
2. Given what you have understood about the Finnish context regarding the management of workforce diversity, together with the perceptions of employees at Petrocom Finland about the importance of workforce diversity issues:
   (i) How would you present the business case for diversity and inclusiveness in the Finnish subsidiary without coming across as over-sensationalizing the issue?
   (ii) How might Finland's standing and recent demographic changes in Finland help or hinder you in the above?
3. What specific methods would you use in efforts to further implement the Group's D&I Initiative whilst taking into account the cultural sensitivities of the Finnish workforce? Can you think of any alternative methods that might be effective?
4. How would you best seek to reconcile Petrocom Finland's desire for a more locally driven approach versus Petrocom Group's "Global Organisation" vision, strategy, and Global D&I Standard?
5. "I don't feel that our task is to be the one who comes and breaks the walls down." Where do (i) Petrocom's, (ii) Petrocom Finland's and (iii) Maria's responsibilities begin and end in terms of changing Finnish employees' attitudes and behaviors about diversity and inclusiveness?

NOTES

1. This case is an abridged version of: Smale, A., Björkman, I., Säntti, R., & Sivasubramanian, N. B. (2018). Implementing a global diversity management initiative in Finland. In L. Castro Christiansen, M. Biron, E. Farndale, & B. Kuvaas (Eds.), *Global human resource management casebook* (Routledge global human resource management series) (2nd ed.) (pp. 64–74). New York: Routledge.

The case is partly based on the fieldwork and findings published in Sippola, A. and Smale, A. (2007) The global integration of diversity management: A longitudinal case study, *International Journal of Human Resource Management*, 18(11): 1895-1916.

The authors have been granted permission to publish findings about this case. However, for confidentiality and teaching purposes, a pseudonym is used and certain details concerning the organization's titles and activities have been altered.

2. Adam Smale, School of Management, University of Vaasa, Finland; Ingmar Björkman, Aalto University School of Business, Finland.

Case 2: RetailCo in the Netherlands[1]

Corine Boon and Deanne N. Den Hartog[2]

BACKGROUND

RetailCo is a Dutch retail organization, founded in the early 1900s in the Netherlands. RetailCo's aim was to open department stores for "ordinary" people, in contrast to other department stores, which were mostly luxury brands focused and aimed at attracting relatively wealthy people. From the start, RetailCo was characterized as optimistic, unique, clear, reliable, accessible, and as typically down-to-earth "Dutch."

RetailCo's mission is to make people's daily lives easier and more enjoyable. The retailer aims to play a key role in the lives of its customers and to offer convenient solutions to many of their everyday problems. Also, RetailCo's management believes that great quality and design should be available to everyone at a great price and that all products they offer need to be both functional and unique. Therefore, the department stores offer convenient, simple, practical, and high-quality products for everyone, using relatively low prices. They have a wide assortment including household and home decorating products, fashion, skin care, and food. The company only offers products that they have designed and branded themselves, to keep the products unique and recognizable. In the Netherlands, most people regularly visit a RetailCo store.

THE SITUATION IN THE EARLY 2000s

By 2007, RetailCo had over 350 stores, with approximately 10,000 employees (more than 85% of them female). Most stores were located in towns and cities throughout the Netherlands. Every year, they opened around 30 new stores, and RetailCo had just begun expanding internationally in the nearby countries of Belgium, Germany, and Luxembourg.

Traditionally, the culture of RetailCo could be described as a family culture, characterized by seven key values: *client orientation, respect and trust, proactivity, results orientation, energy, working systematically, and loving the job.* Top management saw – and still sees – RetailCo's culture and heritage as key to the company's success. Their HR strategy was to strive for high performance by offering employees enjoyable jobs. Thus, the focus was to make work enjoyable and keep employees satisfied and committed, assuming this would enhance the company's performance.

This focus on employees resulted in RetailCo's reputation as an employer being very positive – this reputation, as well as the unique and typically Dutch culture, attracted many applicants. The turnover rate was very low as employees were very loyal to RetailCo and the specific store they worked in. RetailCo strived to maintain this culture by selecting new employees based on culture fit and by putting a lot of effort into the organizational socialization process. RetailCo also strongly preferred internal development and promotion of employees. RetailCo tried to make its jobs diverse and offered relatively high salaries and good benefits compared to other retailers. Employees were also offered job security and the company paid great attention to employee well-being.

There were also some drawbacks to their approach, however. For example, RetailCo's focus on making work enjoyable and keeping employees satisfied was also reflected in the fact that employees had considerable influence over their work schedule. Most of the time, employees could choose their own working hours to match their individual needs. For RetailCo, it was, however, sometimes challenging to accommodate everyone's wishes and at the same time, staff the stores at peak hours. Also, most employees always received positive performance evaluations from their managers, as a result of which RetailCo did not have a clear overview of which employees were perhaps under- or overperforming.

THE TAKE-OVER AND INTERNATIONAL EXPANSION

Over time, the pressure on margins in the retail industry had increased, forcing RetailCo to work more efficiently. In 2007 and 2008, the typically Dutch firm RetailCo was taken over twice in two years by investment firms from the United States (the first take-over) and then from the United Kingdom (the second take-over). The market pressure and the take-overs had a major impact on how RetailCo was managed and the investment firms shifted their focus to more tightly managing efficiency, output, and costs. Consequently, RetailCo reduced their investment in their employees and aimed to staff the stores more efficiently, which created some tensions.

The strategy also changed. To survive as a company in this changing environment and more competitive market, sales volume became increasingly important. Thus, the investment firm decided that RetailCo needed to grow more rapidly than previously. To meet this goal, the investment firm decided to prioritize fast international expansion. The international stores were all franchises, with staff being employed locally rather than as part of the parent company. Their employment conditions could thus differ from those of employees in the Netherlands. As a result of this strategy, RetailCo opened approximately 50 new stores each year and expanded into several new countries. Ten years later, in 2018, almost 300 of RetailCo's 800 stores were outside of the Netherlands and RetailCo owned almost 800 stores in 10 different countries, including France, Spain, Hong Kong, China, and the United Arab Emirates. In total, RetailCo by then had around 20,000 employees and RetailCo stores were visited by more than six million customers every week.

Over time, the investment firm from the UK aimed to improve RetailCo's performance while also maintaining the RetailCo brand and strong culture. A new set of values was introduced by the investment firm to enable this new balance: *our customer first, quality in everything we do, we keep things simple, we do what we say, we win together, and every penny counts*. These new values aim to reflect RetailCo's history and at the same time create a culture that is more customer-centric than before, as well as emphasizing high efficiency and performance more than previously.

Changes were also made in the HRM strategy to increase efficiency and reduce costs. RetailCo now expects more flexibility from employees. For example, employees' scheduling preferences are taken into account less often, and employees are typically scheduled to work across more days but fewer hours each day to cover busy store hours. A new performance appraisal system has been introduced that differentiates more between high and low performers. Also, there is a new collective bargaining agreement with lower salaries and benefits for new employees who enter the company.

THE CURRENT CHALLENGE

RetailCo employees are unhappy with the changes they are experiencing and many have become less satisfied with their work and less committed to RetailCo. The employees feel that the culture over time is changing from a family-type culture in which they were appreciated, to a purely performance-oriented culture. In 2015, a trade union survey among RetailCo employees showed that the majority believed that their working conditions had deteriorated. They experienced increased work pressure and complained about irregular work hours and having to be available for work all the time. Several employees indicated that more work needed to be done with fewer people, and there was no replacement when someone was sick. This situation on the workfloor also had negative consequences for customers, who complained about stores being messy and unclean. Moreover, in 2019, starting salaries for new employees were decreased, as did maximum salaries of store employees and store managers. This caused additional dissatisfaction among employees – many of whom felt they were being let down by RetailCo. RetailCo employees in the Netherlands also noticed that RetailCo was prioritizing international expansion over investing in the Dutch stores and employees.

RetailCo's management team is now worried about the changes and the effects they are having on employee morale. The labor unions have received an increasing number of complaints from RetailCo employees about work pressure, and absenteeism and employee turnover have increased substantially. While the brand is still successful in the Netherlands, winning prizes for best brand and best retail chain, financial returns have started to decrease over the last couple of years. The COVID-19 pandemic has put even more pressure on financial returns. Also, the decrease in employee satisfaction and the changing corporate culture seem to be affecting customer satisfaction, which is also a threat to the business.

At the same time, increased efficiency is still needed in order to survive in the current market, so going back to the old culture and HRM strategy is not a realistic option. The management team wonders what to do to move the company forward:

1. How can they retain the unique culture of the firm and perhaps even reinvigorate Dutch employees' engagement and loyalty, while at the same time becoming even more efficient in their operations?
2. What HRM initiatives could they introduce in the Netherlands to decrease absenteeism and turnover, taking into account costs and the need for efficiency?
3. What effect is international expansion having on the employee and customer experience in the Dutch stores and how might this be improved?

NOTES

1. This case is an abridged version of Boon, C., & Den Hartog, D. N. (2018). HRM and culture at RetailCo. In L. Castro Christiansen, M. Biron, E. Farndale, & B. Kuvaas (Eds.), *Global human resource management casebook* (Routledge global human resource management series) (2nd ed.) (pp. 43–52). New York: Routledge.
2. Amsterdam Business School, University of Amsterdam, the Netherlands.

Case 3: Trimo's global talent management transformation formula[1]

Robert Kaše[2]

INTRODUCTION

The sun was just setting behind the Burj Al Arab, when Sonja Klopčič, Competencies Development Manager at Trimo, was taking off from Dubai airport. Admiring the intense golden color of the glowing desert, she was reflecting on the events over the last days.

Dubai was a venue to an important step in Trimo's continuous internationalization process. Just hours before heading back home, Sonja has finalized everything to hire Šenaj Avdić as the first third country national (TCN) to ever head a subsidiary in Trimo's international network. The appointment of the new Managing Director of Trimo's United Arab Emirates subsidiary was a result of an intense recruiting and selection process that lasted for several months and came to closure in the last three days. One evening after a hard day of interviewing, Sonja was interrupted by a phone call from Marta Strmec, Director of HR and General Affairs at Trimo. She told her that Tatjana Fink, Trimo's General Manager, is planning a meeting on Monday to discuss the next steps of Trimo's internationalization process and asked her to prepare a proposal for what the company should do to develop and maintain a pipeline of global talent.

The phone call triggered a range of questions running through Sonja's mind. What can an ambitious multinational enterprise (MNE) from a small country do to gain recognition and successfully compete on the global expatriate market? What could make a company like Trimo attractive to global talent? Can a small MNE retain global talent? Should headquarters move to a global talent hot spot (such as Paris, New York, or London) to be able to attract global talent? Juggling around these questions the flight attendant interrupted her with a familiar question: "Pasta or chicken?"

THE BACKGROUND

Trimo, headquartered in Trebnje, Slovenia, is one of the leading European providers of original and complete solutions in prefabricated steel buildings, roofs, façades, steel constructions, and containers. Trimo's business model provides its global clients with everything from initial ideas and design through manufacturing and assembly to after-sale service. The company is an innovative player in its segment as it follows the principles of a learning organization and open-innovation, investing heavily in competences and product development.

In 1991, after the short war for independence in Slovenia, the company lost its established Yugoslav markets overnight and had to internationalize intensely. Trimo was entering foreign markets first through sales representatives and sales subsidiaries, later also by joint ventures and manufacturing subsidiaries to increase the radius of its reach. In 2009, when this case unfolds, Trimo was already directly present in 27 countries, exporting to 45 countries, and creating 77% of all revenues abroad (see Figure C3.1).

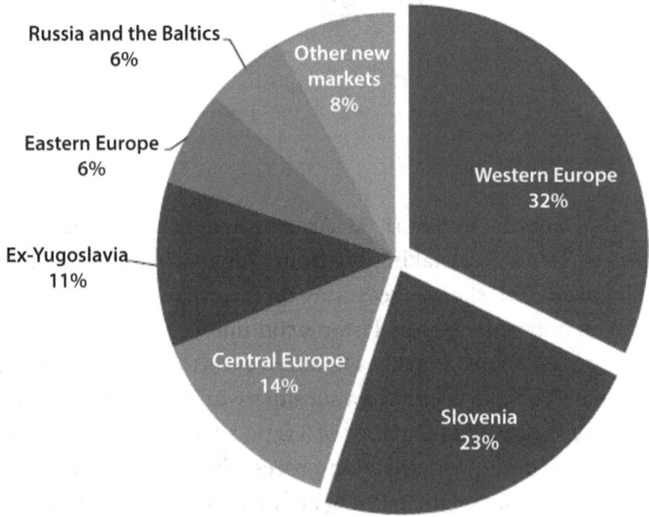

Figure C3.1   Trimo's international sales structure in 2009

In 2009, Trimo employed 522 employees at the headquarters and an additional 691 employees abroad as a part of the Trimo Group; 85% of employees were employed permanently and full-time; 47% had a college or university degree; and 70% of its workforce was male. The average age of employees was 40. While having a majority share of foreign employment and contractually collaborating with many experts from abroad (engineers, designers, researchers, architects), Trimo's top management team remained composed of parent country nationals (PCNs). In 2009, staff turnover in the parent company was 9.2%, compared to 19.5% in its affiliated companies.

When recruiting, Trimo benefits from a reputation of being one of the best employers in Slovenia, although it is still working on its recognition on the global expatriate markets. The company runs international awards for best research theses, architectural solutions, and urban space visions, from which it attracts future employees. Similarly, Trimo's scholarships attract top students very early in their career. Trimo uses traditional and new media to recruit applicants for open positions, including their corporate web page, various employment portals, business-related social networking applications (LinkedIn) and presentation videos on

YouTube. Trimo's experts are frequently speakers at university, professional and networking events, which enables them to be alert to potential future Trimo employees.

Development at Trimo is based on a company-specific competency model and performance appraisal process, both of which are driven by the employees and facilitated by management. These processes focus on employees not only learning new skills but also instilling Trimo's corporate values. Trimo also provides extensive training opportunities with carefully tailored customized training programs to all their employees. Over 94% of training is organized on-site with internal or external trainers. Trimo's base pay is above the industry and regional average. Apart from base pay, employees can earn individual pay for performance (up to 30%), 13th month pay (if the company's profits permit), rewards for extra project work, and vacation allowance. Each year, on average, 20% of employees are given a raise as a result of promotion.

THE PROBLEM

Trimo is one of many internationalized Slovenian companies including several important regional MNEs, some niche global leaders, ambitious small and medium-sized firms, and a vibrant globalized start-up community. One of the biggest obstacles these companies face is the lack of PCNs that are available, capable, and willing to accept a long-term international assignment. The chairman of one Slovenian MNEs commented: "Our young associates, who are willing to accept international assignments, often lack knowledge and experience, while their older colleagues with families have very high demands in terms of international assignment premiums and allowances for living abroad, along with those to provide for the family."

Not having a sufficient pool of expatiates is a bottleneck for many Slovenian MNEs. The reasons lie with the country of origin, the destination country, and the company:

1. It is in Slovene national culture to avoid uncertainty, which is a major issue that discourages international assignees.
2. The absolute number of potential Slovenian PCNs is small due to the size of the country and limited labor market mobility.
3. Approximately 90% of Slovenians own their apartment or house, which is a consequence of a traditional style of living. This creates high opportunity costs for potential expatriates and increases their housing allowance demands.
4. Slovenian MNEs most frequently offer expatriate assignments in Southeastern Europe, which for Slovenians is still considered a less attractive (or even a hardship) post. Moreover, there is a general (subjective) opinion among Slovenians that the quality of living in their home country is still considerably better than at other locations for which expatriate posts are offered. Slovenia offers a very diverse landscape in a very small area (i.e., mountains, sea, lakes, rivers, forests, plains, karst), which is hard to find nearby, along with an attractive combination of (sub)urban and countryside experiences.
5. Slovenian MNEs often lack experience of effective expatriate management and developing and maintaining a pipeline of global talent.

An often-agreed compromise for Slovenian MNEs is the international commuter assignment, where assignees still reside at home but drive (or fly) on a weekly or fortnightly basis to affiliated companies. In the longer term, this situation may improve, given the high percentage of Slovenian students on study abroad programs and experiencing mobility early in their life, as well as increasing numbers of students from neighboring countries that study in Slovenia. There are, however, also fears that these developments could lead to a more intense brain drain: A frequent reaction of Slovenian business school students when asked about their interest in becoming corporate expatriates is that they would rather consider becoming self-initiated expatriates and customize their global work experience. Nevertheless, since international assignments are considered part of fast-track careers for young talent, the future prospects for building a potential international assignee pool look more promising, provided returning expatriates are able to demonstrate to potential future expatriate candidates that international assignments are indeed worth pursuing.

IN SEARCH FOR A WINNING GLOBAL TALENT MANAGEMENT FORMULA...

Trimo intends to pursue further internationalization by extending its focus to selected overseas markets. To make the next step a more realistic possibility, the company needs to be able to augment its current human capital with global talent. Trimo needs to address the questions that Sonja was struggling with as she was thinking about the forthcoming meeting.

Your task is to help Sonja to prepare a viable proposal for the Monday meeting. Propose a robust draft strategy for attracting and retaining global talent. You might find the following questions helpful: How can Trimo become more attractive for global talent? How should Trimo source global talent? What kind of work arrangements should be used to attract global talent? How can Trimo keep its global talent engaged? What should Trimo do to retain global talent?

NOTES

1. This case is an abridged version of: Kaše, R. (2018). On becoming a truly global player: the global talent management challenge at Trimo. In L. Castro Christiansen, M. Biron, E. Farndale, & B. Kuvaas (Eds.), *Global human resource management casebook* (Routledge global human resource management series) (2nd ed.) (pp. 165–176). New York: Routledge. Some of the situations in the case study have been changed to facilitate learning process and do not completely reflect reality.
2. School of Economics & Business, University of Ljubljana.

Case 4: Short-term work at the Robert Bosch Group: an example of the German industrial relations system[1]

Marion Festing[2]

It is my intention, apart from the alleviation of all kinds of suffering, to promote the moral, physical and intellectual development of the people.
(Robert Bosch, Founder of Robert Bosch Group 1935)

Robert Bosch Group (hereafter Bosch) was known in Germany for its focus on recruiting, retaining, motivating and training talent. Education and life-long learning were viewed as the major principles of HRM. Thus, investing in human capital, supported by long-term employee and management development, represented the core strategic goals of the firm. However, when the Global Financial Crisis (GFC) hit around 2008, it was extremely difficult to stay true to this philosophy when all costs, including personnel costs, had to be reduced to ensure the long-term survival and competitiveness of the firm.

"Keeping our core workforce throughout the crisis" was the firm's declared goal, as the GFC hit the automotive division toward the end of 2008. In September 2008, the first discussions started with the works councils on possible reactions to the crisis. Initial negotiations focused on a temporary reduction in working time in accordance with decreased production volume, known as "short-time work."

SHORT-TIME WORK

In Germany, there are specific regulations related to short-time work. Companies affected by a significant loss of work can reduce the working time of their employees, who are compensated with short-time work benefits from the German state. These benefits amount to 60% of net income loss for single persons, or up to 67% of the respective net wage cut for employees with children.

Usually, the firm and the employees agree on short-time work for a period of six months. Changes are subject to short-term notice, that is, within 14 days, and other rules can apply if new production orders arrive. These regulations are an important device for a company to maintain flexible employment during a crisis, and from the employee's perspective they enable individual workers not only to plan their time schedule, but also keep on top of their own financial situation. During the GFC, the maximum period of short-time work was increased substantially by the German government from six to 24 months, as stipulated by law.

The implementation of these regulations does not, however, result in a proportional reduction in the non-labor costs for the employer; the company still has to bear additional mandated costs, such as vacation pay or bonuses, as well as – depending on the duration of short-time work – a proportion of social security contributions. Thus, this solution is expensive for the employer. At Bosch, these residual costs constituted 36% of the regular hourly personnel costs starting from the seventh month of short-time work, or 26% of regular costs if the employee was a trainee during this period.

The regulations are perhaps somewhat beneficial for employees. During short-time work, they usually receive a wage/salary for the hours worked from their employer plus a 60–67% short-time working allowance from the German state. This means that for the hours they are laid off, they nevertheless receive around two-thirds of the pay they would normally have received if working. Nevertheless, this still represents a substantial unexpected cut in pay.

BOSCH'S CHALLENGES

The calculations that resulted from the short-time work regulations imposed during the GFC represented a true challenge to Bosch's HR department. New software had to be developed as part of a very time-consuming process. Furthermore, before related expenses were partially reimbursed by the state, they had to be borne by the firm. This sometimes challenged the liquidity of a firm. Thus, it was important for the company to find alternative ways of reducing working time, without placing an additional financial burden on the employer.

Another regulation, the regional tariff agreement for employment security, permitted a reduction in working time from 35 to 30 hours, or – in some tariff zones – even down to 29 hours per week. For the company, this option was more attractive, as it resulted in decreasing personnel costs almost proportionally to the reduction in working time.

There was a third set of regulations that affected how Bosch could respond to the GFC situation. The relevant collective bargaining agreement on employment security pertaining to Bosch's operations stipulated that working time reductions should be agreed at site level. The result of the negotiations between Bosch and the company's works council (*Gesamtbetriebsrat*) in October 2008 was that the first 15–20% of the working time reduction should be based on the tariff agreement, while the remainder could be based on short-time work legislation.

At the end of 2008, these regulations were rolled out at several locations. Thus, from late 2008 – when the after-effects of the GFC worsened – various groups of employees started short-time work. Simultaneously, the working hours of full-time employees (with 40 hours per week contracts) was reduced from 40 to 35 hours per week. Overall, by the end of 2009, 31% of the working hours of 32,700 employees had been reduced based on the short-time work regulations and tariff agreements. While the first target group included production employees, from 2009, non-production employees working in administrative functions and at the company's headquarters were also affected.

One year later, the crisis was still ongoing. There was an intense ongoing dialogue between the company and employee representatives. In order to maintain long-term competitiveness, and to keep the core workforce despite cyclical employment problems, further negotiations with the company works council were initiated. The aim was to find a solution in line with Bosch's corporate values.

Case study questions

1. What is Bosch's general HRM philosophy as underpinned by the corporate values?
2. What are the core elements of the "short-time work" regulations of the German government?
3. What did the "regional tariff agreement" allow and why do you think this concession was made?
4. What was the role of the company's works council in finding a solution to the challenges Bosch faced as a result of the GFC?
5. Discuss the advantages and disadvantages of short-time work for Bosch, for the employees, and for broader German society.
6. How might Bosch maintain employee engagement during the short-term work period when employees were suffering substantial income loss?

NOTES

1. This case is an abridged version of: Festing, M. (2018). Learning about talent retention in times of crisis – opportunities for the Robert Bosch Group in the context of the German industrial relations system, in L. Castro Christiansen, M. Biron, E. Farndale, & B. Kuvaas (Eds.), *Global human resource management casebook* (Routledge global human resource management series) (2nd ed.) (pp. 22–31). New York: Routledge. The author would like to thank Mr. Fröhlecke, Vice President Corporate Department Human Resources Management – Executives, Ms. Köpnick, Vice President Corporate Department Labour Law and Industrial Relations, and Ms. Litobarski, Senior Consultant Corporate Department Labour Law and Industrial Relations (all Bosch Group Germany) for their cooperation and support for this case study.
2. ESCP Business School, Berlin, Germany.

REFERENCES

Abo, T. (1994). *Hybrid factory: The Japanese production system in the United States.* Oxford: Oxford University Press.

Addison, J. X., & Siebert, W. S. (1994). Recent developments in social policy in the new European Union. *Industrial and Labor Relations Review, 48,* 5-27.

Adler, N. (2011). Women leading and managing worldwide. In A.-W. Harzing, & A. Pinnington (Eds.), *International human resource management* (3rd ed.) (pp. 507-514). London: Sage.

Adler, N. J. (1984). Women in international management: Where are they? *California Management Review, 26,* 78-89.

Adler, N. J., & Ghadar, F. (1990). Strategic human resource management: A global perspective. In R. Pieper (Ed.), *Human resource management in international comparison* (pp. 235-260). Berlin: De Gruyter.

Adler, P. S. (2003). Making the HR outsourcing decision. *MIT Sloan Management Review, 45*(1), 53.

Aguinis, H., & Glavas, A. (2012). What we know and don't know about corporate social responsibility: A review and research agenda. *Journal of Management, 38*(4), 932-968.

Aguinis, H., & Kraiger, K. (2009). Benefits of training and development for individuals and teams, organizations, and society. *Annual Review of Psychology, 60*(1), 451-474.

Aharoni, Y. (1994). How small firms can achieve competitive advantage in an interdependent world. In T. Agmon, & R. Drobnick (Eds.), *Small firms in global competition* (pp. 9-18). New York: Oxford University Press.

AIRINC (2019). Mobility Outlook Survey. Cambridge, MA: AirInc. https://www.air-inc.com/library/2019-mobility-outlook-survey/.

Ales, E., & Dufresne, A. (2012). Transnational collective bargaining: Another (problematic) fragment of the European multi-level industrial relations system. *European Journal of Industrial Relations, 18*(2), 95-105.

Allen, D., & Raynor, M. E. (2004). Preparing for a new global business environment: Divided and disorderly or integrated and harmonious? *Journal of Business Strategy, 25*(5), 16-25.

Andersen, S. K., Kaine, S., & Lansbury, R. D. (2017). Decentralised bargaining in Denmark and Australia: Voluntarism versus legal regulation. *Australian Bulletin of Labour, 43*(1), 45.

Antal, A. B., & Izraeli, D. (1993). A global comparison of women in management: Women managers in their homelands and as expatriates. In E. A. Gagenson (Ed.), *Women in management: Trends, issues and challenges in managerial diversity.* Newbury Park, CA: Sage.

Ariño, A., & Reuer, J. J. (2004). Designing and renegotiating strategic alliance contracts. *Academy of Management Executive, 18,* 37-48.

Arshad, R. (2016). Psychological contract violation and turnover intention: Do cultural values matter?. *Journal of Managerial Psychology, 31*(1), 251-264.

Au, K. (1999). Intra-cultural variation: Evidence and implications for international business. *Journal of International Business Studies, 30,* 799-812.

Au, K., & Fukuda, J. (2002). Boundary spanning behavior of expatriates. *Journal of World Business, 37,* 285-296.

Aust (Ehnert), I., Matthews, B., & Muller-Camen, M. (2020). Common good HRM: A paradigm shift in sustainable HRM? *Human Resource Management Review, 30*(3).https://doi.org/10.1016/j.hrmr.2019.100705.

Aycan, Z. (2005). The interplay between cultural and institutional/structural contingencies in human resource management practices. *International Journal of Human Resource Management, 16*(7), 1083-1119.

Azumi, K., & McMillan, C. J. (1975). Culture and organizational structure: A comparison on Japanese and British organizations. *International Studies of Management and Organization, 5*(1), 35-47.

Bacon, N., & Hoque, K. (2005). HRM in the SME sector: Valuable employees and coercive networks. *International Journal of Human Resource Management, 16*(11), 1976-1999.

Bailey, J. R., Chen, C. C., & Dou, S. G. (1997). Conceptions of self and performance related feedback in the U.S., Japan, and China. *Journal of International Business Studies, 28,* 605-625.

Baird, P. L., Geylani, P. C., & Roberts, J. A. (2012). Corporate social and financial performance re-examined: Industry effects in a linear mixed model analysis. *Journal of Business Ethics, 109*(3), 367–388.

Baker & McKenzie International (2006). Worldwide guide to termination, employment discrimination, and workplace harassment laws. DigitalCommons@ILR: https://digitalcommons.ilr.cornell.edu/lawfirms/46.

Baker, C., & Ciuk, S. (2015). Keeping the family side ticking along: An exploratory study of the work–family interface in the experiences of rotational assignees and frequent business travellers. *Journal of Global Mobility, 3*(2), 137–154.

Barkema, H. G., Bell, J. H. J., & Pennings, J. M. (1996). Foreign entry, cultural barriers, and learning. *Strategic Management Journal, 17*, 151–166.

Barkema, H. G., Shenkar, O., Vermeulen, F., & Bell, J. H. J. (1997). Working abroad, working with others: How firms learn to operate international joint ventures. *Academy of Management Journal, 40*, 426–442.

Barney, J. (1991). Firm resources and sustained competitive advantage. *Journal of Management, 17*(1), 99–120. https://doi.org/10.1177/014920639101700108.

Barrett, R. (2015). Small firm training: just meeting the day-to-day needs of the business. *Employee Relations, 37*(50), 547–567. https://doi.org/10.1108/ER-05-2014-0048.

Bartlett, C. (1986). Building and managing the transnational: The new organizational challenge. In M. Porter (Ed.), *Competition in global industries* (pp. 367–401). Boston, MA: Harvard Business School Press.

Bartlett, C. A., & Ghoshal, S. (1989). *Managing across borders: The transnational solution.* Boston, MA: Harvard Business School Press.

Bartlett, C. A., & Ghoshal, S. (1998). Beyond strategic planning to organization learning: Lifeblood of the individualized corporation. *Strategy & Leadership, 26*, 34–39.

Baruch, Y., Altman, Y., & Tung, R. L. (2016). Career mobility in a global era: Advances in managing expatriation and repatriation. *The Academy of Management Annals, 10*(1), 841–889.

Bastida, M. (2018). Yes, they can do it! Exploring female expatriates' effectiveness. *European Research on Management and Business Economics, 24*(2), 114–120. https://doi.org/10.1016/j.iedeen.2018.03.001.

Baumgarten, K. (1995). Training and development of international staff. In A.-W. Harzing, & J. Van Ruysseveldt (Eds.), *International human resource management* (pp. 205–228). London: Sage.

Bean, R. (1985). *Comparative industrial relations.* Beckenham, UK: Croom Helm.

Beaver, W. (1995). Levi's is leaving China. *Business Horizons*, pp. 35–40.

Beechler, S. (1992). International management control in multinational corporations: The case of Japanese consumer electronics firms in Asia. *ASEAN Economic Bulletin, 9*(2), 149–168.

Beechler, S. L., & Iaquinto, A. L. (1994). *A longitudinal study of staffing patterns in U.S. affiliates of Japanese transnational corporations.* Paper presented to the International Management Division of the Academy of Management, Dallas.

Beer, M. (1981). Performance appraisal: Dilemmas and possibilities. *Organizational Dynamics, Winter*, 25–33.

Beer, M., Spector, P. R., Lawrence, D., Mills, D. Q., & Walton, R. E. (1984). *Managing human assets.* New York: Free Press.

Belasco, J. A., & Stayer, R. C. (1994). *Flight of the buffalo: Soaring to excellence, learning to let employees lead.* New York: Grand Central Publishing.

Belizon, M.J., Gunnigle, P., & Morley, M. (2013). Determinants of central control and subsidiary autonomy in HRM: The case of foreign owned multinational companies in Spain. *Human Resource Management Journal, 23*(3), 262–278.

Bell, B. S., Tannenbaum, S. I., Ford, J. K., Noe, R. A., & Kraiger, K. (2017). 100 years of training and development research: What we know and where we should go. *Journal of Applied Psychology, 102*, 305–323.

Benet-Martínez, V., Leu, J., Lee, F., & Morris, M. W. (2002). Negotiating biculturalism: Cultural frame switching in biculturals with oppositional versus compatible cultural Identities. *Journal of Cross-Cultural Psychology, 33*(5), 492–516. https://doi.org/10.1177/0022022102033005005.

Benson, G. S., & Pattie, M. (2008). Is expatriation good for my career? The impact of expatriate assignments on perceived and actual career outcomes. *International Journal of Human Resource Management, 19*(9), 1636–1653.

Benson, P. G. (1978). Measuring cross-cultural adjustment: The problem of criteria. *International Journal of Intercultural Relations, 2*(1), 21–37.

Berdrow, I., & Lane, H. W. (1993). Iceverks: Ben & Jerry's in Russia. Richard Ivey School of Business Case.

Berger, P.L., & Luckman, T. (1966). *The social construction of reality.* London: Penguin Books.

Bernardin, J. H., & Cascio, W. F. (1984). Personnel appraisal and the law. In R. A. Schuler, & S. A. Youngblood (Eds.), *Readings in personnel and human resource management* (pp. 229–240). St. Paul, MN: West.

Bernthal, P. R., Rogers, R. W., & Smith, A. B. (2003). *Managing performance: Building accountability for organizational success.* Pittsburgh, PA: Developmental Dimensions International.

Beugelsdijk, S., Kostova, T., Kunst, V. E., Spadafora, E., & van Essen, M. (2018). Cultural distance and firm internationalization: A meta-analytical review and theoretical implications. *Journal of Management, 44*(1), 89–130.

BGRS (2020). Talent Mobility Trends. Extended Business Travel: BGRS Pulse Survey.

Bhaskar-Shrinivas, P., Harrison, D. A., Shaffer, M. A., & Luk, D. M. (2005). Input-based and time-based models of international adjustment: Meta-analytic evidence and theoretical extensions. *Academy of Management Journal, 48,* 257–281.

Bidwell, M., & Mollick, E. (2015). Shifts and ladders: Comparing the role of internal and external mobility in managerial careers. *Organization Science, 26*(6), 1629–1645.

Biemann, T., & Braakmann, N. (2013). The impact of international experience on objective and subjective career success in early careers. *International Journal of Human Resource Management, 24*(18), 3438–3456. doi:10.1080/09585192.2013.775176

Birkinshaw, J. (2000). *Entrepreneurship in the global firm.* London: Sage.

Birkinshaw, J., Bresman, H., & Håkanson, L. (2000). Managing the post-acquisition integration process: How the human integration and task integration processes interact to foster value creation. *Journal of Management Studies, 37,* 395–425.

Birkinshaw, J., Nobel, R., & Ridderstråle, J. (2002). Knowledge as a contingency variable: Do the characteristics of knowledge predict organizational structure? *Organization Science, 13,* 274–289.

Björkman, I., & Lu, Y. (2001). Institutionalization and bargaining power explanations of HRM practices in international joint ventures: The case of Chinese–Western joint ventures. *Organization Studies, 22*(3), 491–512.

Björkman, I. (2006). International human resource management research and institutional theory. In G. Stahl, & I. Björkman (Eds.), *Handbook of international human resource management* (pp. 463–474). Cheltenham, UK and Northampton, MA, USA: Edward Elgar Publishing.

Björkman, I., & Lervik, J. E. (2007). Transferring HR practices within multinational corporations. *Human Resource Management Journal, 17,* 320–335.

Black, J. S., & Mendenhall, M. (1989). A practical but theory-based framework for selecting cross-cultural training methods. *Human Resource Management, 28*(4), 511–539.

Black, J. S., & Gregersen, H. B. (1991). Antecedents to cross-cultural adjustment for expatriates in Pacific Rim assignments. *Human Relations, 44*(5), 497–515.

Black, J. S., & Gregersen, H. B. (2000). High impact training: Forging leaders for the global frontier. *Human Resource Management, 39,* 173–184.

Blake, R. R., & Mouton, J. S. (1984). Overcoming group warfare. *Harvard Business Review, 62,* 98–108.

Bleeke, J., & Ernst, D. (1995). Is your strategic alliance really a sale? *Harvard Business Review, 73,* 97–105.

Bonache, J. (2006). The compensation of expatriates: A review and a future research agenda In I. Björkman, & G. Stahl (Eds.), *Handbook of research in international human resource management* (pp. 158–175). Cheltenham, UK and Northampton, MA, USA: Edward Elgar Publishing.

Bonache, J., & Stripe, L. (2012). Compensating global employees. In G. K. Stahl, I. Björkman, & S. Morris (Eds.), *Handbook of research in international human resource management* (2nd ed.) (pp. 162–182). Cheltenham, UK and Northampton, MA, USA: Edward Elgar Publishing.

Bonache, J., & Zárraga-Oberty, C. (2017). The traditional approach to compensating global mobility: Criticisms and alternatives. *International Journal of Human Resource Management, 28*(1), 149–169.

Bonciu, F. (2020). Challenges in designing economic strategies for the post-Covid-19 era. *Global Economic Observer, 18*(1), 19–23.

Bond, M. H., & King, A. Y. C. (1986). The social psychology of the Chinese people. In M. H. Bond (Ed.), *The psychology of the Chinese people* (pp, 213–264). Hong Kong: Oxford University Press.

Borchert, D., & Stewart, E. (1986). *Exploring ethics*. New York: Macmillan.

Borg, M., & Harzing, A. W. (1995). Composing an international staff. In A. W. Harzing, & J. V. Ruysseveldt (Eds.), *International human resource management* (pp. 179-204). London: Sage.

Boroditsky, L. (2001). Does language shape thought: Mandarin and English speakers' conceptions of time. *Cognitive Psychology, 43*(1), 1-22.

Boselie, P., Farndale, E., & Paauwe, J. (2012). Performance management. In C. Brewster, & W. Mayrhofer (Eds.), *Handbook of reserach on comparative human resource management* (pp. 369-392). Cheltenham, UK and Northampton, MA, USA: Edward Elgar Publishing.

Boselie, P., Farndale, E., & Paauwe, J. (2018). Comparing performance management across contexts. In C. Brewster, W. Mayrhofer, & E. Farndale (Eds.), *Handbook of research in comparative human resource management* (pp. 164-183). Cheltenham, UK and Northampton, MA, USA: Edward Elgar Publishing.

Boxall, P., & Purcell, J. (2003). *Strategy and human resource management*. Basingstoke, UK: Palgrave Macmillan.

Boyacigiller, N. (1990). The role of expatriates in the management of interdependence, complexity and risk in multinational corporations. *Journal of International Business Studies, 21*, 357–381.

Brannen, M. Y. (2004). When Mickey loses face: Recontextualization, semantic fit, and the semiotics of foreignness. *Academy of Management Review, 29*, 593-616.

Brenner, S. N., & Molander, E. A. (1977). Is the ethics of business changing? *Harvard Business Review, 55*(1), 57-71.

Brewster, C. (2004). European perspectives on human resource management. *Human Resource Management Review, 14*, 365–382.

Brewster, C. (2006). Comparing HRM policies and practices across geographical borders. In G. Stahl, & I. Björkman (Eds.), *Handbook of international human resource management* (pp. 68-90). Cheltenham, UK and Northampton, MA, USA: Edward Elgar Publishing.

Brewster, C. (2007). Comparative HRM: European views and perspectives. *International Journal of Human Resource Management, 18*(5), 769–787.

Brewster, C., Bonache, J., Cerdin, J. L., & Suutari, V. (2014). Exploring expatriate outcomes. *International Journal of Human Resource Management, 25*(14), 1921-1937.

Briody, E. K., & Chrisman, J. B. (1991). Cultural adaptation on overseas assignments. *Human Organization, 50*(3), 264-282.

Briscoe, D., Schuler, R., & Tarique, I. (2012). *International human resource management: Policies and practices for multinational enterprises*. New York: Routledge.

Briscoe, J. P., & Hall, D. T. (2006). The interplay of boundaryless and protean careers: Combinations and implications. *Journal of Vocational Behavior, 69*(1), 1-18.

Brislin, R. W., MacNab, B. R., & Nayani, F. (2008). Cross-cultural training: Applications and research. In P. B. Smith, M. F. Peterson, & D. C. Thomas (Eds.), *The handbook of cross-cultural management research* (pp. 397-410). Thousand Oaks, CA: Sage.

Broad, G. (1994). Japan in Britain: The dynamics of joint consultation. *Industrial Relations Journal, 25*, 26-38.

Brock, D. M., Shenkar, O., Shoham, A., & Siscovick, I. C. (2008). National culture and expatriate deployment. *Journal of International Business Studies, 39*(8), 1293-1309.

Brookfield Global Relocation Services. (2012). *Global relocation trends: 2012 survey report*. Woodridge, IL: Brookfield Global Relocation Services, LLC

Brookfield Global Relocation Services. (2016). *Global mobility trends: 2016 survey report*. Woodridge, IL: Brookfield Global Relocation Services.

Bücker, J., Poutsma, E., Schouteten, R., & Nies, C. (2020). The development of HR support for alternative international assignments. *Journal of Global Mobility: The Home of Expatriate Management Research, 8*(2), 249-270. doi:10.1108/JGM-02-2020-0011

Buckley, P., & Najumdar, R. (2018). The services powerhouse: Increasingly vital to world economic growth. Deloitte Insights https://www2.deloitte.com/insights/us/en/economy/issues-by-the-numbers/trade-in-services-economy-growth.html.

Budhwar, P. S., Varma, A., & Patel, C. (2016). Convergence–divergence of HRM in the Asia-Pacific: Context-specific analysis and future research agenda. *Human Resource Management Review, 26*(4), 311-326.

Burmeister, A., & Deller, J. (2016). A practical perspective on repatriate knowledge transfer: The influence of organizational support practices. *Journal of Global Mobility, 4*(1), 68-87. doi:10.1108/JGM-09-2015-0041

Burmeister, A., Lazarova, M. B., & Deller, J. (2018). Repatriate knowledge transfer: Antecedents and boundary conditions of a dyadic process. *Journal of World Business, 53*(6), 806-816. https://doi.org/10.1016/j.jwb.2018.06.004.

Burnett, M., & Von Glinow, M. A. (2011). Total rewards in international context. In A.-W. Harzing, & A. H. Pinnington (Eds.), *International human resource management* (3rd ed.) (pp. 468-504). London: Sage.

Burns, T., & Stalker, C. M. (1961). *The management of innovation.* London: Tavistock.

Burt, R. S. (1992). *Structural holes: The social structure of competition.* Cambridge, MA: Harvard University Press.

Bush, J. T. (2020). Win–win–lose? Sustainable HRM and the promotion of unsustainable employee outcomes. *Human Resource Management Review,* 30(3). https://doi.org/10.1016/j.hrmr.2019.100705.

Caligiuri, P. (1997). Assessing expatriate success: Beyond just 'being there'. In Z. Aycan (Ed.), *New approaches to employee management (Vol 4): Expatriate management theory and research* (pp. 117-140). Greenwich, CT: JAI Press.

Caligiuri, P. M., & Tung, R. L. (1999). Comparing the success of male and female expatriates from a US-based multinational company. *International Journal of Human Resource Management, 10*(5), 763-782.

Caligiuri, P. M. (2000). The Big Five personality characteristics as predictors of expatriate's desire to terminate the assignment and supervisor-rated performance. *Personnel Psychology, 53,* 67-88.

Caligiuri, P.M., & DiSanto, V. (2001). Global competence: What is it and can it be developed through global assignments? *Human Resource Planning, 24*(3), 27-38.

Caligiuri, P. M., Phillips, J., Lazarova, M., Tarique, I., & Bürgi, P. (2001). The theory of met expectations applied to expatriate adjustment: The role of cross-cultural training. *International Journal of Human Resource Management, 12,* 357-372.

Caligiuri, P.M. (2006). Developing global leaders. *Human Resource Management Review, 16,* 216-228.

Caligiuri, P. M., & Tarique, I. (2006). International assignee selection and cross-cultural training and development. In G. K. Stahl, & I. Björkman (Eds.), *Handbook of research in international human resource management* (pp. 302-322). Cheltenham, UK and Northampton, MA, USA: Edward Elgar Publishing.

Caligiuri, P., & Tarique, I. (2009). Predicting effectiveness in global leadership activities. *Journal of World Business, 44,* 336-346.

Caligiuri, P., Tarique, I., & Jacobs, R. (2009). Selection for international assignments. *Human Resource Management Review, 19*(3), 251-262.

Caligiuri, P. M., & Tarique, I. (2012a). International assignee selection and cross-cultural training and development. In G. K. Stahl, I. Björkman, & S. Morris (Eds.), *Handbook of research in international human resource management* (2nd ed.) (pp. 321-342). Cheltenham, UK and Northampton, MA, USA: Edward Elgar Publishing.

Caligiuri, P., & Tarique, I. (2012b). Dynamic cross-cultural competencies and global leadership effectiveness. *Journal of World Business, 47*(4), 612-622.

Caligiuri, P., Mencin, A., & Jiang, K. (2013). Win–win–win: the Influence of company-sponsored volunteerism programs on stakeholders. *Personnel Psychology, 66*(4), 825-860.

Caligiuri, P., & Dragoni, L. (2015). Global leadership development. In P. Caligiuri, G. Wood, & D. G. Collings (Eds.), *The Routledge companion to international human resource management* (pp. 226-239). Abingdon, Oxon: Routledge.

Caligiuri, P., Baytalskaya, N., & Lazarova, M. B. (2016). Cultural humility and low ethnocentrism as facilitators of expatriate performance. *Journal of Global Mobility, 4*(1), 4-17.

Caligiuri, P., & Bonache, J. (2016). Evolving and enduring challenges in global mobility. *Journal of World Business, 51*(1), 127-141. doi:http://dx.doi.org/10.1016/j.jwb.2015.10.001.

Caligiuri, P., & Tarique, I. (2016). Cultural agility and international assignees' effectiveness in cross-cultural interactions. *International Journal of Training and Development, 20*(4), 280-289.

Caligiuri, P., Mencin, A., Jayne, B., & Traylor, A. (2019). Developing cross-cultural competencies through international corporate volunteerism. *Journal of World Business, 54*(1), 14-23.

Caligiuri, P., De Cieri, H., Minbaeva, D., Verbeke, A, & Zimmerman, A. (2020). Editorial: International HRM insights for navigating the COVID-19 pandemic: Implications for future research and practice. *Journal of International Business Studies, 51*, 697-713.

Calori, R., Lubatkin, M., & Very, P. (1994). Control mechanism in cross-border acquisitions: An international comparison. *Organization Studies, 15*, 361-379.

Cameron, K., Mora, C., Leutscher, T., & Calarco, M. (2011). Effects of positive practices on organizational effectiveness. *The Journal of Applied Behavioral Science, 47*(3), 266-308. https://doi.org/10.1177/0021886310395514.

Cappelli, P., & Keller, J. R. (2017). The historical context of talent management. In D. G. Collings, K. Mellahi, & W. F. Cascio (Eds.), *The Oxford handbook of talent management* (pp. 23-42). Oxford: Oxford University Press.

Caprar, D.V. (2011). Foreign locals: A cautionary tale on the culture of MNC local employees. *Journal of International Business Studies, 42*(5), 608-628.

Cardon, M. S., & Stevens, C. E. (2004). Managing human resources in small organizations: What do we really know? *Human Resource Management Review, 14*, 295-323.

Cardy, R. L., & Dobbins, G. H. (1994). Performance appraisal: The influence of liking on cognition. *Advances in managerial cognition and organizational information processing, 5*, 115-140.

Care, L., & Donohue, R. (2017). Expatriate Performance. In J. Selmer, & Y. McNulty (Eds.), *Research Handbook of Expatriates* (pp. 106-132). Cheltenham, UK and Northampton, MA, USA: Edward Elgar Publishing.

Carlson, D. S., Upton, N., & Seaman, S. (2006). The impact of human resource practices and compensation design on performance: An analysis of family-owned SMEs. *Journal of Small Business Management, 44*(4), 531-543.

Carpenter, M. A., Sanders, W. G., & Gregersen, H. B. (2001). Bundling human capital with organizational context: The impact of international assignment experience on multinational firm performance and CEO pay. *Academy of Management Journal, 44*(3), 493-511.

Carter, D. E., & Baker, B. S. (1991). *Concurrent engineering: The product development environment for the 1990's.* Reading, MA: Addison-Wesley.

Cartwright, S., & Cooper, C. L. (1996). *Managing mergers, acquisitions and strategic alliances: Integrating people and cultures.* Oxford: Butterworth-Heinemann.

Cascio, W. F. (2006). Performance management systems. In G. Stahl, & I. Björkman (Eds.), *Handbook of research in international human resource management* (pp. 176-196). Cheltenham, UK and Northampton, MA, USA: Edward Elgar Publishing.

Cascio, W. F. (2012). Global performance management systems. In G. K. Stahl, I. Björkman, & S. Morris (Eds.), *Handbook of research in international human resource management* (2nd ed.) (pp. 183-204). Cheltenham, UK and Northampton, MA, USA: Edward Elgar Publishing.

Cassell, C., Nadin, S., Gray, M., & Clegg, C. (2002). Exploring human resource management practices in small and medium sized enterprises. *Personnel Review, 32*(6), 671-692.

Caudron, S., Gale, S. F., Greengard, S., & Hall, J. E. (2002). 80 people, events and trends that shaped HR. *Workforce, 81*(1), 28.

Cerdin, J. L., Diné, M. A., & Brewster, C. (2014). Qualified immigrants' success: Exploring the motivation to migrate and to integrate. *Journal of International Business Studies, 45*(2), 151-168.

Cerdin, J. L., & Sharma, K. (2014). Inpatriation as a key component of global talent management. In A. Al Ariss (Ed.), *Global talent management: Challenges, strategies, and opportunities (management for professionals)* (pp. 79-92). Cham: Springer.

Chan, D. K. S., Gelfand, M. J., Triandis, H. C., & Tzeng, O. (1996). Tightness and looseness revisited: Some preliminary analyses in Japan and the United States. *International Journal of Psychology, 31*(1), 1-12.

Chandler, G.N., & Hanks, S.H. (1994). Market attractiveness, resource-based capabilities, venture strategies, and venture performance. *Journal of Business Venturing, 9*(4), 331-349.

Chen, C. C. (1995). New trends in reward allocation preferences: A Sino–U.S. comparison. *Academy of Management Journal, 38*, 408-428.

Chen, E. (2009). NGOs in China: The rise of civil-awareness. *People's Daily*, May 26, 2009.

Chiang, F. F. T., van Esch, E., Birtch, T. A., & Shaffer, M. A. (2018). Repatriation: What do we know and where do we go from here. *International Journal of Human Resource Management, 29*(1), 188-226. doi:10.1080/09585192.2017.1380065

Child, J., & Kieser, A. (1979). Organization and managerial roles in British and West German companies. In C. J. Lammers, & D. J. Hickson (Eds.), *Organizations are alike and unlike* (pp. 455-477). London: Routledge and Kegan Paul.

Child, J., & Faulkner, D. (1998). *Strategies of cooperation*. Oxford: Oxford University Press.

Chinese Culture Connection (1987). Chinese values and the search for culture-free dimensions of culture. *Journal of Cross-Cultural Psychology, 18*(2), 143-164.

Chung, S. W. (2016). Industrial relations (IR) changes in China: A foreign employer's perspective. *Employee Relations, 38*(6), 826-840.

Church, A. T. (1982). Sojourner adjustment. *Psychological Bulletin, 91*(3), 540-572.

Chusmir, L. H., & Frontczak, N. T. (1990). International management opportunities for women: Women and men paint different pictures. *International Journal of Management, 7*(3), 295-301.

Clark, H. H. (1996). *Using language*. Cambridge: Cambridge University Press.

Clark, P. F., Stewart, J. B., & Clark, D. A. (2006). The globalization of the labour market for health-care professionals. *International Labour Review, 145*, 37.

Claus, L., & Briscoe, D. (2009). Employee management across borders: A review of relevant academic literature. *International Journal of Management Reviews, 11*(2), 175-196.

Clegg, H. A. (1976). *Trade unionism under collective bargaining: A theory based on comparisons of six countries*. Oxford: B. Blackwell.

Cohen, D. (2001). Cultural variation: Considerations and implications. *Psychological Bulletin, 127*, 451-471.

Cole, N. D. (2011). Managing global talent: Solving the spousal adjustment problem. *International Journal of Human Resource Management, 22*(7), 1504-1530.

Cole, N. D. (2012). Expatriate accompanying partners: The males speak. *Asia Pacific Journal of Human Resources, 50*, 308-326.

Collings, D., & Scullion, H. (2006). Global staffing. In G. Stahl, & I. Björkman (Eds.), *Handbook of international human resource management* (pp. 141-157). Cheltenham, UK and Northampton, MA, USA: Edward Elgar Publishing.

Collings, D. G., & Isichei, M. (2018). The shifting boundaries of global staffing: Integrating global talent management, alternative forms of international assignments and non-employees into the discussion. *International Journal of Human Resource Management, 29*(1), 165-187. doi:10.1080/09585192.2017.1380064

Combs, C., Liu, Y., Hall, A., & Ketchen, D. (2006). How much do high performance work practices matter? A meta-analysis of their effects on organizational performance. *Personnel Psychology, 59*(3), 501-528.

Cooke, F. L. (2011). Social responsibility, sustainability and diversity of human resources. In A.-W. Harzing, & J. Van Ruysseveldt (Eds.), *International human resource management* (pp. 583-624). London: Sage.

Cooke, W. N., & Noble, D. S. (1998). Industrial relations systems and US foreign direct investment abroad. *British Journal of Industrial Relations, 36*(4), 581-609.

Cooke, W. N. (2001). Union avoidance and foreign direct investment in the USA. *Employee Relations, 23*(6), 558-580.

Cooke, F. L. (2014). Chinese multinational firms in Asia and Africa: Relationships with institutional actors and patterns of HRM practices. *Human Resource Management, 53*(6), 877-896.

Conyon, M. J., Haß, L. H., Vergauwe, S., & Zhang, Z. (2018). Foreign experience and CEO compensation. *Journal of Corporate Finance, 57*, 102-121. https://doi.org/10.1016/j.jcorpfin.2017.12.016.

Cranet International Report (2017). Cranet survey on comparative human resource management. Unpublished International Executive Report.

Creswell, J. (2001). When a merger fails: Lessons from sprint. *Fortune* (April 30), 185–187.

Crichton, A. (1968). *Personnel management in context*. London: B. T. Batsford.

Croucher, R., & Cotton, E. (2009). *Global unions, global business: Global union federations and international business*. Middlesex, UK: Middlesex University Press.

Croucher, R., & Rizov, M. (2012). Union influence in Eastern Europe. *Industrial & Labor Relations Review, 65*(3), 630-650.

Crowley-Henry, M. (2012). Re-conceptualizing the career development of self-initiated expatriates: Rivers not ladders. *Journal of Management Development, 31*(2), 130-141. doi:10.1108/02621711211199476

Crowley-Henry, M., Heaslip, G., & Martin, J. (2014). Short-term international assignments. Military perspectives and implications for international human resource management. *European Management Journal, 32*(5), 752-760. https://doi.org/10.1016/j.emj.2014.02.002.

Cunningham, L. X. (2011). Managing human resources in SMEs in a transition economy: Evidence from China. *International Journal of Human Resource Management, 21*(12), 2120-2141.

Daniels, J. D., Radebaugh, L. H., & Sullivan, D. P. (2011). *International business: Environments and operations.* Upper Saddle River, NJ: Prentice Hall/Pearson.

Davis, G. F., Whitman, M. V., & Zald, M. N. (2006). The responsibility paradox: Multinational firms and global corporate social responsibility. Ross School of Business Working Paper 1031: https://papers.ssrn.com/sol3/papers.cfm?abstract_id=899112.

Deal, T. E., & Kennedy, A. A. (1982). *Corporate cultures: The rites and rituals of corporate life.* Harmondsworth, UK: Penguin.

Debrah, Y. (2000). Management in Ghana. In M. Warner (Ed.), Management in emerging countries. *International encyclopedia of business and management* (pp. 189–197). London: Thomson Learning Business Press.

De Cieri, H., Dowling, P. J., & Taylor, K. F. (1991). The psychological impact of expatriate relocation on partners. *International Journal of Human Resource Management, 2*(3), 377-414.

De Cieri, H., & Lazarova, M. (2020). 'Your health and safety is of utmost importance to us': A review of research on the occupational health and safety of international employees. *Human Resource Management Review*, 100790. https://doi.org/10.1016/j.hrmr.2020.100790.

De Leon, C. T., & McPartlin, D. (1995). Adjustment of expatriate children. In J. Selmer (Ed.), *Expatriate management: New ideas for international business* (pp. 197-214). Westport, CT: Quorum Books.

Deloitte (2018). Back to the future. Assessing the predicted 2018 global mobility trends and their continued impact in 2019. https://www2.deloitte.com/content/dam/Deloitte/uk/Documents/tax/deloitte-uk-tax-assessing-the-predicted-2018-global-mobility-trends-and-their-continued-impact-in-2019.pdf.

Deloitte (2020). Understanding the COVID-19 impact for global mobility. https://www2.deloitte.com/content/dam/Deloitte/uk/Documents/energy-resources/deloitte-uk-er-covid-19-global-mobility.pdf.

de Nijs, W. (1995). International human resource management and industrial relations: A framework for analysis. In A.-W. Harzing, & J. Van Ruysseveldt (Eds.), *International human resource management* (pp. 271-290). London: Sage.

DeNisi, A. S. (1996). *Cognitive processes in performance appraisal: A research agenda with implications for practice.* London: Routledge.

DeNisi, A. (2000). Performance appraisal and performance management: A multilevel analysis. In S. W. J. Kozlowski, & K. J. Klein (Eds.), *Multilevel theory, research, and methods in organizations: Foundations, extensions, and new directions* (pp. 121-156). San Francisco, CA: Jossey-Bass

Dery, K., Tansley, C., & Hafermalz, E. (2014). Hiring in the age of social media: New rules, new game. *University of Auckland Business Review, 17*(1), 45-51.

Dessler, G. (2011). *Human resource management* (13th ed.). Upper Saddle River, NJ: Prentice Hall.

Dewettinck, K., & Remue, J. (2011). Contextualizing HRM in comparative research: The role of the Cranet network. *Human Resource Management Review, 21*, 37-49.

Diamantidis, A. D., & Chatzoglou, P. D. (2011). Human resource involvement, job related factors, and their relation with firm performance: Experiences from Greece. *International Journal of Human Resource Management, 22*(7), 1531-1553.

Dickmann, M., Suutari, V., Brewster, C., Mäkelä, L., Tanskanen, J., & Tornikoski, C. (2018). The career competencies of self-initiated and assigned expatriates: Assessing the development of career capital over time. *International Journal of Human Resource Management, 29*(6), 2353-2377. 10.1080/09585192.2016.1172657.

Diller, J. (2008). A social conscience in the global marketplace? Labour dimensions of codes of conduct, social labelling and investor initiatives. *International Labour Review, 138*(2), 99-129.

DiMaggio, P. J., & Powell, W. W. (1983). The iron cage revisited: Institutional isomorphism and collective rationality in organizational fields. *American Sociological Review, 48*, 147-160.

Dobbs, R., Goedhart, M., & Suonio, H. (2006). A re companies getting better at M&A? *McKinsey Quarterly.* http://www.mckinseyquarterly.com/Are_companies_getting_better_at_M_A_1886.

Dobbs, R., Remes, J., Smit, S., Manyika, J., Woetzel, J., & Agyenim-Boateng, Y. (2013). Urban world: The shifting global business landscape. McKinsey Global Institute. https://www.mckinsey.com/featured-insights/urbanization/urban-world-the-shifting-global-business-landscape#.

Doherty, N., Dickmann, M., & Mills, T. (2011). Exploring the motives of company backed and self-initiated expatriates. *International Journal of Human Resource Management, 22*(3), 595-611.

Doherty, N. T., & Dickmann, M. (2012). Measuring the return on investment in international assignments: An action research approach. *International Journal of Human Resource Management, 23*(16), 3434-3454.

Donaldson, T. (1989). *The ethics of international business.* New York: Oxford University Press.

Donaldson, T. (1996). Values in tension: Ethics away from home. *Harvard Business Review, 74*, 48-64.

Donnelly, T. Morris, D., & Donnelly, T. (2005). Renault–Nissan: A marriage of necessity. *European Business Review, 17*(5), 428-440.

Dowling, P. J. (1988). International HRM. In L. Dyer (Ed.), *Human resource management: Evolving roles and responsibilities* (pp. 228-258). Washington, DC: BNA.

Dowling, P. J., Festing, M., Engle, A. D., & Gröschl, S. (2009). *International human resource management: A Canadian perspective.* Toronto: Nelson Education.

Downes, M., & Thomas, A. (1999). Managing organizational assignments to build organizational knowledge. *Human Resource Planning, 22*(4), 33-48.

Doz, Y. L., & Hamel, G. (1998). *Alliance advantage: The art of creating value through partnering.* Boston, MA: Harvard Business School Press.

Dragoni, L., Oh, I.-S., Tesluk, P. E., Moore, O. A., VanKatwyk, P., & Hazucha, J. (2014). Developing leaders' strategic thinking through global work experience: The moderating role of cultural distance. *Journal of Applied Psychology, 99*(5), 867-882.

Du, J., & Choi, J. N. (2010). Pay for performance in emerging markets: Insights from China. *Journal of International Business Studies, 41*(4), 671-689.

Dundon, T., & Gollan, P.J. (2007). Re-conceptualizing voice in the non-union workplace. *International Journal of Human Resource Management, 18*(7), 1182-1198. 10.1080/09585190701391925.

Dunlop, J. (1958). *Industrial relations systems.* Carbondale, IL: Southern Illinois University Press.

Dunphy, D. (1987). Convergence/divergence: A temporal review of the Japanese enterprise and its management. *Academy of Management Review, 12*, 445-459.

Edstrom, A., & Galbraith, J. (1977). Transfer of managers as a coordination and control strategy in multinational firms. *Administrative Science Quarterly, 22*, 248-263.

Edwards, T. (1998). Multinationals, labour management and the process of reverse diffusion: A case study. *International Journal of Human Resource Management, 9*, 696-709.

Edwards, T. (2004). The transfer of employment practices across borders in multinational companies. In A.-W. Harzing, & J. Van Ruysseveldt (Eds.), *International human resource management* (2nd ed.) (pp. 389-410). London: Sage.

Edwards, T., Almond, P., Clark, I., Colling, T., & Ferner, A. (2005). Reverse diffusion in US multinationals: Barriers from the American business system. *Journal of Management Studies, 42*, 1261-1286.

Edwards, T., & Rees, C. (2006). *International human resource management: Globalization, national systems and multinational companies.* Harlow, UK: Prentice Hall.

Edwards, T., Edwards, P., Ferner, A., Marginson, P., & Tregaskis, O. (2010). Multinational companies and the diffusion of employment practices from outside the country of origin: Explaining variation across firms. *Management International Review, 50*, 613-634.

Edwards, T., & Tempel, A. (2010). Explaining variation in reverse diffusion of HR practices: Evidence from the German and British subsidiaries of American multinationals. *Journal of World Business, 45*, 19-28.

Edwards, T. (2011). The transfer of employment practices across borders in multinational companies. In A.-W. Harzing, & A. H. Pinnington (Eds.), *International human resource management* (3rd ed.) (pp. 267-290). London: Sage.

Edwards, T., Sánchez-Mangas, R., Jalette, P., Lavelle, J., & Minbaeva, D. (2016). Global standardization or national differentiation of HRM practices in multinational companies? A comparison of multinationals in five countries. *Journal of International Business* Studies, *47*(8): 997-1021

Eichhorst, W., Rodríguez-Planas, N., Schmidl, R., & Zimmermann, K. F. (2015). A road map to vocational education and training in industrialized countries. *ILR Review, 68*(2), 314-337.

Eisenhardt, S. N. (1973). *Tradition, change, and modernity.* New York: Wiley.

Ellegard, K., Jonsson, D., Enstrom, T., Johansson, M., Medbo, L., & Johansson, B. (1992). Reflective production in the final assembly of motor vehicles: An emerging Swedish challenge. *International Journal of Operations and Production Management, 12*(7-8), 117-133.

Ellis, D. R., Thorn, K., & Yao, C. (in press). Repatriation of self-initiated expatriates: Expectations vs. experiences. *Career Development International*. 10.1108/CDI-09-2019-0228

Empson, L. (2000). Mergers between professional service firms: Exploring an undirected process of integration. *Advances in Mergers and Acquisitions, 1*, 205-237.

Enderwick, P. (1982). Labour and the theory of the multinational corporation. *Industrial Relations Journal, 13*(2), 32-43.

English, H. B. (1958). *A comprehensive dictionary of psychological and psychoanalytical terms.* New York: David McKay.

Enloe, W., & Lewin, P. (1987). Issues of integration abroad and readjustment to Japan of Japanese returnees. *International Journal of Intercultural Relations, 11*(3), 223-248.

Erez, M., & Earley, P. C. (1993). *Culture, self-identity and work.* New York: Oxford University Press.

Erez, M., & Shokef, E. (2008). The culture of global organizations. In P. B. Smith, M. F. Peterson, & D. C. Thomas (Eds.), *Handbook of cross-cultural management research* (pp. 285-300). Thousand Oaks, CA: Sage.

European Commission (2001). European competitiveness report 2001: Internal market, industry, entrepreneurship and SMEs. https://ec.europa.eu/growth/content/european-competitiveness-report-2001 -0_en.

Evans, P., Pucik, V., & Barsoux, J.-L. (2002). *The global challenge: Frameworks for international human resource management.* New York: McGraw-Hill.

Evans, P., Pucik, V., & Björkman, I. (2011). *The global challenge: International human resource management.* New York: McGraw-Hill Irwin.

Evenett, S. (2019). Protectionism, state discrimination, and international business since the onset of the global financial crisis. *Journal of International Business Policy, 2*(1), 9-36.

Fagnani, J., & Letablier, M. T. (2004). Work and family life balance: The impact of the 35-hour laws in France. *Work, Employment and Society, 18*(3), 551-572.

Farndale, E., & Paauwe, J. (2007). Uncovering competitive and institutional drivers of HRM practices in multinational corporations. *Human Resource Management Journal, 17*(4), 355-375.

Farndale, E., Brewster, C., & Poutsma, E. (2008). Coordinated vs. liberal market HRM: The impact of institutionalization on multinational firms. *International Journal of Human Resource Management, 19*, 2004-2023.

Farndale, E., Paauwe, J., & Hoeksema, L. (2009). In-sourcing HR: Shared service centres in the Netherlands. *International Journal of Human Resource Management, 20*(3), 544-561.

Farndale, E., Paauwe, J., Morris, S. S., Stahl, G. K., Stiles, P., Trevor, J., & Wright, P. (2010). Context-bound configurations of corporate HR functions in multinational corporations. *Human Resource Management, 49*(1), 45-66.

Farndale, E., Scullion H., & Sparrow, P. (2010). The role of the corporate HR function in global talent management. *Journal of World Business, 45*(2), 161-168.

Farndale, E., Brewster, C., Ligthart, P., & Poutsma, E. (2017). The effects of market economy type and foreign MNE subsidiaries on the convergence and divergence of HRM. *Journal of International Business Studies, 48*(9), 1065-1086.

Farndale, E., Panayotopoulou, L., & Nikandrou, I. (2020). Talent inflow across countries. In E. Galanaki, I. Nikandrou, & L. Panayotopoulou (Eds.), *Volume in honor of Professor Nancy Papalexandris: An anthology on human resource management, organizational behavior and special issues in management* (pp. 40-57). Athens, Greece: Editions Benou.

Farnham, A. (1994). Global or just globaloney? *Fortune*, 97-100.

Faulkner, D., Pitkethly, R., & Child, J. (2002). International mergers and acquisitions in the UK 1985-94: A comparison of national HRM practices. *International Journal of Human Resource Management, 13*, 106-122.

Fee, A. (2020). How host-country nationals manage the demands of hosting expatriates: An exploratory field study. *Journal of Global Mobility: The Home of Expatriate Management Research, 8*(1), 25-54. https://doi.org/10.1108/JGM-09-2019-0045.

Feldman, D. C., & Thomas, D. C. (1992). Career management issues facing expatriates. *Journal of International Business Studies, 23*, 271-293.

Fenwick, M. (2004). International compensation and performance management. In A.-W. Harzing, & J. V. Ruysseveldt (Eds.), *International Human Resource Management* (2nd ed.) (pp 307-332). London: Sage.

Ferner, A., & Varul, M. (2000). Vanguard subsidiaries and the diffusion of new practices: A case study of German multinationals. *British Journal of Industrial Relations, 38*, 115-140.

Ferrell, O. C., & Fraedrich, J. (1994). *Business ethics: Ethical decision making and cases.* Houghton Mifflin.

Festing, M., & Barzantny, C. (2008). Performance management in Germany and France. In A. Varma, P.S. Budhwar, & A. S. DeNisi (Eds.), *Performance management systems: A global perspective* (pp. 147-167). London: Routledge.

Festing, M., Engle, A. D., Dowling, P. J., & Sahakiants, I. (2012). HRM activities: Pay and rewards. In C. Brewster, & W. Mayrhofer (Eds.), *Handbook of reserach on comparative human resource management* (pp. 139-163). Cheltenham, UK and Northampton, MA, USA: Edward Elgar Publishing.

Festing, M., & Sahakiants, I. (2013). Path-dependent evolution of compensation systems in Central and Eastern Europe: A case study of multinational corporation subsidiaries in the Czech Republic, Poland and Hungary. *European Management Journal, 31*(4), 373-389. https://doi.org/10.1016/j.emj.2013.01.005.

Fink, G., Meierewert, S., & Rohr, U. (2005). The use of repatriation knowledge in organizations. *Human Resource Planning, 28*, 30-36.

Fischer, K. (2003). Transforming HR globally: The center of excellence approach. *People and Strategy, 26*(2), 9.

Fischer, M. M., & Stirböck, C. (2006). Pan-European regional income growth and club-convergence. *The Annals of Regional Science, 40*(4), 693–721.

Fischlmayr, I. C., & Puchmüller, K. M. (2016). Married, mom and manager – how can this be combined with an international career? *International Journal of Human Resource Management, 27*(7), 744-765. 10.1080/09585192.2015.1111250.

Fitzgerald, W. (1992). Training versus development. *Training and Development, May 1992*: 82-84. http://lms.powercam.cc/sysdata/user/42/irisli/blog/doc/6aaf13ba58c720ef/attach/160.pdf.

Fletcher, C., & Perry, F. (2001). Performance appraisal and feedback: A consideration of national culture and a review of contemporary and future trends. In N. Anderson, D. Ones, H. Sinanagil, & C. Viswesvaran (Eds.), *International handbook of work and organizational psychology* (pp. 127-144). Beverly Hills, CA: Sage.

Florkowski, G. W., & Fogel, D. S. (1999). Expatriate adjustment and commitment: The role of host-unit treatment. *International Journal of Human Resource Management, 10*(5), 783–807.

Fombrun, C. J., Tichy, N. M., & Devanna, M. A. (1984). *Strategic human resource management.* New York: Wiley.

Forth, J., Bewley, H., & Bryson, A. (2006), *Small and medium-sized enterprises: Findings from the 2004 workplace employment relations survey.* London: Routledge.

Franko, L. (1973). Who manages multinational enterprises? *Columbia Journal of World Business, 8*, 30-42.

Frederick, W. C. (1991). The moral authority of transnational corporate codes. *Journal of Business Ethics, 10*, 165–177.

Freeman, R. B., & Katz, L. F. (1994). Rising wage inequality: The United States vs. other advanced countries. In R. B. Freeman (Ed.), *Working under different rules* (pp. 29–62) New York: Russell Sage Foundation.

Freeman, R. B., & Kane, J. (1995). An alternative approach to expatriate allowances: An international citizen. *International Executive, 37*(3), 245-259.

Friedman, M. (2002). *Capitalism and freedom: Fortieth anniversary edition.* Chicago, IL: University of Chicago Press.

Friedman, T. L. (1999). *The lexus and the olive tree.* New York: Farrar, Strauss & Giroux.

Friedman, T. L. (2005). *The world is flat: A brief history of the twenty first century.* New York: Farrar, Strauss & Giroux.

Froese, F. J., & Peltokorpi, V. (2013). Organizational expatriates and self-initiated expatriates: Differences in cross-cultural adjustment and job satisfaction. *International Journal of Human Resource Management, 24*(10), 1953-1967.

Fuentes-García, F. J., Núñez-Tabales, J. M., & Veroz-Herradón (2008). Applicability of corporate social responsibility to human resources management: Perspective from Spain. *Journal of Business Ethics, 82*, 27-44.

Fulton, L. (2020). National Industrial Relations, an update. Labour Research Department and ETUI (online publication). https://www.worker-participation.eu/National-Industrial-Relations/Countries/

Belgium/Collective-Bargaining#:~:text=Collective%20bargaining%20in%20Belgium%20is,some %20companies)%20at%20the%20bottom.

Furusawa, M., & Brewster, C. (2016). IHRM and expatriation in Japanese MNCs: HRM practices and their impact on adjustment and job performance. *Asia Pacific Journal of Human Resources, 54*(4), 396-420. 10.1111/1744-7941.12106.

Furusawa, M., & Brewster, C. (2019). The determinants of the boundary-spanning functions of Japanese self-initiated expatriates in Japanese subsidiaries in China: Individual skills and human resource management. *Journal of International Management, 25*(4), 100674.

Galanaki, E., & Papalexandris, N. (2005). Outsourcing of human resource management services in Greece. *International Journal of Manpower, 26*(4), 382-396. doi:10.1108/01437720510609564.

Gallagher, M., Giles, J., Park, A., & Wang, M. (2013). *China's 2008 labor contract law: Implementation and implications for China's workers.* Washington, DC: The World Bank.

Garengo, P., Biazzo, S., Simonetti, A., & Bernardi, G. (2005). Benchmarking on managerial practices: A tool for SMEs. *The TQM Magazine, 17*(5) 440-455. https://doi.org/10.1108/09544780510615942.

Gaur, A. S., Delios, A., & Singh, K. (2007). Institutional environments, staffing strategies, and subsidiary performance. *Journal of Management, 33*, 611-636.

Geary, J., & Aguzzoli, R. (2016). Miners, politics and institutional caryatids: Accounting for the transfer of HRM practices in the Brazilian multinational enterprise. *Journal of International Business Studies, 47*(8), 968-996.

Geary, J., Aguzzoli, R., & Lengler, J. (2017). The transfer of 'international best practice' in a Brazilian MNC: A consideration of the convergence and contingency perspectives. *Journal of International Management, 23*(2), 194-207.

Gelfand, M. J., Raver, J. L., Nishii, L. et al. (2011). Differences between tight and loose cultures: A 33 nation study. *Science, 332*, 1100-1104.

Gelfand, M., Gordon, S., Li, C., Choi, V., & Prokopowicz, P. (2018). One reason mergers fail: The two cultures aren't compatible. *Harvard Business Review Digital Articles*, October 2, pp. 30-35.

George, C. S. (1968). *The history of management thought.* Englewood Cliffs, NJ: Prentice Hall.

Gerhart, G., & Fang, M. (2005). National culture and human resource management: Assumptions and evidence. *International Journal of Human Resource Management, 16* (6), 971-986.

Gerhart, G. (2008). Cross cultural management research: Assumptions, evidence, and suggested directions. *International Journal of Cross-Cultural Management, 8*, 259-274.

Gertsen, M. C., Söderberg, A.-M., & Torp, J. E. (1998). Different approaches to understanding of culture in mergers and acquisitions. In M. C. Gertsen, A.-M. Söderberg, & J. E. Torp (Eds.), *Cultural dimensions of international mergers and acquisitions* (pp. 17-38). Berlin: de Gruyter.

Ghauri, P. N., & Prasad, S. B. (1995). A network approach to probing Asia's interfirm linkages. *Advances in International Comparative Management, 10*, 63-77.

Gibson, C. B. (1994). The implications of national culture for organization structure: An investigation of three perspectives. *Advances in International Comparative Management, 9*, 3-38.

Glassock, G., & Fee, A. (2015). The decision-making processes of self-initiated expatriates: A consumer behaviour approach. *Journal of Global Mobility, 3*(1), 4-24.

Global Relocation Trends (2010). *Survey Report.* Brookfield Global Relocation Services: Woodbridge, IL.

Global Relocation Trends (2011). *Survey Report.* Brookfield Global Relocation Services: Woodbridge, IL.

Global Relocation Trends (2012). *Survey Report.* Brookfield Global Relocation Services: Woodbridge, IL.

GMAC, NFTC, & SHRM Global Forum (2004). *Ten years of Global Relocation Trends: 1993-2004.* Oak Brook, IL: GMAC Global Relocation Services.

Goldstein, J. (1999). Emergence as a construct: History and issues. *Emergence, 1*(1), 49-72.

Gomez-Mejia, L. R., & Welbourne, T. (1991). Compensation strategies in a global context. *Human Resource Planning, 14*(1), 29-41.

Gomez-Mejia, L., & Wiseman, R. M. (1997). Reframing executive compensation: An assessment and outlook. *Journal of Management, 23*, 291-375.

Gong, Y. (2003). Toward a dynamic process model of staffing composition and subsidiary outcomes in multinational enterprise. *Journal of Management, 29*, 259-280.

Gooderham, P. N., Nordhaug, O., & Ringdal, K. (1999). Institutional and rational determinants of organizational practices: Human resource management in European firms. *Administrative Science Quarterly, 44*, 507-531.

Gooderham, P., & Nordhaug, O. (2011). One European model of HRM? Cranet empirical contributions. *Human Resource Management Review, 21,* 27–36.

Gooderham, P., Grøgaard, B., & Nordhaug, O. (2013). Competencies and knowledge transfer. In P. Gooderham, B. Grøgaard, & O. Nordhaug, *International management: Theory and practice* (pp. 207–229). Cheltenham, UK: Blackwell.

Gooderham, P. N., Mayrhofer, W., & Brewster, C. (2019). A framework for comparative institutional research on HRM. *International Journal of Human Resource Management, 30*(1), 5–30.

Goulet, P. K., & Schweiger, D. M. (2006). Managing culture and human resources in mergers and acquisitions. In G. K. Stahl, & I. Björkman (Eds.), *Handbook of research in international human resource management* (pp. 405–429). Cheltenham, UK and Northampton, MA, USA: Edward Elgar Publishing.

Gregersen, H. B., Hite, J. M., & Black, J. S. (1996). Expatriate performance appraisal in U.S. multinational firms. *Journal of International Business Studies, 27,* 711–738.

Griffin. R. W., & Pustay, M. W. (2013). *International Business* (7th ed.). Upper Saddle River NJ: Prentice Hall.

Gullahorn, J. T., & Gullahorn, J. E. (1963). An extension of the U-curve hypothesis. *Journal of Social Issues, 19,* 33–47.

Gunnigle, P., Murphy, K., Cleveland, J. N., Heraty, N., & Morley, M. (2002). Localization in human resource management: Comparing American and European multinational corporations. *Advances in International Management, 14,* 259–284.

Hadjimichael, D., & Tsoukas, H. (2019). Toward a better understanding of tacit knowledge in organizations: Taking stock and moving forward. *Academy of Management Annals, 13*(2), 672–703.

Hall, E. T. (1966). *The hidden dimension* (Vol. 609). Garden City, NY: Doubleday.

Hall, P. A., & Sokice, D. W. (2001). *Varieties of capitalism: The institutional foundations of comparative advantage.* Oxford: Oxford University Press.

Hamill, J. (1984). Labour relations decision making in multinational corporations. *Industrial Relations Journal, 15*(2), 30–34.

Hann, D., Hauptmeier, M., & Waddington, J. (2017). European works councils after two decades. *European Journal of Industrial Relations, 23*(3), 209–224.

Hannon, E. (2011). International and comparative employee voice. In T. Edwards, & C. Rees (Eds.), *International human resource management: Globalization, national systems and multinational companies* (2nd ed.) (pp. 229–252). Harlow, Essex: Pearson Education.

Harding, D., & Rouse, T. (2007). Human due diligence. *Harvard Business Review, 85,* 124–131.

Harpaz, I. (1990). The importance of work goals: An international perspective. *Journal of International Business Studies, 21*(1), 75–93.

Harris, H., & Brewster C. (1999). The coffee-machine system: How international selection really works. *International Journal of Human Resource Management, 10*(3), 488–500.

Harris, H. (2004). Global careers: Work–life issues and the adjustment of women international managers. *Journal of Management Development, 23*(9), 818–832.

Harris, H. (2006). Issues facing women on international assignments: A review of the research. In G. K. Stahl, & I. Björkman (Eds.), *Handbook of research in international human resource management* (pp. 265–282). Cheltenham, UK and Northampton, MA, USA: Edward Elgar Publishing.

Harvey, M. (1982). The other side of foreign assignments: Dealing with the repatriation dilemma. *Columbia Journal of World Business, 17*(1), 53–59.

Harvey, M. (1989). Repatriation of corporate executives: An empirical study. *Journal of International Business Studies, 20,* 131–144.

Harzing, A. K. (1995a). The persistent myth of high expatriate failure rates. *International Journal of Human Resource Management, 6*(2), 457–474.

Harzing, A. W. (1995b). Strategic planning in multinational corporations. In A. W. Harzing, & Van Ruysseveldt (Eds.), *International human resource management* (pp. 25–50). London: Sage.

Harzing, A.-W. (2001a). An analysis of the functions of international transfer of managers in MNCs. *Employee Relations, 23,* 581–598.

Harzing, A.-W. (2001b). Of bears, bumblebees, and spiders: The role of expatriates in controlling foreign subsidiaries. *Journal of World Business, 36,* 366–379.

Harzing, A.-W., & Noorderhaven, N. (2006). Geographical distance and the role and management of subsidiaries: The case of subsidiaries down-under. *Asia Pacific Journal of Management, 23,* 167–185.

Harzing, A. W., Pudelko, M., & Sebastian Reiche, B. (2016). The bridging role of expatriates and inpatriates in knowledge transfer in multinational corporations. *Human Resource Management, 55*(4), 679-695.

Haspeslagh, P., & Jemison, D. E. (1991). *Managing acquisitions: Creating value for corporate renewal.* New York: Free Press.

Hayton, J.C. (2003). Strategic human capital management in SMEs: An empirical study of entrepreneurial performance. *Human Resource Management, 42*(4), 375-391.

He, B., An, R., & Berry, J. (2019). Psychological adjustment and social capital: A qualitative investigation of Chinese expatriates. *Cross Cultural & Strategic Management, 26*(1), 67-92.

Hechanova, R., Beehr, T. A., & Christiansen, N. D. (2003). Antecedents and consequences of employees' adjustment to overseas assignment: A meta-analytic review. *Applied Psychology: An International Review, 52*(2), 213-236.

Heenan, D. A., & Perlmutter, H. V. (1979). *Multinational organizational development.* Reading, MA: Addison-Wesley.

Hemmasi, M., & Downes, M. (2013). Cultural distance and expatriate adjustment revisited. *Journal of Global Mobility, 1*(1), 72-91.

Hickson, D.J., & McMillan, C.J. (1981). *Organizations and nation: The Aston programme IV.* Farnborough, UK: Gower.

Hickson, D. J., & Pugh, D. S. (1995). *Management worldwide: The impact of societal culture on organizations around the globe.* London: Penguin Books.

Hill, R., & Stewart, J. (2000). Human resource development in small organizations. *Journal of European Industrial Training, 24*(2-4), 105-117.

Hippler, T., Caligiuri, P. M., Johnson, J. E., & Baytalskaya, N. (2014). The development and validation of a theory-based expatriate adjustment scale. *International Journal of Human Resource Management, 25*(14), 1938-1959. 10.1080/09585192.2013.870286.

Hippler, T., Haslberger, A., & Brewster, C. (2017). Expatriate adjustment. In Y. McNulty, & J. Selmer (Eds.), *Research handbook of expatriates* (pp. 83-105). Cheltenham, UK and Northampton, MA, USA: Edward Elgar Publishing.

Hofstede, G. (1980). *Culture's consequences: International differences in work related values.* Beverly Hills, CA: Sage.

Hofstede, G. (1983). National cultures in four dimensions: A research-based theory of cultural differences among nations. *International Studies of Management & Organization, 13*(1-2), 46-74. 10.1080/00208825.1983.11656358.

Hofstede, G., Neuijen, B., Ohayv, D.D., & Sanders, G. (1990). Measuring organizational cultures: A qualitative and quantitative study across twenty cases. *Administrative Science Quarterly, 35*(2), 286-316.

Hofstede, G. (1991). *Cultures and organizations: Software of the mind.* Maidenhead, UK: McGraw-Hill.

Hofstede, G. (2001). *Culture's consequences: Comparing values, behaviors, institutions, and organizations across nations* (2nd ed.). Thousand Oaks, CA: Sage.

Hofstede, G., & Minkov, M. (2010). *Cultures and organizations. Software of the mind: Intercultural cooperation and its importance for survival.* New York: McGraw Hill.

Hollinshead, G. (2010). *International and comparative human resource management.* New York: McGraw-Hill.

Holten, A.-L., & Crouch, C. (2014). Unions in small- and medium-sized enterprises: A family factor perspective. *European Journal of Industrial Relations, 20*(3), 273-290. https://doi.org/10.1177/0959680113519639.

Hon, A. H. Y., & Lu, L. (2010). The mediating role of trust between expatriate procedural justice and employee outcomes in Chinese hotel industry. *International Journal of Hospitality Management, 29*(4), 669-676. doi:https://doi.org/10.1016/j.ijhm.2010.01.002.

Hon, A. H. Y., & Lu, L. (2015). Are we paid to be creative? The effect of compensation gap on creativity in an expatriate context. *Journal of World Business, 50*(1), 159-167.

Hon, A. H. Y., Lu, L., & Chan, W. W. H. (2015). Does cultural value exacerbate or mitigate the effect of perceived compensation gap between locals and expatriates in hotel industry? *International Journal of Hospitality Management, 48*, 83-91.

Horak, S., Farndale, E., Brannen, M. Y., & Collings, D. (2019). International human resource management in an era of political nationalism. *Thunderbird International Business Review, 61*(3), 465-470.

House, R. J., Hanges, P. J., Javidan, M., Dorfman, P. W., & Gupta, V. (2004). *Culture, leadership, and organizations: The GLOBE study of 62 societies.* Thousand Oaks, CA: Sage.

House, R. J., Dorfman, P., Javidan, M., Hanges, P .J., & Sully de Luque, M. (2014). *Strategic leadership across cultures: The GLOBE study of CEO leadership behavior and effectiveness in 24 countries.* Thousand Oaks, CA: Sage.

Howard, G. (1991). Culture tales: A narrative approach to thinking, cross-cultural psychology and psychotherapy. *American Psychologist, 46,* 187-197.

Howard, M., & Willmott, M. (2001). Ethical consumption in the twenty first century. In T. Bentley, & S. D. Jones (Eds.), *The moral universe* (pp. 1-8). London: Demos.

Hualing, F., & Choy, D. W. (2001). From mediation to adjudication: Settling labor disputes in China. *China Labor, 6,* 5-825.

Hui, H. C., & Cheng, I. W.M. (1987). Effects of second language proficiency of speakers and listeners on person perception and behavioural intention: A study of Chinese bilinguals. *International Journal of Psychology, 22,* 421-430.

Humphrey, J. (1995). The adoption of Japanese management techniques in Brazilian industry. *Journal of Management Studies, 32*(6), 767-787.

Huntington, S.P. (1996). The West unique, not universal. *Foreign Affairs, 75*(6), 28-46.

Huo, P. Y., & Von Glinow, M. A. (1995). On transplanting human resource practices to China. *International Journal of Manpower, 16*(9), 3-13.

Husted, B. W., & Allen, D. B. (2006). Corporate social responsibility in the multinational enterprise: Strategic and institutional approaches. *Journal of International Business Studies, 37,* 838–849.

Hyman, R. (2004). Varieties of capitalism, national industrial relations systems and transnational challenges. In A.-W. Harzing, & J. V. Ruysseveldt (Eds.), *International Human Resource Management* (2nd ed.) (pp. 411-432). London: Sage.

Iles, P., Xin, C., & Preece, D. (2010). Talent management and HRM in multinational companies in Beijing: Definitions, differences and drivers. *Journal of World Business, 45*(2), 179-189.

Inglehart, R., & Baker, W. E. (2000). Modernization, cultural change, and the persistence of traditional values. *American Sociological Review, 65,* 19-51.

Inkpen, A. C., & Tsang, E. (2005). Social capital, networks, and knowledge transfer. *Academy of Management Review, 30,* 146–165.

Inkson, J. H. K., Arthur, M. B., Pringle, J., & Barry, S. (1997). Expatriate assignment versus overseas experience: Contrasting models of international human resource development. *Journal of World Business, 32*(4), 351-368.

Inversi, C., Buckley, L. A., & Dundon, T. (2017). An analytical framework for employment regulation: Investigating the regulatory space. *Employee Relations, 39*(3), 291-307.

Jacoby, S. M. (1985). *Employing bureaucracy: Managers, unions, and the transformation of work in American industry, 1900–1945.* New York: Columbia University Press.

Jacoby, S. M. (2005). *The embedded corporation: Corporate governance and employment relations in Japan and the United States.* Princeton, NJ: Princeton University Press.

Jemison, D. B., & Sitkin, S. B. (1986). Corporate acquisitions: A process perspective. *Academy of Management Review, 11,* 145-163.

Jiang, C. (2014). Transfer of HRM practices in French multinational companies: The case of French subsidiaries in China. In R. Taylor (Ed.), *The globalization of Chinese business* (pp. 123-145). Oxford: Chandos Publishing.

Jones, G. R. (1986). Socialization tactics, self-efficacy, and newcomers' adjustment to the organization. *Academy of Management Journal, 2,* 262-279.

Kabst, R., Wehner, M. C., Meifert, M., & Kötter, P. M. (2009). Personalmanagement im internationalen Vergleich. Ergebnisbericht der siebten Erhebung des Cranfield Project on International Human Resource Management (Cranet). Giessen: Justus-Liebig-Universität Giessen. 2017.10.1093/oxfordhb/9780198758273.013.13.

Kaminska, M. E. (2013). Regional regulation. The EU and NAFTA. In C. Frege, & J. Kelly (Eds.), *Comparative employment relations in the global economy* (pp. 407-424). Abingdon, UK: Routledge.

Kang, H., & Shen, J. (2016). International performance appraisal practices and approaches of South Korean MNEs in China. *International Journal of Human Resource Management, 27*(3), 291-310.

Kang, H., Shen, J., & Benson, J. (2017). Not all expatriates are the same: non-traditional South Korean expatriates in China. *International Journal of Human Resource Management, 28*(13), 1842-1865.

Kang, H., & Shen, J. (2018). Antecedents and consequences of host-country nationals' attitudes and behaviors toward expatriates: What we do and do not know. *Human Resource Management Review, 28*(2), 164-175.

Katz, D., & Kahn, R. L. (1978). *The social psychology of organizations.* New York: Wiley & Sons.

Kaufman, B. E. (2016). Globalization and convergence–divergence of HRM across nations: New measures, explanatory theory, and non-standard predictions from bringing in economics. *Human Resource Management Review, 26*(4), 338-351.

Kay, I. T., & Shelton, M. (2000). The people problem in mergers. *McKinsey Quarterly,* (4), 26-37.

Keller, B. K., & Kirsch, A. (2020). Employment relations in Germany. In R. D. Lansbury, C. F. Wright, G. J. Bamber, & N. Wailes (Eds.), *International and comparative employment relations: National regulation, global changes* (pp. 179-207). Abingdon, UK: Routledge.

Kets de Vries, M., Vrinaud, P., & Florent-Treacy, E. (2004). The global leadership life inventory: Development and psychometric properties of a 360-degree feedback instrument. *International Journal of Human Resource Management, 15*(3), 475-492.

Khan, Z., Wood, G., Tarba, S. Y., Rao-Nicholson, R., & He, S. (2019). Human resource management in Chinese multinationals in the United Kingdom: The interplay of institutions, culture, and strategic choice. *Human Resource Management, 58*(5), 473-487.

Kierner, A. (2018). Expatriated dual-career partners: Hope and disillusionment. *Journal of Global Mobility: The Home of Expatriate Management Research, 6*(3/4), 244-257. 10.1108/JGM-02-2018-0011.

Killing, P. (2003). Improving acquisition integration: Be clear on what you intend and avoid 'best of both' deals. *Perspectives for Managers, 97.* Lausanne: IMD.

King, K. A., & Vaiman, V. (2019). Enabling effective talent management through a macro-contingent approach: A framework for research and practice. *Business Research Quarterly, 22*(3), 194-206.

Klein, N. (2000). *No logo: Taking aim at the brand bullies.* New York: Taylor & Francis.

Kluckhohn, C., & Strodtbeck, K. (1961). *Variations in value orientations.* Westport, CT: Greenwood Press.

Kogut, B., & Zander, U. (1992). Knowledge of the firm, combinative capabilities, and the replication of technology. *Organization Science, 3,* 383-397.

Kosterlitz, J. (1998). Unions of the world unite. *National Journal, 30,* 1134-1154.

Kostova, T. (1999). Transnational transfer of strategic organizational practices: A contextual perspective. *Academy of Management Review, 1999,* 308-324.

Kostova, T., & Roth, K. (2002). Adoption of an organizational practice by subsidiaries of multinational corporations: Institutional and relational effects. *Academy of Management Journal, 45,* 215-233.

Kostova, T., & Roth, K. (2003). Social capital in multinational corporations and a micro–macro model of its formation. *Academy of Management Review, 28,* 297-317.

Kostova, T., Roth, K., & Dacin, T. (2008). Institutional theory in the study of MNCs: A critique and new directions. *Academy of Management Review, 33*(4), 994-1007.

KPMG (1999). Unlocking Shareholder Value: Mergers & Acquisitions: A Global Research Report. London: KPMG International.

KPMG (2018). Global Assignment Policies and Practices Survey: 2018 Results. KPMG International.

KPMG (2019). Global Assignment Policies and Practices Survey: 2019 Results. KPMG International.

Kraimer, M. L., Shaffer, M. A., & Bolino, M. C. (2009). The influence of expatriate and repatriate experiences on career advancement and repatriate retention. *Human Resource Management, 48*(1), 27-47.

Kraimer, M. L., Shaffer, M. A., Harrison, D. A., & Ren, H. (2012). No place like home? An identity strain perspective on repatriate turnover. *Academy of Management Journal, 55*(2), 399-420.

Krishnan, H. A., Miller, A., & Judge, W. Q. (1997). Diversification and top management team complementarity: Is performance improved by merging similar or dissimilar teams? *Strategic Management Journal, 18,* 361-374.

Krishnan, T.A., & Scullion, H. (2014). Talent management and dynamic view of talent in small and medium enterprises. *Human Resource Management Review, 27*(3), 431-441.

Kristensen, P. H., & Zeitlin, J. (2005). *Local players in global games: The strategic constitution of a multinational corporation.* Oxford: Oxford University Press.

Krug, J. A., & Hegarty, W. H. (1997). Post-acquisition turnover among U.S. top management teams: An analysis of the effects of foreign vs. domestic acquisitions of U.S. targets. *Strategic Management Journal, 18,* 667-675.

Kühlmann, T., & Dowling, P. J. (2005). DaimlerChrysler: A case study of a cross-border merger. In G. K. Stahl, & M. E. Mendenhall (Eds.), *Mergers and acquisitions: Managing culture and human resources* (pp. 351-363). Stanford, CA: Stanford University Press.

Kwon, B., & Farndale, E. (2020). Employee voice viewed through a cross-cultural lens. *Human Resource Management Review, 30*(1). doi.org/10.1016/j.hrmr.2018.06.002.

Lam, H., & Khare, A. (2010). HR's crucial role for successful CSR. *Journal of International Business Ethics, 3*(2), 3-15.

Lamare, J. Ryan, Farndale, E., & Gunnigle, P. (2014). Employment relations and international human resource management. In D. G. Collings, G. Wood, & P. Caligiuri (Eds.), *The Routledge companion to international human resource management* (pp. 99-120). London: Routledge.

Latta, G. W., & Danielson, T. A. (2003). Treatment of expatriate tax: A look at U.S., U.K. and Canadian practices. *Compensation and Benefits Review, 35,* 54-59.

Lauring, J., & Selmer, J. (2010). The supportive expatriate spouse: An ethnographic study of spouse involvement in expatriate careers. *International Business Review, 19*(1), 59-69.

Lauring, J., Selmer, J., & Kubovcikova, A. (2019). Personality in context: effective traits for expatriate managers at different levels. *International Journal of Human Resource Management, 30*(6), 1010-1035.

Lawrence, P., & Lorsch, J. (1967). Differentiation and integration in complex organizations. *Administrative Science Quarterly, 12,* 1-47.

Lazarova, M., & Caligiuri, P. (2001). Retaining repatriates: The role of organization support practices. *Journal of World Business, 36*(4), 389-401.

Lazarova, M., & Tarique, I. (2005). Knowledge transfer upon repatriation. *Journal of World Business, 40*(4), 361-373.

Lazarova, M. B. (2006), International human resource management in global perspective. In M. J. Morley, N. Heraty, & D. G. Collings (Eds.), *International human resource management and international assignments* (pp. 24-51). Basingstoke, UK: Palgrave Macmillan.

Lazarova, M. B., & Cerdin, J.-L. (2007). Revisiting repatriation concerns: Organizational support versus career and contextual influences. *Journal of International Business Studies, 38,* 404-429.

Lazarova, M. B., Westman, M., & Shaffer, M. A. (2010). Elucidating the positive side of the work–family interface on international assignments: A model of expatriate work and family performance. *Academy of Management Review, 35,* 93-117.

Lazarova, M. (2015). Taking stock of repatriation research. In D. Collings, P. Wood, & P. M. Caligiuri (Eds.), *The Routledge companion to international human resource management* (pp. 378-398). London: Routledge.

Lazarova, M., McNulty, Y., & Semeniuk, M. (2015). Expatriate family narratives on international mobility: Key characteristics of the successful moveable family. In L. Mäkelä, & V. Suutari (Eds.), *Work and family interface in the international career context* (pp. 29-51). Dordrecht: Springer International Publishing.

Lazarova, M., Mayrhofer, W., Briscoe, J., Dickmann, M., Hall, D. T., & Parry, E. (2018). Comparative career studies: Conceptual issues and empirical results. In C. Brewster, W. Mayrhofer, & E. Farndale (Eds.), *Handbook of research in comparative human resource management* (pp. 257-282). Cheltenham, UK and Northampton, MA, USA: Edward Elgar Publishing.

Lazerson, M. (1995). A new phoenix? *Administrative Science Quarterly, 40,* 34-59.

Leana, C., & Van Buren, H. (1999). Organizational social capital and employment practices. *Academy of Management Review, 24,* 538-555.

Lee, P. N. (1987). *Industrial management and economic reform in China, 1949-1984.* New York: Oxford University Press.

Legge, K. (1978). *Power, innovation, and problem-solving in personnel management.* London: McGraw-Hill.

Leksell, L. (1981). *Headquarter–subsidiary relationships in multinational corporations.* Stockholm: Stockholm School of Economics.

Lemanski, M., Björkman, I., & Stahl, G. (2011). *How do HRM practices diffuse from MNC subsidiaries?* Unpublished manuscript, Vienna University of Economics and Business.

Lepak, D. P., Bartol, K. M., & Erhardt, N. L. (2005). A contingency framework for the delivery of HR practices. *Human Resource Management Review, 15*(2), 139-159.

Leroy, F., & Ramanantsoa, B. (1997). The cognitive and behavioral dimensions of organizational learning in merger: An empirical study. *Journal of Management Studies, 34,* 871-894.

Leung, A. (2003). Different ties for different needs: Recruitment practices of entrepreneurial firms at different developmental phases. *Human Resource Management: Published in Cooperation with the School of Business Administration, The University of Michigan and in alliance with the Society of Human Resources Management, 42*(4), 303-320.

Leung, K., Lin, X., & Lu, L. (2014). Compensation disparity between locals and expatriates in China: A multilevel analysis of the influence of norms. *Management International Review, 54*(1), 107-128.

Levy, O., Beechler, S., Taylor, S., & Boyacigiller, N. A. (2007). What we talk about when we talk about 'global mindset': Managerial cognition in multinational corporations. *Journal of International Business Studies, 38*, 231-258.

Lewis, A. C., Cardy, R. L., & Huang, L. S. (2019). Institutional theory and HRM: A new look. *Human Resource Management Review, 29*(3), 316-335.

Ligthart, P. E. M., Pendleton, A., & Poutsma, E. (2018). Financial participation: the nature and causes of national variation. In C. Brewster, W. Mayrhofer, & E. Farndale (Eds.), *Handbook of research in comparative human resource management* (pp. 283-302). Cheltenham, UK and Northampton, MA, USA: Edward Elgar Publishing.

Lincoln, J. R., Olson, J., & Hanada, M. (1978). Cultural effects of organizational structures: The case of Japanese firms in the United States. *American Sociological Review, 43*, 829-847.

Lindsay, V., Sharma, R. R., & Rashad, S. (2019). How likely am I to return home? A study of New Zealand self-initiated expatriates. *Asia Pacific Journal of Human Resources, 57*(1), 57-84. https://doi.org/10.1111/1744-7941.12148.

Linehan, M., & Walsh, J. (2001). Key issues in the senior female international career move: A qualitative study in European context. *British Journal of Management, 12*, 85-95.

Littrell, L. N., Salas, E., Hess, K. P., Paley, M., & Riedel, S. 2006. Expatriate preparation: A critical analysis of 25 years of cross-cultural training research. *Human Resource Development Review, 5*(3), 355-388.

Liu, M. (2013). China. In C. Frege, & J. Kelly (Eds.), *Comparative employment relations in the global economy* (pp. 324-347). Abingdon, UK: Routledge.

Lo, C. W. H., Egri, C. P., & Ralston, D. A. (2008). Commitment to corporate, social and environmental responsibilities: An insight into contrasting perspectives in China and the U.S. *Organization Management Journal, 5*, 83-98.

Lopez-Cabrales, A., & Valle-Cabrera, R. (2020). Sustainable HRM strategies and employment relationships as drivers of the triple bottom line. *Human Resource Management Review, 30*(3). https://doi.org/10.1016/j.hrmr.2019.100705.

Lorange, P., & Roos, J. (1990). Formation of cooperative ventures: Competence mix of the management teams. *Management International Review, 30*(Special issue), 69-86.

Lowe, K. B., Downes, M., & Kroeck, K. G. (1999). The impact of gender on the willingness to accept overseas assignments. *International Journal of Human Resource Management, 10*, 223-234.

Lubatkin, M., Calori, R., Very, P., & Veiga, J. F. (1998). Managing mergers across borders: A two-nation exploration of a nationally bound administrative heritage. *Organization Science, 9*, 670-684.

Lublin, J. S. (2000, June 27). In choosing the right management model, firms seesaw between product and place. *Wall Street Journal*, A1-A4.

Luce, E. (2004, September 15). IKEA's grown up plan to tackle child labour. *Financial Times*.

Lysgaard, S. (1955). Adjustment in a foreign society: Norwegian Fulbright grantees visiting the United States. *International Social Science Bulletin, 7*, 45-51.

Ma, R., & Allen, D. G. (2009). Recruiting across cultures: A value-based model of recruitment. *Human Resource Management Review, 19*(4), 334-346.

Mabey, C., & Ramirez, M. (2012). Comparing national approaches to management development. In C. Brewster, & W. Mayrhofer (Eds.), *Handbook of research on comparative human resource management* (pp. 185-210). Cheltenham, UK and Northampton, MA, USA: Edward Elgar Publishing.

Maitland, A. (2003, September 29). No hiding place for the irresponsible business: Companies are trying to pre-empt trouble over social, environmental and ethical issues. *Financial Times*, 2.

Mäkelä, K., Björkman, I., & Ehrnrooth, M. (2010). How do MNCs establish their talent pools? Influences on individuals' likelihood of being labeled as talent. *Journal of World Business, 45*, 134-142.

Mäkelä, L., Bergbom, B., Saarenpää, K., & Suutari, V. (2015). Work–family conflict faced by international business travelers: Do gender and parental status make a difference? *Journal of Global Mobility, 3*(2), 155-168. 10.1108/JGM-07-2014-0030.

Mäkelä, L., Suutari, V., Brewster, C., Dickmann, M., & Tornikoski, C. (2016). The impact of career capital on expatriates' perceived marketability. *Thunderbird International Business Review, 58*(1), 29–40.

Mäkelä, K., Barner-Rasmussen, W., Ehrnrooth, M., & Koveshnikov, A. (2019). Potential and recognized boundary spanners in multinational corporations. *Journal of World Business, 54*(4), 335–349.

Marginson, P., Hall, M., Hoffmann, A., & Muller, T. (2004). The impact of European works councils on management decision making in UK and US based multinationals: A case study comparison. *British Journal of Industrial Relations, 42*(2), 209–233.

Marín, G. S. (2008). The influence of institutional and cultural factors on compensation practices around the world. In L. R. Gomez-Mejia, & S. Werner (Eds.), *Global compensation: Foundations and perspective* (pp. 3–17). New York: Routledge.

Marks, M. L., & Mirvis, P. H. (1998). *Joining forces: Making one plus one equal three in mergers, acquisitions, and alliances.* San Francisco, CA: Jossey-Bass.

Marks, M. L., & Mirvis, P. H. (2010). *Joining forces: Making one plus one equal three in mergers, acquisitions, and alliances* (2nd ed.). San Francisco, CA: Jossey-Bass.

Markus, H. R., & Kitayama, S. (1991). Culture and the self: Implications for cognition, emotion, and motivation. *Psychological Review, 98*(2), 224–253.

Marler, J. H. (2009). Making human resources strategic by going to the Net: reality or myth? *International Journal of Human Resource Management, 20*(3), 515–527.

Marlow, S., & Gray, C. (2005). *Information and consultation in small and medium-sized enterprises.* Milton Keynes, UK: The Open University.

Marschan, R. (1996). *New structural forms and inter-unit communication in multinationals.* Helsinki: Helsinki School of Economics.

Marschan-Piekkari, R., Welch, D., & Welch, L. (1999). Adopting a common corporate language: IHRM implications. *International Journal of Human Resource Management, 10*(3), 377–390.

Martin, G., Farndale, E., Paauwe, J., & Stiles, P. (2016). Corporate governance and strategic human resource management: Four archetypes and proposals for a new approach to corporate sustainability. *European Management Journal, 34*(1), 22–35.

Matten, D., & Moon, J. (2008). Implicit and explicit CSR: A conceptual framework for a comparative understanding of corporate social responsibility. *Academy of Management Review, 32*, 404–424.

Mayer, D., & Cava, A. (1993). Ethics and the gender equality dilemma for U.S. multinationals. *Journal of Business Ethics, 12*, 701–708.

Mayrhofer, H., Hartmann, L. C., Michelitsch-Rield, G., & Kollinger, I. (2004). Flexpatriate assignment: A neglected issue in global staffing. *International Journal of Human Resource Management, 15*, 1371–1389.

Mayrhofer, W., Brewster, C., Morley, M.J., & Ledolter, J. (2011). Hearing a different drummer? Convergence of human resource management in Europe: A longitudinal analysis. *Human Resource Management Review, 21*, 50–67.

Mayrhofer, W., Reichel, A., & Sparrow, P. (2012). Alternative forms of international working. In G. K. Stahl, I. Björkman, & S. Morris (Eds.), *Handbook of research in international human resource management* (2nd ed.) (pp. 293–320). Cheltenham, UK and Northampton, MA, USA: Edward Elgar Publishing.

Maznevski, M. L., DiStefano, J. J., & Nason, S. W. (1993). *The cultural perspectives questionnaire: Summary of results using CPQ3.* Paper presented at the annual meeting of Academy of International Business, Hawaii.

McCall, M. W. (1998). *Highfliers: Developing the next generation of global leaders.* Boston: Harvard Business School Press.

McClelland, D. C. (1962). The achievement motive in economic growth. In G. Nielson (Ed.), *Proceedings of the XIV International Congress of Applied Psychology*, 2 (pp. 60–80). Oxford: Munksgaard.

McDonald, F., Tüselmann, H. J., & Heise, A. (2003). Employee relations in German multinationals in an Anglo-Saxon setting: Toward a Germanic version of the Anglo-Saxon approach? *European Journal of Industrial Relations, 9*(3), 327–349.

McDonald, K. S., & Hite, L. M. (2018). Conceptualizing and creating sustainable careers. *Human Resource Development* Review, *17*(4), 349–372.

McDonnell, A., Lamare, R., Gunnigle, P., & Lavelle, J. (2010). Developing tomorrow's leaders: Evidence of global talent management in multinational enterprises. *Journal of World Business, 45*(2), 150–160.

McGaugley, S. L., & De Cieri, H. (1999). Reassessment of convergence and divergence dynamics: Implications for international HRM. *International Journal of Human Resource Management, 10*(2), 235–250.

McKinsey Global Institute (2020). What 800 executives envision for the post-pandemic workforce. https://www.mckinsey.com/featured-insights/future-of-work/what-800-executives-envision-for-the -postpandemic-workforce.

Mcleod, S., Fisch, K., & Bestler (2009). XPLANE, *Economist*. http://mediconvergence.economist.com.

McNulty, Y. M., & Tharenou, P. (2004). Expatriate return on investment. *International Studies of Management & Organization, 34*(3), 68–95.

McNulty, Y., De Cieri, H., & Hutchings, K. (2013). Expatriate return on investment in the Asia Pacific: An empirical study of individual ROI versus corporate ROI. *Journal of World Business, 48*(2), 209–221.

McNulty, Y., Rason, J., & Lockwood, R. (2014). Localizing expatriates: Pitfalls, problems & policy planning. In Santa Fe Group Working Paper: Santa Fe Group.

McNulty, Y., & Brewster, C. (2017). Theorising the meaning(s) of 'expatriate': Establishing boundary conditions for business expatriates. *International Journal of Human Resource Management, 28*(1), 27–61.

McNulty, Y., & Moeller, M. (2018). A typology of dual-career expatriate (trailing) spouses: The 'R' profile. In M. Dickmann, S. Vesa, & O. Wurtz (Eds.), *The management of global careers* (pp. 257–290). London: Palgrave Macmillan.

Meaning of Work International Research Team (1987). *The meaning of working: An international view.* New York: Academic Press.

Mellahi, K., Demirbag, M., Collings, D. G., Tatoglu, E., & Hughes, M. (2013). Similarly different: A comparison of HRM practices in MNE subsidiaries and local firms in Turkey. *International Journal of Human Resource Management, 24*(12), 2339–2368. doi:10.1080/09585192.2013.781434.

Mellahi, K., Frynas, J. G., & Collings, D. G. (2016). Performance management practices within emerging market multinational enterprises: The case of Brazilian multinationals. *International Journal of Human Resource Management, 27*(8), 876–905.

Mendenhall, M., & Oddou, G. (1985). The dimensions of expatriate acculturation: A review. *Academy of Management Review, 10*(1), 39–47.

Mendenhall, M. E., & Stahl, G. K. (2000). Expatriate training and development: Where do we go from here? *Human Resource Management, 39*, 251–265.

Mendenhall, M., & Osland, J. (2002). June. *Mapping the terrain of the global leadership construct.* Paper presented at the Academy of International Business, San Juan Puerto Rico.

Mendenhall, M. E., Osland, J. S., Bird, A., Oddou, G. R., & Maznevski, M., L. (2008). *Global leadership: Research, practice and development.* New York: Routledge.

Mendenhall, M. E., & Oddou, G. R. (2012). Global leadership development. In M. E. Mendenhall, J. Osland, A. Bird, G. R. Oddou, M. L. Maznevski, M. Stevens, & G. K. Stahl (Eds.), *Global leadership: Research, practice, and development* (2nd ed.) (pp. 215–239). London: Routledge.

Mendonca, M., & Kanungo, R. N. (1996). Impact of culture on performance management in developing countries. *International Journal of Manpower, 17*, 65–75.

Menipaz, E., & Menipaz, A. (2011). *International business.* Thousand Oaks, CA: Sage.

Mercer (n.d.) Paying expatriates: Understanding split pay. https://mobilityexchange.mercer.com/Insights/article/Paying-Expatriates-Understanding-Split-Pay.

Meyskens, M., Von Glinow, M. A., Werther, W., & Clarke, L. (2009). The paradox of international talent: Alternative forms of international assignments. *International Journal of Human Resource Management, 20*, 1439–1450.

Michie, J. (2009). HRM and national economic performance. In A. Wilkinson, N. Bacon, T. Redman, & S. Snell (Eds.), *The SAGE handbook of human resource management* (Part III, pp. 407–420). London: Sage.

Milkovich, G. T., & Bloom, M. (1998). Rethinking international compensation. *Compensation and Benefits Reviews, 30*(1), 15–23.

Milkovich, G. T., & Newman, J. M. (2008). *Compensation.* New York: McGraw-Hill.

Mill, J. (1863). *Utilitarianism.* Indianapolis: Bobbs-Merrill.

Miller, J. (1975). Isolation in organizations: Alienation from authority, control, and expressive relations. *Administrative Science Quarterly*, 260–271.

Minbaeva, D., Pedersen, T., Björkman, I., Fey, C. F., & Park, H. J. (2003). MNC knowledge transfer, subsidiary absorptive capacity, and HRM. *Journal of International Business Studies, 34*(6), 586-599.

Minbaeva, D. (2007). Knowledge transfer in multinational corporations. *Management International Review, 47*(4), 567-594.

Mirvis, P. H., & Marks, M. L. (1994). *Managing the merger: Making it work.* Upper Saddle River, NJ: Prentice Hall.

Moeller, M., & Reiche, B. S. (2017). Inpatriates: A review, synthesis and outlook of two decades of research. In Y. McNulty, & J. Selmer (Eds.), *Research handbook of expatriates* (pp. 218–240). Cheltenham, UK and Northampton, MA, USA: Edward Elgar Publishing.

Mol, S. T., Born, M. P., Willemsen, M. E., & Van der Molen, H. T. (2005). Predicting expatriate job performance for selection purposes: a quantitative review. *Journal of Cross-Cultural Psychology, 35*(5), 590-620.

Moore, M. J. (2002). Same ticket, different trip: Supporting dual-career couples on global assignments. *Women in Management Review, 17*(2), 61-67.

Morris, M. A., & Robie, C. (2001). A meta-analysis of the effects of cross-cultural training on expatriate performance and adjustment. *International Journal of Training and Development, 5*(2), 112-125.

Morris, S. S., Snell, S. A., & Wright, P.M. (2006). A resource-based view of international human resources: Toward a framework of integrative and creative capabilities. In G. K Stahl, & I. Björkman (Eds.), *Handbook of research in international human resource management* (pp. 433-449). Cheltenham, UK and Northampton, MA, USA: Edward Elgar Publishing.

Morrison, A. J. (2000). Developing a global leadership model. *Human Resource Management, 39*, 117-131.

Muller, M. (1998). Human resource and industrial relations practices of UK and US multinationals in Germany. *International Journal of Human Resources Management, 9*(4), 732-749.

Murphy, K. R., & Cleveland, J. N. (1995). *Understanding performance appraisal: Social, organizational and goal-based perspectives.* Thousand Oaks, CA: Sage.

Murphy, K. R., & DeNisi, A. S. (2008). A model of the appraisal process. In A. Varma, P. S. Budhwar, & A. S. DeNisi (Eds.), *Performance management systems: A global perspective* (pp. 81-96). London: Routledge.

Murray, V. V., Jain, H. C., & Adams, R. J. (1976). A framework for the comparative analysis of personnel administration. *Academy of Management Review, 19*, 47-57.

Nahapiet, J., & Ghoshal, S. (1998). Social capital, intellectual capital and the organizational advantage. *Academy of Management Review, 23*, 242-266.

Naisbett, J. (1994). *Global paradox.* New York: William Morrow.

Naisbett, J., & Aburdene, P. (1990). *Megatrends 2000: Ten new directions for the 1990's.* New York: Avon.

Napier, N. K. (1989). Mergers and acquisitions, human resource issues and outcomes: A review and suggested typology. *Journal of Management Studies, 26*, 271-289.

Napier, N. K., & Peterson, R. B. (1991). Expatriate re-entry: what do repatriates have to say? *Human Resource Planning, 14*, 19-28.

Napier, N. K., & Taylor, S. (2002). Experiences of women professionals abroad: Comparisons across Japan, China, and Turkey. *International Journal of Human Resource Management, 13*, 837-851.

Napier, N. K., & Thomas, D. C. (2004). *Managing relationships in transition economies.* New York: Praeger.

Naumann, E. (1993). Antecedents and consequences of satisfaction and commitment among expatriate managers. *Group and Organization Management, 18*(2), 153-187.

Neeley, T. (2012). Global business speaks English. *Harvard Business Review, 90*(5), 116-124.

Neeley, T. B., Hinds, P. J., & Cramton, C. D. (2012). The (un)hidden turmoil of language in global collaboration. *Organizational Dynamics, 41*(3), 236-244. doi:http://dx.doi.org/10.1016/j.orgdyn.2012.03.008.

Newman, K. I., & Nollen, S. D. (1996). Culture and congruence: The fit between management practices and national culture. *Journal of International Business Studies, 27*, 753-778.

Nicholson, N., & Imaizumi, A. (1993). The adjustment of Japanese expatriates to living and working in Britain. *British Journal of Management, 4*, 119-134.

Nienhüser, W. (2020). Works councils. In A. Wilkinson, J. Donaghey, T. Dundon, & R. B. Freeman (Eds.), *Handbook of research on employee voice* (pp. 259-276). Cheltenham, UK and Northampton, MA, USA: Edward Elgar Publishing.

Nikandrou, I., & Panayotopoulou, L. (2012). Recruitment and selection in context. In C. Brewster, & W. Mayrhofer (Eds.), *Handbook of research in comparative human resource management* (pp. 121-138). Cheltenham, UK and Northampton, MA, USA: Edward Elgar Publishing.

Nikandrou, I., & Panayotopoulou, L. (2018). Recruitment and selection in context. In C. Brewster, & W. Mayrhofer (Eds.), *Handbook of research in comparative human resource management* (2nd ed.) (pp. 121-138). Cheltenham, UK and Northampton, MA, USA: Edward Elgar Publishing.

Nonaka, I., & Takeuchi, H. (1995). *The knowledge creating company: How Japanese companies create the dynamics of innovation.* Oxford: Oxford University Press.

OECD (2019). Trade unions: Trade union density (edition 2018). OECD Employment and Labour Market Statistics. https://doi.org/10.1787/fc807e2a-en.

Oddou, G., & Mendenhall, M. E. (2000). Expatriate performance appraisal: Problems and solutions. In M. E Mendenhall, & G. Oddou (Eds.), *Readings and cases in international human resource management* (3rd ed.) (pp. 213-223). Cincinnati, OH: South Western.

Ohmae, K. (1995). *The end of the nation state.* Cambridge, MA: Free Press.

Oliver, N., & Wilkinson, B. (1992). *The Japanization of British industry: New developments in the 1990s.* Oxford: Blackwell.

O'Reilly, M. (1996). Expatriate pay: The state of the art. *Compensation and Benefits Review, 12*(1), 54-60.

Osland, J. S., & Bird, A. (2000). Beyond sophisticated stereotypes: Cultural sensemaking in context. *Academy of Management Executive, 14*, 65-79.

Osman, I., Ho, T., Galang, M. C. (2011). Are human resource departments really important? An empirical study on Malaysian small and medium enterprises (SMEs) in the service sector. *International Journal of Business and management, 6*(2), 147-153.

Ott, D. L., & Michailova, S. (2016). Expatriate selection: A historical overview and criteria for decision-making. In Y. Guo, P. J. Dowling, & H. G. Rammal (Eds.), *Global talent management and staffing in MNEs* (pp. 1-24). London: Emerald Publishing.

Ouchi, W. (1981). *Theory Z: How American business can meet the Japanese challenge.* Reading, MA: Addison-Wesley.

Ouyang, C., Liu, M., Chen, Y., Li, J., & Qin, W. (2019). Overcoming liabilities of origin: Human resource management localization of Chinese multinational corporations in developed markets. *Human Resource Management, 58*(5), 543-561.

Paauwe, J., & Boselie, P. (2003). Challenging (strategic) human resource management and the relevance of the institutional setting. *Human Resource Management Journal, 13*(3), 56-70.

Paik, Y., & Sohn, J. D. (2004). Expatriate managers and MNC's ability to control international subsidiaries: The case of Japanese MNCs. *Journal of World Business, 39*(1), 61-71.

Park, H., Sun, D. H., & David, J. M. (1993). Local manager selection for U.S. firms in Korea. *Multinational Business Review, 1*(2), 57-65.

Parker, B. (2005). *Introduction to globalization and business: Relationships and responsibilities.* London: Sage.

Parry, E., Dickmann, M., & Morley, M. (2008). North American MNCs and their HR policies in liberal and coordinated market economies. *International Journal of Human Resource Management, 19*, 2024-2040.

Patel, C., Budhwar, P. S., Witzemann, A., & Katou, A. A. (2019). HR outsourcing: Achieving standardization in terms of harmonization of HR activities post outsourcing. *Journal of Business Research, 103*, 397-406. https://www.sciencedirect.com/journal/journal-of-business-research/vol/103/suppl/C.

Patel, P., Sinha, P., Bhanugopan, R., Boyle, B., & Bray, M. (2018). The transfer of HRM practices from emerging Indian IT MNEs to their subsidiaries in Australia: The MNE diamond model. *Journal of Business Research, 93*, 268-279.

Paz-Aparicio, C., Ricart, J. E., & Bonache, J. (2017). Understanding the decision to offshore human resource activities: A coevolutionary perspective. *International Journal of Physical Distribution & Logistics Management, 47*(2/3), 175-197.

Peiperl, M. A., & Jonsen, K. (2007). Global careers. In H. P. Gunz, & M. A. Peiperl (Eds.), *Handbook of career studies* (pp. 350-372). Thousand Oaks, CA: Sage.

Pelto, P. J. (1968). The difference between tight and loose societies. *Transaction, April*, 37-40.

Peltokorpi, V. (in press). Host country national employees' prosocial behavior toward expatriates in foreign subsidiaries: A common ingroup identity model perspective. *International Business Review, 29*(2). https://doi.org/10.1016/j.ibusrev.2019.101642.

Pendleton, A., & Poutsma, E. (2012). Financial participation. In C. Brewster, & W. Mayrhofer (Eds.), *Handbook of reserach on comparative human resource management* (pp. 345-368). Cheltenham, UK and Northampton, MA, USA: Edward Elgar Publishing.

Peng, G. Z., & Beamish, P. W. (2014). MNC subsidiary size and expatriate control: Resource-dependence and learning perspectives. *Journal of World Business, 49*(1), 51-62.

Peng, M. W. (2000). *Business strategies in transition economies.* Thousand Oaks, CA: Sage.

Peretz, H., & Rosenblatt, Z. (2011). The role of societal cultural practices in organizational training and development: A comparative study in 21 countries. *Journal of Cross-Cultural Psychology, 42,* 817-831.

Perlmutter, H. V. (1969). The tortuous evolution of the multinational corporation. *Columbia Journal of World Business, 4*(1), 9-18.

Peters, T. J., & Waterman, R. H. (1982). *In search of excellence.* New York: Harper & Row.

Peterson, M. F. (2004). Culture, leadership and organizations: The GLOBE study of 62 societies [Book Review]. *Administrative Science Quarterly, 8,* 641-647.

Peterson, R. B., Napier, N., & Won, S. (1995). *Expatriate management: The differential role of national multinational corporation ownership.* Paper presented at the annual meeting of the Academy of International Business, Seoul, Korea.

Petricevic, O., & Teece, D. (2019). The structural reshaping of globalization: Implications for strategic sectors, profiting from innovation, and the multinational enterprise. *Journal of International Business Studies, 50*(9), 1487-1512.

Phatak, A., & Habib, M. (1998). How should managers treat ethics in international business? *Thunderbird International Business Review, 40*(2), 101-117.

Piekkari, R., & Tietze, S. (2012). Language and international human resource management. In G. Stahl, I. Björkman, & C. G. Morris (Eds.), *Handbook of research in international human resource management* (2nd ed.) (pp. 550-565). Cheltenham, UK and Northampton, MA, USA: Edward Elgar Publishing.

Pinker, S. (1994). On language. *Journal of Cognitive Neuroscience, 6*(1), 92-98.

Piraro, D. (2008). Pirates [cartoon]. Published on November 4, 2008 at: https://www.bizarro.com/pirates.

Pless, N. M., Maak, T., & Stahl, G. K. (2011). Developing responsible global leaders through international service-learning programs: The Ulysses experience. *Academy of Management Learning & Education, 10*(2), 237-260.

Pless, N. M., Maak, T., & Stahl, G. K. (2012). Promoting corporate social responsibility and sustainable development through management development: What can be learned from international service-learning programs? *Human Resource Management, 51*(6), 873-903.

Pless, N.M., & Borecká, M. (2014). Comparative analysis of International Service-Learning Programs. *Journal of Management Development, 33*(6), 526-550.

Podgorodnichenko, N., Edgar, F., & McAndrew, I. (2020). The role of HRM in developing sustainable organizations: Contemporary challenges and contradictions. *Human Resource Management Review, 30*(3). https://doi.org/10.1016/j.hrmr.2019.100705.

Poe, A. C. (2000). Welcome back. *HR Magazine, 45*(3), 94-105.

Poole, M. (1986). Managerial strategies and styles in industrial relations: A comparative analysis. *Journal of General Management, 12*(1), 40-53.

Population Division of the United Nations Secretariat (2006). *Trends in Total Migrant Stock: The 2005 Revision* (POP/DB/MIG/Rev.2005), database in digital form.

Porter, M. E. (1986). Changing patterns of international competition. *California Management Review, 28*(2), 9-40.

Prahalad, C. K., & Doz, Y. L. (1999). *The multinational mission: Balancing local demands and global vision.* New York: The Free Press.

Pringle, T. (2011). *Trade unions in China: The challenge of labour unrest.* London: Routledge.

Prouska, R., & Psychogios, A. (2019). Should I say something? A framework for understanding silence from a line manager's perspective during an economic crisis. *Economic and Industrial Democracy, 40*(3), 611–635. https://doi.org/10.1177/0143831X17752869.

Psychogios, A., Szamosi, L.T., Prouska, R., & Brewster, C. (2016), A three-fold framework for understanding HRM practices in South-Eastern European SMEs. *Employee Relations, 38*(3), 310-331. https://doi.org/10.1108/ER-07-2014-0078.

Pucik, V. (1985). Evolution of multinational human resource management. In H. V. Wortzel, & L. H. Wortzel (Eds.), *Strategic management of multinational corporations: The essentials* (pp. 424-435). New York: Wiley.

Pucik, V. (1988). Strategic alliances, organizational learning, and competitive advantage: The HRM agenda. *Human Resource Management, 27,* 77-93.

Pucik, V., & Evans, P. (2004). The human factor in mergers and acquisitions. In P. Morosini, & U Steger (Eds.), *Managing complex mergers* (pp. 161-187). London: Financial Times Management.

Pucik, V., Evans, P., Björkman, I., & Stahl, G. K. (2011). Human resource management in cross-border mergers and acquisitions. In A.-W. Harzing, & A. Pinnington (Eds.), *International human resource management* (3rd ed.) (pp. 119-152). London: Sage.

Pucik, V., Evans, P., Björkman, I., & Morris, S. (2016). *The global challenge: International human resource management* (3rd ed.). Chicago: Chicago Business Press.

Puck, J. F., Mohr, A. T., & Hotbrügge, D. (2006). Cultural convergence though web-based management techniques? The case of corporate web site recruiting. *Journal of International Management, 12*(2), 181-195.

Puck, J. F., Kittler, M. G., & Wright, C. (2008). Does it really work? Re-assessing the impact of pre-departure cross-cultural training on expatriate adjustment. *International Journal of Human Resource Management, 19,* 2182-2197.

Pudelko, M., & Harzing, A.-W. (2007). Country-of-origin, localization, or dominance effect? An empirical investigation of HRM practices in foreign subsidiaries. *Human Resource Management, 46,* 535-559.

Pugh, D. S., Hickson, D. J., Hinings, C. R., MacDonald, K. M., & Turner, C. (1963). Dimensions of organization structure. *Administrative Science Quarterly, 13,* 65-105.

Punnett, B. J. (1997). Towards effective management of expatriate spouses. *Journal of World Business, 32*(3), 243-257.

Punnett, B. J., Crocker, O., & Stevens, M. J. (1992). The challenge for women expatriates and spouses: Some empirical evidence. *International Journal of Human Resource Management, 3*(3), 585-592.

Putnam, R. (1993). *Making democracy work: Civic traditions in modern Italy.* Princeton, NJ: Princeton University Press.

PwC Global (2020). What does COVID-19 mean for global mobility? https://www.pwc.com/gx/en/services/tax/publications/covid-19-mean-for-global-mobility.html.

Radulescu, R., & Robson, M. (2013). Does labour market flexibility matter for investment? A study of manufacturing in the OECD. *Applied Economics, 45*(5), 581-592.

Ragazzi, F. (2014). A comparative analysis of diaspora policies. *Political Geography, 41,* 74–89.

Ran, S., & Huang, J. L. 2019. Enhancing adaptive transfer of cross-cultural training: Lessons learned from the broader training literature. *Human Resource Management Review, 29*(2), 239-252.

Redding, S.G., Norman, A., & Schlander, A. (1994). The nature of individual attachment to the organization: A review of East Asian variations. In H. C. Triandis (Ed.), *Handbook of industrial/organizational psychology* (2nd ed., vol. 4) (pp. 647-688). Palo Alto, CA: Consulting Psychologists Press.

Reiche, B. S. (2006). The inpatriate experience in multinational corporations: An exploratory case study in Germany. *International Journal of Human Resource Management, 17*(9), 1572-1590.

Reiche, B. S. (2011). Knowledge transfer in multinationals: The role of inpatriates' boundary spanning. *Human Resource Management, 50*(3), 365–389.

Reiche, B. S., & Harzing, A.-W. (2011). International assignments. In A.-W. Harzing, & A. Pinnington (Eds.), *International human resource management* (3rd ed.) (pp. 187-226). London: Sage.

Reiche, B. S., Kraimer, M., & Harzing, A. W. (2011). Why do international assignees stay? *Journal of International Business Studies, 42,* 521-544.

Reilly, P. A., Tamkin, P., & Broughton, A. (2007). *The changing HR function: Transforming HR?* London: Chartered Institute of Personnel and Development.

Renesch, J. (Ed.) (1992). *New traditions in business.* San Francisco, CA: Berrett-Koehler.

Reynolds, C. (1997). Expatriate compensation in historical perspective. *Journal of World Business, 32*(3), 118-132.

Richbell, S., Szerb, L., & Vitai, Z. (2010). HRM in the Hungarian SME sector. *Employee Relations, 32*(3), 262-280.

Robertson, R. (1995). Glocalization: Time–space and homogeneity–heterogeneity. In M. Featherstone, S. Lash, & R. Robertson (Eds.), *Global modernities* (pp. 25-44). London: Sage.

Rock, C. P., & Solodkov, V. (2001). Monetary policies, banking, and trust in changing institutions: Russia's transition in the 1990s. *Journal of Economic Issues, 35*(2), 451-458.

Rogers, A. A., Ha, T., & Ockey, S. (2020). Adolescents' perceived socio-emotional impact of COVID-19 and implications for mental health: Results from a U.S.-based mixed-methods study. *Journal of Adolescent Health.* https://doi.org/10.1016/j.jadohealth.2020.09.039.

Rogers, J., & Streeck, W. (1995). *Works councils: Consultation, representation, and cooperation in industrial relations.* London: The University of Chicago Press.

Ronen, S., & Shenkar, O. (2013). Mapping world cultures: Cluster formation, sources and implications. *Journal of International Business Studies, 44*(9), 867-897.

Rosenzweig, P. M., & Nohria, N. (1994). Influences on human resource management practices in multinational corporations. *Journal of International Business Studies, 25,* 229-251.

Rosenzweig, P. M., & Singh, J. V. (1991). Organizational environments and the multinational enterprise. *Academy of Management Review, 16*(2), 340-361.

Roth, K. (1995). Managing international interdependence: CEO characteristics in a resource-based framework. *Academy of Management Journal, 38*(1), 200-231.

Roth, K., & O'Donnell, S. (1996). Foreign compensation strategy: An agency theory perspective. *Academy of Management Journal, 39,* 678-703.

Rowley, C., Poon, I. H.-F., Zhu, Y., & Warner, M. (2011). Approaches to HRM. In A.-W. Harzing, & A. Pinnington (Eds.), *International human resource management* (3rd ed.) (pp. 153-182). London: Sage.

Rozin, P. (1998). Evolution and development of brains and cultures. In M. S. Gazzaniga, & J. S. Altman (Eds.), *Brain and mind* (pp. 111–123). Strasbourg, France: Human Frontier Science Program.

Rutherford, M. W., Buller, P. F., & McMullen, P. R. (2003). Human resource management problems over the life cycle of small to medium-sized firms. *Human Resource Management, 42*(4), 321-335.

Ryan, A. M., Reeder, M. C., Golubovich, J., Grand, J., Inceoglu, I., Bartram, D., Derous, E., Nikolaou, I., & Yao, X. (2017). Culture and testing practices: Is the world flat? *Applied Psychology, 66*(3), 434-467.

Sagiv, L., & Schwartz, S. H. (1995). Value priorities and readiness for outgroup social contact. *Journal of Personality and Social Psychology, 69,* 437-448.

Sagiv, L., & Schwartz, S. H. (2000). A new look at national culture: Illustrative applications to role stress and managerial behavior. In N. N. Ashkanasy, C. Wilderom, & M. F. Peterson (Eds.), *The handbook of organizational culture and climate.* Newbury Park, CA: Sage.

Sahakiants, I., Festing, M., Engle Sr, A. D., & Dowling, P. J. (2018). Comparative total rewards policies and practices. In C. Brewster, W. Mayrhofer, & E. Farndale (Eds.), *Handbook of research in comparative human resource management* (pp. 143-163). Cheltenham, UK and Northampton, MA, USA: Edward Elgar Publishing.

Saini, D. S., & Budhwar, P. S. (2008). Managing the human resource in Indian SMEs: The role of indigenous realties. *Journal of World Business, 43,* 417-434.

Sajdev, S. (2006). International corporate social responsibility and employment relations. In T. Edwards, & C. Rees (Eds.), *International human resource management: Globalization, national systems and multinational companies* (pp. 262-284). Harlow, Essex: Pearson Education.

Sajdev, S. (2011). International corporate social responsibility and HRM. In T. Edwards, & C. Rees (Eds.), *International human resource management: Globalization, national systems and multinational companies* (2nd ed.) (pp. 253-271). Harlow, Essex: Pearson Education Limited.

Salimäki, A., & Heneman, R. L. (2008). Pay for performance for global employees. In L. R. Gomez-Mejia, & S. Werner (Eds.), *Global compensation: Foundations and perspective* (pp. 158-166). New York: Routledge.

Salt, J., & Millar, J. (2006). International migration in interesting times: The case of the UK. *People and Place, 14*(2), 14-25.

Sanchez-Vidal, M. E., Sanz-Valle, R., & Barba-Aragon, M. I. (2018). Repatriates and reverse knowledge transfer in MNCs. *International Journal of Human Resource Management, 29*(10), 1767-1785. 10.1080/09585192.2016.1216876.

Santa Fe Relocation (2019). *The Global Mobility Survey 2019 REVISION: Mobility through the looking glass.* https://www.santaferelo.com/en/mobility-insights/global-mobility-survey/.

Scanlon, J. (2009). How Hewlett-Packard turns strategy into action. Bloomberg. https://www.bloomberg.com/news/articles/2009-09-23/how-hewlett-packard-turns-strategy-into-action.

Schein, E. H. (1985). *Organizational culture and leadership.* San Francisco, CA: Jossey-Bass.

Schein, E. (1996). Career anchors revisited: Implications for career development in the 21st century. *Academy of Management Executive, 10*(4), 80-88.

Schmitt, J., & Mitukiewicz, A. (2012). Politics matter: Changes in unionisation rates in rich countries, 1960-2010. *Industrial Relations Journal, 43*(3), 260-280.

Schmitter P. C. (1979). Still the century of corporatism? In P. C. Schmitter, & G. Lembruch (Eds.), *Trends towards, corporatist intermediation* (pp. 7-52). London: Sage.

Schuler, R.S., & MacMillan, I.C. (1984). Gaining competitive advantage through human resource management practices. *Human Resource Management, 23*, 241-255.

Schuler, R.S., & Rogowsky, N. (1998). Understanding compensation practice variations in firms: The impact of national culture. *Journal of International Business Studies, 29*, 159-177.

Schuler, R. S. (2001). HR issues in international joint venture and alliances. In J. Storey (Ed.), *Human resource management: A critical text* (2nd ed.) (pp. 314-336). London: ITL.

Schuler, R. S., Jackson, S. E., & Luo, Y. (2004). *Managing human resources in cross-border alliances.* London: Routledge.

Schuler, R.S., & Tarique, I. (2006). International joint venture system complexity and human resource management. In G. K. Stahl, & I. Björkman (Eds.), *Handbook of research in international human resource management* (pp. 385-406). Cheltenham, UK and Northampton, MA, USA: Edward Elgar Publishing.

Schwan, R., & Soeters, J. (1994). The strategy of vacancy-filling from internal and external labor market sources: An empirical assessment of the recruitment strategy of different types. *Scandinavian Journal of Management, 10*(1), 69-85.

Schwartz, S. H. (1992). Universals in the content and structure of values: Theoretical advances and empirical tests in 20 countries. In M. P. Zanna (Ed.), *Advances in Experimental Social Psychology* (pp. 1-65). San Diego, CA: Academic Press.

Schwartz, S. H. (1994). Beyond individualism/collectivism: New dimensions of values. In U. Kim, H. C. Triandis, C. Kağitçibaşi, S. C. Choi, & G. Yoon (Eds.), *Individualism and collectivism: Theory applications and methods* (pp. 85-119). Newbury Park, CA: Sage.

Schwartz, S. H., & Bilsky, W. (1990). Toward a universal psychological structure of human values. *Journal of Personality and Social Psychology, 53*, 550-562.

Schwartz, S. H., & Sagie, G. (2000). Value consensus and importance: A cross-national study. *Journal of Cross-Cultural Psychology, 31*(4), 465-497.

Schweiger, D. M., & DeNisi, A. S. (1991). The effects of communication with employees following a merger: A longitudinal field experiment. *Academy of Management Journal, 34*, 110-135.

Schweiger. D. M., Atamer, T., & Calori, R. (2003). Transnational project teams and networks: Making the multinational organization more effective. *Journal of World Business, 38*, 127-140.

Schweiger, D. M., & Goulet, P. K. (2005). Facilitating acquisition integration through deep-level cultural learning interventions: A longitudinal field experiment. *Organization Studies, 26*, 1477-1499.

Schweiger, D. M., & Lippert, R. L. (2005). Integration: The critical link in M&A value creation. In G. K. Stahl, & M. E. Mendenhall (Eds.), *Mergers and acquisitions: Managing culture and human resources* (pp. 17-45). Stanford, CA: Stanford University Press.

Scullion, H. (1991). Why companies prefer to use expatriates. *Personnel Management*, 32-35.

Scullion, H., & Starkey, K. (2000). In search of the changing role of the corporate human resource function in the international firm. *International Journal of Human Resource Management, 11*, 1061-1081.

Scullion, H., & Brewster, C. (2001). The management of expatriates: Messages from Europe? *Journal of World Business, 36*(4), 36-365.

Seddon, J. (1987). Assumptions, cultures and performance appraisal. *Journal of Management Development, 6*, 47-54.

Selmer, J., Torbiorn, I., & de Leon, C. T. (1998). Sequential cross-cultural training for expatriate business managers: Predeparture and post-arrival. *International Journal of Human Resource Management, 9*(5), 831-840.

Selmer, J., Ebrahimi, B. P., & Mingtao, L. (2002). Career management of business expatriates from China. *International Business Review, 11*, 17-33.

Selmer, J., & Lam, H. (2004). 'Third-culture kids': Future business expatriates? *Personnel Review, 33*(4), 430-445.

Selmer, J., Chiu, R. K., & Shenkar, O. (2007). Cultural distance asymmetry in expatriate adjustment. *Cross Cultural Management: An International Journal, 14*(2), 150-160. doi:10.1108/13527600710745750.

Selmer, J. and Lauring, J. (2009). Cultural similarity and adjustment of expatriate academics. *International Journal of Intercultural Relations, 33*(5), 429-436.

Sekiguchi, T., Froese, F. J., & Iguchi, C. (2016). International human resource management of Japanese multinational corporations: Challenges and future directions. *Asian Business & Management, 15,* 83–109.

Serapio, M. G., & Cascio, W. F. (1996). Endgames in international alliances. *Academy of Management Executive, 10,* 62–73.

Sethi, S. P (1975, Spring). Dimensions of corporate social performance: An analytic framework. *California Management Review, 17,* 58–64.

Shaffer, M. A., & Harrison, D. A. (2001). Forgotten partners of international assignments: Development and test of a model of spouse adjustment. *Journal of Applied Psychology, 86*(2), 238–254.

Shaffer, M., Kraimer, M., Chen, Y.-P., & Bolino, M. C. (2012). Choices, challenges, and career consequences of global work experiences: A review and future agenda. *Journal of Management, 38*(4), 1282–1327.

Shaw, W. (1996). *Business ethics* (2nd ed.). Belmont, CA: Wadsworth.

Shen, J., & Jiang, F. (2015). Factors influencing Chinese female expatriates' performance in international assignments. *International Journal of Human Resource Management, 26*(3), 299–315. 10.1080/09585192.2011.581637.

Shih, H. A., Chiang, Y. H., & Kim, I. S. (2005). Expatriate performance management from MNEs of different national origins. *International Journal of Manpower, 26,* 157–176.

Shimizu, K., Hitt, M. A., Vaidyanath, D., & Pisano, V. (2004). Theoretical foundations of cross-border mergers and acquisitions: A review of current research and recommendations for the future. *Journal of International Management, 10,* 307–353.

Shortland, S. (2016). The purpose of expatriation: why women undertake international assignments. *Human Resource Management, 55*(4), 655–678.

Shortland, S., & Perkins, S. J. (2016). Long-term assignment reward (dis)satisfaction outcomes: Hearing women's voices. *Journal of Global Mobility, 4*(2), 225–250.

Shortland, S. (2018a). Women's participation in organisationally assigned expatriation: An assignment type effect. *International Journal of Human Resource Management,* 1–27. 10.1080/09585192.2018.1510849.

Shortland, S. (2018b). What seals the deal? How compensation and benefits affect women's decisions to accept expatriation in the oil and gas industry. *Personnel Review, 47*(3), 765–783.

Sidanius, J. (1993). The psychology of group conflict and the dynamics of oppression: A social dominance perspective. In S. Iyenger, & W. McGuire (Eds.), *Explorations in political psychology* (pp. 183–219). Durham, NC: Duke University Press.

Silzer, R., & Church, A. H. (2009). The pearls and perils of identifying potential. *Industrial and Organizational Psychology, 2*(4), 377–412.

Sinangil, H. K., & Ones, D. S. (2003). Gender differences in expatriate job performance. *Applied Psychology: An International Review, 52*(3), 461–475.

Sinetar, M. (1981). Mergers, morale and productivity. *Personnel Journal, 60,* 863–867.

Sisson, K. (2006). International employee representation – a case of industrial relations systems following the market? In T. Edwards, & C. Rees (Eds.), *International human resource management: Globalization, national systems and multinational companies* (pp. 242–261). Harlow, Essex: Pearson Education.

Smircich, L., & Calas, M. B. (1986). Organizational culture: A critical assessment. *Annual Review of Sociology, 2,* 228–263.

Smith, A., Whittaker, J., Loan Clark, J., & Boocock, G. (1999). Competence based management development provision to SMEs and the providers' perspective. *Journal of Management Development, 18*(6), 557–572. https://doi.org/10.1108/02621719910279653.

Smith, P. B., & Meiskins, P. (1995). Systems, societal and dominance effects in cross-national organizational analysis. *Work, Employment and Society, 9,* 241–267.

Smith, P. B., & Bond, M. H. (1999). *Social psychology: Across cultures* (2nd ed.). Needham Heights, MA: Allyn & Bacon.

Sparrow, P., Schuler, R., & Jackson, S. (1994). Convergence or divergence: human resource practices and policies for competitive advantage worldwide. *International Journal of Human Resource Management, 5*(2), 267–299.

Sparrow, P. R., & Hiltrop, J. M. (1997). Redefining the field of European human resource management: A battle between national mindsets and forces of business transition? *Human Resource Management:*

Published in Cooperation with the School of Business Administration, *The University of Michigan and in alliance with the Society of Human Resources Management*, 36(2), 201-219.

Sparrow, P., Brewster, C., & Harris, H. (2004). *Globalizing human resource management*. London: Routledge.

Sparrow, P., & Braun, W. (2008). HR sourcing and shoring. In M. Dickmann, P. Sparrow, & C. Brewster (Eds.), *International human resource management: A European perspective* (pp. 39-66). London: Routledge.

Sparrow, P., Farndale, E., & Scullion, H. (2013). An empirical study of the role of the corporate HR function in global talent management in professional and financial service firms in the global financial crisis. *International Journal of Human Resource Management, 24*(9), 1777-1798.

Sparrow, P., Schuler R., & Collings, D. G. (Eds.) (2018). *Macro talent management in emerging and emergent markets: a global perspective*, pp. 1-16. London: Routledge.

Sparrow, P., Vaiman, V., Schuler R., & Collings, D. G. (2018). Introduction. Macro talent management in developed markets: Foundations for a developing field. In V. Vaiman, P. Sparrow, R. Schuler, & D. G. Collings (Eds), *Macro talent management in emerging and emergent markets: A global perspective* (pp. 1-16). London: Routledge.

Spencer, J. (2018, November 14). 3 ways companies are analyzing social media to make hiring decisions. https://www.entrepreneur.com/article/323189.

Spurk, D., Hirschi, A., & Dries, N. (2019). Antecedents and outcomes of objective versus subjective career success: Competing perspectives and future directions. *Journal of Management, 45*(1), 35-69.10.1177/0149206318786563.

Stahl, G. K., & Cerdin, J.-L. (2004). Global careers in French and German multinational corporations. *Journal of Management Development, 23*, 885-902.

Stahl, G. K., Pucik, V., Evans, P., & Mendenhall, M. E. (2004). Human resource management in cross-border mergers and acquisitions. In A.-W. Harzing, & J. V. Ruysseveldt (Eds.), *International human resource management* (2nd ed.) (pp. 89-114). London: Sage.

Stahl, G. K., Björkman, I., Farndale, E., Morris, S. S., Paauwe, J., Stiles, P., Trevor, J., & Wright, P. M. (2007). Global talent management: How leading multinationals build and sustain their talent pipeline. Faculty & Research Working Paper, INSEAD, 2007/34/OB.

Stahl, G. K. (2008). Cultural dynamics and impact of cultural distance within mergers and acquisitions. In P. B. Smith, M. F. Peterson, & D. C. Thomas (Eds.), *The handbook of cross-cultural management research* (pp. 431-448). Thousand Oaks, CA: Sage.

Stahl, G., Björkman, I., Farndale, E., Morris, S. S., Paauwe, J., Stiles, P., … & Wright, P. (2012). Six principles of effective global talent management. *Sloan Management Review, 53*(2), 25-42.

Stahl, G., Brewster, C. J., Collings, D. G., & Hajro, A. (2020). Enhancing the role of human resource management in corporate sustainability and social responsibility: A multi-stakeholder, multidimensional approach to HRM. *Human Resource Management Review, 30*(3). https://doi.org/10.1016/j.hrmr.2019.100705.

Stam, L. (2018). Social media and recruitment. https://www.canadaemploymenthumanrightslaw.com/2018/05/social-media-recruitment/.

Starr, T. L., & Currie, G. (2009). 'Out of sight but still in the picture': Short-term international assignments and the influential role of family. *International Journal of Human Resource Management, 20*(6), 1421-1438.

Stavrou-Costea, E. (2004). The challenges of human resource management towards organizational effectiveness: A comparative study in Southern EU. *Journal of European Industrial Training, 29*(2), 112-134.

Stavrou-Costea, E., & Manson, B. (2006). HRM in small and medium enterprises: Typical, but typically ignored. In H. H. Larsen, & W. Mayrhofer (Eds.), *Managing human resources in Europe* (pp. 107-130). London: Routledge.

Steers, R. M., Shin, Y. K., & Ungson, G. R. (1989). *The chaebol*. New York: Harper-Business.

Steiner, D. D., & Gilliland, S. W. (1996). Fairness reactions to personnel selection techniques in France and the United States. *Journal of Applied Psychology, 81*(2), 134-141.

Stopford, J. M., & Wells, L. T. (1972). *Strategy and structure in multinational enterprise*. New York: Basic Books.

Storey, J. (1992). *Developments in the management of human resources: An analytical review*. London: Blackwell.

Stroh, L. K., Varma, A., & Valy-Durbin, S. J. (2000). Why are women left at home: Are they unwilling to go on international assignments. *Journal of World Business, 35*(3), 241-255.

Sumelius, J., Smale, A., & Björkman, I. (2009). The strategic role of HR in MNC subsidiaries in China between 1999 and 2006. *Chinese Management Studies, 3*(4), 295-312. https://doi.org/10.1108/17506140911007477.

Suutari, V., & Brewster, C. (2000). Making their own way: International experience through self-initiated foreign assignments. *Journal of World Business, 35*(4), 417-436.

Suutari, V., Brewster, C., Riusala, K., & Syrjäkari, S. (2013). Managing non-standard international experience: Evidence from a Finnish company. *Journal of Global Mobility, 1*(2), 118–138.

Suutari, V., Brewster, C., Mäkelä, L., Dickmann, M., & Tornikoski, C. (2018). The effect of international work experience on the career success of expatriates: A comparison of assigned and self-initiated expatriates. *Human Resource Management, 57*(1), 37-54. 10.1002/hrm.21827.

Svetlik, I., & Alas, R. (2006). The European Union and HRM: Impact on present and future members. In H. H. Larsen, & W. Mayrhofer (Eds.), *Managing Human Resources in Europe* (pp. 21–43). London: Routledge.

Tachibanaki, T. (1987). Labour market flexibility in Japan in comparison with Europe and the US. *European Economic Review, 31*(3), 647-678.

Tadmor, C. T., & Tetlock, P. E. (2006). Biculturalism: A model of the effects of second-culture exposure on acculturation and integrative complexity. *Journal of Cross-Cultural Psychology, 37*, 173-190.

Tahvanainen, M., Welch, D., & Worm, V. (2005). Implications of short-term international assignments. *European Management Journal, 23*(6), 663-673.

Takeuchi, R., & Hannon, J. M. (1996). *The antecedents of adjustment for Japanese expatriates in the United States.* Paper presented to the annual meeting of the Academy of International Business, Banff, Canada.

Takeuchi, R., Yun, S., & Tesluk, P. E. (2002). An examination of crossover and spillover effects of spousal and expatriate cross-cultural adjustment on expatriate outcomes. *Journal of Applied Psychology, 87*(4), 655-666.

Takeuchi, R., Tesluk, P. E., Yun, S., & Lepak, D. P. (2005). An integrative view of international experience. *Academy of Management Journal, 48*(1), 85-100.

Takeuchi, R., Lepak, D. P., Wang, H., & Takeuchi, K. (2007). An empirical examination of the mechanisms mediating between high-performance work systems and the performance of Japanese organizations. *Journal of Applied Psychology, 92*(4), 1069–1083. https://doi.org/10.1037/0021-9010.92.4.1069.

Takeuchi, R. (2010). A critical review of expatriate adjustment research through a multiple stakeholder view: Progress, emerging trends, and prospects. *Journal of Management, 36*(4), 1040-1064.

Takeuchi, R., Li, Y., & Wang, M. (2019). Expatriates' performance profiles: Examining the effects of work experiences on the longitudinal change patterns. *Journal of Management, 45*(2), 451-475.

Tarique, I., & Schuler, R. S. (2010). Global talent management: Literature review, integrative framework, and suggestions for further research. *Journal of World Business, 45*(2), 122-133.

Taylor, S., Beechler, S., & Napier, N. (1996). Toward an integrative model of strategic human resource management. *Academy of Management Review, 21*, 959-985.

Taylor, S., & Napier, N. (1996). Working in Japan: Lessons from women expatriates. *Sloan Management Review, 37*, 76-84.

Teague, P., & Donaghey, J. (2018). Brexit: EU social policy and the UK employment model. *Industrial Relations Journal, 49*(5-6), 512-533.

Templin, N. (1996). GM strike hits Mexican output as talks on settlement resume. *Wall Street Journal,* March 20, p. A3

Tharenou, P., & Caulfield, N. (2010). Will I stay or will I go? Explaining repatriation by self-initiated expatriates. *Academy of Management Journal, 53*(5), 1009-1028. 10.5465/amj.2010.54533183.

Thomas, A. (2017). Conglomerate unions and transformations of union democracy. *British Journal of Industrial Relations, 55*(3), 648-671.

Thomas, D. C. (1994). The boundary-spanning role of expatriates in the multinational corporation. *Advances in International Comparative Management, 9*, 145-170.

Thomas, D. C. (1998). The expatriate experience: A critical review and synthesis. *Advances in International Comparative Management, 12*, 237-273.

Thomas, D. C., Au, K., & Ravlin, E. C. (2003). Cultural variation and the psychological contract. *Journal of Organizational Behavior, 24*, 451-471.

Thomas, D. C., Lazarova, M. B., & Inkson, K. (2005). Global careers: New phenomenon or new perspectives? *Journal of World Business, 40,* 340-347.

Thomas, D. C. (2008). *Cross-cultural management: Essential concepts.* Thousand Oaks, CA: Sage.

Thomas, D. C., Elron, E., Stahl, G., Ekelund, B. Z., Ravlin, E. C., Cerdin, J.-L., et al. (2008). Cultural intelligence: Domain and assessment. *International Journal of Cross-Cultural Management, 8*(2), 123-143.

Thomas, D. C., & Fitzsimmons, S. R. (2008). Cross-cultural skills and abilities: From communication competence to cultural intelligence. In P. B. Smith, M. F. Peterson, & D. C. Thomas (Eds.), *The handbook of cross-cultural management research* (pp. 201-218). Thousand Oaks, CA: Sage.

Thomas, D. C., & Lazarova, M. B. (2008). Expatriate adjustment and performance: A critical review. In G. K. Stahl, I. Björkman, & S. Morris (Eds.), *Handbook of research in international human resource management* (2nd ed.) (pp. 247-264). Cheltenham, UK and Northampton, MA, USA: Edward Elgar Publishing.

Thomas, D. C., & Inkson, K. (2009). *Cultural intelligence: Living and working globally.* San Francisco, CA: Berrett-Koehler.

Thomas, D. C. (2010). Cultural intelligence and all that jazz: A cognitive revolution in internal management research? *Advances in International Management, 23,* 169-187.

Thomas, D. C., Fitzsimmons, S. R., Ravlin, E. C., Au, K. Y., Ekelund B. Z., & Barzanty, C. (2010). Psychological contracts across cultures. *Organization Studies, 31*(12), 1-22.

Thory, K. (2008). The internationalisation of HRM through reverse transfer: Two case studies of French multinationals in Scotland. *Human Resource Management Journal, 18,* 54-71.

Toh, S. M., & DeNisi, A. S. (2003). Host country national reactions to expatriate pay policies: A model and implications. *Academy of Management Review, 28*(4), 606-621.

Toh, S. M., & DeNisi, A. S. (2007). Host country nationals as socializing agents: A social identity approach. *Journal of Organizational Behavior, 28,* 281-301.

Torbiörn, I. (1982). *Living abroad: Personal adjustment and personnel policy in the overseas setting.* New York: John Wiley & Sons.

Torbiörn, I. (1985). The structure of managerial roles in cross-cultural settings. *International Studies of Management & Organization, 85*(1), 52-74.

Tornikoski, C., Suutari, V., & Festing, M. (2014). Compensation package of international assignees. In D. G. Collings, G. T. Wood, & P. M. Caligiuri (Eds.), *The Routledge companion to international human resource management* (pp. 289–307). Abingdon, UK: Routledge.

Tregakis, O. (2003). Learning networks, power & legitimacy in multinational subsidiaries. *International Journal of Human Resource Management, 14*(3), 431-447.

Tregaskis, O., Glover, L., & Ferner, A. (2005). *International HR networks in multinational companies.* London: Chartered Institute of Personnel Development.

Tregaskis, O., & Brewster, C. (2006). Converging or diverging? A comparative analysis of contingent employment practice in Europe over a 10-year period. *Journal of International Business Studies, 37,* 111-126.

Tregaskis, O., & Heraty, N. (2018). Human resource development: National embeddedness. In C. Brewster, W. Mayrhofer, & E. Farndale (Eds.), *Handbook of research in comparative human resource management* (pp. 184-199). Cheltenham, UK and Northampton, MA, USA: Edward Elgar Publishing.

Triandis, H. C. (1994). Cross-cultural industrial and organizational psychology. In H. C. Triandis, M. D. Dunnette, & L. M. Hough (Eds.), *Handbook of industrial and organizational psychology* (pp. 103-172). Palo Alto, CA: Consulting Psychologists Press.

Triandis, H. C. (1995). *Individualism and collectivism.* Boulder, CO: Westview.

Trompenaars, F., & Hampden-Turner, C. (1998). *Riding the waves of cultures: Understanding diversity in global business.* Upper Saddle River, NJ: Prentice Hall.

Tsai, C-J. (2010). HRM in SMEs: Homogeneity or heterogeneity? A study of Taiwanese high-tech firms. *International Journal of Human Resource Management, 21*(10), 1689-1711.

Tung, R. L. (1981). Selection and training of personnel for overseas assignments. *Columbia Journal of World Business, 16,* 68-78.

Tung, R. L. (1998). A contingency framework of selection and training of expatriates revisited. *Human Resource Management Review, 8*(1), 23-37.

Tyson, S., & Fell, A. (1986). *Evaluating the personnel function.* London: Hutchinson Radius.

Ulrich, D. (1997). *Human resource champions: The next agenda for adding value and delivering results.* Boston, MA: Harvard Business School Press.

Ulrich, D., & Brockbank, W. (2005). *The HR value proposition*. Boston, MA: Harvard Business Press.

UNCTAD Investment Trends Monitor (2019). Global FDI flows flat in 2019. https://unctad.org/system/files/official-document/diaeiainf2020d1_en.pdf.

Vaara, E. (2003). Post-acquisition integration as sensemaking: Glimpses of ambiguity, confusion, hypocrisy, and politicization. *Journal of Management Studies, 40*, 859-894.

Vaara, E., Tienari, J., & Säntti, R. (2003). The international match: Metaphors as vehicles of social identity-building in cross-border mergers. *Human Relations, 56*, 419-452.

Valk, R. (2019). The global mobility function: From tightrope walker performing a balancing act towards knowledge broker and linchpin. *Journal of Global Mobility: The Home of Expatriate Management Research, 7*(2), 194-212.

van Bakel, M. (2019). It takes two to tango: A review of the empirical research on expatriate-local interactions. *International Journal of Human Resource Management*, 30(21), 2993-3025. 0.1080/09585192.2018.1449763.

Vance, C. M., & Paik, Y. (2011). *Managing a global workforce: Challenges and opportunities in international human resource management*. Armonk, NY: M.E. Sharpe.

Van den Berg, A., Grift, Y., & Van Witteloostuijn, A. (2011). Managerial perceptions of works councils' effectiveness in the Netherlands. *Industrial Relations: A Journal of Economy and Society, 50*(3), 497-513.

Van der Klink, M., & Mulder, M. (1995). Human resource development and staff policy in Europe. In A.-W. Harzing, & J. Van Ruysseveldt (Eds.), *International human resource management* (pp. 156-178). London: Sage.

van der Velde, M. E. G., Bossink, C. J. H., & Jansen, P. G. W. (2005). Gender differences in the determinants of the willingness to accept an international assignment. *Journal of Vocational Behavior, 66*(1), 81-103.

van Odenhoven, J. P., & deBoer, T. (1995). Complementarity and similarity of partners in international mergers. *Basic and Applied Social Psychology, 17*(3), 343-356.

Varma, A., & Stroh, L. K. (2001). The impact of same sex LMX dyads on performance evaluations. *Human Resource Management, 12*, 84-95.

Varma, A., Budhwar, P. S., & DeNisi (2008). *Performance management systems: A global perspective*. New York: Routledge.

Varma, A., & Budhwar, P.S. (2011). Global performance management In A.-W. Harzing, & A. H. Pinnington (Eds.), *International human resource management* (3rd ed.) (pp. 440-467). London: Sage.

Verbeke, A., Coeurderoy, R., & Matt, T. (2018). The future of international business research on corporate globalization that never was.... *Journal of International Business Studies, 49*(9), 1101-1112.

Vernon, G. (2011). International and comparative pay and reward. In T. Edwards, & C. Rees (Eds.), *International Human Resource Management: Globalization, National Systems and Multinational Companies* (2nd ed.) (pp. 207-228). Harlow, UK: Pearson.

Vidović, M., & Farndale, E. (2016). HR departments in multinational corporations. In C. Zheng (Ed.), *International human resource management: Practices, trends and future directions* (pp. 21-43). New York: Nova Science Publishers.

Vijayakumar, P. B., Morley, M., J., Heraty, N., Mendenhall, M., E., & Osland, J., S. 2018. Leadership in the global context: Bibliometric and thematic patterns of an evolving field. In J. Osland, M. Mendenhall, & M. Li (Eds.), *Advances in global leadership* (Vol. 11, pp. 31-72). London: Emerald Publishing.

Von Glinow, M. A., & Teagarden, M. B. (1988). The transfer of human resource technology in Sino–U.S. cooperative ventures: Problems and solutions. *Human Resource Management, 27*, 201-229.

Vora, D. (2008). Managerial roles in the international context. In P.B. Smith, M. F. Peterson, & D. C. Thomas (Eds.), *Handbook of cross-cultural management research* (pp. 411-430). Thousand Oaks, CA: Sage.

Wagar, T. H. (1998). Determinants of human resource management practices in small firms: Some evidence from Atlantic Canada. *Journal of Small Business Management, 36*(2), 13-23. http://ezaccess.libraries.psu.edu/login?url=https://www.proquest.com/docview/221009499?accountid=13158.

Wan Hooi, L., & Sing Ngui, K. (2014). Enhancing organizational performance of Malaysian SMEs: The role of HRM and organizational learning capability. *International Journal of Manpower, 35*(7), 73-995. https://doi.org/10.1108/IJM-04-2012-0059.

Ward, C., & Kennedy, A. (1993). Where's the culture in cross-cultural transition? Comparative studies of sojourner adjustment. *Journal of Cross-Cultural Psychology, 24*(2), 221-249.

Warner, M. (1993). Human resource management 'with Chinese characteristics'. *International Journal of Human Resource Management, 4*(1), 45-65.

Watson, J. (1997). *Golden arches east: McDonald's in East Asia.* Stanford, CA: Stanford University Press.

Weeks, K. P., Weeks, M., & Willis-Muller, K. (2009). The adjustment of expatriate teenagers. *Personnel Review, 39*(1), 24-34.

Weiss, S. E. (1993). Analysis of complex negotiations in international business: The RBC perspective. *Organization Science, 2,* 269-300.

Welch, D. E., & Worm, V. (2006). International business travellers: A challenge for IHRM. In G. H. Stahl, & I. Björkman (Eds.), *Handbook of research in international human resource management* (pp. 283-301). Cheltenham, UK and Northampton, MA, USA: Edward Elgar Publishing.

Welch, D. E., Welch, L. S., & Worm, V. (2007). The international business traveller: A neglected but strategic human resource. *International Journal of Human Resource Management, 18*(2), 173-183.

Westney, D. E. (1993). Institutionalization theory and the multinational corporation. In S. Goshall, & E. Westney (Eds.), *Organization theory and the multinational corporation* (pp. 53-75). New York: St. Martin's Press.

Whorf, B. L. (1956). *Language, thought, and reality: selected writings of...* (Edited by John B. Carroll). Cambridge, MA: Technology Press of MIT.

Wiechmann, D. Ryan, A. M., & Hemingway, M. (2003). Designing and implementing global staffing systems: Part 1 – leaders in global staffing. *Human Resource Management, 42*(1), 71-83.

Willis, H. L. (1984). Selection for employment in developing countries. *Personnel Administrator, 29*(7), 55.

Wilson, M. S., & Yip, J. (2010). Grounding leader development: Cultural perspectives. *Industrial and Organizational Psychology, 3*(1), 52-55.

Wilson, Y. Y., & Jones, R. G. (2008). Reducing job-irrelevant bias in performance appraisals: Compliance and beyond. *Journal of General Management, 34*(2), 57-70.

Wong, E. (2010). Official in China says Western-style democracy won't take root there. *New York Times,* March 21 (online edition). http://www.nytimes.com/2010/2003/2021/world/asia/2021china.html.

Woodall, J. 2011. International management development. In T. Edwards, & C. Rees (Eds.), *International human resource management: Globalization, national systems and multinational companies* (2nd ed.) (pp. 163-183). Harlow, UK: Pearson Education.

World Trade Organization (2012). *WTO annual report.* Geneva: Author.

Wu, L. (1999). Guanxi: A cross-cultural comparative study. Unpublished doctoral dissertation, University of Auckland, New Zealand.

Xi, M., Xu, Q., Wang, X., & Zhao, S. (2017). Partnership practices, labor relations climate, and employee attitudes: Evidence from China. *ILR Review, 70*(5), 1196-1218.

Yanadori, Y. (2014). Compensation and benefits in the global organization. In D. G. Collings, G. T. Wood, & P. M. Caligiuri (Eds.), *The Routledge companion to international human resource management* (pp. 190-209). London: Routledge.

Yamazaki, Y. (2005). Learning Styles and Typologies of Cultural Differences: A Theoretical and Empirical Comparison. *International Journal of Intercultural Relations, 29*(5), 521–48.

Zhou, J., & Martocchio, J. J. (2001). Chinese and American managers' compensation award decisions: A comparative policy-capturing study. *Personnel Psychology, 54,* 115-145.

Zhu, C. J., & Dowling, P. J. (2002). Staffing practices in transition: Some empirical evidence from China. *International Journal of Human Resource Management, 13*(4), 569-597.

Zhu, J., Wanberg, C. R., Harrison, D. A., & Diehn, E. W. (2016). Ups and downs of the expatriate experience? Understanding work adjustment trajectories and career outcomes. *Journal of Applied Psychology, 101*(4), 549-568.